Transformations of Urban and Suburban Landscapes

Transformations of Urban and Suburban Landscapes

Perspectives from Philosophy, Geography, and Architecture

Edited by
Gary Backhaus and John Murungi

LEXINGTON BOOKS
Lanham • Boulder • New York • Oxford

LEXINGTON BOOKS

Published in the United States of America
by Lexington Books
4720 Boston Way, Lanham, Maryland 20706

12 Hid's Copse Road
Cumnor Hill, Oxford OX2 9JJ, England

British Library Cataloguing in Publication Information Available

Library of Congress Cataloging-in-Publication Data

Transformations of urban and suburban landscapes /
edited by Gary Backhaus and John Murungi.
    p. cm.
  ISBN 0-7391-0335-0 (cloth : alk. paper)—ISBN 0-7391-0336-9 (pbk. : alk. paper)
    1. Human geography—United States—Congresses. 2. Landscape changes—
United States—Congresses. 3. City planning—United States—Congresses.
4. Public spaces—United States—Congresses. 5. United States—Environmental
conditions—Congresses. I. Backhaus, Gary, 1953– II. Murungi, John, 1943–
III. Annual Philosophy and Geography Conference (Towson University)

  GF27 .T73 2002
  307.76—dc21

                                                            2001038965

Printed in the United States of America

♾™ The paper used in this publication meets the minimum requirements of American
National Standard for Information Sciences—Permanence of Paper for Printed Library
Materials, ANSI/NISO Z39.48–1992.

Contents

Figures   vii

Preface   ix

1   Introduction: Landings   1
Gary Backhaus and John Murungi

2   On the Question of Land: A Philosophical Perspective   19
John Murungi

3   Where the Beaver Gnaw: Predatory Space
in the Urban Landscape   35
James Hatley

4   The Deceptive Environment: The Architecture of Security   55
Ruth Connell

5   Getting Nowhere Fast? Intrinsic Worth, Utility,
and Sense of Place at the Century's Turn   81
Francis Conroy

6   Auto-Mobility and the Route-Scape: A Critical Phenomenology   97
Gary Backhaus

7   Having a Need to Act   125
John A. Scott

8   Municipal Parks in New York City: Olmsted, Riis, and the
Transformation of the Urban Landscape, 1858-1897   153
Mary Hague and Nancy Siegel

9   Walking the Urban Environment: Pedestrian Practices
and Peripatetic Politics   193
David Macauley

10 Valid Research in Human Geography and the Image of the
Ideal Science   227
Derek Shanahan

Selected Bibliography   253

Index   263

About the Contributors   267

Figures

Figure 4.1   Chowan County Courthouse,
Edenton, North Carolina, begun 1767   64

Figure 4.2   Randolph County Courthouse,
Asheboro, North Carolina, 1908-1909   65

Figure 4.3   Warren B. Rudman U.S. Courthouse,
Concord, New Hampshire   65

Figure 4.4   Ronald Reagan Federal Building and Courthouse,
Santa Ana, California   66

Figure 4.5   La Crosse County Courthouse, La Crosse, Wisconsin   67

Figure 4.6   U.S. Embassy, Muscat, Oman, 1985-1989   73

Figure 8.1   Central Park before construction, c. 1860. Photograph.
Museum of the City of New York   179

Figure 8.2   Frederick Law Olmsted and Calvert Vaux, landscape
architects, "Greensward" Plan for Central Park,
New York City, 1858. Pen and ink. New York City
Department of Parks, The Arsenal   180

Figure 8.3.   Jacob Riis, *Dens of Death,* c. 1890s. Photograph.
Museum of the City of New York   181

Figure 8.4.   Jacob Riis, *Mulberry Bend,* c. 1880s. Photograph.
Museum of the City of New York   182

Figure 8.5.   Jacob Riis, *The Mulberry Bend Became a Park,* c. 1897.
Photograph. Museum of the City of New York   183

Preface

The chapters in this anthology are selected from presentations given at the First Annual Philosophy and Geography Conference held at Towson University in Towson, Maryland. They are drawn not only from philosophers and geographers, but also from conference participants from other disciplines. Since what philosophers and geographers do has implications on what others do, it was only proper that the invitations be extended to contributors in other disciplines. The presenters at the conference were informed in advance that the conference would be interdisciplinary and they were asked to prepare their presentations to meet the needs of a wide audience. The expectations were that contributors would extend their thoughts beyond the confines of their own disciplines so that cross-disciplinary bridges could be formed. The conference was designed also as a forum for conversations in order to provide the opportunity for researchers to informally cross the disciplinary divides. It is in this same spirit that these essays have been selected, which is in support of the core objective of the Society for Philosophy and Geography. This volume is a step in realizing our interdisciplinary ideal.

Readers of this volume are asked to adjust their "lenses" to accommodate philosophical speculation, case study empirical description, ethical argumentation and prescription, phenomenological description, and metatheoretical discussion. All of these approaches constitute a rich *scientia,* which when interfaced in a single volume, helps us to envision the great potential of exchange and the integration of knowledge bases.

We would like to express appreciation to the cofounders of the Society for Philosophy and Geography, Jonathan M. Smith and Andrew Light, for their encouragement and support. We express our appreciation to the administration and various departments at Towson University for their financial support and for their recognition of the importance of international, interdisciplinary conferences. We want to thank all of those scholars and friends who have attended our conferences. And, we thank Jason Hallman at Lexington Books who has exhibited great foresight in encouraging this new burgeoning dialogue between philosophy and geography.

Chapter 1

Introduction: Landings

Gary Backhaus and John Murungi

Philosophy and Geography

This collection of essays investigates processes of experience and meaning that inscribe urban and suburban landscapes. Placiality, or the meaningful organization of life as an environmental nexus, both affects and effects personal and collective identities as well as modal processes of social and environmental relations. Through its placial qualities, a landscape exhibits its own identity, which has been called *genius loci* by Norberg-Schulz.[1] But on the other hand, human activities obviously continually modify landscapes. So, the processes of landscapes as human expressive activities result in objectivations that modify the *genius loci*, which, in turn, modify human identities and relations. This dialectical relation or mutual implication is the undergirding principle in the chapters that follow.

The spatial characteristics of the various forms of human interaction and social orientation involve primary and secondary (technologically enhanced) zones of operation, the worlds of actual and potential (restorable and attainable) reach.[2] These necessary spatial structures of experience are formed upon the basis of the lived-body. However, these structures are qualitatively organized in relation with empirical geographical conditions, which are necessarily imposed. The lived-body always finds itself situated in a particular qualitatively organized geography, from which relational structures of implacement (or the collusion of lived-body and place) autochtonously emerge.[3] The concrete spatial organization of the life-world is a fundamental condition for the possibility of our social interaction and orientation. But the geographical component does more than provide a spatial situation or an occasion; by conditioning the relational form, it affects the contents of social relations. The social world is constructed through a dialectical process of externalization, objectivation, and internalization.[4] Yet, these processes are only possible in a natural/social/cultural *geographic* context that structures the horizon or limit for all our pragmatically motivated interests and indirectly for all of our interests, since the everyday life-world is the paramount reality.[5] Human expression is a spatial expression; it exudes its *geographicity*. We must be careful not to partition form and content when talking about space, because we then make the mistake of treating the geographical component as a formal container wherein events take place.[6] Human events are sociogeographical; they are at once producers and products of spatial relations. It is out of connected, yet discontinuous temporally and spatially modified and stratified social relations that this very introduction has been created. What are the philosophical underpinnings of this point? We can illustrate our thesis through referring to our own project of preparing this volume.

Epistemologically, we are claiming that theoretical thought does not transcend its context. Yet, it can be argued that the objective meaning of this introduction can be apprehended without any reference to the spatial or geographical conditions that provided the "occasion" for its creation. The putative paradigmatic example of an objective meaning is that, $1 + 1 = 2$, regardless of who thinks it when, where, and how the objective formula is presented. But such an abstraction of a meaning from the life-world context can be interpreted as a metonym for the crisis of Western *scientia*—the theoretical posit of an objective, contextless world "above" the life-world context.[7] The canon of modern *scientia* is, in fact, number, and all meanings are to be reduced and quantified by laws of mathematics. Either a qualitative meaning is stripped of its non-reality through a reduction to number, or it is inherently and merely subjective and thus discounted. This epistemology has informed the geographies that reduce place to a homogeneous spatial container where dots and lines map objective reality.[8] This charge should not be misconstrued as a rejection of quantitative methodologies. However, we are pointing out a philosophic bias that would limit science to quantitative analyses. Seduced by the idea of objectivity and the operational procedure of gathering "simple facts," the correlates of the atom of natural science, the positivist strains of the later developed "human sciences" abnegated philosophy (metaphysics/speculation). Ironically, the alleged abnegation of philosophy is a form of philosophical objectivism and more than that it rests on a speculative foundation concerning the nature of reality. The abstraction of "objectivism" is a highly suspect philosophical path. The modern sciences (both natural and human) assume a philosophical orientation and foundation like the fellow who does not know that all along he has been speaking prose.

Due to our admitted interest in the geographical context of meanings, we could be accused by philosophers of another form of reductionism, not psychologism, biologism, sociologism, or historicism, but "geographism"—the reduction of all meanings to their geographical textuality. Reductionism is the relativization of theoretical thought by taking a circumscribed sphere of empirical investigation and hypostatizing it to the realm of ultimate reality. Both those who would engage in geographical reductionism and those who would be firm in their polemic against it seem to presuppose that geography is essentially static and thus do not treat it as a dynamic process. Can we settle, once and for all, what geography is?

There are "germs" for a geographical reductionism in Kant and Hegel.[9] Even though geography has not gained its due because of the temporocentrism of Western culture, perhaps the "discovery" of the importance of geographical placiality will result in yet another reductionistic attempt. We do not deny that the "relative-objective meaning" of the introduction can be interpreted without an investigation of the spatial material conditions that provided the context for the objectivation of subjective expression. However, the epistemological tradition that ignores the fundamental structures of the life-world, which consist of placiality, historicality, and sociality, has become bankrupt. This epistemological tradition that does not subordinate thought to any supra-theoretical factors is the paradigmatic "excellence" of the Enlightenment, its *Weltanschauung,* through which modern science emerges. But the aforementioned supra-theoretical modalities of experience are not merely conditions for the possibility. The historicity of experiential modalities enters into the shaping of the act-objectivations and artifacts of human endeavor. Historically, the economic component of material existence became the first condition in modernity to be taken seriously as a determinant of the contents of consciousness (thought). However, every aspect of empirical life that qualitatively conditions the necessary structures of the life-world must be seriously investigated. We do not intend, then, that geography is to be understood as any more or less important in this respect. Our intention, however, is to highlight the geographical contextualization of the life-world, and thus, emphasize the subordination of thought to Being from the standpoint of the geographic modality of experience. So, as an objectivated product of human expression, it would be a mistake to merely apprehend its objective sense, and it would be a mistake to think that its objective sense can be reduced to some component of its genesis. Insightful knowledge has a much more difficult task.

Just as the introduction has been created through sociogeographical processes, the thematic synthesis of philosophy and geography involves an interrelation between disciplines. A social relation must emerge whereby researchers deterritorialize their "own disciplines" and enter into an interpretive and explicative space of interinvolvement. This volume of essays has been conceived as an experiment in deterritorialization. But, the supra-theoretical contents of this interdisciplinary sociality are already interrelated prior to a commitment to interact. The I-me relation is already a social one, for the recognition of a "me" is carved out of social categories.[10] The recognition of the identity of a discipline is carved out from socially recognized regions of phenomena. Thus, the social relation is formed in the very forming of an identity. But an identity becomes fragmented, if it no longer maintains a distance from itself. In the psychology of mind-altering drugs, it is said that the ego becomes fragmented when it can no longer separate itself from the objects that it perceives. The disciplines become fragmented when after their initial carving out of an identity, they do not distance themselves from their own regions. The convergence of I and me is a loss of identity, a useless endeavor to become god-like (in-itself-for-itself as Sartre has described it),[11] which ends in the fragmentation of identity. The overemphasis of a discipline (spontaneous subjective activity of the I/ego) *to be* its territory (the objectified me) actually results in a dysfunctional or lost identity. The recognition of the non-monadological context of a discipline generates theoretical transformation. It is through relations that an open system self-organizes and grows to new systemic levels; it needs diversification in order to develop its identity. To treat a discipline as a closed system is to have it suffer from entropy and identity-reduction. Disciplines have both internal and external horizons and the development of internal horizons alone leads to a dysfunctional narcissistic existence. The academic institutionalization of disciplines, each fortifying its own territory, encourages an intellectual narcissism, and a crisis in the academy. Narcissistic ideology threatens to conceal the relational significance in the discovery of both the "individual" and social reality as open dynamic systems.

But this transformational discovery involves a difficult task. The academic partitioning of disciplines has led to the social segregation of scholars. Each discipline has developed and has institutionalized its own specialized language to the point of mummification. Language must be revived in a way that the disciplines can re-establish a living contact with each other. "The increasing number and complexity of sub-universes make them increasingly inaccessible to outsiders. They become esoteric enclaves."[12] Outsiders are to be kept out and the insiders kept in. Interdisciplinary study renders the hermetically sealed walls of text permeable, but only by great effort. Technical languages reflect the hierarchical model of expert versus layperson, and it is difficult to relinquish this buttressing of territorial power.

In cross-disciplinary discussions, there seems to be an uneasiness that pervades the horizon of the conversations, which at any moment threatens the progress of constructing, or envisioning, social bridges. For the practitioners are called out of their disciplines, which means calling into question their identities. Existentially we still want to cling to the illusion of a center and so to participate in an experience that involves the de-centering of identity is met with psychological resistance. How can any work get accomplished by calling into question its meaning in a way that entails the problematizing of one's own being?

A living relation between philosophy and geography allows each to further develop an identity. Philosophy becomes what it will develop into in its relation to geography and geography will develop into what it will develop into in its relation to philosophy. So, this volume provides space for philosophy to explore what it is through its interaction with geography, and vice versa. The anthology is constituted at the expense of academic fortifications for the sake of renewing the social process of identity. Drawing from the later Husserl, Merleau-Ponty characterizes the relation between science and philosophy as a reciprocal envelopment.[13] He is not thinking from the standpoint of a bipolar relation between disciplines or groups of professionals. A reciprocal envelopment is a continuum of the interpenetration of philosophical and scientific attitudes. Any thinker or group of practitioners finds their query along a continuum that is both scientific and philosophical, or if you want to attempt to think beyond the categories of the modern bifurcation, neither scientific nor philosophical (in traditional senses). No longer can philosophy retreat to the foundations while science builds the edifice. The "building metaphor" no longer symbolizes a viable paradigm. A better metaphor for the symbolization of reality is the warp and woof of an ever-changing weaving pattern. The epistemological program for positivism only saw isolated data; it could not see relations and processes. And thus the sciences carved out regions (rooms in the house) in which certain kinds of isolated facts were to be collected and stored. But from the standpoint of the new paradigm, no region can any longer maintain its identity without taking into account the whole. Yet, the whole is a process that is too complex to grasp in its entirety and each attempt at envisioning an embedded, contextual reality leads to its modification. There is no view from above (sorry philosophy, you have lost the possibility to build foundations) and there is no window from which objects are objectively transparent (sorry science, it is no longer prudent to dominate or control through prediction and manipulation). Thus philosophy and science both must step down from their respective *hubris*. Philosophy is empty without science and science is blind without philosophy. There is no *philosophia* that does not entail *scientia* and no *scientia* that does not entail *philosophia*. Any attempt to separate these attitudes is abstractive. Any attempt to break apart the lifeworld into non-related regions of being is abstractive. And both of these abstractive *praxes* are egregious distortions. Here we have borrowed the language of Kant, but our project is not Kantian. We are not in the business of demonstrating how objective scientific knowledge is possible. We are in the processs of articulating a new synthesis of philosophy and science, wisdom and knowledge (*sophia* and *phronesis*), by which neither play their traditional roles and in a way that envelops both, which will create categories that only the future will be able to describe.

Postmodern thought emphasizes the non-privilege of any single voice, and places emphasis on the plurality of voices. The postmodernism that posits that all reality is text may be guilty of hyperbole, but this assertion is not wholly wrong. The cultural crisis that corroborates the crisis of science is what Baudrillard has called the simulacrum. Our abstractions have developed in such a way that symbols symbolize other symbols and reality is simulated and dissimulated in a purely constructive manner.[14] But the play of which Derrida speaks is not frivolity; it is the de-centering principle of structures.[15] Heidegger speaks of Western metaphysics being emptied of its original meaning in technological thinking and practice. But what needs to be added is that technology is emptied in a semiotic nihilism. The seriousness of this state-of-affairs can be witnessed through the abstractive development of our economic system. "Xenomoney, floating, and inconvertible to anything outside itself, signifies itself. More specifically, it signifies possible relations it can establish with future states of itself. Its 'value' is the relation between what it *was* worth, as an index number in relation to some fixed and arbitrary past state taken as an origin, and what the market judges it *will* be worth at different points in the future."[16] The origins of money are merely traces and its value is to be crossed out (the Derridean erasure).[17] Only a very small percentage of money transactions have anything to do with goods and services—a remnant of nonsymbolic reality that is a mere glitch in the simulacra. But the postmodern critique that captures the meaning of this kind of phenomena is dependent upon the abstractive mistakes of modernity. Seeing that the reality of which modernity speaks doesn't exist, it then confuses the empirical-historicality of our age, the self-referencings of symbolic systems and their de-constructions, with the structures of systems as such.

However, supra-theoretical reality is best understood as an open dynamic system—this new paradigm of *scientia* is on the verge of taking hold and post-modernity has been only a stepping zone toward a new optimism for theoretical progress, which hopefully is not too late. But it is no longer justified, as post-modern thinkers have pointed out, to connect "reality" with the metaphor of the mirror when discussing the legitimacy of theoretical concepts. The new paradigm dissolves the dualism on which such an epistemological problem is raised. It is through reflection on this scientific paradigm shift with its transformations that our cross-disciplinary project has been formulated.

'Philosophy'—from the Greek word, 'philo,' has been translated roughly as 'love,' and from the Greek word, 'sophia,' which has been translated as 'wisdom.' This endeavor is the fundamental reflective, questioning and problematizing attitude of humankind. 'Geography'—from the Greek, 'geo,' has been translated as 'earth,' and from 'graphein,' which means to write. Geography is the open dynamic spatiality that spans the earth's surface and the discipline of geography investigates this earthly whereness. As an earthbound science, it implicates everyone, including geographers and philosophers, for every human being is earthbound. Geographers, through mapping the earth, map themselves as well as the human. So, wherever geographers and philosophers gather for dialogue and conversation, no human being is a stranger and every discipline should recognize its kinship with other disciplines. Those practitioners in other disciplines that do not recognize their kinship do not fully understand themselves.

But the placiality of the academy is based upon a no longer viable epistemological and ontological paradigm and so its landscape is one of segregated "departments" of study. The fact that the segregated academy has produced territorialized researchers who defend intellectually constructed abstractions should not deter us from reformulating the problematic. The spatial textuality of the earth belongs exclusively to no department or discipline. Since reality is a whole, an interrelated open dynamic system, all "disciplines" have something to contribute to the relation of philosophy and geography and any particular problematic that is conceived through their relation. The theoretical approximation of the open system network of reality is greatly enhanced through a diversity of "academic departments" contributing to the same problematic. So, philosophy and geography must be conceived in such a way as to include all voices as an integral part of the conversation. For the most part, philosophical questioning had been extirpated from the trained minds of scientists, and scientific investigation and its evidences had been extirpated from the theoretical work of philosophers. The new thinker/researcher will transcend the still institutionalized nineteenth century contrivance of academic disciplines and the alienation of philosophy and will synthesize a higher systemic level of research. Academia need not tear down its disciplines but it needs to emphasize external horizons, which means the destructuring of territorialization. Nothing less than the transformation of *scientia* allows for us to discuss the transformation of urban and suburban landscapes in a fertile manner.

Transformation, Landscape, and
Urban and Suburban Phenomena

The Meaning of 'Transformation'

Inexorable motion and change, the universal flux, is the ground upon which relatively stable systems and relations of systems emerge. A relatively stable system exhibits fundamental principles of organization that must be maintained in order for the system to remain in existence. In one of his famous papers on gestalt principles, Wolfgang Köhler explains that "each local event" in a fragile soap bubble must dynamically "know" the "behaviors" of the others. This is what is meant by self-organization. Each event must play its respective part in establishing equilibrium against the air currents that both support and threaten the bubble's existence.[18] At some point the chaos introduced into the inwardly/outwardly functional system is too much and at that very moment the soap bubble bursts. Most relatively stable systems are much more complex and are better at meeting external changes with inner adaptations, which allows for a continued existence. What about the changing qualities determining existence? Some changes do not maintain the gestalt-character, which means that the elements become reorganized in accordance with a new set of system-level principles. For example, various vectors of change resulted in a systems-level transformation from feudalism to the system of commercialism. Change at the systems-level, which results in the reorganization of the whole bringing about newly emergent meanings of the parts, is what we mean by transformation.

The editors specifically employ the word, 'transformations,' to be contrasted with the words, 'changes,' and 'modifications.' If the theoretical conception apprehends landscape as an openly organized dynamic whole, then some forms of change would rearrange the parts but in a way that the quality of the system as a whole is maintained. However, what is meant by 'transformation' is a qualitative destructuring of the whole, a process in which the weave (reality) formulates a new pattern. Another way of saying this is that a 'transformation' implies something like a paradigm shift, but in this context a new system emerges in the spatial mapping of the life-world. Paradigm shifts do admit of degrees. A qualitative reorganization of a system can result in a whole that is quite different from the prior patterning, or it can alter the whole in a more subtle way. Of course all changes alter the whole, but not in terms of reorganization at the systems level. Systems are characterized in terms of a continuum from the relatively stable to the highly unstable. But open dynamic systems are systems that de-systematize themselves, due to the fact that they are self-organizing. Chaos is an important positive factor, for it is a catalyst for the spontaneous emergence of a new systems level that cannot be reduced to, or explained by, the prior level of organization. Novelty emerges out of these disorganizing dynamics. In terms of transformations of landscapes, an investigator must look for features that tend to produce a chaotic disequilibrium in a sustaining pattern, for those are the characteristics that portend a fundamental reorganization of the landscape. The chapters included in this collection are investigations of features that exhibit transformational properties.

We are aware that a systems approach became fashionable in the 1970s in both geography and interdisciplinary development. Ingrid Leman Stefanovic writes, "Surveying the literature from the 1970s, one is reminded of the much lauded 'systems approach' to interdisciplinary problem solving."[19] But the theory has continued to develop and the weaknesses that seemed to show themselves in the 1970s foray are much in the past.[20] We do not develop it in any technical sense in this work; we find the open dynamic systems paradigm, however, to be the most supportive basis for our conception of transformations.

A fundamental characteristic of the twentieth century is the acceleration of change. Is humankind capable of controlling, monitoring, or contending with these changes? Many theoreticians, experts, and laypersons are very concerned with the rapid growth of human populations, the rising levels of consumption, and the rapid depletion of the natural world, the gravity of environmental problems, the rapid introduction of technologies, and the global form of economic development. The speed of change coupled with its variety and complexity has led to a greater volume of transformational trends, undulatory currents, and newly introduced elements. The following chapters provide examples of these transformational qualities of speed, variety, and complexity. But, the selection of trends, currents, and elements are more subtle than the concerns mentioned above, and thus might be overlooked when the macroscopic viewpoint is taken. The contributors begin with landscape dynamics that they have experienced either by living-through or by living-the-result-of, which then are submitted to theoretical reflection.

To illustrate this point, I (Backhaus) offer a painful memory concerning a transformation that occurred over a period of seven years from 1964 to 1971. My parents moved from the city out into the "country." There was a wood behind my house filled with snakes, turtles, birds, and mammals. At the top of our single street, which had just been carved out of an idyllic setting, there was a cornfield and next to that was grazing land for sheep. On the other side of the street from our house behind those newly built houses that stood opposite to ours, there stretched across the landscape a beautiful apple orchard. I had no idea at first that my family had moved into the suburbs—like the first arrow shot at the beginning of a battle, ours was the first street to usher in the transformation. The country landscape quickly changed and much much more of the landscape has been transformed over the years. I remember in 1971 climbing on top of the roof of our house and seeing *nothing but* other rooftops. By then there were no snakes, no turtles, none of the animals, no woods and wooded paths, and no food being grown—just roads, driveways, cars, and houses. "Place identity answers the question—Who am I?—by countering—Where am I? or Where do I belong? From a social psychological perspective, place identities are thought to arise because places, as bounded locales imbued with personal, social, and cultural meanings, provide a significant framework in which identity is constructed, maintained, and transformed."[21] The placial meanings that were forming my identity as a child were obliterated in a transformation in which my own family was an accomplice. This "self-destruction" is what I realized in

1971 as I gazed from our rooftop. The very fact that such transformations of landscapes do engender an incredibly deep psychological impact testifies to how fundamentally the placiality of landscape is interwoven in the meaning of life itself. But what is offered in chapter 6 is not a phenomenological description of this experience. Rather, the experience serves as a catalyst for a transposition to another level—to the treatment of suburbia as a system made possible by the transformational effects of auto-mobility. James Hatley (chapter 3) is an avid backpacker, which serves as a catalyst for the transposition of this experience into a meditation concerning the asymmetry/symmetry of edibility and the transformational possibilities for a new ethic.

The Meaning of 'Landscape'

'Landscape' is a term of cultural geography that begins with the fact that the "physical earth" (an ideal limiting concept) is always an interpreted phenomenon—it is always a supra-physical reality. This statement does not entail anthropomorphic or anthropocentric standpoints, for even ecocentric standpoints are interpretations. Landscape is generally a holistic concept and if it is differentiated from the term 'environment,' it is because the perceptual, i.e., tangible relations of elements, are emphasized.[22] Lowenthal has examined how human values are embedded in landscape through cultural interpretations.[23] Landscape experiences influence cultures and are symbolically interpreted and modified through cultures. Donald W. Meinig reads landscapes as texts through historical methodology and discourse analysis. Meinig unpacks "not only the physical information contained in landscapes, but also the beliefs, values, shared habits, and preferences that different cultures exhibit in the ways their landscapes are arranged."[24]

Let us relate this general understanding of 'landscape' to our notion of 'transformations.' A natural occurrence, such as a volcanic eruption, can alter the whole (the landscape) such that a new ecological organization emerges. Human intervention also qualitatively alters geographical organization at the systems level. Major paradigm shifts would be the emergence of the humanized landscape of agriculture, the creation of cities as human centers, the emergence of the suburb, counter-urbanization, edge-cities, and the megalopolis. Some researchers have looked into the loss of the commons, factory farming, deforestation, or the loss of wetlands through the expansion of ecosystem altering human activities. These transformational practices portend paradigm shifts of grave ecological consequences. J. B. Jackson in an article (1953) in *Landscape* describes the modifications in consciousness toward the farm in three generations of a family. Nehemiah thought of the farm as "a fragment of creation which he is to redeem, support himself from, and pass on to his progeny." Pliny thought of the farm as "an expanding organism, the victory of one individual over Nature." Ray thought of the farm as "an instrument for the prompt and efficient conversion of natural energy . . . into economic energy."[25] Roger Paden has described four kinds of policies concerning natural areas that have been historically practiced in the United States: the developmental policy, the conservation

policy, the policy of product preservation, and the policy of process preservation.[26] Landscape is the earth's textuality, a geographic organization of the life-
world that is at once both natural and social. The landscape as a text is a hermeneutic between humans and the meaning-sedimented life-world (natural/social).
Transformation of landscapes mutually and dialectically entails transformations
of beings for whose Being is at issue as a landed-being. And even though human
beings are *condemned* to meanings, as Maurice Merleau-Ponty teaches, all beings are mutually implicated in these transformations.

The Meaning of 'Urban' and 'Suburban'

The themes of these chapters concern urban and suburban landscapes, which
are treated as dynamic processes. In context, 'suburban' signifies a twentieth-
century phenomenon that for the most part applies to "overly-developed" first
world countries, especially the United States. This is because the growth of the
suburbs has depended upon technologies such as the ownership of the automobile, and a postwar defense strategy that formulated the project of moving people out of the center of cities. Suburban living has become the symbol for a
higher standard of living and a greater level of consumption. But the growth of
the suburbs has transformed the meaning of the urban. Technologies, such as
radio and television, have led to new forms of social experience that are much
less dependent on immediate human interaction. American culture, the culture of
consumerism and economically driven manipulative forms of entertainment,
relies upon technological mediums of information transmission. We cannot, of
course, develop any of this content here in the introduction. We do want to point
out, however, that these rapid transformations outstrip the time needed for reflective valuations. Theoretical life cannot keep up with practical life, and an
important aspect of this volume is to discover who and what we have become
through these geographical transformations.

The great cultural thinkers at the turn of the twentieth century were able to
witness the rapid growth that transformed the old-world cities, which in many
cases were more like villages, into modern urban centers. At the end of the
twentieth century there are still thinkers commenting on this transformational
phenomenon. Joseph Grange notes: "What marks the difference between a city
as opposed to a village is both the size of its semiotic system as well as the way
in which space shrinks into increasingly smaller distances and time collapses
into increasingly shorter durations."[27] Intersubjectivity is intensified through the
media of signs. "The city's lines of communication become ever more critical.
Meaning (which is another term for the cultural) becomes the neural network
governing all forms of interaction. Because of its critical mass, communication
becomes the primary form of energy transformation."[28] Earlier in the introduction we described the geographical context of the placial, temporal, and social
stratifications of the life-world. In just these few sentences Grange is able to
describe the modifications of these experiential modalities in the geographical
organization of the city. We also established the point that our identities are es-

tablished socially through our relations with others and that these relations are conditioned through the geographical context. Georg Simmel, who witnessed the rapid transformation of Berlin into a modern urban center, corroborates our points as well as those of Grange. In 1903 Simmel writes:

> Lasting impressions . . . consume, so to speak, less mental energy than the rapid telescoping of changing images, pronounced differences within what is grasped in a changing glance, and the unexpectedness of violent stimuli. To the extent the metropolis creates these psychological conditions—with every crossing of the street, with the tempo and multiplicity of economic, occupational and social life—it creates . . . a deep contrast with the slower, more habitual, more smoothly flowing rhythm of the sensory-mental phase of small town and rural existence. Thereby the essentially intellectualist character of the mental life of the metropolis becomes intelligible as over against that of the small town.[29]

The reorganization of psychological habitualizations transforms identity traits and the "me" of the I-me dialectic becomes recognizable as an ideal type.

> Thus the metropolitan type . . . creates a protective organ for itself against the profound disruption with which the fluctuations and discontinuities of the external milieu threaten it. Instead of reacting emotionally, the metropolitan type reacts primarily in a rational manner, thus creating a mental predominance through the intensification of consciousness. . . . The reaction . . . is moved to the sphere of mental activity which is least sensitive and which is furthest removed from the depths of the personality.[30]

The production of modern cities results as an objectivated typology that manifests in their *genius loci*, which then informs consciousness and the lived-body, and thus transforms the parameters of human identities.

The newer form of geographic organization, the suburb, has superseded the city, bringing with it a transformation that implicates the meaning of both. By identifying potentially transformational currents within the urban/suburban landscapes, human beings can become aware of their responsibilities, for we already recognize responsibility for ourselves, and we are implicated in the landscape. Until we become conscious of these currents, we do not understand our own identity and we allow objectivated currents, which have taken on a "life" of their own, decide our identity for us. Do we want to be these landscapes that we are?

Overview of the Volume

In terms of a brief schematic, the volume contains three chapters (2, 7, and 10) that are more theoretical in nature. In chapter 2, Murungi shows that the transformational processes of urban and suburban landscapes are inexorably linked to a fundamental hermeneutic of human identity and meaning. In chapter 7, Scott focuses upon the nature of transformation and what is required of its agents. In chapter 10, Shanahan presents the transformational trends in geographical research, which certainly affects how transformations of landscapes are to be apprehended and interpreted. Chapter 3, Hatley, and chapter 5, Conroy, call for ethical transformations in the landscapes based upon their respective observations of sedimented axiologies exhibited in our contemporary landscapes. Chapter 4, Connell, and chapter 8, Hague and Siegel, offer two fine case studies of transformational trends. In chapter 6, Backhaus, and chapter 9, Macauley, descriptions of transformational experiences of auto-mobility and walking, respectively, corroborate one another by displaying a complementary contrast.

Our volume begins with John Murungi's chapter, "On the Question of Land: A Philosophical Perspective." In raising the question, "who is land?" Murungi invites us to reconstruct our thinking about land in a way that bridges the abyss that has opened up in the West—an ontological (Being) abyss that creates an ontic (beings) gap between human being and landscape. Through raising this question we are summoned to reconstruct the way we think about and approach ourselves. This hermeneutic bridging raises the possibility of understanding the ontological bond between the Being of human and the Being of land and it generates the thinking about praxes that reveal their intertwining. The question of the who-ness of landscape transformations is the general concern of all of the chapters in this volume.

The next chapter addresses an axiological crisis in the overlapping of human and natural landscapes. In his chapter, "Where the Beaver Gnaw: Predatory Space and the Urban Landscape," James Hatley raises the problematic concerning two orders of goodness: the ordering of landscape according to asymmetrical and symmetrical predation. The attempt to erect a boundary whereby humans eat but are not eaten (and this is extended to being bitten and stung or to having one's homes and gardens threatened by hungry beings) conceals a crisis, a problematic in the very attempt to partition human and natural space. The feeling of uncanniness occurs when the "other" encroaches upon what humans have tried to keep separate. When we feel uncanny we are outside ourselves and we cannot re-enter our own space. But the uncanny is also an uncovering because it reveals that identity is only formed in relations with the identities of others, even those we encounter in the more-than-human-landscapes. Hatley argues that a new ethic must be realized—an ethic that is not built upon a repression of predation. In a revealing way, Hatley's concern leads to the discussion of the next paper that involves transformations based on human to human "predation."

In her chapter, "The Deceptive Environment: The Architecture of Security," Ruth Connell documents the expanding phenomenon of building unseen or unrecognized elements into architectural designs. She describes the elements of security design and their implementation in various types and particular sites of buildings. Connell raises social, political, and ethical implications as grist for the reader's reflection. One aspect of possible transformation is that the more buildings become fortress-like, environmental security retreats to the "inside." Since the fortress is segregated from the "outside," the public streets become less safe—the public-private fluid relation evaporates and forms a geographical segregation. Obviously, this trend can lead to a transformation of the public/private spheres and their relation. We ask the question who and what will we become when we know that we are spatially manipulated for purposes of "security design," and moreover that we may not know by whom, for what reason, where, how, or when? Are we building landscapes of suspicion? Do we create boundaries of control, or is it that we want to create landscapes of responsibility and prudence? Here we set up at least a couple of asymmetries: the watchers and the watched, and the protectors and the protected. Who watches the watchers and who protects the protectors? Inscribed in the landscape is the policing function. Is this policing function inscribed in the landscape necessary to ensure also the inscription of a security function? Looking back to the previous paper we recognize here another kind of attempt at sealing ourselves off from the Other. The more fortressing and monitoring we introduce in the landscape, the more we implicate others in our own being in a particular way. If others are to be watched, which could be argued as a dehumanizing activity, do we not dehumanize ourselves? This specific concern over security design opens up the broader concern of the next chapter: transformation of the landscape through the geographical mapping of values based upon ethical instrumentalism.

In his chapter, "Getting Nowhere Fast? Intrinsic Worth, Utility, and Sense of Place at the Century's Turn," Francis Conroy distinguishes "homes" from "settings-in-which-we-are-interchangeable-parts." He argues that the home setting correlates with the ethical orientation of intrinsic worth and that the interchangeable parts setting correlates with the ethics of utility. He argues that both types of settings are necessary for the geographic organization of life, but that a transformational trend in which the interchangeable parts setting has become exaggerated and dominant has led to a loss of a very deep aspect of our Being— dwelling. The ethics of instrumentality now dominates our lives, because its inscription in the landscape has become hegemonic. At the end of his chapter, Conroy calls for a new synthesis of these forms of settings. We might add that his proposed geographical transformation then calls for a new ethical paradigm that transcends the intrinsic and instrumental debate. Looking backwards at the previous chapter we could apply Conroy's distinctions to security design. Perhaps we need to look at what form of ethics solicits the security-designed landscapes. Conroy's study leads to the more specific concerns of the next chapter, which aids this thesis by a case study that exhibits certain consequences in the spatial mapping of instrumental values.

In his chapter, "Auto-mobility and the Route-scape: A Critical Phenomenology," Gary Backhaus synthesizes environmental philosophy, critical theory, and phenomenology in order to investigate the automobile landscape. He argues that the over dependence upon auto-mobility uproots us from place, and this uprootedness leads to insensitivity toward issues of placiality, especially environmental problems. The fundamental relation of the ambulatory upright posture to the landscape is nearly replaced by automobile use. This transformation is hardly noticed within our everyday adaptations. Yet, harkening back to Murungi's chapter, the "who" that is the landscape may just be a machine, the automobile, for it dominates the landscape. The insensitivity to the mediating function of the automobile in determining the collusion between the lived-body and place specifically alienates us from taking seriously the environmental crisis, which is implicated in the very object that uproots us. A phenomenological investigation of auto-mobility is carried out for the purposes of exposing the structure of uprootedness embedded in this mode of transportation. The costs to the environment due to automobile use are tolerated, for in its very use we are distanced (alienated) from the environment. The issue of uprootedness leads to the concerns of the next chapter, which investigates the need to act in order to dwell in a manner of belonging.

In his chapter, "Having a Need to Act," John A. Scott maintains that the transformations of landscapes need to be founded upon living well or dwelling. Like Heidegger, he is critical of the substitution of construction or building for dwelling. Perhaps Conroy's distinction between homes and settings of interchangeable parts is again germane. Whereas Heidegger claims that we must await Being in order to relinquish the manipulative domination that has uprooted us as dwelling beings, Scott claims that waiting "for the weal that has withdrawn" is inadequate for living well, and that in order to dwell, we must act. Scott returns to Aristotle in order to describe the integrative, dynamic, reflective process that promotes a transformation of human being. This requires both *scientia* and *praxis*; dwelling is a knowing that shapes living. But the shaping is to be based on needing, the needing of a home, and the needing involves a teleology of belonging. Urban and suburban landscapes must belong to us fully, as something loved in order to live well, for only then will we live an integrated being, that is, as a full human community. Scott's concern for an active dwelling leads to the next chapter's discussion of specific actions and sites that put the philosophy of needing to act into practice.

In their chapter, "Municipal Parks in New York: Olmsted, Riis, and the Transformation of the Urban Landscape, 1858-1897," Mary Hague and Nancy Siegel investigate the repercussions of the dense gridiron geography of New York, which was built to serve a growing industrialized economic organization. The accelerated development of the business sector did not take into consideration the physical, psychological, and sociological needs of the people who worked and lived in the city. This chapter presents a fine case study in the sub-field, geographies of health, through exploring the geographically mapped philosophies and politics of Frederick Law Olmsted and Jacob Riis, who promoted the inclusion of open spaces, parks, and playgrounds within the urban environs. The lesson to learn is that society must continually guard against the threatening possibility that the geographical mappings of economic transformations take precedence over a healthy human ecology in urban and suburban landscapes. The operative concern here is the construction and maintenance of the healthy landscape, or what Wilbert Gessler has called the therapeutic landscape.[31] The theme of active involvement and political geography is taken up in the next chapter.

In his chapter, "Walking the Urban Environment: Pedestrian Practices and Peripatetic Politics," David Macauley discusses the fundamental activity of walking as a political and environmental practice. He discusses walking cities and then pits these forms against our "technological somnambulism" and our "technomadic" lifestyles. His message is simple, but yet so profound: if you want to deeply understand cities and their surroundings, the politically mapped geography, you should walk them. Macauley uncovers the close connection between walking and place by investigating the decline of the walkers' world that characterizes our contemporary landscapes. To walk in the withdrawal of the walkers' world reveals an authoritarian hegemony and control. This internalized socialization ironically succeeds by the fact that the transformed land-scape has produced a society of non-walkers who are oblivious to the oppression they suffer. Walk the non-walking landscape and you can become liberated from its ideology that you have lived unconsciously. Do you know really who you are if you are oblivious to the need for an ideological unmasking concerning our fundamental question: who is the landscape?

In the last chapter, "Valid Research in Human Geography and the Image of an Ideal Science," Derek Shanahan provides a perfect complement to the introduc-tion to our volume. He discusses transformations in the manner in which we conduct scientific inquiry, which of course has impact on our interpretations of the transformations of landscapes. Shanahan investigates alternative orientations within the discipline of geography that have been misunderstood and dismissed from the standpoint of the dominant paradigm of positivism. The argument cen-ters on phenomenological methodology and Shanahan's apology for phenome-nology takes the strategy of showing phenomenology's affinity with the posi-tivistic emphasis on evidence while at the same time avoiding the positivist dogmatic.

Notes

1. Christian Norberg-Schulz, *Genius Loci: Towards a Phenomenology of Architecture* (New York: Rizzoli International, 1984).
2. Alfred Schutz and Thomas Luckmann, "Spatial Arrangement of the Everyday Life-World," in *The Structures of the Life-World*, trans. Richard M. Zaner and H. Tristram Engelhardt Jr. (Evanston, Ill.: Northwestern University, 1973), 36-45.
3. For an explication of the notion of implacement, see Edward S. Casey, *Getting Back Into Place* (Bloomington: Indiana University Press, 1993).
4. Peter L. Berger and Thomas Luckmann, *The Social Construction of Reality* (Lon-don: Anchor, 1966), 60-61.
5. In his theory of sub-universes, William James introduces the concept of paramount reality. See William James, "The Paramount Reality of Sensations," in *The Principles of Psychology,* vol. 2 (New York: Dover, 1950), 299-306.
6. Kant is mistaken when he makes space a form of experience. But this follows from the fact that he only admits of a formal a priori. Merleau-Ponty states, "We cannot under-stand . . . the experience of space either in terms of the consideration of contents or of that of some pure unifying activity; we are confronted with that third spatiality . . . which is neither that of things in space, nor that of spatializing space, and which, on this ac-count, evades the Kantian analysis." Maurice Merleau-Ponty, "Space," in *Phenomenol-ogy of Perception*, trans. Colin Smith (London: Routledge & Kegan Paul, 1962), 248.
7. Psychologism attempted to reduce the ideality of meanings to real psychological events. This was an erroneous way to frame the problem of context. In his, "Prolegomena to Pure Logic," Husserl thoroughly defeats psychologism, which saved the ideality and objectivity of meanings. See Edmund Husserl, *Logical Investigations,* vol. 1, trans. J. N. Findlay (London: Routledge & Kegan Paul, 1970), 53-247. Nevertheless, through the doctrine of intentionality, Husserl sets up the proper framework for the problem of con-text. All meanings are constituted, which means that the subjective acts that constitute objective meanings are essential to the grounding of meanings. See Edmund Husserl,

"Logical Investigation VI," in *Logical Investigations,* vol. 2, trans. J. N. Findlay (London: Routledge & Kegan Paul, 1970), 677-834. Because objectivist thought is inherently an abstraction, Husserl's work erroneously appears to those of that position as subjectivism. Husserl later develops the crisis of the sciences as the development of a theoretical "knowledge" that has lost its connection to the life-world, that is, de-contextualized thought. See, Edmund Husserl, *The Crisis of European Sciences and Transcendental Phenomenology,* trans. David Carr (Evanston, Ill.: Northwestern University Press, 1970).

8. For a discussion of modern epistemology in terms of its conception of space, see Edward S. Casey, "Part Three: The Supremacy of Space," in *The Fate of Place* (Berkeley: University of California Press, 1998), 133-93.

9. For an illuminating discussion of Kant's geography, see Robert Burch, "On the Ethical Determination of Geography: A Kantian Prolegomenon," in *Philosophy and Geography I: Space, Place, and Environmental Ethics,* ed. Andrew Light and Jonathan M. Smith (Lanham, Md.: Rowman & Littlefield, 1997), 15-47. See Georg Wilhelm Friedrich Hegel, "Geographical Basis of History," in *The Philosophy of History,* trans. J. Sibree (New York: Dover, 1956), 79-102.

10. For the definitive discussion of the socially mediated I-me structure, see George Herbert Mead, "The Self," in *Mind, Self, and Society,* ed. Charles W. Morris (Chicago: University of Chicago Press, 1934), 135-226.

11. Jean-Paul Sartre, "The Desire to be God," in *Existentialism and Human Emotions,* trans. Hazel E. Barnes (New York: Philosophical Library, 1985), 60-67.

12. Berger and Luckmann, *Social Construction,* 87.

13. See Maurice Merleau-Ponty, "The Philosopher and Sociology," in *Signs,* trans. Richard C. McCleary (Evanston, Ill.: Northwestern University Press, 1964), 98-113.

14. Jean Baudrillard, *Simulations,* trans. Paul Foss, Paul Patton, and Philip Beitchman (New York: Semiotexte, 1983).

15. We agree with Derrida's point that play involves disruption. Play functions analogously to chaos in open dynamic system theory. However, we disagree with Derrida when he states, "Being must be conceived as presence or absence in the basis of the possibility of play and not the other way around." Jacques Derrida, "Structure, Sign and Play in the Discourse of the Human Sciences," in *Writing and Difference,* trans. Alan Bass (Chicago: University of Chicago Press, 1976), 292. We conceive of a dialectical relation where neither is the basis of the other. Structures (meanings) are achieved, but due to their openness, destructuring is inherent to them.

16. Brian Rotman, *Signifying Nothing: The Semiotics of Zero* (Stanford: Stanford University Press, 1987), 92.

17. Derrida's concept, sous rature, is used to mean the already absent presence. Derrida denies that a sign can reveal objects; signs can only refer to other signs. The furthest development of economic symbols seems to exhibit this emergent property.

18. See the discussion by Maurice Merleau-Ponty, *The Structures of Behavior,* trans. Alden L. Fisher (Boston: Beacon Press, 1963), 143-44. See, Wolfgang Kohler, "Physical Gestalten," in *A Source Book of Gestalt Psychology,* ed. Willis D. Ellis (New York: Harcourt Brace, 1938), 17-54.

19. Ingrid Leman Stefanovic, Safeguarding Our Common Future: Rethinking Sustainable Development (Albany: SUNY, 2000), 61.

20. Systems theorists have been able to incorporate the latest of findings as well as various important theories, e.g., chaos theory, into its approach. Furthermore, prominent phenomenologists see the theories of open dynamic systems and self-organizing systems as complementary to phenomenology. See Anna-Teresa Tymieniecka, "The New Paradigm: The Ontopoiesis of Life as a New Starting Point of Philosophy," in *Phenomenological Inquiry,* 22 (October 1998): 12-59. Also, Ralph D. Ellis, "Integrating the Physiological and Phenomenological Dimensions of Affect and Motivation," in *The Caldrons of*

Consciousness, ed. Ralph D. Ellis and Natika Newton (Amsterdam: John Benjamins, 2000), 3-26.

21. L. Cuba and D. Hummon, "A Place to Call Home: Identification with Dwelling, Community, and Region," *Sociological Quarterly* 34, 112.

22. Reginald G. Golledge and Robert J. Stimson, "Landscape Perception," in *Spatial Behavior: A Geographic Perspective* (London: Guilford, 1997), 392.

23. D. Lowenthal, "Past Time, Present Place," in *The Geographic Review,* 65 (1975): 1-36.

24. Golledge and Stimpson, *Spatial Behavior,* 392. See D. W. Meinig, ed., *The Interpretation of Ordinary Landscapes: Geographical Essays* (New York: Oxford University Press, 1979).

25. J. B. Jackson, "The Westward-moving House," in *Landscapes,* ed. Ervin H. Zube (Amherst: University of Massachusetts Press, 1970), 37-38.

26. Roger Paden, "Wilderness Management," in *Philosophy and Geography I: Space, Place, and Environmental Ethics,* ed. Andrew Light and Jonathan M. Smith (Lanham, Md.: Rowman & Littlefield, 1997), 175-87.

27. Joseph Grange, *The City An Urban Cosmology* (Albany: State University of New York Press, 1999), xxix.

28. Grange, *The City,* xxviii.

29. Georg Simmel, *On Individuality and Social Forms,* ed. Donald N. Levine (Chicago: University of Chicago Press, 1971), 325.

30. Simmel, *On Individuality,* 326.

31. Robin A. Kearns and William M. Gessler, eds., *Putting Health into Place: Landscape, Identity, and Well-Being* (Syracuse, N.Y.: Syracuse University Press, 1998).

Chapter 2

On the Question of Land:
A Philosophical Perspective

John Murungi

Whether explicitly or implicitly, when we speak about the transformations of urban and suburban landscapes we inevitably concern ourselves with land. How we concern ourselves with land reveals not only our understanding of land, but also an understanding of ourselves. This intertwining double understanding is not self-evident, and one might add, it is not always explicit. In regard to land, normally, we concern ourselves with what we are doing to the land, on the land, with the land, or what is happening to it. Normally, we do not pay attention to what we are doing to ourselves, or to what is happening to us in our dealings with land. When the opposite occurs, that is, when the question of land appears to affect us, it is only in an inessential way. For example, when we acknowledge that our survival is dependent on land, what we normally have in mind is mostly survival in the same sense that any other living being is dependent on land for survival. It is not that this sense of survival should be trivialized. It is indeed a necessary condition for every other sense of survival. But it is not the only necessary condition, and we should not be held hostage to it. There are other land-based experiences that open up other dimensions of our being—dimensions that are also essential for other aspects of our survival.

Other than the biological significance for survival, the question of land appears to be exterior to what we are, and the question of our being appears exterior to the question of land. That the question of land is essentially the question of being human, and that the question of being human is essentially the question of land, may strike us as absurd. What seems absurd, however, may conceal a more elemental experience of truth as it pertains to us and to land. To be sure, that the question of the one is the question of the other, points to the uncanny way of the questioning that is at stake. It also points to an uncanny experience of truth. Provided that the uncanny is not dismissed outright as a hindrance to the manifestation of truth, it may set us on a productive course. If the path that leads to where the truth of what land is, is at the same time, the path that leads to where the truth of what being human is, a possibility opens up in which we can ask not only *what* land is, but also *who* land is. The intertwining of what is understood as land, and of what is understood as human may render this possibility possible. This possibility has been rendered impossible by a conventional view in which what is human and what is not human, i.e., land, are portrayed not only as different, but also as being in opposition to each other. There is nothing immutable about this conventional wisdom. The possibility for the non-duality of what is human and what is land is to be retrieved from the reservoir of possibilities—a reservoir whose existence may lie concealed under the dominion of the possibilities that are presently fashionable. Such a retrieval is not only something that we do. It opens us to what is essential about us. We are the reservoir of possibilities. At the same time, this reservoir of possibilities is what is essential about land.

Land. What is it, or should one ask, who is it? This "or" confuses matters, doesn't it? As an interrogative, "who" is a pronoun that applies to persons, the grammarians tell us, whereas "what" applies to impersonal beings. But must grammarians, especially the conventional ones, be given the last word when it comes to the usages of words? Assuming that the answer is affirmative, from whence do they derive their authority? Who is it, or what is it that legitimizes their authority? How are we to address land, or how is land to address us? Who or what answers these questions? Does land have any say in how the question is formulated? And how can an entity such as land have a say in how a question is to be formulated? Doesn't having a say apply more appropriately to human beings? And assuming that it is conceded that having a say applies to human beings, are we so sure that what being human is, is so self-evident that we can intuitively demarcate the province of what being human is, and set it apart from what is not human? Moreover, on the basis of this assumption, how is it to be determined whether the human formulation of the question of land is a formulation that will yield the truth about land? To what extent does land allow herself to be subjected to human formulation? That is, to what extent does the being of land, or the truth of the being of land, subject to humanism? Is land a *tabula rasa* upon which human beings have to inscribe meaning? And assuming that this is the case, to whom or to what is land a *tabula rasa?* If, as appears to be the case, it is to a human being that she has to appear as such, what can be said about such a being? Could such a being be itself a *tabula rasa*, and hence acquire meaning as it inscribes meaning to land? And should this be the case, isn't it the case that in giving land meaning, the land also gives meaning to who or what gives her meaning? Apparently, neither predates the other. What predates both has no witness, and it is to it that both owe their being. As the genes of an ancestor are carried over by the offspring, so does land and human being bear the genes of that which is without witness. Neither human being nor land is or is not intelligible without the presence of that which is without witness. Language witnesses. That which is without witness poses a problem for language, for it cannot be subject to an expression in and by language. This is not to say that it is in opposition to language. It is that from which language arises. It is what sustains the being and the truth of language. In witnessing, language witnesses itself as that which is without witness. In this latter witnessing, being human too has a home. At this home, what is uncanny ceases to be uncanny. Even the questioning that would, otherwise, be uncanny ceases to be uncanny at this home.

It should be obvious now that, in drawing attention to the question of land, this drawing draws attention to our being. How we stand in relation to the question of land, we stand in such a way that our own being stands in relation to itself. It is both natural and proper to appropriate our relationship with land in a manner that preserves not only the questionableness of our being but also the questionableness of this relationship. The language of this relationship is not only questionable; it is also a questioning language. A claim that when we ask who is land is absurd, and a violation of the rules of language ignores the richness of language, and does an injustice to who and to what we are. It is also an injustice to who, and to what land is. The ordering of language that is dictated by conventional grammar may be a violation of language, if it fails to take direction from language itself. Grammar is in the service of language and not vice versa. It is only as such that it can truthfully exhibit what is called forth by language.

To the extent that our relationship with land is a matter of language, it should not readily be conceded that grammarians or linguists in general have a monopoly in determining what is essential about language, nor should it be readily conceded that language is exclusively a matter of human beings. Our humanistic conception of language may conceal the possibility that what is not human has an essential role to play in revealing what is essential about language. This revelation may be concealed by human hubris—a hubris that works against the truth of what is essential about being human. When the truth of what is human is compromised, the compromise is extended to truth of whatever is posited as the subject of human inquiry. To assume that speech is uniquely human may testify to the possibility that the assumption fails to grasp what is essential about speech, and to what is essential about being human. Because assumptions are what they are, namely, assumptions, they betray a problematic ground from which they arise. What grammarians tell us is more than a mere statement of language. It is also a statement of what being human is—a statement that is incomprehensible without taking into account the world in which human beings exist. Our modern grammar-ians, however, appear oblivious of this situation. They appear to abstract lang-uage from that which endows language with being and with meaning. What they say cannot be divorced from their understanding of being human, or from their understanding of the world in which human beings have their being.

What can be said about human beings or about land cannot be divorced from the traditions into which our language and understanding are rooted. The con-

stitution and the interpretations of being human, as is the case with the constitution and interpretations of land, do not take place outside our respective traditions. Traditions are torchlights of hermeneutics. And it can equally be said that
hermeneutics is the torchlight of traditions. Just as hermeneutics lights up a tradition, a tradition lights up hermeneutics. In either case, lighting brings into relief what is fundamental. Given the heterogeneity of our traditions, how we understand ourselves, as is the case with how we understand land, is subject to this
heterogeneity. In some fundamental way, each tradition is what it is by being
open to every other tradition. This openness is a rich ground for the availability
of an understanding that may lay concealed under what appears on the surface of
any tradition.

Let us provisionally treat the question about land as a fundamental question.
To do so is to bring seriousness to bear on the question. All fundamental questions summon seriousness. When seriousness is brought to bear on a question,
philosophy is brought to bear on it. And we will provisionally concede that philosophy does not have a monopoly on seriousness. Other disciplines may also
bring their brand of seriousness to bear on fundamental questions. For example,
science brings seriousness to the questions that it raises. As sciences, both geography and geology exhibit seriousness when they take up the question of land.
What is important is to take note of the multiple senses of seriousness to which
fundamental questions are subject. Taking note of the multiplicity alerts us to the
danger of confusing senses of seriousness, and also alerts us to the danger of
mistaking one sense for the other. To the extent that it is possible, I will seek to
confine myself to the seriousness that pertains to philosophy. The fundamental
question of land will be taken up philosophically, and philosophical seriousness
will be brought to bear on it. As is the case with every philosophical undertaking,
how such seriousness is to be understood, remains problematic. Consensus
among philosophers on the nature of a philosophical undertaking remains elu-
sive. Elusiveness, however, is not accidental to this undertaking. It is what determines this undertaking in regard to what it is. What philosophy says about any
fundamental question implicates the fundamental question about the nature of
philosophy. Thus, it should not surprise us that the fundamental question of land
implicates and is implicated in the fundamental question of philosophy. Every
project that is pursued by philosophy harbors within itself a pursuit of a project
regarding the nature of philosophy. This subtext exhibits one's understanding of
philosophy.

Bringing philosophical seriousness to bear on the fundamental question of
land brings us to an uncanny ground. In conventional wisdom, philosophy is not
expected to raise and explore the question of land in any serious way. The concern with the transformations of urban and suburban landscapes, for example,
does not normally strike us as a matter that should be taken up by philosophers.
When the transformations of urban and suburban landscapes occur, it is not normally expected that philosophy would have anything to do with constituting and
clarifying them. Normally, when issues regarding these transformations are

raised, philosophy is not expected to make a contribution to the clarification, or to participate in the quest for solutions to the problems raised by these issues. Hence, the vulgar view that philosophy bakes no bread. We leave serious issues about land to the sciences of nature, that is, nature as constructed by the sciences. The normal province of the question land is the province of natural/physical sciences. It is the experts in these sciences to whom modern societies turn for guidance in formulating and implementing policies that bear on land. Generally, society relies on these experts in conceptualizing land and in urban and suburban planning and management. Philosophical guidance or assistance is not normally sought. However, we ignore philosophy at our own peril—a peril not readily understood. Philosophers must bear a part of the responsibility for this ignorance. For the most part, they ignore the range of what is at stake in philosophizing. If they are not aware of this peril, it cannot be expected that they will be in a position to bring it to the attention of others. By taking up the question of land as a fundamental philosophical question, those of us in philosophy may contribute to our own education, and in the course of doing so, others may equally benefit. By abandoning the inquiry on the nature of land to the empirical sciences, philosophy has impoverished not only our understanding of land, but also our understanding of philosophy. To understand itself, philosophy needs to question itself, and this includes interrogating what philosophy deems fundamental. At stake in this interrogation is not simply having a detached attention to what is fundamental, but having an experience, or more appropriately, experiencing what is fundamental. In philosophy one experiences the question that one is asking if the asking is fundamental. To ask what is fundamental about land is to expose ourselves to an experience of what is fundamental about land.

In an essay entitled "Introduction to Metaphysics," the twentieth century German philosopher Martin Heidegger points the way to a philosophical understanding of fundamental questions. He tells us that questions and particularly fundamental questions do not just occur like stones and water. Questions are not found ready-made like shoes and clothes and books. Questions are, and are only, as they are actually asked. A leading into the asking of the fundamental questions is consequently not a going to something that lies and stands somewhere; no, this leading-to must first awaken and create the questioning. The leading is itself a questioning advance, a preliminary questioning. It is a leading for which in the very nature of things there can be no following.[1]

Fundamentally, the question of land, which should be a question only as it is actually being asked, does not lie ahead of me or ahead of you. Its locus is precisely where I am, and where you are. It is raised from my standpoint and from your standpoint. Each of these standpoints is being awakened by the question we raise. As it is awakened, we thereby get awakened onto ourselves. Because the question does not lie and stand somewhere other than where we are, it is not only a question that touches on the question of our being; it is also a question whose answer lies where we are. As Heidegger reminds us, in regard to any fundamental question, there can be no following in the quest for the understanding of this question, or in the quest for an answer to it. With all the risks that may be entailed, if there is any following, it is a following of oneself. This following of oneself is not a subjectivist path. It is a path into which each one of us individually and communally all of us are drawn—a path that draws everything that is of concern to us into itself, and in which all that is draws us into itself. It is in the very nature of the fundamental questions to have answers from the same place where questions are located. If indeed fundamental questions have their location in us, it is also in us that the answers are to be found, if they are to be found at all. Thus, as a fundamental question, the question of land is to be found where we are.

The implication of these observations should be obvious. You are not to look to me or to anyone to provide the answer to the question we are raising. You and I are to look at where we are both individually and communally for the understanding of the question, and for the answer to the question. This is how we must hear the question, and this is how we must set out to look for an answer to the question. To look at ourselves individually and communally for the proper grounding of the question and for an answer to the question we are raising does not imply "turning away from." It is not a matter of withdrawing into ourselves so that the question of land can be understood and answered. To do so is to misunderstand ourselves, and to the extent that the question of land is bound to the question of our being, when we misunderstand ourselves, we misunderstand land.

"Turning into" is not always "turning away from." To hear a fundamental question truly is to experience oneself placed where "turning into" and "turning away from" cease to exist as opposites. It is to experience oneself as placed where "turning into" and "turning away from" are unified. It is out of this unity that the fundamental question of land arises, and it is from it that a fundamental answer can be provided. As long as we think that we are here and that the land is there, or conversely, that land is there and we are here, there will not be fundamental questioning or fundamental answering. If the fundamental question of land is truly heard, it must be heard fundamentally. It is only such a hearing that can yield the answer we are after.

In philosophy, hearing, as is the case with every other mode of philosophical sensing, is not simply a matter of physiology. Conventionally, it is matter of one's cultural tradition, and to the extent that philosophy is culturally rooted, hearing is a matter of one's philosophico-cultural tradition. Our hearing is deeply rooted in our cultural traditions. Philosophical hearing is no less deeply rooted in our cultural traditions. Given the multiplicity of our cultural traditions and the attendant multiplicity of our philosophical traditions, it should not come as a surprise that in the context of this multiplicity, hearing and understanding interculturally and inter-traditionally is a formidable task. This is especially the case when cultures and traditions are experienced or construed monadically. Moreover, where certain cultural traditions deem themselves superior to other cultures, and when they assume the right to speak on behalf of other cultures, crosscultural hearing and understanding are severely compromised. Furthermore, the matter is more complicated by the fact that it is not only we who are cultured. Land too is cultured. Land is culturally constituted. A culture-free land, that is a land that is not an embodiment of this or that cultural tradition is an imaginary land. But even in the world of imagination, culture is not an outcast. Imagination is thoroughly cultural. A cultural hermeneutic of land is therefore quite appropriate, and should not be construed as a hermeneutic that obscures the truth of land. Land is what it is and becomes intelligible in the context of cultural landscape. This is the case whether land has or has not been domesticated by human beings. It is the case whether land has or has not been subjected to urbanization. A virgin land is still a cultured land since virginity is a cultural phenomenon. Nothing is inherently virgin. Virginity is a contingent patina of meaning that is placed on what is inherently without meaning. It is only by an act of violence that what is inherently nonvirgin is made to appear as if virginity is its essential nature.

There is no pure land, just as there is no pure human being. Even the proverbial Garden of Eden is not and was not a pure land. It is a land already subjected to a cultural divine—not to the divine in general, but to a specific cultural divine—a Judeo/Christian/Islamic cultural divine. And because the divine is the divine for the human, divinized land is human land. No land anti-dates the human, for what anti-dates the human, anti-dates the human humanly. Anti-dating the human is a human projection. The uninhabited land is still a human land whether it is or it is not habitable. Land, after all, is not land-in-itself. It is land only in the context of the human. Even more radically stated, land is human. Another way of stating this is to say a human being is a landed being. It is in landing that a human being is a human being. If this is fully understood, then grammarians who tell us that the question, "who land is?" is unintelligible, misunderstand themselves as human beings. A human being is not a landed being because he or she lives on land, or because he or she lives off land. And it is not simply because he or she is buried on land. Although it may not be immediately obvious, he or she inhabits the land in the same way that I inhabit my body. I inhabit my body in such a way that it is nonsensical to say that I am in my body. What makes sense is to say that I am my body, and my body is what I am. Similarly, land is more than a container of human beings. We do not solely have an external relation to land. We are our lands. Land expresses us in the same way that the bodies express us. In land, what addresses us and who addresses us are united, and out of this unity, we rise and are preserved, and the land is, and is preserved. The rising and the preservation are at the same time human and land events. Transformations of urban and suburban landscapes are what they are as transformations of what is essentially human, as apparitions of what is human. Landscapes give birth to who and to what we are, and when they are transformed, we thereby get transformed. Urbanization and suburbanization are human processes in which what is human humanizes itself. Urbanization, as is the case with suburbanization, is a humanization. But this is not exclusively a human process. It is also a land process. It is a landing of the land. What is urban as is the case with what is suburban is a generated by and from the transformation of land. Such generation and transformation would not come about if it were not the case that land already exists as a possibility for urbanization and suburbanization. The already urbanized land, as is the case with an already suburbanized land, retains this possibility. It is also a possibility that is retained by those who become urbanized or suburbanized. Being urbanized, as is the case with being suburbanized, is a realization of human possibility, and it is a realization that does not exhaust the possibility that human beings are. It is a realization that is not fully a realization. The possibility of being human is the possibility of land, and the possibility of land is the possibility of being human.

When one looks at this nexus of possibilities, what does one see today? Today, land has increasingly fallen under the regime of science (natural and social) and technology. The urban and suburban landscapes are the showcases of scientific and technological achievements. Although not fully understood, what could be urbanization other than the flourishing and the triumph of techno-scientific genius? Could what has been referred to as the suburban sprawl be other than a spread of this genius? This is a genius that produces not only urbanized and suburbanized land, but also a genius that produces a mode of being human for whom this urbanized and suburbanized land is a home. And in either case, do we not see a transformation of land and a transformation of human being resulting in a landscape that responds to the techno-scientific imperative? But what is this imperative if not an imperative stemming from a particular conception of what land is, and of a particular conception of what a human being is? It is also an imperative with an imperial mission—a mission to bring into subjection all land and all human beings. It is an imperative of modernity. One of the proofs of modernization is urbanization. Those who resist modernization are threatened with extinction.

The triumph of this imperative, however, is achieved at the expense of another imperative—the imperative of another nexus of the possibilities of land and possibility of being human. This other imperative rests on a nexus of possibilities in which land is not there simply as a resource for techno-scientific exploitation and manipulation, and in which human beings do not exist as exploiters and manipulators of land. It is an imperative that summons the being human and the being of land to common repose—a repose that for human beings is a homeland. In this homeland human beings are born and sustained. Herein, land becomes motherland for human beings and human beings become land's mother.

It is more than metaphorical to refer to land as motherland. It is land that gives us life, and it is land that sustains us. In addition to giving us birth and sustaining us, it also holds us within itself and exhibits us as belonging to it. The "it" pertains not to a thing out there, but to what we ourselves are. The "it" is "us," and "we" are "it." The ontological bond that is hereby affirmed is not a material or a physical bond. And it is not a spiritual bond, if by spiritual we are contemplating what is other than, or what is in opposition to, the physical. It is not a Hegelian synthesis, or a synthesis of matter and spirit. It is an onto-existential bond that calls for an ethical imperative. To care for human beings without caring for land is to betray ignorance of both what is human and what is land. Conversely, to care for land without caring for human beings is to betray the same type of ignorance. Land too cares for us. To understand how land cares for us, however, presupposes a radical understanding of what we are. We inhabit the land, and the land inhabits us. This is not simply a matter of holding an anthropomorphic view of land. One is not imposing what is human on what is not human, or what is not human on what is human. It is a matter of affirming what is elemental about human as belonging to what is elemental about land, and necessarily affirming what is elemental about land as belonging to what is elemental about human. It is on the basis of this mutually implicating elementals that one can found not only an authentic aesthetics, but also an authentic environmental ethics. An environmental ethics that is not so founded remains derivative and lacks essential seriousness. For an environmental ethics that is serious, there is a prerequisite. The prerequisite is that human beings be viewed not as inhabitants of the environment but as the environment itself. A human being is an environing being. This is not because he or she lives in an environment, but because he or she is an environment. A human being is an environing being. To exist is to exist environmentally. It is only as such that a human being is a landed being. Environment is synonymous with land. Hence, an environing being, the being that being human is, is a landing being. When projected as a container of human beings and of other phenomena, environment is an abstraction, and, in it, human beings and other phenomena are equally abstractions. We thereby lose intimacy with ourselves by losing intimacy with environment. Being intimate with ourselves is being intimate with environment, and being intimate with environment is being intimate with ourselves.

The divorce of the being of humanity from the being of land—a divorce that results in the estrangement of human beings from themselves and, by implication, in the estrangement of land from itself has many faces. Here, I briefly mention and highlight two of them. The first one is attested by the rise of a humanism, in which being human is defined soulfully or spiritually. In this humanism, what is essential about being human is the soul or the spirit. Either of these conceptions of being human is portrayed not only as what is other than the physical but also, at times, the portrayal is framed in terms of the opposition to what is physical. There is a longstanding interpretation of Plato that stands for this point of view. Human beings, according to this view, are distinguished from other beings in that they have a soul—an incorporeal being that belongs to the intelligible realm. It is as a soul that a human being is truly human. The spatio-temporal realm is the physical realm—a realm in which human body has its membership. What is essential about being human is not to be found in this realm. It is to be found in the intelligible realm. This feature of Platonism has been taken up by Christians as the gospel truth to be propagated throughout the world. Regardless of his self-professed philosophical radicalism, Descartes is a propagator of this gospel. It is he who is one of the major architects of modern Western philosophy—a phase of the history of Western philosophy whose major problematic is the mind-body dualism. In the context of this type of thinking, land is portrayed essentially as a physical phenomenon, and since being human is not being physical, being human is cut off from the being of land. Although, under this type of thinking, it is conceded that human beings live on land, the assumption is that human beings literally live "on" it. They may be in land but they are not of it. Land may give us food, water, air, and shelter but not what truly defines what is essential about us. The Cartesian "I think, therefore I am" excludes land from the determination of what is truly human. Human beings are essentially strangers to land. Land is an absolute "it"—the absolute other, the thing that does not think. Thus, one can profess to care for what is truly human without caring for land. To be sure, land is the source of resources that sustain human life, but life in this case is understood in a biological sense. Land does not offer any resource for human sustenance—the sustenance that human beings need to be truly human. The Platonized-Christianized-Cartesianized land is the view of land that appears to be presupposed in the Western world.

The second face that attests for the divorce of humans from land is technico-scientific. Although technology and science have been aspects of human life for thousands of years, the technico-scientific view as it applies to land today, is largely associated with Westerners. This association has reached a point where it is generally and wrongly assumed that techno-scientific view is exclusively Western. The view is a dominant, if not the dominant, feature of modern life. As one of the major architects of modernity Descartes has made a significant contribution to this view. By radicalizing the distinction between *res cogitans* and the *res extensa*, he opened the possibility of cultivating *res extensa* in its own right. Hence, the development of the physical science—a science that has been built up as the final arbiter on the issue of what is physical. To the extent that land is construed exclusively as physical, it is relegated to physical science. And to the extent that human beings are construed as physical, they are lumped together with other physical beings. Those who have fought against this anthropology, that is, those who have fought to rescue human beings from physicalism have often fallen into the trap of Cartesian dualism. They have affirmed a spiritual order as to what is distinctively human, and have posited it in opposition to the physical order. They have put human beings at odds with land. The result has been one of estranging human beings from themselves, since, as previously stated, to be human is to be landed, estrangement from being human is, at the same time, estrangement from land. The techno-scientific orientation caters to techno-scientific person—a person that it constitutes and that it uses to legitimize itself. It also caters to a techno-scientific conception of land that reinforces its self-stipulated legitimacy.

Indeed, contrary to the view that Christianity and modern science are in opposition to each other, one finds a shared conception of land—land construed solely as a physical entity. Descartes may be viewed as one of the major architects of the reconciliation between Christianity and modern science. Christianity and modern science have always operated under the assumption that land is what is other than human, and that it stands out there as an object of manipulation, exploitation, and as an object. Under the guidance of science and technology, the modernity construes mathematics as the instrument par excellence for carrying out these processes. The domination of land by mathematics is one of the major features of modern society, and it should be evident that without mathematics we would not have the advances that we have in science and technology. It is incontestable that without mathematics we would not have the urban and suburban provinces. Mathematics governs these provinces. One notices therein calculation, measuring, and surveying. Geometrics governs here. With the blessing of Christianity, we have surrendered the understanding and transformation of land and of the earth generally to geometrics and to science and technology. We readily succumb to the dominant view that the transformations of urban and suburban landscapes is a matter of scientific and technical practices. We leave it to techno-scientists to formulate, understand, and to direct these transformations. The construction/deconstruction of urban and suburban areas, and the construction/deconstruction of the relation between urban and suburban areas have been construed as the prerogative of these experts.

Since it appears to be taken for granted that not every one is an expert on these matters, we see a concentration of expertise into fewer and fewer hands, raising the very real possibility that our societies are becoming less and less democratic. As land processes, the transformations of urban and suburban landscapes are increasingly becoming less and less democratic. It is not that the public is not consulted, for indeed, it is consulted. But the consultation is based and guided by information that is given by the experts, the same agents who act on the public decisions they have engineered. The very notion of the public has lost its publicness, and perhaps, it has never been truly public. In capitalist societies, the public has been determined and is determined by capitalism. The transformations of urban and suburban landscapes have primarily been directed and have served capitalist interests. Land is capitalized and is secured in its being by capital. Under the dictatorship of capital, land-scaping has been a capitalist scaping. In a capitalist society transformations of urban and suburban landscapes are capitalist transformations, and they are transformations of capitalistic modes of being human. Capitalism is a humanism, and at our time, it has become the most aggressive form of humanism. Its triumph in urban and suburban landscapes is a triumph of a humanism.

The humanism that has triumphed is not humanism in general, but rather, a male-centered humanism. Just as the public in the capitalist order has been a capitalist construction, in a patriarchal society—the type of society that prevails in the human community today, what is public is construed and driven by the male imperative. Both urban and suburban areas are visibly gendered. Symbolically, both areas are phallocentric. High-rise buildings that rise from the earth characterize them. In both urban and suburban areas we erect the buildings. The high-rises may be construed as erectiles. Architects appear to compete with each other to see who can erect the sturdiest, the tallest erectile, and one that can withstand the elements and not collapse before old age has overtaken it. Third World countries appear to compete for admission to modernity by erecting skyscrapers as if to prove their masculinity. A classic example of this phenomenon is the city of São Paulo in Brazil. Flying in and out of this city, one witnesses a forest of skyscrapers—tall skinny buildings that appear to look scornfully on the surrounding land. Any open space appears to call for an erectile. São Paulo must catch up with New York, with London, with Paris to demonstrate that in the tropics too, super-erections are possible. Males, for the most part white males, are primarily the prime movers of this architecture. The deployment of white male power is not only exemplified in the erection of buildings and other structures. Urbanization has become a metaphor for masculinization of land. Unurbanized land has been construed as virgin. It is in this context that the spread of urbanization is portrayed as the encroachment of virgin territory. In the West, the virgin has primarily been portrayed as a woman. The protection of virginity, a protection that has for the most part been undertaken by men, therefore, has been primarily a protection of the woman. In this reasoning, a woman is to be protected because she is incapable of protecting herself. Thus, it should not come as a surprise that in both urban and suburban areas, planning and implementing are led by males (mostly white), while females and non-white people play a subservient role. The latter are predominantly a service people.

In the United States, the males that mostly matter are white. What one sees here is not only the gendering of people in a way that favors males in landscaping, but also a racialization of landscapes. Accordingly, the transformations of the urban and suburban landscapes in the United States are gendered, and racialized. Genderism and racism must be taken into account if one is to have an accurate understanding of urbanization and suburbanization of the United States. The resulting landscapes are gender and racial landscapes. To gender-scaping and race-scaping, one must add class-scaping to fully grasp the process of landscaping. The tragic dramas of gender, race, and class conflicts are not simply played out on urban and suburban landscapes. They are expressions of these landscapes. The resolution of these conflicts is not likely to take place if there is not a radical transformation in the understanding and constitution of these landscapes. It is not that one has to come before the other. Each is the expression of the other. We see ourselves in our landscapes. The problems that beset us are landscaped. If we fail to see this, perhaps, it is because we fail to see who and what we are, and what the landscapes are.

It is evident to any casual observer that both urban and suburban areas in the United States exhibit a deployment of wealth in such a way that certain areas are set for the rich and other are set for the poor. There is a remarkable difference in the landscapes where the two classes reside. Each class is where it resides. One sees well paved roads, neat lawns, and good housing where the rich live, and one sees grassless yards, unrepaired roads, and dilapidated houses and stores where the poor live. The streets where the rich live are clean and safe while the streets where the poor live are filthy and unsafe. This division appears to parallel the racial division. For the most part, the poor areas are inhabited by African Americans and by other people of color. For the most part, white people inhabit the wealthy areas. The movement of middle class African Americans or the movement of the people of color does not do away with the class divide. It merely solidifies it.

If it is accepted that the rise of modern urbanism and suburbanism is unintelligible if racism, classicism, and genderism are not taken into account, it appears to be the case that the problems that are generated by modern urbanism and suburbanism are inseparable from the problems associated with the constructions of race, gender, and class. But, as human problems, these problems are understood superficially if we fail to understand them as the problems of land. In bringing up race, class, and gender to bear on land, there is a likely charge that one is mystifying the nature of land, and it is precisely this mystification that techno-science is the antidote. But doesn't this charge conceal the manner in which techno-science has concealed the nature of land? Land does not have a meaning that lies beyond human beings if only because such a beyond is inconceivable by human beings. Since human beings are landed beings, matters of race, class, and gender intrinsically bear on land. How they are land matters, however, remains unthought and inadequately understood, if only because being human remains unthought and inadequately understood. Genderism, racism, and classism freeze human beings into immutable categories—categories that are projected as set by nature, just as land is projected as one entity in nature among other entities in nature. Christianity and techno-scientism have demonstrated inability to reveal this unthoughtfulness and inadequacy. Neither of them has demonstrated any interest in overcoming this inability, if only because neither of them recognizes this inability as inability.

The one-dimensional conception and presentation of land embedded in the Christian view and the techno-scientific view of us conceal not only what we are but also what land is. This intertwining and unified concealment reflects intertwining and unified estrangement from the truth of human being and the truth of land. In this context, one can see the illusory nature of what appears to the tension between urbanism and suburbanism. Suburbanism is depicted as a new frontier where human beings can escape from the diabolical and horrible conditions in urban areas and where self-reconstruction can take place as suburbia is constructed. Urban areas—areas that once stood for civilization, for the domestication of human beings, for the triumph over what was regarded as mere animal world, and for the highest achievement of human beings on land (for a transformation of and for transformed land)—areas where human beings showcased themselves, are now portrayed as citadels of neo-barbarism, areas from which the friends of civilization should flee. Urban land, the land that human beings domesticated as they domesticated themselves, appears to have reverted to the undomesticated state, and that has become the home of the wild, untamed, and perhaps, untamable human beings is now to be abandoned, and to be left to the inferior human races, and to the scum of the earth. Here, one sees the failure of the Hobbesian project where human beings, believing that urbanism is anti-dote to the state of nature, now find themselves haunted by what they thought they were fleeing. Suburbia is the new mecca, where the glory of man shines brilliantly and where the salvation of man lies. The urban area, it should not be forgotten, was once a mecca to which human beings fled. Now that human beings appear to flee from it, one can reasonably suspect that suburbia—the new mecca—may similarly, in the course of time, be eclipsed by a new wildness, and human beings will make an effort to construct a sub-suburbia. When this too becomes unbearable still another effort will be made to construct a sub-suburbia. Provided that this process has not stymied reflection, an occasion may arise and force us to question precisely what it is that we are fleeing, and indeed, whether the flight is not an illusion to justify living. It may dawn on us that this process is nothing other than a reenactment of the Oedipal process.

We are yet to take to heart the teaching of Sophocles. Oedipus tried to run away from killing his father and bedding his mother, and used all conceivable avenues available to a rational being. He ended up killing his father and bedding his mother. Perhaps it is precisely this human condition that Sartre refers to as bad faith.[2] As a flight from self, bad faith is an attempt to attain what is impossible. Perhaps the problems we normally associate with racism, classicism, and genderism are nothing more than symptoms of a more deeply rooted problem: the problem of fleeing from what we are. We ask of land that it be the vehicle of this flight. The forays of land are the forays of our being. If this is not evident, perhaps it is, in part, that we have constructed a disguise that conceals the forays of our being. It should not surprise us that the conventional conception of land is a disguise of what land is. Sartrean study of human ontology provides a basis for further reflection on this matter.[3] To Sartre, a human being is not what he is, and he is what he is not.[4] He is nothing more than the possibility of being, a possibility that is a useless passion—useless in the sense that this possibility can never be realized. According to him, this is the project of attempting to be God. Racists are people in flight from who and what they are. It is precisely this same project that is pursued by classicists and by misogynists. They too have adopted a project of bad faith, a project that is destined to fail.

Sartre, however, never fully developed an understanding of bad faith. He polarized us to what is not human, that is, to what is in-itself. He was mistaken about this polarity. He was mistaken about what it is to be human and was also mistaken about what it is to not be human. He regarded this polarity as essential whereas it is merely contingent. If he was mistaken it is not a mistake made by an isolated individual. It is a mistake rooted in his tradition—the western European tradition. The divide between human and physical sciences, the polarization of human beings and land, the polarization of urban/suburban and the rest of land, are western phenomena. The transformations of urban and suburban landscapes in the West are western phenomena and so are the problems that are generated by them. To understand them is to understand the manner in which the western man understands and practices his self-understanding. His dealings with land are his autobiography. Landscapes are scapes of self. The transformations are cultural transformations of self. As this cultural self has acquired a global imperial dimension, to challenge it from within and from a non-western perspective is to open up the possibility of raising a more fundamental question about being human and about how being human inhabits and understands land.

In our obsession with smart growth—conservation and preservation of biosphere and human monuments, the quest for clean water and clean air, open space, and war on the cannibalization of rural or virgin land, this question remains concealed. It is, in part, this obsession that has stilled the voice of philosophy, a voice that seeks to reawaken the question that we are to ask if a proper diagnosis of what ills us is to take place. This redemptive voice will continue to be silenced as long as we abandon our understanding of land to scientific geography, scientific geology, and to other physical sciences. An elemental geography is a geography that hearkens unto this voice. An elemental geography is intelligible on the basis of an elemental geology, a geology that is extra-scientific. Such a geography and a geology have their foundation in philosophy, and such a philosophy is founded in an elemental geography, which in turn, is founded in an elemental geology. Being founded, in this context, is not a matter of reductionism, whereby one discipline is made the foundation of the other. It is transdiscipline experience of that soil that gives rise to disciplines. As experienced, philosophy, geography, and geology in this context are not subject to the discipline of the academy. They are not academic disciplines among others in the academy. From the standpoint of the academy they are non-disciplined. They are wild not in the sense that they stand in opposition to what is domesticated or tamed, but wild in a primordial non-oppositional sense. Accordingly, it is only as wild that human beings are drawn to them. The wild philosopher, the wild geographer, and the wild geologist inhabit this wildness and are guarded by it as they guard it. It is this wildness that announces what is yet to be fully experienced as the essence of land. Transformations of urban and suburban landscapes presuppose this experience of land. Such an experience points to land as the inexhaustible not understood as a resource in the modern sense but as non-modern and poetic. It is the experience from which urban and suburban landscapes emerge and to which they subside. Here too, human beings have a home. A primordial home in which being human and not-being human converge, unify, and annihilate their opposition so that each can be truly what it is. Out of this annihilation there arises the questionableness that is native to both human being and land. Questionableness is the reservoir of possibility in which human being and land derive their common destiny. What resides in questionableness resides in openness, and remains as such. This is the way of being of the land. Out of it land trajectories arise and subside. We too, thereby, arise and subside.

Notes

1. Martin Heidegger, *Introduction to Metaphysics*, trans. Ralph Manheim (New Haven, Conn.: Yale University Press, 1959), 19.

2. Jean Paul Sartre, *Being and Nothingness*, trans. Hazel Barnes (New York: Washington Square Press, 1956), 86-116.

3. See generally, Sartre, *Being and Nothingness.*

4. Sartre, *Being and Nothingness*, 735.

Chapter 3

Where the Beaver Gnaw: Predatory Space in the Urban Landscape

James Hatley

O wonderful! O wonderful! O wonderful!
I am food! I am food! I am food!
I eat food! I eat food! I eat food![1]

The Space of the Edible

In his essay, "Wildness," Wendell Berry argues that human beings are intimately involved in the wild even as this involvement incessantly leads to moments of threatening incongruence and opposition: "Our problem, exactly, is that the human and natural are indivisible, and yet are different."[2] But how challenging this difference in intimacy can become and how oddly it may at times reorient what is involved in being ethically responsible deserves much amplification if the full force of Berry's claim is to be understood. Particularly revealing in this regard is the issue of predation and edibility. Nothing could be more intimate and natural than to be eaten by an animal in the wild, yet nothing could be more terrifying and seemingly outside the normal scope of human experience (at least in Western culture) than this event.[3] In fact, it can be argued that the very bounding of the urban, the suburban, and even the rural is based upon the articulation of a predatory space that is asymmetric:[4] in a humanized landscape nature is to be eaten and we are to be its eaters.

Americans have been understandably insistent that they do not become prey. This insistence in turn is articulated not only in our individual actions to prevent such occurrences, but also in the thoroughgoing cultural appropriation of space in various guises that eradicate the possibility of human "victimization" by animals. In this mode of thinking, a space is morally ordered only if society has intervened to exclude animals' (and by extension, other humans') becoming predators of humans.[5] In the space of human habitation, the moral urgency to produce an asymmetry of predation is everywhere at work. While authors such as Holmes Rolston tend to see the rural as between the urban and the wild landscape, a "hybrid" of the natural and the cultural,[6] the claim that is being made here is that the rural is fully on the side of the urban in regards to edibility. In fact, the very work of the rural—even more than the urban—is to render nature edible for humans in a thoroughgoing manner. In rural areas, Holmes argues, the wilds become domesticated nature, which in turn is envisioned as "a fertile field of human labor."[7] But even if in the rural we find ourselves working creatively in conjunction with nature's pliability and diversity, profiting from its powers and properties, we should also recognize that the nature that would eat us is kept resolutely at bay in this process. Only in the establishment of wilderness areas, and to a lesser extent in the maintenance of marginal spaces—the spaces described by Berry as modes of trans-species "democratic diversity," in which "limits are set on human intention"[8]—is the cultural insistence on the inediblity of humans allowed a tentative reversal. The otherwise insistent moral duty to repress predation undergoes a temporary lapse and produces in varying degrees a moral crisis. For in becoming hospitable to wild animals and their intentions, in allowing their "wild lives" to intermingle with our own "wild play," we inevitably confront that they are hungry and intend to eat.

Thus, when predation lifts its head, opens up its maws, bares its fangs, arms its stinger within the American urban landscape, a crisis is sure to ensue that puts into question the very modes by which we draw a line between ourselves and the wilds. Often, the perception of humans in the wake of this epiphany is that the very fabric of space itself is unraveling.

> How can I live a human life if my children are continually subjected to predation by
> rattlesnakes, or if my cat might be carted off at any moment by a hungry coyote, or
> my cattle slaughtered by ravenous wolves? It is *as if* anywhere I turn, a force is at
> work that would destroy my capacity to walk freely within my own home place. Let
> the wilds be out there somewhere beyond my landscape but do not let them stray too
> close to my home and my chattel.[9]

What is meant explicitly by the "wilds" in this mode of address is a landscape where edibility is freely at play, and where humans get caught up in its ebb and flow. In his *Practice of the Wild*, Gary Snyder speaks of a wild beyond "eating berries in the sunlight," one in which is found "the ball of crunched bones in a scat, the feathers in the snow, the tales of insatiable appetite."[10] To walk on this "dark side of nature," as Snyder puts it, is to court contact with its digestive and fermentative dimensions, with life that eats life. To find oneself the prey of animals is to experience a mode of disorientation that bites into the very heart of what humans strive so hard to achieve—a landscape in tune with our desires and supportive of our security. A landscape where the "wild play" of children does not mean they will be in danger for their lives and well-being. Seemingly, the space of wildness is utterly at odds with human habitation. And yet, as Berry points out, the very wildness that we would exclude by redrawing yet again the line whereby its place is distinguished from ours, is something in which we are inextricably caught up. Indivisible and yet at odds with nature, we must both exclude and yet include it and its denizens. We would feed it and be fed by it, coax it to come near for our spiritual edification, but also object strenuously when it bites our hand.

The Beaver Predators

A whimsical example of this crisis in spatiality recently surfaced as several beaver began to make their home within a supposedly marginal area of an urban landscape—the Tidal Basin of Washington, D.C. First reported in the Metro section of the *Washington Post*,[11] the story moved to the front page by the next day, as well as airing on national television in Willard Scott's live, on-the-scene report of the happenings. What was newsworthy about the beaver was not their appearance so near the halls of governmental power but their behavior. The beaver were gnawing down one by one the beloved cherry trees whose blossoming is an annual event for the entire nation. The Cherry Blossom Festival was being crashed by predators.

For that was what the beaver were accused of being, albeit humorously, on the second day of the story—"voracious," "tree-chomping," "tree-predators" (the last term coined by Earle Kittleman of the park service)—who were "terrorizing" the basin by "gnawing deep valleys" into cherry trees.[12] No doubt, to the frustration of the beaver, the felled trees were being dragged away by park service personnel as quickly as they were being discovered. Not so much in an effort to deny the beaver the fruits of their labor as to keep tourists flocking to the cherry groves from "tripping on the stumps." As if to add insult to injury, just at the moment the story about the beaver was breaking, a red-tailed hawk had the bad manners to make himself at home on the White House grounds. Here he was preying on "squirrels and weaker birds" (including ducks) in plain sight of tourists and the White House staff. A picture of the hawk in the act of downing "duck carpaccio" was printed in the *Post*[13] along with the statement that the bird's behavior left "White House employees disgusted." Like the beaver, the hawk was envisioned to have "chomped" on his prey.

As humorous and merely diverting as this series of events may first seem, darker realities are at play in their unfolding. These realities invite, or perhaps, better put, corner us into asking questions about the very meaning of our being embodied creatures who are part and parcel of a wild spatiality in spite of our best efforts to the contrary. In confronting these beaver the D.C. community began to find problematic the manner in which it had drawn the line between predator and prey even to the point of feeling a certain dark eagerness to be under the threat of being edible, of being wild. As noted above, what made the event of the invasion of the beaver predators newsworthy in the first place was not the appearance of the beaver, not the sudden burgeoning of natural beings at the edge of a city landscape. Rather, it was the ensuing behavior of the beaver and most importantly the effect of that behavior upon the sensibilities of those humans who witnessed it. The ensuing narrative elaborated by the newspaper emphasizes the reaction of various individuals to the circumstance of a treasured grove of blossoming trees not only being destroyed but also being ingested by furry interlopers. What makes this reaction so delightful, or at least newsworthy, is its complicated affect: One is both fascinated and disgusted that the cherry trees are being eaten. The beaver must absolutely be stopped, but they are also to be encouraged. The beaver are destroying a national heritage, but they are part of our national heritage. The beaver are pests to be disposed of, and they are respectable family members acting to nurture their own kith and kin. As an editorial in the *Washington Post* put it: "We're sorry, of course, about the damage they've caused. But we're sort of glad they stopped by."[14]

Much could be made concerning how the narrative space in which the beaver are working is itself tied into a series of political issues flurrying through the capitol at the same moment as the beaver's appearance. The beaver's story ties into concerns as disparate as the debate over family values and the anxieties and moral outrage at play in the NATO bombing of Kosovo. The beaver, wild or no, are also cultural artifacts and are taken up in our words about them in a manner that tells as much and perhaps more about ourselves than it does about the beaver. But what also provokes our interest is the manner in which this story of beaver tree-predators pictures how a customary differentiation of two types of predatory space is being probed at and tested. And, how the very threat of the beaver crossing a certain line that we have elaborated between those two spaces becomes culturally disturbing. In this mode of reading the story, the beaver themselves assert their agency and we are left with them face-to-face or tooth-to-tooth to consider the meaning of their spontaneous intervention. To repeat the obvious: Humans do not wish to be eaten. By proxy, we do not wish our gardens, our tulips, our pets, and especially our sacred groves, the very groves in which ironically we are accustomed to celebrate the processes of nature, the changing of the seasons, to be eaten. And yet, once the line is crossed and the predators have arrived, we are obviously fascinated and perhaps a bit ashamed. For nature itself defies our enculturation of it, unravels the orientation that we so carefully groom into it, and reminds us in Berry's terms of *wildness*, of a nature both different from and yet indivisible with us.

Uncanny Edibility

Let us return to the notion of being eaten. For, as the beaver's narrative makes clear, the very affect of edibility is not one of simple disgust but of disgust intimately tied to fascination, even of delight. Put otherwise, the possibility of being eaten is uncanny, especially in the sense of this term as Freud develops it. As Kristeva makes us aware, the Freudian uncanny precipitates a crisis in which the very capacity to set a boundary for one's own self is undermined by the logic of a doubled lapse or confusion.[15] In the uncanny, I am utterly outside of myself to the point that *I am an other* and/or the other is so utterly inside me that *no space remains where I can be myself.* In just the *threat* of being eaten one finds oneself in this situation—the very body that sustains one's own life suddenly is also the body that is to be ingested in order that another's life might be sustained. What was most intimate becomes most strange and what was most strange becomes most intimate. One looks (or imagines oneself looking) into the face of one's predator and finds her or him already lurking in the very coursing of one's blood through one's veins, in the very softness and saltiness of one's tissues. In that look the claim of the animal's flesh momentarily overturns one's own claim to oneself. What is one to make of this sudden, chilling awareness?

Surreptitiously, the beaver who briefly settled on the shores of Washington, D.C.'s ceremonial region posed this question and in doing so precipitated a crisis in our habitual notion of spatiality. This crisis is rooted not simply in the fact that an other-than-human animal was making a claim to land that was already claimed by a human animal. For after all, many other creatures are immediately welcomed, even encouraged, in their projects to make themselves at home in the many marginal areas of the nation's capital, whether it be the president's back yard or a bit of beach along the Potomac. What made the beaver not welcomed was their insistence on eating us, if not out of house and home, at least out of our sacred, ceremonial grove. In our refusal of hospitality to them (or was it merely a deferral of hospitality since the beaver ultimately were trapped and placed elsewhere in the D.C. area?), we were reminded of how our control over predatory space is tentative. And, we were reminded that in the natural order, the very order that we are cultivating in the maintenance of marginal spaces in our urban landscape, symmetrical rather than asymmetrical predation is at work. The very dynamic of the wild is to intercross predator with prey, eating with being eaten, until every creature is satisfied by the appropriation of every other creature for the purpose of nourishment, for the very sustenance of life.

What both threatens and fascinates humans about the wild is precisely its massive indifference to the claims of a holy grove not to be eaten and, by implication to our own insistent discomfort with being edible. But in spite of our most concerted efforts to the contrary, we remain edible, as anyone who has just been bitten by a horsefly, mosquito, or especially a brown recluse spider can assuredly testify. Our flesh is quite vulnerable to the tearing of incisors, to the fanged injections of toxins, to the prickly and poisoned darts of thorns. In nature, which is to say, in the wilds, which is to say, in a predatory space no longer groomed for the convenience of men and women, house cats and pet cherry trees, space itself changes in its orientation. In full-blown predatory space, a space where you and I might be eaten as well as eat, the issue is not only that the claims of one species disinherit the other, that space does not have enough space to hold their distinct bodies and their competing intentions. But also the issue is that the eating of one species by another functions to let both species flourish.

This last observation leads to a perhaps provocative and certainly radical claim: In wild space we encounter another sort of goodness, a goodness caught up in the circle of edibility articulated in the food chain. Wild predatory space is revealed to be a massive nurturing of every form of life by means of every other form of life. Without edibility and consumption the very building up of a world of diverse biological entities could not have occurred. One suspects that without the eating of one life form by another, life itself would have remained at its most primitive levels. And the evolutionary emergence of humans onto the stage of this world of diverse entities is itself directly due to the fact that we have eaten others in order to become ourselves. One might say that from the purely human perspective of a goodness based upon respect for an inviolable other that there is too much space in the wilds. Which is to say, there are too many hungers lacing through space, veering bodies into one another, bringing humans into closer proximity with other animals than we may want to risk. In wild space we encounter a space co-oriented by non-human others, hungry others. In wild space, we watch our step, we become attentive to our surroundings, and we touch the beings around us, if at all, tentatively and with respect of another sort than we perhaps reserve for our fellow humans. Wild space and, by implication, the space of the marginal, the space Berry so dearly wishes to keep in contact with our more humanized landscapes, is a space permeated with threat. The very orientation of this space insists on the vulnerability of all creatures, including ourselves, to being claimed by other life forms as their very flesh. .

The Significance of the Uncanny

This last observation takes us back to the carnival, the bacchanalia, or what the *Washington Post* termed the "Beavermania,"[16] of the sudden, although merely temporary, reversal of human control over predatory space. For particularly the threat of being edible drew crowds of people to watch the drama of eater and eaten be played out. People, one might phrase it this way, were hungry to watch hunger at work. What gave the beaver their particular moment in the public eye was the fact that the public was tired of its public eye, tired of its massive repression of its own edibility. It wanted to be somewhere wild and it found itself somewhere wild the moment animals started eating beings in proximity to humans.

If we turn to the philosophy of Merleau-Ponty, we can begin to appreciate that this turn to the wild is much more than a passing fascination for that uncomfortable moment (at least for us). Where one is momentarily threatened with being eaten, momentarily fascinated by that supposedly abnormal turn of events that we strive so resolutely to exclude from our humanized landscapes. As Merleau-

Ponty points out, the very matter of our orientation in space and ultimately of our encounter with space itself only comes about as our phenomenal bodies, which is to say, our bodies in their eruption into seeing, smelling, tasting, touching, and hearing, intercross phenomenally with the bodies surrounding us. Chiasmatic in nature, always returning, however incompletely, upon themselves to be themselves, our perceived and perceiving bodies only find themselves in space by means of all the other perceived and perceiving bodies whose masses and movements and gestures provide a context, a phenomenal map, by which space itself can come to be articulated. Space in the first instance and in its most true expression is not the objective, abstract ordering of things according to a homogenous grid of coordinates. Rather, space is the very manner in which motility and intention bends and is focused, flees and is dissipated by the corporeal beings with whom we are in contact. My hands, then, are revealed to me in their *lived meaning*, in their phenomenal embodiment, not as a technical apparatus built according to a preconceived plan. But rather as an active grasp and passive sensitivity whose very movement toward another is reflexively given palpability in the touch of the other's body against my own. And one distinct possibility given in that palpability is the very submission of my flesh to the needs of other flesh to nourish itself. The hand or paw or claw of the other may make my flesh its own.

In the context of this phenomenal body, the earlier claim that my own edibility is uncanny is now revealed to be more than a merely psychological observation. The very registering of the uncanny is possible only for a creature whose very orientation to itself is given through its orientation to others, in which the very placement of its identity is in its nomadic intercrossing with the flesh of other beings, both human and nonhuman. Only a being so permeable to others can find its own identity already so deeply claimed by another. As Merleau-Ponty hints in his notes at the end of *The Visible and the Invisible*:

> There is not the For Itself and the For the other. They are each the other side of the other. This is why they incorporate one another—There is that line, that frontier surface at some distance before me, where occurs the veering I-Other Other-I.[17]

The veering of the other's body into my own and my own body into the other's is not a delusion, not a bad moment or an interesting metaphorical excursion into the nearly psychotic. Rather, it is the very articulation of my flesh, the very orientation whereby my body is first given a whither from which to gather itself into its own where. The chiasmic nature of this interconnecting between myself and the other undermines any straightforward antithesis in which the "for oneself" is placed in opposition to the "for the other," in which a "rivalry," i.e., a *polemos*, a differing whose incompossibility divides and sets at odds, is the ultimate significance of my encounter with the other, even with the other who would eat me. At odds with being at odds, my flesh is caught up in what Merleau-Ponty terms a "co-functioning," in which my being is first a "Wild Being" (Merleau-Ponty's own term) without impermeable restrictions, a being in which I and the other exist in a co-exchange, in which the boundaries between one and the other are both diffused and reversible.[18]

But the very articulation of this reversibility, of a co-veering of diverse beings into the being and flesh of one another, is given a new twist in edibility. For here submission to the appetite of the other's flesh initiates a veering so extreme and so final that my phenomenal body exceeds itself in its actually becoming the nutriment for the flesh of the other. My edibility implicitly involves me in the *threat* of being ingested. In the actualization of this threat, there is no recuperation across a difference of who I am. Instead, the very articulation of my being is one of abjection, of a being swallowed *beyond* the point of nullification. One is not even given the space to be *nothing* but becomes the *other*. In the flesh.[19] In the carnival of Beavermania human beings begin to sense their investment in an embodiment that is quickened by feeding upon and being fed upon. The very fecundity of nature is revealed to be subversive and yet sustaining. Teetering on the lip of psychosis, caught up in an edibility that seems to make one's own flesh utterly alien to itself, one confronts what Kristeva would term an abject origin, an origin whose very articulation was already for the famished other, even as it gave me myself.[20] In confronting this abjection one is now moved *for the sake of another who is in one*. One becomes aware that the very mouth of the other is nourished even as one's own flesh is given up to her or him. One is perhaps disgusted, as the hawk tears into the very duck who might just as well have been ourselves. Even though most of us would also have gladly ingested that very same flesh as a dish of Peking duck, or perhaps one served up in Serbian style, on a moment's notice.[21] And given this second thought, one is also perhaps inspired in this moment by how life feeds life even as it is fed upon. One senses in one's eating an order of goodness that eludes the grasp of how we might speak of it within the merely inter-human sphere.

How One Dies

But before edibility can be characterized as an order of goodness, some thought needs to be given to how death is significant for human beings and how the notion of uncanniness helps one to appreciate that significance. And in order to do that, the uncanniness of being flesh and so already given to the hunger of others needs to be distinguished at least in part from the existential uncanniness made popular by Heidegger's discussion of human mortality in *Being and Time*. In making this distinction, it is important to note that generally, as has been indicated in the discussion above, the uncanny precipitates a crisis in space—one does not know how to find one's place because one cannot distinguish it from all the other places or at least one other place. The space between places seems to have contorted itself or simply collapsed. In this contortion or collapse, the decisiveness of limit itself finds its limit. The boundaries that have been drawn to put and keep the world in order are suddenly shown to be fragile and deceptive. At an ontic or more superficial level, the collapse of boundaries within the uncanny appears, as has been argued above, as the onset of psychosis. The clock's face suddenly sprouts eyes and watches us wherever we turn. But it should not be forgotten that the very capacity to undergo the breakdown of boundaries characteristic of psychosis can only occur for a being for whom boundary itself is continually in question. The practices of the Crow tribe in their Sun Dance, for example, seemingly precipitates a moment of psychosis, when on the third day of having abstained from water and food, participants are pushed to their limit and suddenly pass out. They are left in this state on the earthen floor of the lodge where they might experience what enlightenment culture would term vivid hallucinations. But given a mode of thinking and feeling more open to the permeability of boundaries, to their trickster moments, these hallucinations become visions and are instructive of how one might proceed in living one's life and finding one's place.[22]

Among the issues to be confronted in moments of vision is finding the manner in which one should die. In both notions of the uncanny, that of Heidegger and the one being developed here, the issue of one's mortality is crucial. For one's impending death quite dramatically puts into question exactly how one draws the boundary between oneself and all the other beings with whom one shares a world. In death, one ceases to be oneself insofar as to be a self is to be embodied and existent. Even if one is insistent upon a spiritual afterlife, the transition from life to death is hardly a simple or ordinary one.

In Heidegger the approach of one's death puts one before what he terms the "completely indefinite."[23] This crisis in limit is in turn interpreted by Heidegger as anxiety, because in death one finds oneself threatened in a manner in which that threat is located in no particular "where" or "thing" (*Seindes*) within the world. In confronting this threat Heidegger claims one is brought out of an "absorption in the world" that hides the deeper existential dimensions of one's being. In reality, one is not at home in the world when it comes to the matter of one's dying and so of one's being. In the registering of the *unheimilichkeit* or uncanniness of one's death, one is radically individuated as that being for whom no other being can die one's death.

While this unassailable existential fact deserves acknowledgment, the notion of the uncanny being developed here would go a step further by asking about the spatial significance of one's death. For the notion of the uncanny developed by Heidegger is mainly a temporal one. Although Heidegger speaks of a nowhere in regard to his experience of anxiety what he actually means is a "nowhen." *Dasein*'s anxiety is not concerned about *where* it will cease to be but *when*. Because it does not know and can never know the *when* of its own death, all particular *wheres* within its world fall away. The deepening of this anxiety into ontological insight then leads Heidegger to characterize *Dasein*, even if its name (Being-there) suggests a where, as an essentially temporal structure. *Dasein* is a mode of being that finds itself thrown into its future against the background of its past between which its present moment finds its orientation. For Heidegger we are nothing less than the articulation of this temporal field in all of its complexity and uncanniness.

But in the abject uncanniness of edibility, one's death is not so much about its *when* as its *where*. When one confronts one's death in the flesh, it is not in terms of a time when one no longer will be but in terms of a flesh that one will become, a flesh that is not oneself and yet is of one's flesh. In this thought, the existential fact of how only one can die one's own death finds a strange, even uncanny, twist. In dying one's own death, one dies so completely, so finally, that one's death is another's life. One's death belongs to the eaters.

Although writing in a very different context, Maurice Blanchot has a similar thought when he argues that the ultimate outcome of Heidegger's existential project is to demonstrate the impossibility of searching for a proper death, that is, a death that belongs to one uniquely. Blanchot argues the ultimate trajectory of death found in Rilke's poetry is a "movement of dispossession," where we are no longer sheltered but "where we are, rather, introduced, utterly without re-serve, into a place where nothing retains us at all."[24] Submitting to this mode of dying, Blanchot argues, "implies an immense responsibility toward things."[25] It is left to thinkers such as Merleau-Ponty to remind us that among the windows and violins celebrated by Rilke are found living entities and that our responsibil-ity to them is fulfilled in more than our songs about them. They need nothing less than our flesh.

Insofar as the significance of this situation strikes home, it leaves one touched by and interwoven with every living being that exists, an involvement that finds one both everywhere and nowhere. In one's flesh, one is taken beyond the thought of a being who is a unique existence dying its own death into a lived realization that one exists only because one is always already the articulation of all other fleshly beings. One should keep in mind the point made in the preced-ing section that the very way in which one's flesh is articulated as flesh involves the incorporation of other bodies into it who in turn are incorporating one's own body into theirs. For this reason, the very movement of one's hands finds a cor-respondence with the flicker of a rat's twitching paws that is unnerving. And if one then thinks of the rat's mouth, of how it gnaws on its food and how it might even gnaw on one's flesh, the correspondence between my flesh and the rat's flesh becomes even more unnerving. In the lived experience of this correspon-dence is the indication of how paw and hand, as well as mouth and mouth, are both of flesh and the order of edibility. This insight is not unlike that of the Bud-dhist notion of *paticca samuppada*, dependent co-arising, in which the existence of each living entity is found to be dependent upon and interconnected with the existence of all other living entities.[26] When Merleau-Ponty speaks above of the cofunctioning of all flesh that sets it beyond rivalry, his words imply the same relationship.

Rather than being a moment of radical individuation, in the abject uncanny one's death involves how the very flesh by which one's being is engendered is revealed as also already the flesh of other beings. In being of the flesh of the world, one's death becomes *the rendering of one's flesh as the other's flesh.* One gazes into the mouths of innumerable stomachs ready to ingest one's life, whether they be microscopic bacteria or immense orcas, and finds that their claim to one's flesh has already been made within one's own flesh. In all of those mouths one comes before an indefinite *where*, but one that is distinctly different than that indefinite no-where of Heideggerian anxiety that leaves *Dasein* alone before its own death. The ambivalent, multidimensional *where* of the flesh is in its own way uncanny—it leaves one insecure in one's home (of which the body is the first instance), but only because the very substance of who one is provides all the other beings with their home as well. Rather than being utterly alone in one's death, one is absorbed (although in a manner differing radically from that thoughtless absorption of inauthentic *Dasein* in a world of mere curiosities and diversions) into the lives of all other life. The hyperfecundity of one's flesh is unnerving and yet inspiring. Its ontic moment, in which paranoia similar to that of unreflective anxiety in Heidegger is at play, could be called disgust. One shivers at the thought of the other's mouth tasting one's own flesh, one's own taste. And one also shivers at the thought of all the other beings one ingests in order to be who one is. Yet in the ontological moment of this disgust, one finds the very eating of one's flesh is the occasion for the dispossession and compassion alluded to above by Blanchot. One finds the significance of one's death transcends one's own life, even as one's own life has in turn been inspired and enfleshed by the lives and flesh of other beings. In this manner one finds the significance of one's birth and death extends beyond the question of one's own particular being and interrupts that question incessantly.

But can this moment of dispossession, of the questioning of the uniqueness of one's human existence, be characterized as good? Some might argue that in sundering humans so definitively from biological existence, Heidegger makes it possible to think the death of humans in a manner that renders them the dignity due to them. Humans are after all not merely another natural creature (and has not this not been claimed above as well?) whose death is nothing more than the recycling of material from one living organism to another. But to argue that the order of edibility is nothing more than the recycling of material for the sake of the one who consumes it, is itself a reduction and betrayal of life itself. Life is not a mechanism by which matter is transferred from one self-sustaining entity to another but an engendering and sustaining of all living entities by means of all other living entities. The Heideggerian anxiety about death leaves humans too alone, too alienated from the reality which engenders them and sustains them not only in ontic bodies but also in ontological ones. For Heidegger, it is as if there is no body there to die in *Dasein*'s death, as if one's anxiety only takes place as a function of one's time. Without a *where* that is always already the tissue of all other *wheres*, which is to say, without a body, Heidegger's thought about the uncanny minimizes the threat of being edible, of finding that one becomes in one's death all the other beings with whom one coexists. One can claim in counterpoint to the argument beginning this paragraph that the Heideggerian solution to preserving human dignity (at least as it is described in this paper) diminishes the significance of that dignity rather than saving it.

In Merleau-Ponty's rereading of Heideggerian ontology lies the dawning of a realization that being human is an achievement that cannot be sundered from its own body or all the other bodies that engender and sustain it as its own. Our bodies are the very sign that nothing that we are is in the first instance provided by ourselves. To be enfleshed is to be already in debt to all other creatures who have not only set the stage for our own emergence into existence but also have given us their very bodies so that we too might have one.[27] And our deaths, when thought against the horizon of our edibility, become an occasion for facing up to this debt, by rendering our flesh back to all other living entities for the sake of their lives too.

While one may not wish to do so and may fight this debt with every breath of one's life, one still cannot escape its hold upon one. Life intervenes before one can decide to accept it or not. The very existence of one's life already signifies an assent to the order of edibility that was given before one could have given it for oneself. One's existence is already in obligation to life itself. That one is then ingested by other entities so that their life might be fed need not and ought not to be thought of in terms of a reductive biologism. But as an order of goodness in which the very capacity to be already puts one in debt to the flesh of all other beings and so finds one responsible to them.[28] Before the array of all these other hungers, the dispossession of one's self by one's oncoming death opens up the capacity to feel compassion for all other living beings. A compassion that is quite different than that which one feels for one's fellow human beings (whom one would not eat or be eaten by) and yet is compassion none the less. In speaking about this order of edibility, Jack Turner reminds his reader of Thoreau's own motto for our reciprocal involvement with the world: "Sympathy with Intelligence." Thinking of how whortleberries and willow feed the moose, who in turn feeds human mouths, Turner expands upon the meaning of Thoreau's motto with the following questions: "How shall we experience an absence of boundaries, a world mutual and shared, an accord and an understanding grounded in feeling? When shall we know a compassion, an allegiance, and a loyalty that is infinite?"[29]

Another Ethics?

How then might the goodness of being edible find its expression within human society, and how might the small drama played out between a human community and three wayward beaver provide some insight into that question? Before proceeding to this point one caveat must be made: to argue for the goodness of being edible does not mean that we should take this order to be the unique standard by which a humane notion of goodness is to be characterized. In Beavermania, the emergence of the wild within the urban landscape, just as Wendell Berry has hinted would be so, induces an encounter with a difference that cannot be cast out, with a threat that is peculiarly intimate, with a nature that is not fully human but remains fully involved in our animation as living beings. The very registering of nature within urban and rural spaces is in terms of a crisis concerning which of two orders of goodness might prevail—a landscape ordered according to symmetrical predation or asymmetrical predation.[30] What is called for in this situation is not the determination of which order of goodness really holds but of how to accommodate two orders of goodness with radically different structures. On the one hand, we do not wish to argue for human cannibalism, and yet, on the other hand, we may want to respect the eating of one's own species when it occurs among crocodiles and guppies. This crisis is not to be put aside as a misunderstanding, as if we might have avoided it if we had only been more in tune with the natural order. We can only become truly responsible if we are willing to live with a sense of the necessity and the incompossiblity of two conflicting orders of goodness, along with at least two conflicting orderings of space. Both are necessary if human culture is to survive and flourish and become morally praiseworthy. The peculiar nature of our obligation to nonhuman entities within the order of edibility does not let us off the hook in regard to other humans. It does not allow us to shed humane responsibilities in the name of an amoral natural order, but complicates and intensifies the very significance of responsibility.

In making their claim to the cherry trees of Washington, D.C., three beaver called an entire community to reflective deliberation about the relative claims of these two orders. In doing so, animals reminded a human community that the issue of how wild spaces are interwoven into urban and suburban environments was not a trivial one, not merely a matter of how much pleasure one might gain in one's recreation. The goodness of the beaver being there, of making their own way in the world as creatures who eat other creatures, inspired the community. This experience suggests that much more should be done within urban and suburban spaces to make a place for the wild. But in doing so, one should remain aware that the intentional interweaving of wild spaces into urban and suburban environments challenges humans to rethink the meaning of their own flesh and to take more seriously the intimacy and the goodness of the act of eating *and of being eaten*. As Turner's words remind us: "This system of food [in which we are 'guest of honor and part of the feast'], which is hidden from the urban mind, is terrifying in its identity and reciprocity. It is a vision that could inform everything from our private spiritual matters to the gross facts of nourishment and death."[31] Unless urban peoples are willing to confront this insight, simply opening up marginal spaces within the urban landscape will not lead to their being sustained as wild spaces. Allied with this opening must come an ethical turn of the heart that desires these spaces to be more than parks in which predatory animals are singled out and eradicated or "managed." We ought to subdue our insistence on not being edible at least to the point that its threat is more palpable. In this tempering of our intentions toward other's—animals' intentions, the "human courtesy"[32] that Berry would have us give them is revealed to involve more than a traditional gesture of hospitality. Hospitality requires that we invite the other into our own home in order to share our food and shelter with her or him. In regard to the wilds, courtesy involves more than the discomfort of sharing one's provender. The host also runs the risk of sharing his or her own flesh, even if this is to no greater extent than in the bite of a spider or the salt-hungered lick of a fly.

How much forbearance should a community exercise in its welcome to beings that eat other beings? Recently at my own university an issue allied to this one came up when several students who are members of the Environmental Studies Association suggested that we start an apiary on the edge of our campus. This suggestion brought an immediate response from a concerned biology professor who insisted the danger of bee stings to a percentage of the human population on campus made the introduction of bees immoral. We should not, he argued, endanger human life for the sake of having a few bee colonies in the neighborhood. He may be right. But we need to acknowledge that precisely the failure to have bee colonies in the neighborhood can also be immoral. Especially when the drive to protect human life from being stung or bit or gnawed upon leads to the impression that our flesh has somehow seceded from the order of edibility, that the pollination of plants and the intermingling of humans with the insect orders can be forgone with little or no effect on our own spiritual and moral lives. What constitutes a tolerable level of risk is up for discussion. That there be no discussion, or that the discussion immediately stops with the objection that people might be harmed, is itself morally questionable.

One is reminded of Kafka's parable in which the temple ceremony is finally changed so that when the leopards arrive, their dashing of the vessels is itself incorporated into the ceremony. This sort of solidarity can only be achieved if we are willing to encounter animals under the uncanny threat of our being edible to them. No kind ranger would intervene with his or her chainsaw to manicure a park where no one might trip inadvertently, nor would the beaver be summarily shipped away. The threat of predation, rather than involving the collapse of an ethical relationship, is the introduction into another sort of ethics, in which the goodness of nutrition, of eating as a universal, *inter-species* phenomenon is acknowledged and affirmed.[33] The fact that many survivors, often severely maimed, of animal "attacks" continue to hold the animals they have encountered in profound respect indicates another notion of goodness than that at play in the intra-human sphere, in intra-human space.[34] Because we have so often insisted on thinking of ethics in terms of the repression of predation (although often in modes of dishonesty and denial—for example, the manner in which meat is sold as hunks of inert matter), accounting for this tone of respect has been an almost impossible task. In bringing us back to our involvement in the edible world the now captured and relocated beaver of the Tidal Basin deserve praise.[35] We too will deserve praise insofar as we learn to negotiate and honestly live within the difficult tension that comes from working out a human morality in a more-than-human landscape.

Notes

1. From the Taittiriya Upanishad. Quoted by Jack Turner, "In Wildness is the Preservation of the World," in *The Great New Wilderness Debate*, ed. J. Baird Callicott and Michael P. Nelson (Athens: University of Georgia Press, 1998), 627. This essay is found in altered form in: Jack Turner, *The Abstract Wild* (Tucson: University of Arizona Press, 1996), ch. 6.

2. Wendell Berry, "Preserving Wildness," in *Home Economics* (New York: Farrar, Straus and Giroux, 1987), 139.

3. This issue is raised in a different context—namely that of wilderness areas—in my essay, "The Uncanny Goodness of Being Edible to Bears" [in *Nature Reconsidered: New Essays in Environmental Philosophy*, Folz and Froedeman, editors (Indiana University Press, forthcoming)].

4. The term "space" is used in this context in a sense differing from that abstract grid of homogeneous locations, characterized by Enlightenment thinkers such as Descartes and Kant. Predatory space is characterized by a unique and symmetrical pre-orientation, in which one has always already found oneself in the flesh of the other's body as much as in one's own. Or conversely, the other's hunger claims one's flesh from within one's flesh. Symmetrical predatory space is highly ambivalent, even uncanny—it both nurtures and feeds upon one's own flesh. One does not take a step into it without having brought other living creatures closer to one's own mouth and one's own flesh closer to their mouths. Within any earthly place (i.e., within any place in which life exists and feeds upon itself), this space is always already articulated. As such it transcends given locations and given places, even as it is found as a constant feature of them. The human attempt to transform the ambivalent symmetry of predatory space so that its orientation is asymmetrical, that is, in favor of the human mouth at the expense of all the other mouths (if a choice must be made), is a necessarily temporary phenomenon but nevertheless a commendable one within certain limits. Here we mark a second sense of predatory space, in which wild places are marked off culturally and administratively from non-wild places in a manner described below. For a while, we put predatory space in its place. This second sense of predatory space is a derivative one but unfortunately is all too often treated as the primary instantiation of the phenomenon.

It could be argued, via the thought of Edward Casey and others [see Edward Casey, *Getting Back into Place* (Bloomington: Indiana University Press, 1993)], that what is being described in this chapter is actually a crisis in place. Insofar as place is thought of as that mode by which particular bodies find themselves in regard to a limit that orients them, this objection has much merit. Predation, found in the fangs or molars (as the case of the beaver show) of other particular mouths, becomes a sort of limit that brings the place of one's body into crisis—one's body is both one's place and the other's place. But space has been kept as the central term in the following argument because a distinction needs to be made in the case being discussed between the many localities in which predatory orientation is at work and the features of that orientation itself which show a more universal quality. In this mode of thought, predation is a crisis in how one can space one's body—that is, create an interval between it and other bodies. This crisis is experienced throughout the earthly places in which human habitation occurs.

5. The very use of the term "predator" in regard to human perpetrators of violence against humans is a profoundly questionable rhetorical move, but one with incredible power within our social landscape. Among other effects, it allows at least one segment of our population to view human perpetrators of violence as "mere" animals. This thought, combined with a history of viewing animals as a disposable resource, opens the way to becoming so hateful toward the perpetrator of violence as to be utterly indifferent to her or his humanity: "He or she is just an animal." This statement does neither the human nor the animal credit. Animal predation, while it may be violent, is not murder and is commendable for that animal. We should desire that bear and beaver eat what is necessary to sustain their existence. The discourse involved in the order of edibility should not be confused with that addressing how one human betrays another in a gesture of violence.

6. Holmes Rolston III, *Conserving Natural Value* (New York: Columbia University Press, 1994), 12.

7. Rolston, *Conserving,* 14.

8. Berry, "Preserving Wildness," 151.

9. These statements can be just as typical for farmers and ranchers as for suburbanites. The nearly successful genocide of the wolf in America over the last century bears witness to this [see, for example, Barry Lopez, *Of Wolves and Men* (New York: Simon & Schuster, 1978), especially ch. 9]. Concerning the reintroduction of wolves into the southwest, rancher Jupe Means argues [in an article titled "Mexican Wolves Return to the Southwest, Despite Ranchers' Howls" (*Washington Post*, 27 January 1998, 3(A))]: "If the wolf has the right to run in this country, we have the right to protect our interests, if you understand what I mean." Consider as well the tone and implication, albeit often humorous, of citizen comments to the U.S. Fish and Wildlife Service about reintroduction of wolves into Idaho and Montana in 1994 [*Missoulian*, 5 August 1994, 1(A)]: (1) "Wolves don't help feed and water the livestock and they don't help raise food for people to eat so what good are they?"; (2) "I'm sure they (wolves) would eat me too if they were hungry, and I'm sure a healthy cow."; (3) "There are too many misconsumptions (*sic!*) about wolves."; (4) "It's like, it's like inviting the AIDS virus."; (5) "I think they are a beautiful animal. I shot one in British Columbia and had it mounted, and I have it in my home. I enjoy looking at it every day"; (6) "It's a little bit like allowing gays into the military, but not if they admit they're gay. Allow wolves into Yellowstone, but only if they don't behave like wolves."

10. Gary Snyder, *The Practice of the Wild* (New York: Farrar, Straus and Giroux, 1990), 110. Also quoted in his *A Place in Space* (Washington, D.C.: Counterpoint, 1995), 169.

11. Linda Wheeler, "Chomping Down on Cherry Blossom Season," *Washington Post,* 7 April 1999, 1(B).

12. Linda Wheeler, *Washington Post*, 8 April 1999, A1. Notice how an herbivore becomes a predator not by a predilection for meat—which would be odd indeed for a beaver—but by its consumption of living entities to which we feel partial and over which we exercise ownership. By analogy, it is as if the beaver were gnawing on our own body, or at least upon the body politic.

13. Annie Groer and Ann Gerhart, "Duck and Hover at the White House," *The Washington Post*, 7 April 1999, 3(C).

14. "Leave It to the Beavers," *Washington Post*, 10 April 1999, 20(A).

15. Julia Kristeva, *Strangers to Ourselves*, Leon Roudiez, trans. (New York: Columbia University Press, 1991), 182ff.

16. Linda Wheeler, "Tree-Chomping Beaver May Have Cohort in Crime," *Washington Post*, 9 April 1999, 1(A), 24(A).

17. Maurice Merleau-Ponty, *The Visible and the Invisible*, Alphonso Lingis, trans. (Evanston, Ill.: Northwestern University Press, 1968), 263.

18. I have argued elsewhere that Merleau-Ponty's very turn to a phenomenological view of the body is effectively an ethics [See "Recursive Incarnation and Chiasmic Flesh: Two Readings of Celan's *Chymsich*," in *Chiasms: Merleau-Ponty's Notion of the Flesh* (Albany: SUNY Press, forthcoming)]. Merleau-Ponty's analysis implies that we most often flee being in touch with the cofunctioning of our bodies with other bodies, precisely because this cofunctioning so deeply undermines our complacent view of being the center of our world and in complete control of our own embodiment. By demonstrating the futility and fundamental dishonesty of this mode of flight, phenomenology serves to bring us into a posture of humility in regard to all other beings. To live in the delusional state of an autonomy that is utterly impermeable to other bodies is to cultivate an insensitivity to the other's sensitivity, inattentiveness to the pangs of her or his or its hunger.

19. One becomes not *literally* the other but *in the flesh* the other. One's flesh is as much the other's flesh!

20. See Kelly Oliver's discussion of abjection in her *Reading Kristeva* (Bloomington: Indiana University Press, 1993), 56 ff. The abject is not "a quality" but "a relationship to a boundary" (56) such as the boundary between mother and child, or in the present case, between prey and predator. The abject threatens identity, threatens the distinction by which the other remains outside of oneself, by threatening the very notion of distinction itself. In abjection, the very flesh of one's being is shown to have at its origin a lack of origin, a lack of particularity that is scandalous and yet inevitable. In Kristeva's example, Kelly claims, "the mother cannot tell whether this other in her [the fetus/child] is her or not; and either alternative seems equally impossible" (57). Similarly, in regard to one's edibility one becomes abject to all other mouths, to all other hungers. Flesh maintains itself by eating and being eaten. In that conjunction there is no easy way to untie the other's investment in my flesh and of my flesh in her or him. While abjection in gestation involves the sundering of one's flesh to become both oneself and the other (one's child), in edibility it involves being ingested by the other to become the other (or ingesting the other to become oneself). In the act of ingestion, one's body both is and is not one's own.

21. This claim should not be read to imply that in all cases eating meat is a good thing or that vegetarianism is a fallacious moral choice. The question here is not whether humans will continue to eat other animals but of how honestly we will face up to the manner in which all flesh feeds upon and feeds all other flesh. The fact of the matter is that the bodies of all the other animals find their way into our mouths, even if we are vegetarians, via the soil itself. Decomposition, as much as predation, is a part of the uncanniness of being edible. And even if we find it moral to eat meat, the issue of how domesticated animals are treated remains crucial. What is more pressing to what is being argued above is whether we can find in ourselves the courage and humility to respect wild animals and their mode of behavior in eating one another. We should be willing to praise the mountain lion for being a predator, to find that mode of life a good one. If we are not, then we will continue to carry a prejudice in favor of the domesticated animal that will be fatal to any long term contact between our civilization and the wilds.

22. See Michael Crummet, *Sun Dance: The 50th Anniversary Crow Indian Sun Dance*, foreword by Heywood Big Day (Helena, Mont.: Falcon Press, 1993), 50-51, where one

particular dancer who is described as "pushing himself to the limit" after three days of dancing collapses and falls deep in his vision: "It was alarming for spectators who did not know what was going on to witness a Sun Dancer not only tumble to the ground, but also to see him left in the sun while the ceremony continued. They did not understand that it was of great benefit when this happened, that it was one of the intended results of going into a Sun Dance." In interpreting these moments as visions, one would in my mind be making a mistake to see them as what enlightenment culture terms "literally true." The epistemological and ontological status of moments of vision can be argued for without asking that they be interpreted as if they were just another waking moment. They are real but not real in the same way. For this very reason, careful reflection about and interpretation of them is necessary.

23. Martin Heidegger, *Being and Time,* trans. John Macquarrie and Edward Robinson (New York: Harper and Row, 1962), 295.

24. Maurice Blanchot, "The Work and Death's Space," in *The Space of Literature,* trans. Ann Smock (Lincoln: University of Nebraska Press, 1989), 141.

25. Blanchot, "The Work and Death's Space," 150.

26. See, for example, Joanna Macy's discussion of this concept and its implications for the contemporary world in her *World as Lover, World as Self* (Berkeley: Parallax Press, 1991), esp. ch. 8.

27. This also occurs in the intra-human sphere through our being engendered. The manner in which flesh gives itself to flesh goes beyond mere edibility and includes the abject origin of human beings in sexual procreation.

28. Holmes Rolston III has argued in a different manner to the same end, namely, that edibility is a form of goodness. But his rationale is put in terms of the language of value and does not emphasize so much the uncanniness of the situation, although he makes an implicit reference to it. He claims that while each animal has "its integral intrinsic value," it can also be "sacrificed in behalf of another life course, when its intrinsic value collapses, becomes extrinsic, and is in part instrumentally transported to another organism" [Holmes Rolston III, "Values Gone Wild," in *Environmental Ethics: Divergence and Convergence* eds. Susan Armstrong and Richard Botzler (New York: McGraw-Hill, 1993), 64; originally found in *Inquiry* 26 (1983): 181-207. Reprinted in his *Philosophy Gone Wild* (Buffalo, N.Y.: Prometheus Books, 1989), 118-43]. Notice how crucial is the collapse and transformation of what was intrinsic to what is extrinsic in Rolston's argument. Here too a notion of the uncanny is implicitly at play. While Rolston provides much insight into the manner in which life has value both for oneself and for all other life, the approach being developed here allows one to think more directly about the very slipperiness of the boundary between intrinsic and extrinsic value. This slipperiness is itself a feature of life that deserves much attention.

29. Jack Turner, "In Wildness is the Preservation of the World," 627.

30. The claim here is that no space is without predation, which is to say, without the consuming of the other's flesh. What distinguishes asymmetrical from symmetrical space is the orientation of predation within it. In asymmetrical predatory space we humans eat others who are not allowed in turn to eat us. In symmetrical predatory space, or wild space, we are subjected to predation, to becoming flesh for the other.

31. Turner, *The Abstract Wild,* 91.

32. Berry, "Preserving Wildness," 151.

33. But to argue that we should be willing to live with the *threat* of predation does not mean that we are willingly to become prey. And allowing the leopards to dash vessels to the ground does not mean that all the vessels need be destroyed. The argument being

given here does not preempt our defending ourselves from the bear that would make us his or her lunch, but our defense can no longer take place in a tone of moral outrage. This outrage is hypocritical in that it would forget its own desire to eat. Ultimately, the very incompossibility of these two orders of goodness, human and wild, demands the most strenuous exercise of *phronesis* and the humility to acknowledge that no harmony is achieved with nature that is entirely nonlethal. In living between two conflicting moral orders, we are asked to continually negotiate covenants between them. For example, as simple a decision as where to draw the line on if and where spiders can live in one's domicile should be fraught with consideration. In a culture attentive to the balances between the differing demands of edibility and human thriving, the very fabric of decision-making would lead to radically different narratives of how the wild is at play within the human context and to different modes of organizing the boundaries between domesticized and wild landscapes.

34. This point has been treated in some detail in my paper, "The Uncanny Goodness of Being Edible to Bears." As for a particular example of the phenomenon of survivors of bear attacks respecting the animals that tried to kill them, see the video of *National Geographic Explorer: Bears*, "Bear Attack," in which Kelley McConnell talks about his sentiments for a bear that killed his mother and nearly killed him in northern British Columbia on August 14, 1997.

35. See Martin Weil and Linda Wheeler, "Tidal Basin Hunt Nets Beaver Family's Big Daddy," *Washington Post,* 13 April 1999, 1(B). Having been finally captured, the beaver were set free at an undisclosed location near Washington, and their ongoing conditions were reported on intermittently over the next two years.

Chapter 4

The Deceptive Environment:
The Architecture of Security

Ruth Connell

"The only thing we have to fear is fear itself."
—Franklin Delano Roosevelt

"Individuals may deceive and be deceived; but no one ever deceived everybody,
nor has everybody ever deceived anyone."
—Pliny the Younger

Introduction

Design for security affects the visual, psychological, and cultural experience of architectural and landscape environments. Recent trends in the use of electronic security systems, proxy elements, and other security design devices are creating an architecture of deception. Appearances *can* be deceiving. Today more environments within our democratic society are being secured by unseen methods in contrast to the legibility of the secured environments of the past. The visibility of security design proves to be a transmutable quality: design for security is seen and unseen, understood or deceptive, or simply disingenuous. This author considers the impact of security issues on the built environment, from an architect's point of view, and is mainly concerned with public environments and American examples of architecture, abroad and at home.

Security issues are of particular interest to Americans, both inside the nation and abroad. In April 1999, the nation grieved for students murdered inside a school building in Littleton, Colorado. The carnage at Littleton was only the next in a series of school murders, following two young people killed in Pearl, Mississippi; three killed in West Paducah, Kentucky; five killed in Jonesboro,

Arkansas; and two killed in Springfield, Oregon."[1] Recent acts of terrorism abroad include the simultaneous truck bombings of the U.S. embassies in Kenya and Tanzania that killed 224 people (August 1998) and the truck bombing of the Khobar Towers housing complex in Saudi Arabia (1996) that killed nineteen U.S. servicemen and injured more than 500 Americans and Saudis.[2]

Could an event like Littleton, Colorado, be mitigated by the design of the environment? Could the devastation of the terrorist truck bombings in Africa have been prevented by the architecture? Can the introduction of security controls into the design of schools, embassies, and their landscapes make a difference? The answer is yes to proponents of CPTED or "Crime Prevention Through Environmental Design."[3]

CPTED is a movement that supports the idea of security through design—design in the broadest sense, from the conceptual site plan to the details of hardware. Experts of "Crime Prevention Through Environmental Design" have studied security issues using the tools of the behavioral sciences and have generated specific physical design guidelines to enhance security. CPTED guidelines concentrate on security through the physical manipulation of design elements that are already at play in any given scenario: access points, window location and design, buffer zones, etc.

The modification of design elements to create a more secure environment is not always evident or perceptible to the observer. Some modifications of specific design elements will be visually obvious, while others will not be perceived or recognized as security measures. The majority of the recommendations on a CPTED "objectives" checklist for school design would be unseen, or unidentifiable regarding their purpose, once implemented.[4] This list includes concepts like "surveillance through physical design," "congestion control," and "territorial identity." Other objectives, like *mechanical surveillance devices*—provide schools with security devices to detect and signal unauthorized entry attempts," would most likely be visible and understood as security elements.

If design for security is addressed as an initial design parameter, not unlike the provision for other basic design parameters such as functional activity relationships, circulation patterns, adequate daylight, climate, existing built context, etc., then the design response to security is less likely to be perceived as a specific response to security than modifications or alterations that arrive later in the design or building process. Ordinarily the design process is a synthetic response to a complex set of design parameters. Often the link between a specific design parameter like security and a particular design response may not be perceived or understood, and most likely the design is an integrated response to many layered demands of different types of design parameters.

Consider the simple design of a corridor width in a school building. The width of the corridor may have been regulated by the egress demands of the prevailing building code, or the width may have been determined by the architect's own assessment of circulation requirements. Perhaps the width was derived from a need for solar gain against an opposing passive solar thermal mass; or maybe it was a response to a favorable viewing angle for human surveillance. The building occupant is unlikely to perceive or to know the controlling reason behind the design of the corridor. In this way many design parameters may be unseen or unknown. Similarly, many design modifications for security may be unseen or unknown.

The Visibility of Security: the Seen, the Unseen, and the Disingenuous

A change in some design elements for security enhancement will be visually obvious, while others will not be perceived or recognized as security measures. A design that coordinates the location of building access points for improved security will not look very different to the casual observer than a building without this design consideration. On the other hand, the addition of a guardhouse with a gate is clearly visible as a functional security control and as a symbol of security.

Elements that are visible and recognizable as to their function add to the legibility of an environment. Unseen elements do not contribute directly to our experience of a space, although our suspicion of invisible surveillance greatly affects our psychological experience of a space. An electronic laser beam fence or electronic eye of a surveillance camera is entirely invisible, and because its presence is unseen, it reveals no information about the security of its environment. A posted sign informing us of the existence of electronic surveillance may reassure us about security precautions or induce the disturbing sensation of being observed by invisible methods.

In order to examine the visual, experiential, and psychological impacts of security issues on the environment, it is necessary to determine what a secure environment looks like. The visibility of security exists on at least three levels: the seen, the unseen, and the disingenuous.

These elements can be illustrated by examples. "The seen" includes fences and gates, guards and guardhouses, razor wire, metal-detector security gates, barred windows, displayed declarations of subscriptive commercial security service. Seen elements are readily perceived as security elements, and are understood as environmental responses to the need for security. The appropriateness of the response is usually related to the context of the building type or landscape function. Thus I am not startled to see razor wire looped on the walls of the county penitentiary, but might be disturbed to find a security metal detector at the entrance of a church.

"The unseen" are most elements of Crime Prevention Through Environmental Design. Because CPTED relies on fundamental design decisions, the results are primarily unseen. This does not imply that the design measures for security are deliberately intended to be unseen or unknown. The location of control points or access points, the location of doors and windows, and the inclusion of buffer zones remain unrecognizable as elements of security because these architectural design decisions are meshed with other design parameters. Our unawareness of the security reason behind the placement of a door is an intrinsic consequence of the multivalent architectural design process. The relative invisibility of these design modifications for security is not deliberate. It is simply a function of the design process.

However some design elements for security are disingenuous, or purposefully deceptive. To be disingenuous is to consciously lack openness in communication—not exactly to be dishonest, but to be lacking in directness or candor. Proxy elements are good examples of "the disingenuous" presence of security elements in the built environment. An example of a proxy element would be a tree that is planted to function as a traffic-blocking bollard. As a security element, the function of these disingenuous objects is unrecognizable to the uninformed eye, and they become ambiguous parts of the environment.

Design for security also applies at the scale of urban design, and can be equally disingenuous at the urban scale. For instance, Napoleon III reconfigured the medieval streets of Paris ostensibly for many social improvements—the installation of sewers, new housing, improved flow of carts and pedestrians. Yet the wide avenues designed under Baron G. E. Haussmann vastly improved surveillance and crowd control in the event of civilian riot.[5]

The unseen becomes the deceptive by human intention, by choice. The invisibility of the electronic laser beam fence presents a startling example. Invisibility is an onboard characteristic of the device; it simply exists without "malice aforethought." Yet the decision to design with invisible security technology may reflect conscious intent to deceive, or at the very least, to be disingenuous. In other words, many layers of visibility and invisibility, or of legibility and deception are found in the built environment.

Architectural design for security has an enormous potential to be willfully deceptive, or disingenuous. The deliberate construction of an ambiguous environment has deep social, political, and ethical implications. There is a high social cost to a free, democratic society for a built environment where appearances are deceiving.

Our perception of security is also dependent on factors outside the realm of the environment. The perception of physical security is a psychological condition. Our conviction that we are in a safe environment reflects our psychology as well as our cultural location. Just as individuals from different cultures have different body languages and different tolerances for human crowding, our perception of security varies by culture. "Freedom from Fear"[6] is both a psychological and cultural condition.

Terrorism

Among the initial effects of entering the post-Cold War period was a decline in international terrorism. Throughout the 1980s American fatalities from terrorism declined, but by the late 1990s terrorist violence was on the increase. According to the *Architectural Record*, it is significant that "business targets have accounted for more incidents in recent years than diplomatic, government, and military ones."[7] Businesses—located in the public realm—have become popular targets of terrorist violence. American businesses are associated with American political and economic dominance. An explanation for this can be found in Thomas Friedman's article on globalization and the new world order.[8] He writes: "In most countries, people can no longer distinguish between American power, American exports, American cultural assaults, American cultural exports and plain old globalization." In the post-Cold War era, the United States, the leader of the Fast World, has become a leading target of attack.

As an example of attacks on commercial businesses, in 1991 in Lima, Peru, three terrorists bombed a Kentucky Fried Chicken (KFC) outlet.[9] This incident is of particular interest because it was so clearly directed against the building itself. The building was seen as a symbol, or icon, of American business interests. The terrorists evacuated all the people from the restaurant before dynamiting the building itself. Although people were injured—people driving by in cars, nearby pedestrians, and people crushed by flying architectural detritus—the injuries were not deliberate, but incidental. The intention was to destroy a symbolic architectural artifact, and not to specifically injure people.

Security issues in architecture have intensified following specific incidents of successful terrorist attacks on public buildings. These were attacks directed at the building itself, a type of architectural terrorism. Usually the tactic was a vehicle-delivered bomb directed at the structure of the building. Some more notorious recent events were the bombing of the Alfred P. Murrah Federal Building, Oklahoma City (1995), the bombing of the World Trade Center in New York (1993), and the bombings of U.S. embassies in Kenya and Tanzania in East Africa (1998). In the case of the World Trade Center, because the building itself is internationally renowned as a masterpiece of architectural design and structural engineering, and is a potent architectural symbol of American economic power, the attack was clearly one of architectural terrorism.

Security issues are not new. Architecture has always been about shelter—and protection. What is new is the technology available to all players, to the design professional and to the perpetrator of civic violence.

An interesting new technology available to the structural engineer is the computer software known as "Bomb Cad."[10] Bomb Cad allows the design professional to run model bomb scenarios against structural diagrams to determine weak points. By identifying the design vulnerability to the well-placed bomb, these areas can be reinforced or blocked from accessibility. As with all technology the tool becomes available to both sides. It can be assumed that the would-be terrorist could access building design files, and could use a Bomb Cad type software with devastating results.

Impregnable Architecture

Buildings can be designed as absolute fortresses. Much of the early history of architecture is a history of fortifications and defensive architecture. The technology and technique exist; it is rather a question of social choice whether to fortify a building or to create an open, civic public space.

Recent examples of impregnable architecture have been built within the urban cores and ghettos of the United States. Camilo Jose Vergara has ventured into the center of our "new American ghettos" with his camera, and has revealed an urban architecture of survival—and defense. The Salvation Army Building[11] on the West Side of Chicago is an example of an impregnable building that gives nothing to the street but a completely closed absolute wall.

Another example of an urban fortress from the documentation work of Camilo Jose Vergara is the Detroit Receiving Hospital. Surrounded by walls and parking lots this building presents a "hard and shiny" persona to its decayed urban surroundings. At an even grander scale, the University of Medicine and Dentistry is sited like a high tech urban castle in a field of car parking.[12]

Because all buildings play a role in the definition of public space and in the delineation of the spatial character of the city, the decision to create closed and impregnable buildings carries a social cost. Public space, and the character of the public street, is important to the identity of a society. Fortified buildings close the space of the street in more than one way. The erection of a visually and physically closed wall removes the potential of human interaction at the boundaries between building and street. In *The Life and Death of Great American Cities*,[13] Jane Jacobs demonstrated how a street with a bar—complete with noisy drinkers coming and going—was much safer than a homogeneous residential street without night life on the street. The social life of the street is the essential ingredient of the safe street. Paradoxically, a fortified building renders its interior space "safe" at the cost of making the public space of the street unsafe. When a building becomes a windowless closed bastion, the "eyes" of the building are removed from the street, and no longer give natural security surveillance to the street.

Examples of contemporary fortified buildings include the Omni Renaissance hotel centers, in Atlanta, Detroit, and elsewhere. These hotels were designed as completely independent mixed-use commercial development centers that could function as economic and physical islands within the city. In this phenomenon of the 1970s and 1980s the interior volumes appeared to balloon into gargantuan atriums while the exteriors became more closed and fortified in appearance. Another building to present massive walls to the street, complete with iron-barred openings, is Robert Stern's Miami government center.

Impregnable buildings also carry a high social cost on the symbolic level. The identity of a democratic society depends on concepts of freedom—freedom of speech, freedom of movement. The closed landscape of a fortified street denies freedom of movement, denies the appearance of open space—i.e., places where choice of movement is not overly restricted or controlled.

Security, Signs, and Symbolism

Signs and symbolism have a fundamental role in architecture and landscape architecture,[14] and are integral aspects in the issues of security. There are many types of architectural symbolism which have been thoroughly discussed elsewhere.[15] The simplest example is the use of signs in the landscape.

Posted signs may proclaim a community's participation in an organized crime-prevention program. The announcement of the community's self-surveillance can be a functional deterrent to criminal activity. On a more abstract level partial walls located at the entrance of a community suggest or symbolize the existence of a comprehensive yet nonexistent perimeter wall. Although the wall is not there, the *idea* of the wall conveys a community status and self-awareness that is prohibitive to crime. The partial gate-walls function as territorial markers, and the concept of territory is basic to the design of secure environments. Yet the reality is false, the perimeter wall does not exist and no one may be at home to enforce the advertised crime-prevention program.

Surveillance cameras are often announced with signs, under a ubiquitous statement that "these premises are under electronic surveillance." Although it might be difficult to quantitatively measure the controlling effect of the signs themselves,[16] certainly there is some increase in security from the signs alone. It then follows that deliberately false signs offer a seductive economy—from the smallest vinyl "Beware of Bad Dog" sign posted at a non-canine household to the proclamation of nonexisting security cameras. In South America, realistic life-size plastic models of security guards are being installed in bank lobbies and on street corners. Inside these security guard decoys are cameras and microphones; the passerby can approach the decoy and ask for directions. Are these objects guards? Or are they decoy guards, cameras that look like people, or familiar cloth-mother monkeys of security? The separations between signs and not-signs, and between deception and reality become confused.

With architectural elements, it is even easier to blur distinctions between deception and honesty. The limits of potential deception are boundless. Consider that in the German Nazi extermination camps, gas chambers were designed to look like showers. Because architecture can be such a powerful tool of social control, the question of how security concerns are to be integrated into the design of our environment must be raised to a social, political, and ethical debate.

Hierarchical Space and Security

The expression of hierarchical space in the design of either buildings or the landscape communicates to the user where he or she is welcome or not welcome. It does this by helping to establish territory. As defined by Leon Pastalan, "A territory is a delimited space that a person or a group uses and defends as an

exclusive preserve. It involves psychological identification with a place, symbolized by attitudes of possessiveness and arrangements of objects in the area."[17]

The pioneering work of Oscar Newman, *Defensible Space,* had this to say
about territory: "Real Versus Symbolic Barriers: There is a language of symbols
which has come to be recognized as instrumental in defining boundaries or a
claim to territory. These boundary definers are interruptions in the sequence of
movement along access paths and serve to create perceptible zones of transition
from public to private spaces. . . . Some represent real barriers: U-shaped buildings, high walls and fences, and locked gates and doors. Others are symbolic
barriers only: open gateways, light standards, a short run of steps, planting, and
changes in the texture of the walking surface. Both serve a common purpose: to
inform that one is passing from a space which is public where one's presence is
not questioned through a barrier to a space which is private and where one's
presence requires justification."[18]

Hierarchical space implies levels of territory, and therefore creates security,
within the built environment. An example of hierarchical space can be found in
the work of Sir Edwin Lutyens. His design for the Viceroy's House and Mughal
Garden built in New Delhi between 1920 and 1931 is an interesting example of
layered space that uses symbolic barriers to define territorial zones. The layering
of zones is first established in the site plan. The public approach to the building
is clearly defined by the strong use of symmetry. Within the building, the inner
residential cores are implicitly secure. In this way, hierarchical space is used to
establish territoriality.

The works of Louis I. Kahn present strong examples of hierarchy in architectural design. At the Salk Institute for Biological Studies (La Jolla, California,
1959-1965) the exquisite centrality of the courtyard uses hierarchy to create
spatial order. Another example of crystalline spatial order is demonstrated at the
capitol of Bangladesh in Dhaka (Dhaka, Bangladesh, 1962-1983).

Use of Hierarchical Space to Establish Territoriality: The Courthouse Example

The secure environment of the past depended in part on the legibility of its
building types. The courthouse is a traditional example of a civic building type.
Historically courthouses have been symbols of public justice—symbols of civic
life. In the past, the symbolic meaning of many historic courthouses was conveyed by a simple architectural iconography.

Different theories abound to explain how buildings acquire symbolic meaning.
In the case of courthouse iconography, the acquisition of symbolic meaning
follows Jon Lang's definition of the "ecological model of perception and cognition."[19] This model maintains that people learn the meaning of particular forms
through social and cultural association. Our collective experience of architectural and landscape environments establishes and renews their meaning. This

also follows Ferdinand de Saussure's concept of a sign, that it is "a two-part entity, consisting of a *signifier* and a *signified*, formally united by social contract."[20]

In the historic courthouse precedent, classical temple fronts and high domes communicated the hierarchical importance of the building in the community. Open colonnades and majestic entrances established both invitation and formal dignity. Consider this iconography more closely, the classical temple front signifies the democracy of the Greeks as transformed through the cultural experiences of the Renaissance and the Enlightenment. The Romans were the first to "borrow" the iconography of the Greek temple front, going so far as to apply its rectilinear mass to the cylindrical form of the Pantheon. The high domes of the traditional nineteenth century courthouse signified civic importance through sheer power of height and dominance in the landscape; the monumental stairs and the use of an elevated *piano nobile* main floor level conveyed the same message.

The following courthouse examples, all from North Carolina, rely on architectural iconography to convey importance, territoriality and security. At the Chowan County Courthouse, Edenton, North Carolina, begun in 1767, the high cupola, tall windows, and central entrance serve this purpose (fig. 4.1). At the Randolph County Courthouse, Asheboro, North Carolina (1908-1909) the dominance of a centrally located sculpture in the landscape, a temple front and monumental stairs to an elevated main floor level communicate hierarchy and territoriality (fig. 4.2). Despite the evolution of stylistic expression, the Union County Courthouse, Monroe, North Carolina, (1886)[21] has a tall central spire and elevated central entrance with a staircase that convey the same message. Hundreds of other historic American courthouses throughout the nation exemplified this important civic building type.

These clearly established and socially accepted architectural symbols serve to identify the building's function and status; equally, the architectural symbolism identifies who the players are within the building. This identification establishes a psychological sense of security. The traditional civic landscape demonstrated by these historic courthouse examples, conveyed order, hierarchy, territoriality, and cultural meaning. Theirs was a legible environment understood by the general population. The meaning of the environment was an accepted social covenant.

In the ensuing one hundred years since the nineteenth century courthouse reached its mature expression as a building type, architectural design and theory embraced the functionalist ethic of modern architecture, only to later forsake modernism for post-modernism, deconstructionism, and the neo-traditionalist mandate of New Urbanism.

Although it is a contemporary design, the Warren B. Rudman United States Courthouse, Concord, New Hampshire[22] uses the traditional language of hierarchy and symbolism to convey territory and meaning (fig. 4.3). The façade is symmetrical; the central entrance is clearly defined and elevated behind a modest staircase.

Fig. 4.1: Chowan County Courthouse, Edenton, North Carolina, begun 1767
(All illustrations drawn by Ruth Connell)

The advent of required handicapped accessibility[23] has largely removed the
monumental staircase as an available expressive element of hierarchy and territoriality. Only with careful site design and detailing can an architect choose to
employ the iconography of the monumental stair. Rarely can new structures
accommodate both handicapped access ramps and expressive flights of stairs.
The Warren B. Rudman United States Courthouse designed by Shepley Bulfinch
Richardson and Abbott/PMR Joint Venture Architects is a successful example.

A handicapped access ramp is smoothly positioned behind a wall, and it can
be assumed that the staircase height was limited to the height that could be accommodated by the ramp's total height gain. This compromise made it possible
to include the stair as a diminished but still iconographic element.

At the Rudman Courthouse, tall windows and a water table masonry detail
express a *piano nobile.* The importance of the central entrance is continued in
the interior with a monumental lobby. Symmetry, monumentality, and indirect

natural lighting enhance the experience of order and hierarchy. Our experience of this courthouse environment is an affirmation of citizenship—our roles within the building are defined and supported by the architecture. A sense of security is created by the fundamental design of the building.

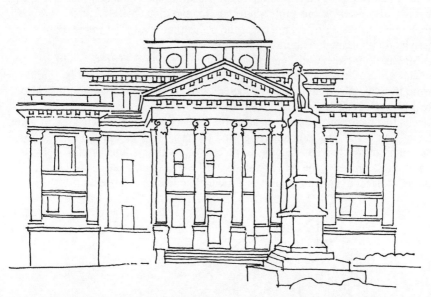

Fig. 4.2: Randolph County Courthouse, Asheboro, North Carolina, 1908-1909

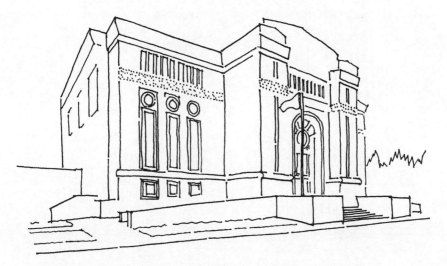

Fig. 4.3: Warren B. Rudman U.S. Courthouse, Concord, New Hampshire

Without the assistance of symbolism and clearly established hierarchy and territory, other contemporary examples of courthouse design rely on the use of proxy elements and electronic surveillance to increase security.

The Ronald Reagan Federal Building and Courthouse, Santa Ana, California[24] is an interesting example (fig. 4.4). This building's symmetry is more legible from a distance or from across the street. Locating the entrance to the site at the corner, and entering the projecting entrance pavilion laterally in the site plan mute the expression of symmetry at the pedestrian level. The impression of entering an important civic building is deflected.

Massive concrete walls on the sides of the building express a visual base, which are a functional as well as a visual deterrent that protects the building from truck bombs. A reinforced concrete wall signifies fortification. It is also a real barrier to penetration from vehicles.

The most surprising design detail at the Reagan Courthouse is the use of palm trees. The palms are judiciously located to serve as proxy elements. They are "unseen" traffic barriers helping to defend the building from a truck-delivered bombing. Ironically, the most natural of all the elements present—the tree—is the most deceptive, being placed as a protective defensive device.

Fig. 4.4: Ronald Reagan Federal Building and Courthouse, Santa Ana, California

The La Crosse County Courthouse[25] continues the functionalist ethic of twentieth century modernism (fig. 4.5). This contemporary Wisconsin courthouse is almost devoid of traditional symbolism or hierarchy associated with the courthouse building type. The building is organized with the simple massing of glass, brick, and block panel areas. A stepped-back central glass volume over a forward glass pavilion houses the inconspicuous entrance. Unarticulated doors that are visually organized into the grid lines of the building afford lateral access. The recognition of entrance into a civic realm is nonexistent. The identity and function of this building as a courthouse is not known to the passerby. The ambiguous presence of the building on the street and in the community cannot be understood—it does not contribute to a legible public environment.

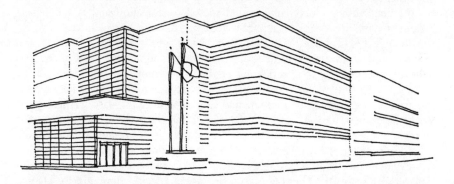

Fig. 4.5: La Crosse County Courthouse, La Crosse, Wisconsin

Closing a Nation's Capital and the Open Space of Democracy

The last several years in Washington, D.C. have witnessed adhoc environmental adaptations to security needs. In 1995, after the Oklahoma bombing of the Alfred P. Murrah Federal Office Building, Pennsylvania Avenue in front of the White House was closed to vehicular access. The closure was executed with the ubiquitous "temporary" concrete traffic dividers known as Jersey barriers, in honor of the New Jersey Turnpike. The streets approaching the Capitol have also been barricaded with Jersey barriers, as well as with oversized reinforced concrete "planters."[26] In 1998 the Washington Monument was surrounded with a double ring of Jersey barriers, following the bombings of the American embassies in Africa. Clearly the response to security threats is taking a toll on the public open spaces of the nation's capital city.

The Supreme Court of the United States is a monumental version of traditional courthouse design. Behind its pristine iconography of a classic temple front and monumental stairs, the entrance is retrofitted with an off-the-shelf metal-detector security gate. The gate stands alone just inside the entrance and is flanked by cloth ropes and security guards. In contrast to the many architectural messages of this building that are conveyed through its symbolism, the retrofit does not add to our psychological sense of security—it is experienced only as a technical barrier.

These "temporary" methods are highly visible manifestations of security issues. The very strangeness of their temporary ad hoc quality exaggerates their visibility. However the meaning and purpose of these adaptations is understood by the public. In this way many of the temporary solutions are very democratic; their function is clear and they are part of legible public environments.

The heart of Washington's public open space is the Mall. The Mall is the organizing spatial center of civic Washington, and it is the site of the nation's most valued memorials. The experience of this place is central to our individual self-identification as citizens of the world's largest democracy. The Mall is a legible environment with a clearly understood spatial organization and is a cohesive system of symbolic ideas. It is a public statement of collective identity.[27]

Although it is organized as a monumental axis on a grand scale, the Mall remains open and accessible in its spatial character. The interior heart of the axis is devoted to green lawns, reflecting pools and monuments. The accessibility and openness of the Mall distinguishes it from a totalitarian or imperialist political space. For example, the monumental axis at New Delhi was a reification of British imperialist power,[28] whereas the Mall has remained symbolic of a democracy. Other examples of authoritarian space can be found in Mussolini's extension of the axis to St. Peter's in Rome, and in Moscow's 1935 plan.[29]

A closing of the Mall—by either a physical change to its borders or by the installation of security technology, seen or unseen—would dramatically change the symbolic meaning of the space.

Public access to the architectural space of the U.S. government is a long tradition, and certainly predates the existence of effective mass media. The most outstanding example of an open, publicly accessible civic architectural space is the Capitol Building of the United States. Only a handful of the world's national legislatures are physically accessible to the public with the ease that a citizen may gain entrance to the interior chambers of the Senate and the House of Representatives. After the October 1999 massacre at Armenia's national legislature, we can assume that one more legislative chamber will be permanently closed to citizen access. [30]

The architecture of the U.S. Capitol uses symbolism and hierarchy to establish social controls on the users of its spaces. However in the recent past it has been necessary to add a retrofitted layer of security. Similar to the use of ad hoc elements at the White House and at the Washington Monument, additional security needs at the Capitol are being met by highly visible, concrete Jersey road barriers, monumental planters that are poorly camouflaged as vehicle barriers, metal detectors, and surveillance cameras. Yet despite the increased surveillance at all building entrances, on July 24, 1998 a man with a .38-caliber revolver entered the Capitol. Within minutes he killed two police officers and wounded a tourist.[31]

This incident revived debate over an elaborate plan for an underground visitor's entrance to the Capitol that had been shelved because of its extraordinary expense. The plan includes several thousand square feet of orientation spaces and exhibition galleries. The facility would be primarily underground, and the visitor would progress into the Capitol building after experiencing many filtering layers of orientation and exhibition. The complexity of the scheme camouflages its primary objective of providing security screening. The impact of the proposal on the authenticity of the Capitol experience is analogous to similar issues raised about the proposed World War II memorial on the Washington Mall site.[32] By adding layers of orientation space and educational environments, the experience of the authentic historic space becomes a manipulated presentation. It could be suggested that the authentic environment is commodified, or transformed into a packaged experience, not unlike the experience of recreational shopping environments, or even like Walt Disney World. In this way the psychological experience of a space can become similar to the consumption of a product.

Immediately following the violent incident described above, there seemed to be a consensus that the Capitol must remain open. According to an editorial in the *New York Times*, "Despite the security searches at every door, the Capitol has an air of openness and accessibility that members of Congress rightfully treasure. It is impossible to walk past the White House's tall fences, guard posts, and traffic barriers without being reminded that ours is a society that has learned to worry constantly about the President's safety. But even though the Capitol has seen sporadic violence, its crowded corridors, meandering tourists, and open lawns speak of a government of the people. That is a symbol in itself, and one that should not given up lightly."[33]

The notion of individual accessibility to the halls of a democratic government is part of the nation's self image. However, access to the architecture and landscapes of government is being altered by security needs. The new visitors center will add layers of social control, both seen and unseen, to the experience of an authentic core architectural site of national identity. A change of cultural significance is occurring as security methods shift to the invisible means of electronic surveillance. Security in the built environment exists as seen, as unseen, and as the disingenuous. The Capitol area is engaged in a slow transition from the seen to the unseen, and may be converging with the disingenuous and the deceptive. The social consequences of this transformation remain unknown.

A democratic society requires environmental legibility. Legibility means that users of a space understand the space, and are not deceived by the space. Democratic space is self-revealing. Democratic space offers freedom of movement— or at least freedom of choice. The reality of contemporary security needs means that some spaces must be closed, and some spaces require relative degrees of closure and control. If the mechanisms of control are self-evident, at least choice of participation in security screening exists.

These two qualities, environmental legibility and freedom of movement, are not inexorably tied to specific spatial configurations. Consider the example of a monumental civic place. Can political context of a civic space be defined by the particulars of a design? Historically we may associate the interlocking axial layouts of the Roman forums with an idea of Roman Imperial space. Since June 1989, the broad reaches of Tianamen Square are historically associated with crushing totalitarian control. We may associate the infinite vistas of Versailles with monarchic space and Lutyen's urban design at New Delhi with imperialist space. Commentary concerning the proposed World War II memorial on Washington's Mall decried the design based on the association of stark neoclassical forms with the Hitler's architect, Albert Speer.[34] As cultural manifestations, architecture and environmental spaces are in a constant state of evolution. Associative links between specific designs and political meanings are subject to change.

Regardless of form, the freedom of movement is a valid characteristic of democratic space. In the context of suburban development, it is difficult to argue that the grid is more democratic than loop roads simply because it offers multiple choices of routes. The grid may symbolize freedom of path choice, but the realities of traffic movement suggest that cul-de-sac and loop road layouts offer more actual freedom and ease of travel through a hierarchy of choice and movement patterns.

Democratic space is free from deceptive social controls. Democratic space allows for freedom of movement without invisible and manipulative social controls.[35] Contrast this idea with the example of Walt Disney World. Within the spaces of Walt Disney World, the environment is designed to generally remove path choices but without the appearance of control. The environment is designed to induce the sensation of easy, natural choice of movement. The park visitor is thus cushioned from "stressful choices." But as participants of this type of consumer space, we have chosen to submit to this type of social control or manipulation. When we enter Walt Disney World, we have made a choice to inhabit that landscape—and we surrender to it. We are also not surprised to find security guards masquerading as costumed Disney characters or concealed in tourist garb.[36] Should there be a qualitative difference between the spatial controls of Walt Disney World and our public civic spaces like the Capitol or the Mall?

A more recently established characteristic of public space in a democracy is that it be "universal space." In other words, this is the mandate of the Americans With Disabilities Act—that all space is universally accessible. A similar code has been adopted in Europe as an admissions requirement to the European Union.

While specific forms evolve and change, it can be extrapolated that democratic space requires environmental legibility, freedom of movement, universal access, and freedom from deceptive social controls.

Technology and Invisible Security

Technology has changed the way the built environment can respond to security needs. Recent years have seen a rapid increase in the use of electronic surveillance and unseen control devices. In many environments it has become the cultural norm to be viewed by surveillance cameras. Typical of these environments are 24-hour convenience stores, banks, ATMs, and parking garages. The use of cameras may or may not be announced with signage.

A key characteristic of the new technologies is the component of invisibility. Electronic surveillance is a powerful but invisible element of the built environment. An environment can appear to be unsecured, open, and inviting when in reality it is highly protected and controlled. In this way the use of invisible security systems begins to create an architecture of deception—an environment where things are not simply as they appear to be.

A distinctive example of the invisibility of electronic security control can be found at the East Wing of the National Gallery of Art, which houses a grand public atrium space experienced by millions of people a year.

The public experiences an open inviting space, with one or two security guards near the entrance. In reality the visitor is under physical and electronic surveillance at all times. Unknown to these visitors, "There are tiny openings in the sides of the escalators which are infrared photocells; if someone should attempt to travel from one level to another during off hours, an alarm is tripped which automatically engages a TV camera that switches to that location."[37] Other electronic controls are "concealed motion detectors in two consecutive door headers, so the alarm system can then determine in which direction the intruder is moving."[38]

Security Abroad: The Embassy

As a building type, the embassy is especially fraught with symbolism. As representative of an open democracy and an outreaching contact point on foreign turf, an embassy needs to be symbolically open and inviting. It must also convey messages of status, power, and hierarchy. Simultaneously it is more vulnerable to attack than domestic civic structures.

The modern architecture of many post-war embassies was open in design, with office blocks raised on exposed columns or *pilotis*, expansive areas of glass walls, flow-through courtyards, and open landscapes. An example is the U.S. embassy in Stockholm (1951-1954) designed by Ralph Rapson and John van der Meulen. Although the architects conceptually segregated the private functions of the embassy from the public functions, in reality a spatially open stair and unsecured lobby elevators blurred the division of territory. Under the guidance of the Architectural Advisory Committee and Pietro Belluschi, embassy design sought to be both an expression of American architecture and reflective of the regional context. The U.S. embassy in Accra, Ghana by Harry Weese (1956-1959) described by Jane Loeffler as "a glass box raised on stilts and wrapped in wooden shutters," is open, accessible, and features design details that attempted to make the regional connection. Other examples are the U.S. embassy in Athens (Walter Gropius, The Architects Collaborative, 1956-1959), and the U.S. consulate in Japan (G. T. Rockrise with Clark & Beuttler, 1958-1960). The modern architecture of these designs symbolized the openness of public diplomacy.[39]

In response to the burgeoning security issues in the 1980s, a special committee lead by retired Admiral Bobby R. Inman, former Deputy Director of Central Intelligence, developed design standards to improve security at all embassies. These standards—known as the Inman standards of 1985—would have increased the fortified appearance of most embassies by requiring remote locations, walled compounds, eliminating windows, and creating one-hundred-foot deep security perimeters. These standards were derisively referred to by some state department staff members as "Inman architecture."[40]

The U.S. embassy in Oman is outside the city of Muscat, Oman, and was designed and built between 1985 and 1989 by Polshek and Partners (fig. 4.6). Early in the design process the architects understood that the sultan of Oman expected that the building would reflect Islamic architectural traditions. The architects were unwilling to simply borrow standard elements of Islamic architecture but were inspired to incorporate the concepts of the traditional regional architecture into an innovative design.

The site plan includes CPTED principles as well as the Inman embassy design standards. A security perimeter is established with an eight-foot-high wall. A continuous buffer zone is "designed to resist breach by vehicles, as well as defeat by climbing, prying, hammering, and sawing."[41] Visitors and staff park outside the walled perimeter. On the roof are security penthouses and sites for surveillance. The floor plan reflects Islamic culture by being organized on a grid, which with four columns in each cell is derivative from mosque design. The inclusion of an interior atrium may be interpreted as a referent to the traditional courtyard dwelling.

Security is enhanced by layers of access and by careful zoning of public to private with "hard line" separations between the zones. Security needs required a massive wall for the exterior. The architect detailed the wall by articulating the structural bays. Segmental arches would have traditionally spanned the square opening, but conventionally supported segmental arches would have been out of place on reinforced concrete bays.[42] Instead tie beams were used to resist the lateral thrust of the arch. These architectural details permitted an expression of open corners and reveals, which articulated the structural bays. The use of deep jambs revealed the thickness of the blast-resistant walls, which can be interpreted as an honest and visible expression of security needs. In this way the embassy design at Oman is legible and comprehensible.

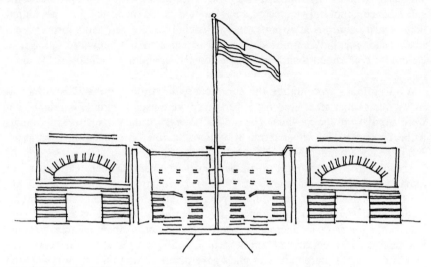

Fig. 4.6: U.S. Embassy, Muscat, Oman, 1985-1989

The U.S. Chancery and Embassy Residence in Amman, Jordan, was designed by Perry Dean Rogers, Architects. It represents an abandonment of the downtown embassy in favor of an absolute compound at a remote location. "The compound is larger than six football fields and is surrounded by a nine-foot wall; it is hardly inconspicuous and is not intended to be."[43] The design follows Inman's version of CPTED guidelines. The embassy is at a remote location, has high perimeter walls at a distance from roads or other buildings, and has as few windows as possible. The architects relied on interior courtyards to gain natural light and spatial relief.

The embassy in Amman does not use hierarchy or monumentality to express its civic importance. The exterior is a simple masonry wall with raised pilasters. A flat cornice is suggested with a continuous row of contrasting masonry squares and contrasting bands over the ubiquitous square windows of the postmodern period.

As an architectural statement, the Amman embassy is far removed from the days when American architecture was considered a vehicle of cultural leadership. James S. Russell, writing for the *Architectural Record*, considered the building to be very contextual but still "defensive, inward-looking," and that "its message about America is ambivalent."[44]

Airports and High Technology Security

The airport is an environment where high technology security and electronic surveillance is not only expected, but also considered the status quo. We anticipate security controls at airports, and are socially concerned about airport security breakdowns.[45] When unseen security is expected and known to the user, it cannot be considered disingenuous but simply as another element of the environment.

As a building type, unlike the courthouse, the airport terminal is comparatively free of historical precedent. Terminals were usually simple buildings that were auxiliary to the hangars. The most renowned of the early airport terminals is the Trans World Airlines terminal by Eero Saarinen completed in 1962 at the John F. Kennedy International Airport.

The design is an example of modern expressionism. Modern expressionism moves somewhat beyond the strict tenets of the functionalist ethic. Not only are the functional needs of the building program emphatically met, but the architecture also attempts to communicate the meaning or spirit of its raison d'etre. Saarinen's reinforced concrete structure created large open volumes for the business of passenger arrival and departure, and was a metaphorical expression of a bird in flight. Large areas of glass gave direct views to the runways. At the time of its design, security issues were almost nonexistent.

The United Airlines Terminal 1 Complex, at O'Hare International Airport in Chicago, designed by Helmut Jahn, was completed in 1988. The expression of structure and the prolific use of clear glazing are conceptually related to Saarinen's work. Security is by controlled access, metal detectors, and electronic surveillance. As is typical of contemporary airports, the fundamental element of security is in the design of the circulation paths. The flow of people through the building is highly directed and controlled, and uses both seen and unseen methods of electronic surveillance.

Security at Home: Residential Trends

Transformations in residential security are happening at different scales. The proliferation of gated communities is a response to security issues at the scale of community planning. A second area is in the proliferation of technological products for home security, which is happening at the scale of a computer chip connected to a laser beam.

Gated communities have obvious implications for a democratic society. The security intervention is highly seen, but the message is contrary to the ideals of an open society. Functionally the effect of the gated community is analogous to the fortified building: in terms of security, conditions may be improved on the interior but are worsened beyond the walls or gates. The resources of the community are removed from the realm of their greater context. A parallel development is the expansion of New Urbanism planning ideas. New Urbanist communities have internal physical design parameters that function like most CPTED elements—porches that open to the street, smaller lot sizes, reduced dimensions of streets to calm traffic and increase community interaction and social surveillance.

These communities have great appeal for being "safe" places to live. However teenagers at the new Disney community of Celebration feel placeless. Among the teens at Celebration was a persistent belief in the existence of surveillance cameras—whether true or not, the rumor reveals a perception of the environmental character.[46]

The growing market of home security products highlights the full extent of the American interest in security. The high-end residential market now incorporates fully integrated high technology security systems as part of standard design procedure.

Author Mike Davis writes "Meanwhile the rich are yearning for high-tech castles. . . . An overriding but discreet goal of the current 'mansionizing' mania on the Westside of Los Angeles—for instance, tearing down $3 million houses to build $30 million mansions is the search for 'absolute security.' Residential architects are borrowing design secrets from overseas embassies and military command posts. One of the features most in demand is the 'terrorist-proof security room' concealed in the house plan and accessed by sliding panels and secret doors. Merv Griffith and his fellow mansionizers are hardening their palaces like missile silos."[47]

Residential security, like security in all other building types, functions at both the seen and the unseen levels.

In some specialized environments, we are accepting of unseen security. In certain environments we expect or even demand security, seen or unseen. In airports, as travelers, we would be alarmed to find out that the security systems were not functioning. At the airport we might accept any level of security because it is perceived as a life or death factor for the collective community of air travelers and air travel professionals.

In other environments, the acceptance of unseen security is part of the consumer "package." Walt Disney World is a considered a safe environment, with security controls that are almost entirely unseen—like the security guards disguised as Disney characters or camouflaged as ordinary tourists. However unsettling this deliberate deception may be, it is not happening in a truly public space but within the domain of a gated commercial environment. At Walt Disney World, unseen security elements are not entirely deceptive in that the unseen security is part of the established social contract of the entertainment park, a part of a consumer transaction with a highly specific environment.

Both of these situations, the airport and the amusement park, are environments that we enter by conscious choice. Presumably it would be a different situation if security guards populated our high schools disguised as students, and if all public spaces were subject to surveillance cameras.

"Good Design" and the Architectural Profession

Both proponents of CPTED and of established architectural practice[48] recommend that security requirements can be mainly satisfied through "good design." The CPTED movement in synchronicity with the architectural profession recognizes that design in the broadest sense, from the conceptual site plan to the details of hardware, can provide enhanced security to the built environment.

The establishment standards of the architectural profession consider not simply design, but "good design" as an effective deterrent to security problems. What do architects understand as "good design?" Despite the evolutionary movements of the architectural profession throughout the twentieth century, certain basic values have remained constant to the profession. The conceptual integrity of an architectural style—including the integrity of the one style that was conceived to supersede the *idea* of style, i.e., modernism—has been a consistent value. This means that Gothic Revival, Neoclassical, Modern, and Deconstructivism are recognizable styles, and that each operates within a paradigm. Each manner of architectural style has an internal integrity of expression. Even a style like Deconstructivism, which is intended to be dynamically unsettled, and devoid of traditional spatial cues, has an internal integrity to its own expression, and to its theoretical guidelines.

This stylistic integrity is achieved by integrating all design decisions, from site orientation to door hardware, into the same mode of architectural expression. Understanding this value of the architectural profession suggests that proponents of "good design" would advocate design integration for security solutions. For the architectural profession, the full integration of security design solutions or features into the design will have a preferred aesthetic impact. The profession is concerned with making "ugly" security elements more aesthetic and even "beautiful." However, with this integration comes the disappearance or relative invisibility of the security function.

Within the established culture of the architectural profession, it is understood that an integrated element is an "unseen" element in that it does not stand out as a foreign object in the integrated landscape of a "good" design. Elements are "unseen" in that they are holistically meshed into the fabric of the design, unless the designer has deliberately chosen to accent that element. As security issues become increasingly pervasive as design criteria for buildings, security design will become a conceptually integral element of normative design process. In this way, proponents of good design—integrated design—are also proponents of an unseen, invisible, security layer within our architectural and landscape environments.

This sublimation of security into the standard design process means that architects will be grappling less with the visibility—and legibility—issue of security design. As explored here, the security dimension of the environment can be seen, unseen, or disingenuous.

An ethical dilemma exists with the control of visibility. The profession of architecture should be concerned with the clarity of security measures, and consider the ethical implications of concealment. How will a democratic society function in landscapes that may have increasingly invisible levels of social control? This ethical question resides in the power of the "unseen" and the process of deception. Many related questions arise. For example, when does the disingenuous become the deliberately deceptive? Who will take responsibility for the choice of visibility, for environments that can be understood and interpreted by citizens of a free society? Will it be the architect, the client, or legislative bodies of the people?

Democratic Space: A Place for Deception?

The need for greater security, especially in public buildings like schools, federal office buildings, and embassies is without precedent in an era of terrorism. The problem is real, and this social requirement for increased security must be satisfied. Yet the landscape of a democratic society calls for a legible and comprehensible environment. What is a democratic society willing to give up for increased security? A democratic society requires freedom from fear—but also freedom of movement, and possibly freedom from surveillance. Freedom from fear cannot come at the cost of a collective paranoia brought on by a deceptive environment, or an environment of surveillance. A free society requires a safe but free environment—to create another environment is to undermine democratic rule.

A review of recent trends in the design of secure environments reveals many contradictory aspects of designing for security, a subject with an implicit ethical moment. The architectural aesthetics of integrated security design—and normative architectural practice—may inadvertently lead to the architecture of deception. The architectural profession has an ethical responsibility to be aware of the social implications of the design process, and a greater obligation to exercise a choice in the creation of the built environment. Architects must carefully weigh the social costs of ambiguity and concealment, and be wary of the political cost of deceptive environments.

[*Author's note:* This investigation of architecture and security began in 1998, resulting in the final edit of this chapter in July 2001.]

The American worldview of security changed on September 11, 2001. New understandings and perceptions of security are having a colossal ripple effect on the built environment. The technological solution—represented by cameras and biological-recognition systems—are exponentially proliferating in the environment, along with Jersey barriers, sandbags, street closures, and every other adaptive element of security. The fundamental questions raised by this chapter have not changed. Critical ethical, social, and political questions about how we will integrate design for security into our civic places, our architecture, and our landscapes still cry out to be answered.

As our society zealously embraces new layers of security systems, it would be helpful to reflect on why existing security components failed at airport access systems on September 11, 2001. And why established governmental agencies, and existing laws and regulations failed to prevent the infiltration of hijackers into the cockpits of four commercial airliners. Newspaper reports document the many occasions when the hijackers violated established laws, and revealed themselves in small ways. Before rushing to add more technology, the failed systems should be understood at every level. Then we can look to the future. Will architects be designing a progressive architecture supportive of healthy urbanism? Will architects be designing livable communities supportive of an open society in this time of fear? Will new public places address the civic needs of a democratic nation? If left unanswered, implicit and fundamental questions of designing for security may have a surprising and irrevocable effect on the landscape of our free society.

Notes

1. David von Drehle, "Two Killers, Model School Was Cruel," *Washington Post*, 25 April 1999, 1(A).

2. Review and Outlook (editorial) "Outrage in Africa," *Wall Street Journal*, 10 August 1998, 14(A).

3. Timothy D. Crowe, *Crime Prevention through Environmental Design* (Stoneham, Mass.: Butterworth-Heinemann and the National Crime Prevention Institute, 1991).

4. Crowe, *Crime Prevention*, 162.

5. Leonardo Benevolo, *History of Modern Architecture*, vol. 1 (Cambridge, Mass.: MIT Press, 1977) 61-95.

6. Franklin Deleano Roosevelt, "The Four Freedoms," State of the Union Address, 6 January 1941.

7. Stuart L. Knoop, "Securing the U.S. Abroad," *Architectural Record* (August 1992): 36.

8. Thomas L. Friedman, "A Manifesto for the Fast World: From the Supercharged Financial Markets to Osama bin Laden, The Emerging Global Order Demands an Enforcer. That's America's New Burden," *New York Times Magazine*, 28 March 1999, 40-44, 61, 70-71, 84, 96-97.

9. U.S. Department of State Bureau of Diplomatic Security, Office of Intelligence and Threat Analysis, *Significant Incidents of Political Violence against Americans*, U.S. Department of State Publications, 1992, no. 9953, 8.

10. Gregory Littleton, "Blast-Free Design," *Architecture* 79, no. 5 (May 1990): 84-85.

11. Camilo Jose Vergara, *The New American Ghetto* (New Brunswick, N.J.: Rutgers University Press, 1995), 121.

12. Vergara, *The New American Ghetto*, 122.

13. Jane Jacobs, *The Death and Life of Great American Cities* (New York: Random House, 1961).

14. For example, see Geoffrey Broadbent, "A Plain Man's Guide to the Theory of Signs in Architecture," 122-40 in *Theorizing a New Agenda for Architecture: An Anthol-*

ogy of Architectural Theory, 1965-1995, ed. Kate Nesbitt (New York: Princeton Architectural Press, 1996).

15. For example, see Jon Lang, Creating Architectural Theory, The Role of the Behavioral Sciences in Environmental Design (New York: Van Nostrand Reinhold, 1987).

16. In the aftermath of the Columbine High School massacre, security camera footage of the shootings was released—and in light of the investigations it may have been a motivational force for the perpetrators to know that their actions were being recorded on video film. See Nancy Gibbs and Timothy Roche, "The Columbine Tapes," Time, 20 December 1999, vol. 154, no. 25, 40-51.

17. Lang, Architectural Theory, 148.

18. Oscar Newman, Defensible Space, Crime Prevention through Urban Design (New York: Macmillan, 1972), 63.

19. Lang, Architectural Theory, 213.

20. Geoffrey Broadbent, "A Plain Man's Guide to the Theory of Signs in Architecture," in Theorizing a New Agenda for Architecture, An Anthology of Architectural Theory 1965-1995, ed. Kate Nesbitt (New York: Princeton Architectural Press, 1996), 133.

21. Catherine W. Bishir, North Carolina Architect (Chapel Hill: University of North Carolina Press for The Historic Preservation Foundation of North Carolina, 1990).

22. Virginia Kent Dorris, "Warren B. Rudman United States Courthouse, Concord, New Hampshire: With a Symmetrical Layout and a Limited Palette of Materials, a New Courthouse Recalls Traditional Civic Structures," Architectural Record 187, no. 3 (March 1999): 122-25.

23. The Americans With Disabilities Act 1990, Public Law 101-336.

24. Dana Holbrook, "Ronald Reagan Federal Building and Courthouse, Santa Ana, California: Designed to Accommodate the County's Needs for the Next 25 Years, This Courthouse Incorporates Technology and Tradition," Architectural Record 187, no. 3 (March 1999): 118-21.

25. John E. Czarnecki, "La Crosse County Courthouse, La Crosse, Wisconsin; A New County Courthouse Consolidates Law Enforcement, Incarceration, and Court Processes Within One Building," Architectural Record 187, no. 3 (March 1999): 126-28.

26. These planters cross the line between the seen and the unseen. Their freakish size belies their existence as floral ornament; perhaps they are to the world of security what floral air spray is to the world of odor control.

27. Lawrence J. Vale, Architecture, Power and National Identity (New Haven, Conn.: Yale University Press, 1992).

28. Hosagrahar Jyoti, "City as Durbar: Theater and Power in Imperial Delhi," 83-105 in Forms of Dominance, On the Architecture and Urbanism of the Colonial Enterprise, ed. Nezar AlSayyad (Aldershot, Eng.: Avebury, 1992).

29. Nezar AlSayyad, "Urbanism and the Dominance Equation, Reflections on Colonialism and National Identity," Forms of Dominance, 1-26.

30. David Hoffman, "Lax Security Is Blamed for Armenia Attack; Officials' Dismissals Demanded," Washington Post, 29 October 1999, 23(A).

31. Francis X. Clines, "Capitol Hill Slayings: The Overview; Gunman Invades Capitol, Killing Two Guards," New York Times, 25 July 1998, 1(A). David Stout, "Capitol Hill Slayings: The Security; Despite History of Violence, Capitol Is a Very Public Place," New York Times, 25 July 1998, 9(A). Editorial, "Keeping the Capitol Safe," 28 July 1998, 14(A).

32. Ruth Connell, "Modern Political Space, Consumption and Authenticity in the Evolution of National Space, Washington, D.C.," in Building as a Political Act, 1997

ACSA International Conference, Berlin, ed. Randall Ott (New York: ACSA Press, 1998) 307-14.

33. Editorial, "Keeping the Capitol Safe," *New York Times,* 28 July 1998, 14(A).

34. Deborah K. Dietsch, "Capital Offense, An Overblown War Memorial Will Destroy a Sacred Site on the National Mall," *Architecture* (March 1997), 63.

35. This has been symbolized in the American culture by the "open range," and the iconography of the wilderness.

36. "One of the most palpable things at WDW is the lack of fear—not just fear of moving vehicles (except, perhaps, at Space Mountain) but fear of other people. . . . People are rarely aware of the security forces around them—some wearing cast garb, others dressed as tourists." Stephen M. Fjellman, *Vinyl Leaves, Walt Disney World and America* (Boulder, Colo.: Westview, 1992), 200.

37. Ira Wolfman, "Insecurities about Security: Face to Face with the Building-Protection Crisis," *Architectural Record* (August 1987): 129.

38. Wolfman, "Insecurities," 129.

39. Jane C. Loeffler, *The Architecture of Diplomacy, Building America's Embassies* (New York: Princeton Architectural Press, 1998).

40. Jane C. Loeffler, "Can an Embassy be Open and Secure?," *New York Times,* 14 August 1998, 21(A).

41. Philip Arcidi, "P/A Awards Update: A Two-fold Solution, A Layered Façade Exemplifies Polshek and Partners' Search for Literate Modernism, Enriched by Both History and Technology," *Progressive Architecture* 7 no. 6 (June 1990), 114-16; Thomas Vonier, "Defensive Designs: Building a Secure Embassy, *Progressive Architecture* 7 no. 6 (June 1990), 118-19.

42. Vonier, "Defensive Designs," 118.

43. Loeffler, *The Architecture of Diplomacy,* 250.

44. James S. Russell, "Chancery and Embassy Residence, Amman, Jordan, Perry Dean Rogers, Architects," *Architectural Record* (May 1993), 68.

45. Don Phillips, "Airport Security Found Lacking, DOT Probers Board Jets Unchallenged," *Washington Post,* 2 December 1999 30(A); "Tightening Airport Security," *Washington Post,* 7 December 1999, Editorial.

46. Andrew Ross, *The Celebration Chronicles, Life, Liberty, and the Pursuit of Property Value in Disney's New Town* (New York: Ballantine, 1999), 206.

47. Mike Davis, *City of Quartz, Excavating the Future in Los Angeles* (London: Verso, 1990), 248.

48. "Security Is in Demand from the White House to Our House," *Progressive Architecture,* (March 1986), 118-22; Thomas Vonier, AIA, "Security: The Next Stage," *Progressive Architecture,* (April 1988), 144.

Chapter 5

Getting Nowhere Fast? Intrinsic Worth, Utility, and Sense of Place at the Century's Turn

Francis Conroy

> The spirit, overcome by the weight of quantity,
> has no longer any other criterion than efficiency.
> —Simone Weil[1]

I want to make a distinction between two kinds of settings. The first has a simple name, "homes," although I will be using the term to refer to a considerably broader category of things than is ordinarily the case. The second kind of setting has no simple name, requiring a longer phrase to designate it: "settings-in-which-we-are-interchangeable-parts" will do.

By "homes," I mean settings in which we are known and cared for with specific affection: for example, families, households, communities, land we know well, buildings that have been created and maintained with specific care. The "we" here refers first to people, but it could also include "we" animals and plants, even "we" creeks, woods, fields, churches, schoolhouses, local stores: all the possible interdependent ingredients of a community. Creeks with names, the neighbor's old dog, the south side of a certain hill with its burst of wild flowers, family members, the freshman seminar room in College Hall: all of these are elements of the settings I will call "homes." I am choosing the term "homes" over other possible terms precisely because of its architectural possibilities. It is a good example of a holistic term, bringing the physical in relation to the social and philosophical.

By "settings-in-which-we-are-interchangeable-parts" I mean the other kind of setting that rapidly began to proliferate in the late twentieth century: "nowhere" is the term James Howard Kuntsler uses to refer to this setting. Malls, highways, and feeder roads, with their industrial-style trees and managed landscapes, head the list. Chain stores—the Wal-Marts, Home Depots, Staples, Riteaids, McDonalds, and Denny's that have replaced local stores everywhere—are prominent among "nowheres." Add many schools and colleges today (wherever we find ourselves filling in those ubiquitous ovals), corporate healthcare systems, and computerized telephone systems (where we sit and wait and push buttons). Include banks with no one to talk to, virtually all glass and steel buildings, airlines, and cruise ships. Throw in most of the world of corporate advertising, plus corporate music, corporate sports; also the settings for industrial farming, industrial poultry production, industrial livestock, industrial fish (most of the food industry, taking over for the family farm and herdsman's pastures). Finally, add many settings where one receives "generic" care rather than care with specific affection: corporate hospitals, insurance companies, chain day care centers, and the like. Clearly, the list goes on and on. In these settings we are not known specifically, or cared for specifically. The "we," again, refers to people, but also to animals, plants, land, and artifacts, which are parts of these settings. If we are, in a way, cared for, it is only in a nonspecific generic way: the way in which Prudential cares about us, AT&T cares about bringing families together, Archer Daniels Midland cares about the earth, the Hospital of the University of Pennsylvania cares about our health, or our political candidates care about "the American people." In these settings, we are "anyone," and inhabitants of "anywhere." We are known by numbers, and our lives are measurable by numbers. We are handled adeptly by new technologies, and we become like cogs in these technologies. There are benefits—so we are told. We can get more of many things: more and more, "no limits," of . . . something. What?—Of the products and services of anywhere/nowhere: the mass-produced material products, the packaged entertainment, the packaged education, the glamorous look; more speed, more "information," quicker communication, greater "efficiency." All these things rolled together constitute "Value" itself, a ubiquitous, unquestioned kind of multipurpose equivalent of all worth—except the kind of worth in the previous paragraph, the worth of homes, families, communities: intrinsic worth.

A crisis of contemporary society seems to lie in the relationship between these two worlds, these two kinds of settings. The two are out of balance, disturbingly and increasingly so. If the home settings are continually diminished, it is clear that something deep is lost—something fundamental concerning who we are and what we are to do. We will first examine the underlying philosophical issue, then come back to sociology and geography.

Bearing significantly on the home/interchangeable parts distinction is an older, philosophical distinction between two kinds of ethics. These are usually called "utilitarian" and "deontological." However, we will use the first term "utilitarian," but modify the second term to "intrinsic-worth" ethics to broaden its scope. If we were to look at utilitarian and intrinsic-worth ethics in the two leading societies of the turn-of-century world, the United States and Japan, we would find that the hegemony of utilitarian ethics is rooted in what I will call "instrumental rationality." It is virtually unchallenged in the United States and spreading considerably to Japan and other societies, and it is increasingly dominant in all major institutions, led by the "neoliberal" trend in economics. On the other hand, intrinsic-worth ethics, rooted in what we will call "full rationality" and connected to the "wisdom" traditions of most societies, has been largely relegated to the background, forgotten, or marginalized.

A utilitarian approach looks at the consequences of an action to determine its moral worth. An intrinsic worth approach looks at the action itself. The term "utilitarian" comes from the word "utility" or "usefulness": the action is useful for something, presumably for producing some kind of pleasure, happiness—or "Value." The term "deontological" comes from the Greek *deon,* duty: the action is good-in-itself, it has intrinsic worth, because it fulfills a standard of justice or rightness that is built into things. The exact way in which this may be "built into things" can, I think, be best described as something of a mystery; but it is a respected, even revered mystery. For many traditions over many generations, much thought, attentiveness, and dialogue have dealt with this mystery.

Let us consider "intrinsic-worth" ethics in a variety of forms from Western and Eastern traditions, focusing on the United States and Japan: Kantian, Platonic, and Christian, from the Western side; and Confucian, Zen, and Shinto from the Eastern side.

The crosscultural unanimity that it is intrinsic-worth ethics, not utilitarian, that constitutes the heart of our moral lives is remarkably clear in traditional thought, East and West. "It is right because it is right" is a possible way of expressing the general form of intrinsic-worth ethics. Yet, the particular variations branching out from such a unity are striking in their diversity, ranging from the strict moralism of some types of Christianity to the gentle naturalism of Lao Tzu's Taoism. For example, the catalogue description of the required ethics course at Gettysburg College a century ago read, "The student is conducted through an examination of utilitarianism and other rejected theories to an immutable basis of truth in the nature of God."[2] At the other extreme, the portrayals of a Taoist master in the *Tao Te Ching* convey an unforced, flowing way to inherent goodness: e.g., "Because he has no goal in mind, everything he does succeeds;" or, "Because she has let go of herself, she is perfectly fulfilled."[3]

For our purposes, we are interested in seeing how the Kantian, Platonic, Christian, Zen, Confucian, and Shinto perspectives each provide entrance from a different side into intrinsic worth. To approach this issue, assume for the moment that there are hidden moral truths, intangibles, beneath or deep within our world. Next, consider that there might be different paths, which are suited for different people.

Immanuel Kant has one approach, a moralistic approach characterized by words like "duty" and "obligation." It appeals to some, but may repel others (feminists, most notably among recent critics). His approach is reason-and-will-oriented, as opposed to, feelings-and-consequences-oriented. It gives us rules of universal obligation. The most famous rules, variations of the so-called "categorical imperative," are, roughly translated, "One ought only to act such that the principle of one's action could become a universal law in a world in which one would hope to live," and, "One ought to treat others as having intrinsic value in themselves, not merely as a means to achieve one's ends." Overall, Kant sketches out for us the glowing possibility of a world one might call the "kingdom of ends," a better world, a fully ennobling human world, that, paradoxically one arrives at precisely by not paying attention to consequences. The moral law that leads toward such a world deserves our reverence, Kant points out. We revere and follow the law and as for "consequences"?—We trust things will work out for the best.

Lurking beneath Kant's perspective is a moral metaphysic that there are hidden foundations, eternal, perfect, unchanging truths, built into our world. It is the Platonic perspective that most clearly makes the case for the existence of such hidden moral things. The side of intrinsic worth that Plato illuminates is mystical, dialogical, and metaphysical. In his famous doctrine of Forms, Plato asserts that there are primordial archetypes, like beacons to us, such as Wisdom, Justice, and Beauty. We can draw close to these through strenuous communal thinking (dialogue or dialectic); yet these truths are ultimately beyond words, and we may need a kind of mystical intuition finally to grasp them. These goods are good for their own sake; the good consequences that may flow from them come as a kind of bonus. From the hidden world, therefore, we derive our meaning in this world; the faint glimmerings we see of that deeper world are our real guides to how we are to live our lives, rather than our own calculations as to how to get to certain consequences. And we need to approach the task with a sense of humility, awe, and lifelong learning.

The Christian approach to intrinsic-worth ethics has a similarity in terms of the cultivation of humility, but is more distinctively characterized by the sense of a divine "Other," and by the qualities of "holiness" and "mystery." A repeated theme in various intrinsic-worth ethics is that this mode of thinking is not calculating, does not move in a controlled way toward outcomes, but rather involves a recognition that in an important sense outcomes are out of one's own control. This aspect is most clearly captured in the Christian perspective by such phrases as "Thy will be done," and, "Results are up to God." In this tradition, what we experience when we try to act rightly, not from our own utilitarian standards but from a deeper standard, is too profound to be contained within our everyday worldly language. So, we find other words—Lord, God, Yahweh—to convey our sense of contingency, as well as our openness and humility. In this process, we are seeking what is holy, i.e., what is pure and whole—not that which just appears "good" by some partial reckoning, but that which is good overall, and for which we hunger. This holy dimension of intrinsic-worth ethics is, in Catholicism, embodied in the ritual of the Eucharist. The ritual is performed not for any utilitarian reasons, but because while we are partaking of the holy communion we are for a short time doing something pure, good, and true. It is self-justifying and self-referential. For a moment we are not separate from God. Other actions in life that can move even a little in the direction of this self-contained goodness of the Eucharist become thereby more sacred, more in tune with the wholeness of the original Creation. And of course all of this is a mystery, for we cannot fully understand it with our minds, but need to embrace it with our whole beings. From the Catholic perspective, we only become what we truly are when we partake of the communion. Finally, we are fully present.

It is this notion of presence that can provide the bridge that takes us from West to East. The Buddhist tradition of intrinsic worth, extending from Siddhartha Gautama in India to Zen in Japan, teaches presence, or full awareness, of the intrinsic nature, or "suchness," of each moment. Buddhism detects that we tend to keep passing over the here and now, sacrificing it, instrumentalizing it in order to get to something else. When we do so, we cut off life, don't really live it. What we need to do is come back from our expectations, calculations, and ambitions, and recover the only real ground we have: our presence. "When you eat, eat." "When you walk, walk." When you attend to another person, or an animal, or a plant, be fully there, attentive . . . present. Never do things merely for the sake of something else; try to fill more and more of your life doing things for their own sake; do nothing that isn't self-referentially good. Such are the advisements of Buddhism that are most emphasized in its distinctively Japanese form, Zen. This is the Zen side of intrinsic-worth ethics.

The Confucian approach to intrinsic worth calls attention to another side of "presence": being fully what one is socially. The Confucian side is characterized by words like "community," "neighborhood," "family," and "tradition." From the Confucian perspective, we are reminded that our being is social. Therefore in seeking what is good or right we need to consider what we are as sons and daughters, sisters and brothers, parents and teachers—as grandchildren who will one day be grandparents. We are called to act in a way that bears witness to our social being through re-creating and renewing it. An action is good when it represents who we are, and not primarily because of its consequences. Our guidance comes from those who have gone before us and left their examples: holistic patterns of trying to find the balance, hit the mark, walk the path, or Tao. Scholars/teachers provide special leadership in trying to study and transmit this. Students are called to learn in a holistic way, not simply extracting from a lesson what seems of utilitarian value to them. Confucius reminds us in *Analects* 2, "A scholar is not a thing of use," i.e., liberal arts learning is a whole, involving investigation of roots as well as branches, including all premises or foundations— it is not just "information" to be cut into pieces according to one's own limited objectives.

Finally we get to Shinto. For the Japanese, Shinto, being Japan's indigenous world view, provided historically the perspective from within which "sides" of Buddhism and Confucianism were selectively appropriated. The Japanese took mainly the "living" side of Buddhism, for example, stressing presence more than nonattachment; and the "neighborhood" side of Confucianism, emphasizing particularity more than universality. As for Shinto itself, its "take" on intrinsic-worth is perhaps best characterized by the words of "vitality" and "place." If we remember how Kant's approach put emphasis on the moralistic, Shinto's approach is almost the opposite. In Western terms it is more akin to Nietzsche's critique of Kant's (possibly deadening) morality on behalf of life. In Shinto, one honors vitality: in nature, in aesthetics, in the generations. From baths to Tori gates, from forest glens to the perpetually new Ise Shrine, Shinto cultivates an appreciation of specific places: local rocks and trees, wind and rain, mountains and forests, as well as the generations of people passing on local nature and culture. Gods (*kami*) are present everywhere; they are specific to every location. There is a special divinity in this waterfall, in that estuary, in yonder bending pine. Honoring that which passes on life is the first requirement of our actions in Shinto. Utilitarian interests, once again, can only be secondary.

Our purpose in briefly examining intrinsic-worth ethics through these six diverse lenses has been to establish their unity around mainly one point: that at the deepest level utilitarian or instrumental thinking is too impoverished, too shallow and partial, for providing the wisdom we need to live. Our ancestors both East and West send us back repeatedly to "being present where we are" and to "doing right because it is right"—back from being away somewhere in our utilitarian absentmindedness.

Now we may proceed to study the nature of utilitarian ethics, or "instrumental rationality," particularly how it is used today, for this kind of thinking is pervasive, in many areas virtually unchallenged, in the turn-of-century ethos. Few Americans today may use the term "utilitarian" to describe their moral thinking. Yet, a one-sidedly utilitarian ethos has slipped in during the last quarter century to the point where it now prevails unreflectively over a broad range of American life, ranging from the social sciences, to the economy, to education.

Although utilitarianism, as expounded early in the modern era by David Hume and John Stuart Mill, may have attempted to frame utilitarian thinking in the broadest possible way, including not only narrow calculation for economic profit or material pleasure, but also more sensitive pleasures of mind and spirit, nevertheless over the years the problem with utilitarian thinking has been that it seems repeatedly to veer toward narrowing human endeavor to what all-too-humans themselves deem as profitable or pleasurable. There is perhaps no a priori reason why utilitarian thinking could not, theoretically, yield as rich and diverse an ethos as intrinsic-worth thinking, perhaps including even a sensitivity to gods, the divine, the hidden, etc. Yet the fact is that the utilitarian way of directing one's attention toward consequences rather than toward the thing itself tends to create a kind of habit of using one thing as an instrument to get to another, of using one moment for the next. Or, to borrow language from Marx, sacrificing real value for market exchange value—and by that route, one soon discovers that life has been sacrificed to an idol. Utilitarian thinking ends up contributing to the genesis of the ubiquitous "Value," something we previously mentioned and which might be defined as wealth, power, educational success, and sex appeal rolled into one and now standing above and against real human life as its new standard of measurement.

Think of the things everybody talks about today as important. Especially consider education and business: things like "acquiring skills," "setting personal goals," "investing time," "achieving measurable outcomes," "becoming a success," "developing leadership," and "managing resources." Add in typical contemporary buzz words like "growth," "no limits," "enhanced life style," "personal freedom," "diversity," "change," and "the future." Such phrases are tossed around constantly in turn-of-century America. They have even seeped out into Japan and the rest of the world. Note that this is entirely a utilitarian terminology. None of these words refers to a good-in-itself. None refers to intrinsic worth. None provides a full context or content that would make one able to evaluate an activity morally. In fact, in an important sense, all of these are either morally ambiguous—they could actually be good or bad, depending on the context—or morally noxious. The latter is possible because many of them deflect one's attention away exactly from presence, from the right-in-itself, from holism. They counsel the partial, encourage only limited vision, as if to say: "Open your eyes only so far."

The utilitarian revolution has changed what up to a generation ago we had meant by the word "thinking," at least in liberal arts contexts. It has narrowed the meaning from what we might call "full thinking," to "partial thinking." Instrumental reason has replaced full reason. In full reason, one thinks about everything. Reflection upon premises and foundations is always appropriate and in fact is the mark of worthy thought. Reflective thought is inherently interesting, challenging, important. Instrumental thinking is reason used only for some preconceived objective, which itself is excluded from the realm of questioning. Therefore, we get the ironic situation, again and again at the turn of the century, that the most "successful" of our young adults may be making smarter and smarter decisions, yet making the world worse and worse. They may be "growing the economy," but at the same time damaging local communities and the environment. They may be figuring out how to ace SAT tests and enhance their portfolios, yet be incapable of noticing the multilayered richness of a Bach violin concerto, a Platonic dialogue, or a Flannery O'Connor short story. They are "successes" in a world measurable in quantities, a world that is seamlessly compatible with new computer technologies; but being raised on television commercials, SAT-prep courses, polls, and outcome assessments, they have been left more hollow than educated people were a generation ago. Their "success" is measured only within the confines circumscribed by the intersecting spheres of high-tech, corporate market economy, and neoliberal ideology. Outside those confines, according to more perennial measures of what a good human being is, such as exercising the wisdom to harmonize within the natural world or to sustain and transmit families and communities, many "successful" young people seem distressingly impoverished. Some are even aware of it.

The popular rationale as to why most of us turn-of-century people do not talk about overall goals, fundamental questions, or "highest goods" is that such matters should be left "up to the individual," are matters of "personal choice." According to the prevailing ideology, society's leadership should go only so far as to sweep away barriers to anyone getting an equal opportunity to compete. Compete for what?—For market "goods," naturally, including material wealth, real estate, education, power, fame, pleasure. Moreover, the prevailing ideology is committed to keeping away all barriers that could impede those who have already accumulated great quantities of such Value from using their acquisitions freely. The pervasiveness of one-sidedly utilitarian approaches to ethics has contributed to this vacuum, by narrowing thinking from whole to partial, by pointing us toward quantity, and by cutting us off from the richness in our traditions.

Finally, we are ready to return to the sociogeographical distinction with which we began: settings that are "homes" versus settings-in-which-we-are-interchangeable-parts. I want to argue that homes draw us toward intrinsic-worth ethics and the practice of intrinsic-worth ethics is a necessary part of the conditions that make a place a home. Settings in which we are interchangeable parts are, on the other hand, the places where utilitarian ethics thrive. Other, more traditional modes of thinking seem to vanish there—they lose their ability to justify themselves, seem "unscientific," not "measurable."

I have been awakened to the sociology of place most of all by the writings of Wendell Berry, the Kentucky poet, essayist, and farmer who starts from the kind of local and regional sense of place that most of us, even if we are sensitive to the issue, can only tap through memory and imagination. Berry defines community as "the commonwealth and common interests . . . of people living together in a place and wishing to continue to do so;" or, in other words, an "interdependence of local people, local culture, local economy, and local nature." He adds that "community, of course, is an idea that can extend itself beyond the local, but it does so only metaphorically," and that "the idea of a national or a global community is meaningless apart from the realization of local communities."[4]

It is with such a definition of community that we can begin to reclaim a more holistic understanding of economy. Berry writes primarily about the economy of the household, community, and region. He observes that "the destruction of community begins when its economy is made . . . subject to a larger external economy."[5] Berry proceeds to note many things that are damaged when the larger industrial economy triumphs over community: "the care of the old, the care and education of children, family life, neighborly work, the handing down of memory, the care of the earth, respect for nature and the lives of wild creatures." He concludes that most precious of all the damaged is perhaps sexual love, which he describes as "the heart of community life—the force that in our bodily life connects us most intimately to the Creation, to the fertility of the world, to farming and the care of animals." In the industrial economy, he notes, "sexual energy is made publicly available for commercial use."[6]

Berry gives us a history of Luddism as an illustration of resistance by local people to becoming subjects of a larger external economy. He insists that the Luddites' nineteenth-century example is again relevant, that settled communities today, such as his own in Henry County, Kentucky, would be well advised to familiarize themselves, as the Luddites did, with the colonialist principles by which their lives are being uprooted. For example, "the assumption that it is permissible to ruin one place for the sake of another;" and that the economic prosperity of nations is measured by "the burgeoning wealth of industrial interests, not according to the success or failure of small local economies." He notes that the global economy today does not exist "to help the communities and localities of the globe. It exists to siphon the wealth of these communities and place it into a few bank accounts." He calls the global economy a "totalitarian economy" and notes that it triumphs with the aid of an ideology one might call "technological determinism." He adds that this is usually mixed with rhetoric of national mysticism about "our destiny" and "the future," but that it really amounts to a denial of democracy and self-determination.[7]

Berry's perspective has its own tradition, most notably flowing out of the 1972 classic *Small Is Beautiful* by E. F. Schumaker. Berry's principle that we should be doing "everything possible to provide ordinary citizens the opportunity to own a small, usable share of the country"[8] echoes Schumaker's earlier suggestion that in a holistically healthy economy, the average amount of capital for establishing a workplace should be no more than the annual earnings of an able and industrious working person.[9] Schumaker observes that such visions of a world composed of human-scale local and regional economies are usually called "uneconomic" by the "realistic" practitioners of the new "science" of economics. He adds, "In the current vocabulary of condemnation there are few words as final and conclusive as 'uneconomic.' If an activity has been deemed uneconomic, its right to existence is not merely questioned but energetically denied."[10] Thus are swept away virtually all practices passed down through the generations such as horticulture, husbandry, artisanship, and small industries and businesses of diverse kinds.

However, the word "economic" used in such a way involves an "extremely *fragmentary* judgement," Schumaker continues. "Out of the large number of aspects which in real life have to be seen and judged together before a decision can be taken, economics supplies only one—whether a thing yields a profit to *those who undertake it* or not." In other words, the word "economic" as employed by its scientific-sounding practitioners these days does not normally look at "whether an activity carried on by a group within society yields a profit to society as a whole."[11] Damage that is inflicted on other parts of the natural or social environment is not included. Such damage is hidden from view as "externalities."

On the other hand, Berry, by starting with community, is able to avoid this unrealistic use of the term "economic," for at the community level that part of community life called "economy" is embedded in local nature, culture, and people. Community economy cannot "succeed" if the rest falls to ruin. What is apparent from ground level, however, is little noticed from the heights of the multinational corporate towers: the possibility of a thriving "economy" while local nature and culture almost everywhere are destroyed is a commonplace assumption in the kind of partial reasoning used by non-holistic economists.

Berry expresses the "scale" issue in terms of affection. Small scale means places, things, plants, and animals can be watched over with specific affection, but as scale grows beyond a certain point everything becomes interchangeable

parts. "Land cannot be properly cared for by people who do not know it intimately," he writes, adding that the quality of the attention decreases as the acre-
age increases and as the level of absenteeism increases.[12] At the scale of what is
today called "global thinking" local nature and local culture appear only statisti-
cally; intrinsic worth is replaced by utilitarian calculation. Land, forests, water,
air become "resources." Even people become "human resources." There is no
specific affection implied in the term "resource."[13]

Berry suggests that the plain term "good work" can help us here.[14] We know,
or at least have a cultural memory of, what "good work" is. Berry cites his late
husbander-neighbor Henry Besuden's daily work of saddling up in the early
morning to "see the bloom," by which he meant check on "a certain visible de-
lectability" of the pastures where his sheep would be grazing that day. "He recognized it, of course, by his delight in it. . . . He was not interested in 'statistical
indicators' of his flock's 'productivity.'"[15] At the consumer end, if we eat this
lamb or use this wool, we are aware of completing a process about which we can
approve. The whole is good—the beginnings of holiness. The entire process
from production to consumption embodies what we have earlier called "intrinsic
worth." It also includes, Berry notes, a wonderful sense of pleasure, even when
the work is difficult.

Contrast this with the settings for industrialized meat production, and the jobs
provided in the mechanized and computerized handling of meat animals. This is
a prime example of "bad work." "The name of our present society's connection
to the earth is 'bad work,'" Berry observes, "work that is only generally and
crudely defined, that enacts a dependence that is ill understood, that enacts no
affection and gives no honor." He admits that we cannot avoid doing some bad
work today, or having it done by other people for us. But he adds, "There is
much good work to be done by every one of us and we must begin to do it."[16]

A bad work epidemic might be a good description of the globe-sweeping process George Ritzer describes in his book *The McDonaldization of Society*. This
is production organized not in the holistic way that Berry describes but in accordance with the principles of "efficiency, calculability, predictability, and control."[17] Ritzer traces the genesis of this approach from early modern bureaucra-
cies as studied by Max Weber, through Taylorism, Ford-style assembly lines,
Levittowns, and the "malling of America," to the McDonaldization of everything from fast food to health care. With narrowly utilitarian thinking, the help
of the latest technologies, and what *Adbusters* magazine aptly calls a very favorable "habitat," McDonaldized corporate production has given us a deluge of
consumer goods. "With no natural enemies, corporations have grown and
thrived," *Adbusters* editors explain. . . . These companies buy and sell each
other's stocks and shares, lobby legislators, bankroll elections, run our air
waves, set our economic and cultural agendas." In the beginning, they add, humans were in control of the relationship with corporations, which could be dis-
solved simply by having their charters revoked. Yet now it has been a hundred
years since this power has been used.[18] As products and services have become
increasingly mass-produced, disposable redundancies, so have people become

mass-produced, disposable redundancies. We have also become accomplices in our own subjugation, as we let more and more of our money work its way toward distant coffers—instead of keeping it as long as possible in local communities, as Berry suggests.

One objection that liberals often make to Berry's thinking is that it might lead to a revival of parochialism and bigotry. His answer to this objection is his call for a "pluralism of settled communities," an important concept that links Berry's localism with an alternative view of the global picture. He points out that the current rhetoric of multiculturalism and globalism actually works against settled communities, because it amounts to a destruction of local culture and nature even as it gives "equal opportunity" to individual Native Americans, Mexicans, Thais, etc. to find jobs or pursue profits in the corporate monoculture. In other words, there are third world counterparts to Henry County, Kentucky, around the globe. For example, Quaker activists George and Lillian Willoughby, returning in early 1998 from conferences in Thailand on "Alternatives to Consumerism" and "Self-reliance," report that resistance is growing to a future of "one borderless mass with no economic barriers." The "Alternatives to Consumerism" conference resolution called for "a restored earth with healthy children, vibrant and creative communities, and valued elders." The "Self-reliance" gathering involved sharing local knowledge that could help to build resistance to "people coming in with offers of big money and jobs." For example, "Anita, from Sri Lanka, told of a commercial soft drink company advertising a new drink. To counter this, Anita and a group of women treated church and other groups with the delicious and healthy drink made from the common hibiscus flower, and provided the recipe which helped popularize the hibiscus drink."[19]

Finally, I want to relate Berry and Ritzer's work to the sociology of landscape architecture developed by James Howard Kuntsler in *The Geography of Nowhere*. The terms community, place, affection, good work, and human scale, as well as the resistance to McDonaldization, all come up from a slightly different angle in Kuntsler's writings. Kuntsler traces how Americans, through a century of increasing architectural and town-planning amnesia accompanied by automobile addiction, have lost our sense of place, have forgotten our understanding of the interconnectedness of architecture and community and our ability to create buildings worthy of affection.

Kuntsler writes about Long Island, Saratoga Springs, and Schuylerville, New York, but his principles, from which we derived our homes/settings-in-which-we-are-interchangeable-parts framework, might well be illustrated by an example taken from my home state of New Jersey. In Burlington and Camden counties where I live and frequent, there are two distinctively different architectural patterns, each of which implies a way of living. One is classically small town: places like Riverton, where I live, Palmyra, Moorestown, or Haddonfield. These towns are constructed as civic places. Their elements include sidewalks, front porches, and back alleys rather than front garages and driveways; what one might call "civic trees," providing a canopy along boulevards; Main Street-type downtown areas with locally owned shops built out to the sidewalks; a central square with benches and gardens; architectural focal points like city hall, churches, the post office, a bandstand, sometimes a train station, and not far away the public school. Even the old local city, Camden, now severely damaged by urban blight, shows many of these same architectural and civic elements.

These towns—there are several dozen of them in Burlington and Camden counties alone—constitute settings I call "homes." They are places, not "anywheres" or "nowheres." At their best they are constructed in ways that honor local nature. The architectural patterns in these towns thrust one out into public life, in a gentle, civilized way—not that there is no privacy, but that too is part of a civic design. Housing was originally designed to provide for a variety of income levels interspersed with each other, including apartments over stores or businesses.

Some towns have managed to stay somewhat protected from the ravages of the automobile, the symbol of the different pattern found all around them. In this other pattern, everything is automobile-oriented. These places have names like Cherry Hill, Mt. Laurel, Cinnaminson, and Marlton. Freeways and highways crisscross them. Getting off of these highways, one finds various feeder roads that lead to malls, strip malls, convenience stores, industrial and office parks, and housing developments. Each of these sectors is segregated from the others so that it would be difficult, if not fearful, for a person to walk from one to another. Businesses are not built out to the sidewalk, but have large parking lots in front of them. The architecture of the vast majority of buildings is a modification of a box-with-a-sign. Civic buildings are not much different. Schools, which can only be reached by car or school bus, have a cinderblock factory look. Houses are set back from sidewalk-less streets. Front porches are gone, and instead there are private decks in the back. The most prominent feature on the front of the house is the two-car garage, projecting a blank face to passerbys and a signal that any link between life inside that house and the outside world will be via the car (or telephone, or internet). Interspersed in this pattern is another arrangement called by names like "Meadow View" or "Fox Run," described by Robert Bellah as a "lifestyle enclave" rather than a community in the full sense.[20] Here people of homogeneous income levels and consumption preferences are grouped together and separated from the outside world. They are excluded from civic life. Most of the land not landscaped into towns many years ago but left open as orchards, farms, and woods is now being converted to this second pattern for living. This is the pattern we have called "settings-in-which-we-are-interchangeable-parts."

In conclusion, the homes/interchangeable parts distinction, and its derivation from the philosophical distinction between intrinsic worth and utility, has implications that spread beyond matters of geography, land use, and place. The analogies in education, for example, are striking. "Homes" become by analogy educational situations in which the student is specifically known through writing, speech, and conversation, and is recommended for higher studies by personal letters passed between people who know each other. The teacher is also specifically known by the administrators as a bearer and propagator of intellectual and moral judgement, of character, and of personality, and as embedded within a community that is relatively permanent. On the other hand, "interchangeable parts settings" become by analogy educational situations in which students are known primarily by objective test scores, GPAs, and SATs, that greatly determine life chances through their influence on admissions and scholarship procedures which work mechanically and anonymously. Students are known primarily as intersections of sets of numbers rather than as creators of essays and bearers of character and personality. Other fields, too—health care, for example—witness parallel developments that need to be critiqued in terms of the distinction between the intrinsic worth of "homes" and the utility of "interchangeable parts."

However, the application to geography seems primary, in that the loss of "home" here affects the landscape in which all else takes place. The loss affects humans' basic relationship with nature and with cultural tradition reflected in place. In the late 1990s and early 2000s, some awareness of this primacy of geography and the importance of "home" seems to have taken root in the culture. A flourish of new books—*Cities and Natural Processes* by Michael Hough (1995), *Ecological Design* by Sim Van der Ryn and Stuart Cowan (1996), *The Ecology of Place* by Timothy Beatley and Kristy Manning and *Sustainability and Cities: Overcoming Automobile Dependence* by Peter Newman and Jeffrey Kenworthy (1999)—have become essential reading in cities, landscape architecture, regional planning, historic preservation, and environmental studies programs. Moreover, the above fields have all begun to link up with each other, becoming one large interdisciplinary cause that is attracting more and more students.

The work of James Howard Kuntsler, George Ritzer, and Wendell Berry in the early 1990s has been absorbed and has become a catalyst for new levels of holistic understanding of the habitat for life. The environmental movement, the simplicity movement, and the anti-corporate globalization movement have attracted more dissenters away from the dominant ideology of growth and interchangeable parts. "Seattle 1999" and "Quebec City 2001" have become symbols of a new gestalt that is slowly taking shape, with its alternative visions of bicycles and hybrid vehicles, solar power and fuel cells, return to towns and disillusionment with sprawl, and renewal of family and community in new inclusive ways.

Kuntsler's *Geography of Nowhere*, having sparked much productive discussion, has more recently been critiqued for its envisioning the future too narrowly in terms of the architectural movement called New Urbanism, or Traditional Neighborhood Design. This model emphasizes laying out of new areas as towns rather than sprawl, but when conceived too narrowly New Urbanism can serve builders' interests more than society's if it neglects to give sufficient attention to social justice and ecological impact issues. An alternative emphasis that some are embracing is on the renewal of decaying and ecologically damaged old cities, such as in my own area Camden, New Jersey, which has many of the elements of traditional neighborhood design but is now broken, with boarded-up row houses and contaminated brownfields. Meanwhile, nearby Philadelphia is experimenting with restoration of urban meadows in parks, emphasizing native grasses rather than lawns.[21]

Ritzer's *McDonaldization of Society* has also sparked a second round of books, including most notably *No Logo: Taking Aim at the Brand Bullies* by Naomi Klein, a centerpiece for the anti-globalization movement.

Finally, Wendell Berry has sparked more Wendell Berry. His *Life Is a Miracle* (2000) draws deeply into the well of Western and regional American culture to argue that mind cannot be abstracted from body and place, an argument reminiscent of Heidegger's in his seminal essay "Building, Dwelling, Thinking." And in Berry's 1996 essay, "Conserving Communities," he prophesizes the emergence of a more genuine two-party system in America with the arising of a party of local community to oppose the Republican-Democrat corporate party. Point nine of his proposed party platform brings this political vision home to intrinsic worth and family life. "See that the old and the young take care of one another," he advises. "The young must learn from the old, not necessarily and not always in school. There must be no institutionalized childcare and no homes for the aged. The community knows and remembers itself by the association of old and young."[22]

Notes

1. Simone Weil, *Gravity and Grace* (New York: Routledge, 1963), 140.

2. Dennis O'Brien, "The Disappearing Moral Curriculum," *The Key Reporter* 62, no. 4 (summer 1997): 1-2.

3. Stephen Mitchell, *Tao Te Ching* (New York: Harper, 1988).

4. Wendell Berry, *Sex, Economy, Freedom and Community* (New York: Pantheon, 1993), 119-20.

5. Berry, *Sex, Economy,* 126.

6. Berry, *Sex, Economy,* 133-36.

7. Berry, *Sex, Economy,* 126-32.

8. Berry, *Sex, Economy,* 17.

9. E. F. Schumaker, *Small Is Beautiful* (New York: Harper and Row, 1973), 35.

10. E. F. Schumaker, *Small,* 41.

11. E. F. Schumaker, *Small,* 43.

12. Berry, *Sex, Economy,* 3-37.

13. Berry, *Sex, Economy,* 19-20.

14. Berry, *Sex, Economy,* 35-36.

15. Berry, *What Are People For?* (New York: North Point, 1990), 140-41.

16. Berry, *Sex, Economy,* 35-37.

17. George Ritzer, *The McDonaldization of Society* (Thousand Oaks, Calif.: Pine Forge, 1996), 9-11.

18. "Editorial," *Adbusters,* July 1998, 1.

19. George and Lillian Willoughby, unpublished newsletter (Deptford, N.J., 1998), 1-3.

20. Robert N. Bellah et al., *Habits of the Heart* (New York: Harper and Row, 1985), 335.

21. Elisa Ung, "Driving Nature Back to Nature," *Philadelphia Inquirer,* 5 November 2000, 1-2(B).

22. Wendell Berry, "Conserving Communities," in *The Case Against the Global Economy,* ed. Jerry Mander and Edward Goldsmith (San Francisco: Sierra Club, 1996), 407-17.

Chapter 6

Auto-Mobility and the Route-Scape: A Critical Phenomenology

Gary Backhaus

In the theory of the location of towns and cities, a question at which we are now arrived, exchange plays a subordinate part and may be regarded simply as the symbolic aspect of transportation. As far as place relations are concerned, transportation determines exchange and not *vice versa*.
—Charles Horton Cooley, "The Theory of Transportation"

Introduction: Theme and Methodology

This chapter concerns meanings that emerge out of the most basic structure of embodied Being-in-the-world: the lived-body in its relation to place. The collusion of the lived-body and the environing landscape, implacement, constitutes the primal preconscious orientation within the place-world.[1] Placiality (the significance of place) involves the qualitative modalities of the lived-body, formed through its upright posture, body asymmetry, body schema, synaesthetic, kinesthetic, and visceral moments in relation to the world horizon and its contents. Implacement sets the parameters for not only *where* and *how* each of us exists with others in the environs, but moreover *who* we shall become together. Specifically, this phenomenological study focusses on the structures of implacement as they are modified through the mediation of auto-mobility. The automobile and other forms of auto-transport are an integral moment of contemporary living. So the automobile has become an aspect of our very own Being, which includes being-with (modalities of social relations) and being-in (modalities of geographic context), for it informs the fundamental structures of our experience of the life-world.[2]

However, these preconscious structures are easily taken for granted, because the very conditions for the genesis of world-experience are opaque to the lived relative-natural world-view.[3] From the standpoint of the everyday commerce with the environing world, conscious life is immersed in pragmatic contexts, which must be bracketed in order to open to conscious reflection that which is ordinarily closed to it.[4] Phenomenological methodology uncovers the material a priori that remains hidden from the standpoint of the natural attitude, both in its everyday and theoretical modalities.[5] Without investigating the fundamental structures pertaining to implacement, we remain naïve as to *how* we have become who we are and thus it follows that we *remain naïve* as to the *who* that we have become.[6] The cultural processes (externalization) that have been created (objectivation) then retroject back into us (internalization), and insight into this dialectical construction of identity allows for a critical assessment of this identity.[7] The concern of this study is to contextualize this dialectic within geographical embodiment, the lived dynamic placialization, which is the cultural embodiment that we *are*.

Auto-mobility modifies how the lived-body relates to the environing world in very fundamental ways, and through the emergent embodied forms of lived experience, the character of our Being-in-the-world is transformed. These transformations are exhibited in the pre-conscious body schema. The body schemata are postures that form fundamental attitudes of meaningful commerce with the environs, prefiguring the interpretive understanding of the world, the *Weltanschauung*. This enforming of the lived-body's intentional structure through technological mediation is the pre-conscious basis or the embodied pre-predicative structuring of meanings that is naively lived within the object-focussed awareness of natural consciousness. This phenomenological investigation reveals that *uprootedness* from place is a systemic feature of the supermodern over-dependence upon auto-mobility. The temporally truncated traversal of place and the technologically mediated transference of work do not inherently incur uprootedness. But it is the frequency and extent, that is, the dependency on the use of auto-mobility with its correlative demands on geographical organization that leads to uprootedness as the general characteristic of the lived-relation to the place-world. Uprootedness is a basic existential character of the cultures of 'supermodernity.'[8]

I employ a methodology that I call 'critical phenomenology.' Phenomenology is a descriptive science that attempts to ascertain the structures of meaning or appearances just as they appear in the experience. The telos of phenomenological description is to avoid theoretical constructions, to remain faithful to intuitive evidence all the while attempting to grasp the essential structures. The word, 'critical,' has to do with the notion that description, the 'is' of appearance, motivates questions of the 'ought.' For example, in investigating essential structures of religiosity if phenomenological inquiry finds religious practices that actually obstruct spirituality, then questions of the ought are critically motivated and implied. By the same token, if auto-mobility is to provide greater access to places, but through its use actually uproots a culture resulting in a deficient sense of place, then an evaluation of this apprehended evidence should lead to oughts that sanction a change in praxis. Interrogatives naturally arise simultaneously with indicatives. Rather than a rigorous attention to only the descriptive contents this critical methodology proceeds to pursue the questions that motivate the formulation of 'oughts,' which arise from questioning the significance in the description. It is beyond the scope of this chapter however to entertain possible solutions to the problems associated with auto-mobility.

An analogous view is held by environmentalist, Holmes Rolston III, who in describing the evolutionary aspect of nature states, "The system is value-able, able to produce value."[9] Critical descriptive phenomenology is value-able, able to produce value by illuminating imperatives for change. Rolston states, "The sharp is/ought dichotomy is gone; the values seem to be there as soon as the facts are fully in, and both alike properties of the system. This conviction, and the conscience that follows from it, can yield our best adaptive fit on earth."[10] The emergence of a scientific paradigm that overturns objectivist abstractions of the moderns and becomes open to the axiological and teleonomic[11] character of the "natural" and "social" worlds offers the possibility for a closer integration of scientific expertise with valuations.

Phenomenology had been created with the recognition that the is/ought dichotomy is based on an objectivist abstraction and thus a distortion when the 'is' of factology (positivism) is legislated as reality. Phenomenology shows that

> perception is affective as well as cognitive, since I apprehend objects, not a neutral husks, but as charged with an affective and vital meaning, as poles of intentionality. In this perceptual field there is no distinction between perceptual objects (facts) and how I perceive them (values). . . . Phenomenology seeks to trace the birth of values and morality in perceptual experience, which, according to Merleau-Ponty's thesis of the primacy of perception, is the ground of all rationality, all descriptions and all values.[12]

In our method of critical phenomenology the 'ought' is a complementary function to a description of the values and moralities already inscribed in the encultured geography under investigation. Pre-predicative experience that pertains to auto-mobility, then, is already pervaded with axiological significance, meanings that must be uncovered if we want to recognize the value-Being that we have come to be. Critical methodology evaluates implications for axiological and ethical progress concerning this phenomenon of the mediated collusion of the lived-body and place through auto-mobility.

The Context and Heuristic: The Environmental Geographic

Let us first place auto-mobility in the larger context of the environmental concerns and the qualitative experience of the life-world. The structuring of landscapes by a culture that relies on auto-transport has had a huge impact on the quality of human and natural ecology. Through automobile travel, the latent effects of industrialism have manifested in an intensive and complex web of paved roads that blanket a vast amount of geographical space, the route-scape. The emergent forms of life based upon auto-transport, most notably, suburban forms have brought about grave environmental consequences.[13]

Environmental problems for the most part are still seen as limited to industrial pollution and consumer waste. Yet, the paving over of vast amounts of land, the filling up of adjacent land with suburban architecture, and the socioeconomic geography by which the automobile has been made a necessity, has transmogrified the natural and human world. It has only been 150 years since a vast amount of humanity has been transformed into an indoor culture. It has only been 100 years that humanity has been building paved roads and highways to the extent that the beauty of the natural world has been dissected with passageways that merely serve the growing stream of automobiles. What sort of culture could ever make such extensive and rapid modifications without caution and reflection through which its own Being and the Being of the natural world are so greatly affected? Is manifest destiny or romanticized technology so determining that this culture will continue with its present material growth such that the vast space of the North American continent (and other continents as well) is to be covered with pavement and road-kill (if any four-legged creatures would be left)?

An ecological voice has emerged in the latter half of the twentieth century: the basic fabric of our cultural organization has been called into question, morally and axiologically. A burgeoning ecological consciousness and conscience has shown with overwhelming evidence that the human world must be made compatible with the health requirements of the natural world, the biosphere, which entails a radical transformation in cultural values and material organization. The first half of the twentieth century became consumed with anxiety and alienation. The catastrophic extent of humanity's destructive capabilities in relation to itself had become apparent through the world wars, ethnic cleansings, and economic dominations. In peace, the dominant values had been reasserted in a cultural renewal that continues to have faith in progress through economic and technological "development." But this scientistic western paradigm runs headfirst into a contradiction. The realization of the environmental crisis in the latter half of the twentieth century has shown that the seemingly most innocuous and ordinary aspects of values, morals, and practical organization inherent to 'supermodern' forms of culture, need to be called into question.[14]

In terms of population growth, the quantitative presence of humanity on this planet has threatened the very biosphere of which other forms of life and humanity depend. The Ehrlich's have indicated that the 6 billion humans now living on earth have already destroyed or appropriated approximately 40 percent of biomass productivity on the land.[15] Such increased appropriation of the biosphere calls into question "business as usual," for it is obvious that the destruction of the rainforests and other human irresponsible practices are linked to the demands that humanity puts on nature for its consumptive practices. As Aldo Leopold has stated, "The trend of evolution is to elaborate and diversify the biota."[16] Human activity since the industrial revolution has undone a large portion of what it took nature (evolution) tens of thousands of years to create.

> Mankind inherited a richer, more diverse world than had ever existed before in the 3.5 billion-year (*sic*) odyssey of life on Earth. What is wrong with anthropogenic species extirpation and extinction is the *rate* at which it is occurring and the *result*: biological impoverishment instead of enrichment.[17]

The new field, conservation biology, which integrates ecology and ethics, calls for nothing less than geographical reorganization if natural environments are to be saved and renewed. Conservation biologist, Norman Meyers, claims that the current rate of anthropogenic extinctions may annihilate as many as a third of the planet's species over the next several decades.[18] After examining twenty wildlife reserves in East Africa, Michael Soulé concluded that as they become habitat islands due to human encroachment, many species become extinct.[19] Edward Grumbine points out that "No park in the U. S. is capable of supporting minimum viable populations of large animals over the long term. And the situation is worsening."[20] There is bad faith in the arrogance of domination over nature, which includes the alleged scientific acumen of predictability in the manipulation and control of nature. But ecologist Frank Egler counters, "Nature is not only more complex than we think, it is more complex than we *can* think."[21] Thomas Fleischner claims that "over 95% of the contiguous United States has been altered from its original state."[22] The general point inherent in this body of environmental research is that humanity has appropriated too much of the earth both quantitatively and qualitatively in a manner that results in grave, harmful consequences for the natural world as well as for its own quality of Being.

The specific point of this investigation establishes that the seemingly innocuous inculcation of auto-mobility in mundane human affairs involves participation in the acceleration of ecological destruction. Automobile use has led to spatial organizations that level the significance of the landscape to that of road-mapping-for-transportation. Auto-mobility is key to the inordinate spreading out of human dominated landscapes. Auto-transport is an aspect of the excesses of supermodernity that appropriates the landscape in order to accommodate the growing forms of suburbanized living; it is the condition for the possibility of the suburban organization of space.

But how can the values inherent to the everyday life-world exhibit insidious consequences?[23] After all, humans have to exist also and need to maintain a culture that is built upon meanings sufficient to satisfy human life. Auto-mobility has made possible a form of affluence generating the great expansion of the size of cities and the suburban sprawl that surrounds cities, that is, the geographical growth of human culture. The building of roads and highways has created the expansion into the mega-metropolis and urban corridors. The eastern seaboard of the United States is close to becoming a pattern of parking lots, roads, and the suburban lawns, which are regularly doused with chemicals so no living creatures will survive. The unlimited expansion of this form of existence, the supposed good life of high consumption, and the unquestioned expectation that an economistic high standard of living equals quality of life, actually leads to its own negation. No longer can the evil of the world be placed on industrial pollution, criminal violence, etc. Supermodern cultural excess camouflages the violence against world ecology, which will no longer sustain life given the increasing expansion of this present form of geographic transformation.[24]

There is no lack of cultural meanings in supermodernity. However, the hyperbolic affront of cultural objectivations levels meaning-qualities in the experience of those who attempt to make sense of their lives. The sheer volume and rhythm of meaning obfuscates value-quality. Life has become a consumption-frenzy. As one small example, the excess of television channels can be interpreted as a metonym for the excess of objectivations in supermodernity. French anthropologist Marc Augé remarks of the curious modifications of placiality in supermodernity in which one finds oneself both everywhere and nowhere at the same time, the emptying of placial-qualties by providing an excess of mobility.

> If a place can be defined as relational, historical and concerned with identity, then a space which cannot be defined as relational, or historical, or concerned with identity is a non-place. The hypothesis advanced here is that supermodernity produces non-places, meaning spaces which are not themselves anthropological places and which, . . . do not integrate the earlier places: instead these are listed, classified, promoted to the status of 'places of memory,' and assigned to a circumscribed and specific position. . . . Non-places are the real measure of our time; one that could be quantified—with the aid of a few conversions between area, volume, and distance—by totaling all the air, rail and motorway routes, the mobile cabins called 'means of transport' (aircraft, trains and road vehicles), the airports and railway stations, hotel chains, leisure parks, large retail outlets, and finally the complex skein of cable and wireless networks that mobilize extraterrestial space for the purposes of a communication so peculiar that it often puts the individual in contact only with another image of himself.[25]

Constructed non-places of supermodernity are a component of uprootedness and our participation in them obfuscates our understanding of the basic need to be rooted, which, in turn, blankets the seriousness of the environmental crisis.

The uprooted modality of our existence keeps us from recognizing the imperative to understand historical modifications in our placial relationship with the natural world. Gary Snyder remarks, "Imposed borders sometimes cut across biotic areas and ethnic zones alike. Inhabitants lost ecological knowledge and community solidarity. In the old ways, the flora and fauna and landforms are *part of culture*."[26] Bioregionalists like Snyder explore the need for reinhabitation, which would consist of "the creation of a culture and way of life based on a very specific, detailed knowledge of the ecological realities of the larger natural community in which the human community participates."[27] But the roads and automobiles of a consumerist society contribute to the leveling of the specific placial-qualities and turn it into the homogeneous, economically appropriated landscape of advanced capitalist culture. Place-significance becomes monolithic through multinational corporations whose aim is to construct consumer markets for their wares, which involves a disregard for, and a destruction of, bioregional values and a scale of place for human-Being.

Culture informs place and place informs culture. But if the architectural spirit is to dominate a place by transforming it into the homogeneous space driven by the capitalist economy fueled on auto-transport, which is a destruction in the name of development, then the spirit of place is lost. An uprooted culture even loses the value to value the spirit of place, unless spirit is to be reduced to the simulacra of entertainment, and other excesses of media consumption. The over dependence upon auto-transport produces a "narcotic" that keeps us from re-membering our lost rootedness. As long as we are on the "high-way" we will never come "down to earth."

By placing our investigation of auto-mobility in this context its importance is elucidated. Rootedness is recognized as a fundamental human value, because Being-in-place is our anchor to the inherent value and significance of the earth. Advanced technology has become insidious only because it has not been imple-mented in the life-world with caution. The automobile is a machine of everyday use and its incorporation into our Being and its effects on the natural world are not recognized, because the importance of place, the anchoring value of genius loci, has been forgotten. We pass it by in our automobiles as we travel from point A to point B in an external environment leveled down to pavement and traffic signals. We spend much of our time in an internal environment that en-slaves us to the task of machine operator and encases us as a passenger in a rolling metal bubble.

Let us summarize the implied argument. The environmental/ecological crisis demands a radical restructuring of forms of existence. The over-dependence upon certain space-appropriating forms of technology and the lifestyle that this creates is a major form of the uprootedness in our relation to place. Our culture is insensitive to the immensity of the environmental crisis due to the lived-uprootedness that is our identity. Only a culture that is rooted in its placiality can be sensitive to environmental values and thus live in a more harmonious way with the demands of the natural world. In order to become sensitive to place, it is first necessary to become aware of the character of uprootedness in specific forms of activities. The supermodern excess of auto-mobility is a major form. By exposing its destructive transformation of implacement, decisions concern-ing this technology can lead us back to the value-rootedness of place. We must now turn to phenomenological analysis to carefully uncover the structures of implacement as they are modified in the lived-body/automobile/environment relation.

Phenomenological Investigation of Auto-Mobility

Zones: Placial Modalities Surrounding the Lived-Body

From the place that the lived-body occupies, which establishes the null-point of placial orientation, there are surrounding zones of placial significance.[28] In the zone of manipulative reach objects are at immediate disposal. Manipulation of objects is accomplished especially with the hands along with other body parts directly altering the immediate environment according to pragmatically pro-jected goals. The surrounding zone of actual reach is within perceptual capabili-ties of the lived-body. The zone of actual reach involves that which is under purview of perceptual immediacy, vision, audition, and olfaction. Zones of po-tential reach transcend the immediate perceptual capacities, which can become zones of actual reach through the mobility of the lived-body. Zones of restora-tive reach are those of potential reach that are already familiar and to which one may return. Zones of attainable reach are zones that as yet have not been directly experienced and can be arranged according to probability for actualization. Each of these zones is a function of the here of the lived-body. The structural differ-ences introduced in the experience of these zones through the mediation of the automobile must be elucidated. Other structures of embodiment in conjunction with these zones are necessary for the investigation of auto-mobility to proceed.

The Relation between the Vertical and the Horizontal

The ability to stand up, the upright posture, establishes the fundamental value of *human* placiality.[29] The upright posture establishes the human form of equi-librium. The upright equilibrium establishes and organizes the placial values of up/down and the horizon. The bipedal vertical position from which the lived-body establishes equilibrium constitutes a unique qualitative relation to the places before the horizon.[30] Standing-up and walking about inform vision with the quality of overseeing the environing zone of actual reach. When sitting down the lived-body is immobilized and vision is directed across the horizontal plane in a positional vector-like fashion. Sitting no longer allows for a gathering of those vectors into a field-like overview (unless statically from above as in the construction of stadiums). The ambulatory potentiality of the upright posture establishes the significance of horizontal orientation, for ambulation is our fun-damental potency for survival and development of human forms of life. The mobile verticality of the lived-body allows for the gathering of perceptual ad-umbrations into a field-synthesis of which we find ourselves amidst. Verticality, as the quality of human ambulation, is the necessary condition for establishing the horizontal quality of human rootedness to the earth. Ambulation constitutes placiality as a *dynamic* field. The lived-body assumes a "dynamic active stand" in relation to the environment, which is the fundamental adaptation for a being that depends on pragmatic intellection for its survival. Obviously, then, the postures of auto-mobility modify this important structure of lived-body rootedness.

The Dynamic/Static and Active/Passive Matrix

The immobile posture of sitting is a static form of embodiment in the lived-body's relation to the environing world. In terms of the zone of actual reach or of converting zones of potential reach into actual reach, the seated posture is a passive form. Nevertheless, the lived-body can be quite active within the zone of manipulation while in the seated posture. The mobile posture of walking is dynamic and active in terms of modifying placial-qualities in the zone of actual reach and in converting zones of potential reach into zones of actual reach. Through the technological mediation of auto-mobility, the passive posture of sitting becomes dynamic in its relation to the environing zones. One is quite active in the manipulatory zone, which is a condition for operating the machinery, but the seated posture remains passive and depends upon the "activity" of the technology, the auto-traversal of spatial sectors. A subtle but important shift occurs in this dynamic/passive matrix. The environing world is experienced as if it comes to the seated lived-body and passes through it rather than the lived-body advancing toward the world. It is a facile gestalt shift while traveling in the automobile to feel as if the automobile is stationary and it is the environing world that is moving toward it, which is facilitated by the passivity of the seated posture. Ambulatory postures actively *participate* in the environing world by continually transforming its *relational* significance. A new value-character emerges in the space traversal of auto-mobility, because it enables the passive but dynamic lived-body to transcend active participation in the environing world. Its dynamic relationship is a nonparticipatory vector-like synthesis, which in terms of the lived-body, the vector points toward it, but in terms of the technology, the vector actually moves forward. The over dependence upon a nonparticipatory dynamic of the lived-body is an aspect of uprootedness. Nonparticipating transformations within the structures of implacement establish praxes of noninvolvement (uprootedness).

Here/There: Com-place and Counter-place

The here, which is always the place of the lived-body, becomes related to a plethora of theres as the landscape surrounding the lived-body becomes articulated. A particular there is established as a com-place when the ambulatory transition that establishes "the there" as "a here" is a smooth one. A there-place is established as a counter-place when the transition that would establish the there-place as here presents difficulties or impossibilities.[31] Lived-body mobility allows for the transition.

In the culture of supermodernity, auto-mobility is the primary means of trans-forming heres into theres outside interior environments. Roads are engineered in a way that accounts for the engineered properties of the automobile. Roads and parking areas are geographically mapped so that the automobile has become intrusive to every geographical form of placiality. Generally, roads and parking areas are the com-places for the automobile and all other place-forms are its counter-places. What obscures the recognition of the import of this partitioning is that roads and parking areas are so intrusive that roads conveniently route us to any of the multitudinous destinations that are available in the supermodern cultural geographic. Bipedal ambulation has been efficiently truncated. The lived-body is transported from one zone of actual reach to another zone of actual reach so that once out of the automobile, ambulation needs only to remain within the immediate environs of actual reach. For most activities involving mobility, people no longer ambulate to convert zones of potential reach into zones of actual reach; this is accomplished by automobile travel. This "conven-ience" is taken for granted and the demand for even greater convenience is ob-vious in the social competition of vying for the closest parking spaces.

What remains unnoticed is that between destinations there exists a vast web of counter-places for ambulation. In this way com-places for ambulation are atom-ized because the connection between places, the auto-route, is a counter-place for them.[32] Empirical substantiation abounds. Recently I walked across the parking lot of one large shopping area and then across the parking lot of another shopping area. Such ambulatory projects are discouraging, because these areas are constructed to keep pedestrians within the bounds of a particular consumer haven. The automobile is to be employed to enter and to exit a circumscribed area. The atomization of ambulatory com-places is further augmented because auto-mobility has led to geographical expansion of the distances between the places of our daily concerns. No longer is there the need for self-contained liv-ing-relations (where you can walk to everything). The greater freedom of the automobile has led to bondage based on this freedom. One cannot walk to all the places one needs to go and one would not want to walk anyway, for places-of-mobility have been made in the image of the automobile. The hegemony of the auto-route creates a grid of counter-places for ambulation. The sidewalk is a fairly weak caveat, for the heat off the asphalt, the noise of the automobiles whizzing by, water spray from the tires of passing automobiles, and other con-ditions (e.g., crossing streets) makes walking an unsuitable underclass of mobil-ity in its spatial juxtaposition to the auto-route. Besides, geographical segmenta-tion means that suburbanites must travel large roads where there is no place to walk.

Geographic organization is based on an economy of consumption whose ma-terial form is made possible through auto-transport. This quantitative enlarge-ment qualitatively diminishes intimate familiarity with the contiguous environs from an established residing-place. The participation in the continually devel-oping auto-mobile consumerist society uproots the individual from an intimate relation with the surrounding environs in a geographical organization that preempts a relational being-in. Instead, intimate familiarity consists of disconnected points on a non-centered grid. Placiality in supermodernity involves a disconnected sum of satellites.

Ambulation and the Near/Far Interpenetration

The lived-body is an asymmetrical pole in the matrix of rootedness to place. Primordial values are constituted through the a priori structural meanings of lived-body asymmetry. One aspect of body asymmetry is its front and its back. The sensory organs face front and locomotion is usually forward. The body moves ahead and leaves behind it the places where it has been. The ahead is the forging of progress in place. Because of body-mobility in relation to carrying out projects, there exists an interpenetration of the near and far. We can get farther from the near, farther from the far, nearer to the near, and nearer to the far. But none of this involves purely quantitative measure, for what is near or far is established through the existential situation.[33] If to find safety one must cross the "parkway" during rush hour, but to cross means dodging moving automobiles, the other side is quite far away in terms of existential significance.

The ambulatory project of the lived-body continually modifies the qualitative meanings of the places that surround it, because of the continuous transformation of object-relations through the near/far context. The pace of walking allows for objects that continually enter and exit the zone of manipulation to be articulated in a "momentary fashion." But this articulation is sufficient to motivate interest in those objects with which one could touch or scrutinize if one wanted to stop and take the time. Entities continually become accessible to the zone of manipulation from the zone of actual reach, which forms a bond of potential and actual immediate intimacy.

The zone of actual reach places the objects in an interconnected context, the placial matrix of sense experiences. When walking the zone of actual reach gathers together the objects that surround the lived-body, but that which is in front of the lived-body and is drawn near, takes on the character of encounter. The horizon sets limits to a far sphere that becomes more vague and ethereal as vision fades. But when walking, objects emerge from the horizon and enter the zone of actual reach unless an obstacle creates a counter-place within the ambulatory project. The horizon domes overhead and around the lived-body so that it is the center of a circumscribed field of directions that are articulated through left/right differentiation. Thus, obstacles are surmounted through the possibility for the reorientation of direction.

Zonal Partitioning of Auto-Mobility and the Structure of Scenery

This particular structure of implacement, near/far, also becomes modified in the activity of operating an automobile. The posture of sitting is assumed for spectatorship, or as a form of rest/reclining, or when active within the zone of manipulation. All three functions are operative components when driving. Within manipulative reach, equipment must be operated. These operations include starting, maintaining, and stopping movement, steering, and signaling (to mention some of the activities). Although place-scapes are traversed when driving, nothing within the zone of manipulation changes. This zone, which is our most intimate environmental contact, remains statically wedded to the mobile cabin of operation from which the appropriate manual activities direct the project of locomotion. The objects within the zone of actual reach never enter the zone of manipulation, for these two zones have been partitioned. Thus, the most intimate, immediate contact with the traversed environment is denied.

The posture of sitting inside the partitioned manipulatory area of the automobile modifies the overall quality of the zone of actual reach. In order to act directly in the zone of actual reach, the automobile must be vacated. The auto-transported person is a seated spectator and this means that the perceived-contents within the zone of actual reach are transformed into a spectacle. The lived-body is removed from its field of perception. This peculiar spectacle of auto-mobility, because it does not engender a meaning-context of spectatorship like a sports event or a dog show, is constituted as scenery. The primary meaning of scenery denotes the backdrops and hangings that represent places and surroundings in a theatrical play. Its secondary meaning has to do with features of a landscape. But this ambiguity is synthesized in terms of auto-mobility, for the places within the zone of actual reach have now become present-at-hand.[34] They become things that are merely named. This is exactly the function of road signs and beltway exits; they label aspects of the landscape that are merely present-at-hand for the passengers of an automobile. Business signs that litter the commercial strips represent the actual place of business from which the auto-motorist has become partitioned. Landscape takes on the quality of the backdrops of a play, a horizon of non-action. When driving, the landscape is like the representations in the wallpaper while we walk down a hallway. However, *lived* place-scapes are not scenery and this contradiction indicates another aspect of uprootedness. If most traversal of space is through auto-transport, and if geographical organization requires a great deal of space traversal, then experiences constitute place as scenery and the *depth of place* is negated. Placial depth is re-established at destinations, but in a quite limited fashion, due to the domination of auto-geography.

Orientation-to-Place: Establishing the Panorama

When driving, the organization of place takes on a peculiarly limited character. The contents of the ahead/behind structure are the continuous stretches of paved road. The operation of the equipment demands that visual perception and attention remain on the affairs of the road, which requires commitment to the frontal/dorsal axis. This paved environment conditions perception, that is, creates a bipartite experiencing of non-road and road. The word, 'route,' is derived from the Latin, 'rumpere,' which means to break apart. In the stationary sitting position, I am constrained to face front. I am predetermined to the ahead as my restrained perceptual character so that the experience of the movement of the automobile is vector-like. I cannot circumrotate in place. In my other lived-spaces where I can get up and walk around, it is because of habitual circumrotation that I move about with ease. A panorama is constituted through the transmutation of directionality. The turning of the head also results in a panorama, but of a wholly different form. In a resting position turning the head creates a panorama-at-a-distance, a projected curvilinear horizontal axis that is established "out there" because left and right are fixed. But the panorama-by-circumrotation is formed intimately around the lived-body through a continuous transition of angles. Left and right are in the process of an ongoing translation. Panorama-by-circumrotation centers the lived-body in place by gathering-in the surrounding places. The encircling relation of the lived-body with its environs is a fundamental activity establishing placial orientation, for all sectors are transmuted through the changing directionality. The lived-body gains equilibrium by establishing the up and down: it gains placial orientation by establishing the panorama, that is, the transmutation of directionality in its fundamental relation to the lived-body. As the integration of environmental context around the lived-body, panoramic kinaesthesia is necessary for embodied rootedness. Driving an automobile denies access to this form of panorama, and thus the primary quality of auto-mobility is that of surmounting linear distance. The panorama-at-a-distance that can be formed by shifting the eyes or head while driving involves an "implosive" process. Linear traversal draws objects near but the sides of the panoramic view collapse and whiz by on both the left and right of the body while the objects in front either remain at a distance if moving or become indirectly encountered if at rest. The panorama of auto-mobility forms a moving arrowhead. The loss of the lived-body's ability for circumrotation does not lead to disorientation, however, for there is compensation in the loss of the integration of environmental context through the provision of a concrete mapping, the paved road. Driving is like retracing the lines that already connect the numbered dots (the automobile follows these roads and not others in reachings its destinations).

While attending graduate school my automobile once broke down and I had to walk along what I thought to be a familiar route. Instead, I had a surprising experience even though I knew exactly where I was headed. The lived-body was becoming intimately oriented to the place-scape, which required the transmutation of directionality. Even though I was walking along the sidewalk of a relatively straight road, turning right angles allowed me to see directly across the street, which resulted in the transfer of the left/right axis mapped to the direction of the street. To grasp the importance of the circumrotative panorama for orientation, think of how one's body is so familiar with one's living quarters. No one needs to think about how to make all the maneuvers through rooms. This is because a panorama-by-circumrotation has been established through the lived-body schema kinesthetically feeling the continuous transition of angles in the transmutation of directionality. The lived-body is at home, because it has established and intuitively saturated the panoramic orientation. I would never be oriented to the route to the university as I am to my intimate living quarters. But through walking the lived-body had become oriented in a way that is qualitatively different than driving, even though walking is usually linearly directed. In driving the route to the university, I first relied on conscious judgments as to how many streets and whether to turn left or right, which eventually became lifeless habit.

In order to travel somewhere by automobile, one learns the directions, which are already articulated judgments. These judgments are filled-in by highly selected percepts, in fact, one disregards percepts that do not fit the signposts that are indicated in the directions. After traveling the route the judgments become habit based on the limited filled-in perception of those landmarks. When we walk, the on-going perceptions are articulated into judgments, if we are to learn a route. We still are looking for specific landmarks, yet the between is filled-in by many more perceptions from which we articulate judgments. In the automobile, we are oriented to the road, which does not need or inspire much articulation. We listen to the radio and concentrate on looking at the signs and road marks. The environs out of which the habitual routes of our daily drives are abstracted cannot be really loved or enjoyed because the environs are merely *passed-by.* Pre-predicative meanings are established upon the lived-body's intimate orientation and not through a linearly distant orientation that requires conscious selection. *Passing-by-the-environs* is another aspect of uprootedness.

The Zone of Manipulation and Perceptual Fulfillment

George Herbert Mead articulates the importance of the zone of manipulation. According to Mead the reality of perception is in its relation to future manipulatory experience. The act of perception carries within it a relational process of an anticipated future experience of actual contact within the zone of manipulation. "The truth of the perception lies in the agreement of the initiated process of handling with the actual process when the separating distance has been actually covered."[35] Perception involves varying distances of objects lying in a perceptual zone outside of the manipulatory area, and it includes the readiness within the intentionality of the lived-body to take up an attitude toward those objects projecting their manifestation within the zone of manipulation. "Perceptual experience is that in which we control our conduct with reference to spatiotemporally distant stimulation by the promise of the contact experience."[36] "Objects of immediate contact *are.* . . . The promise and fulfillment are both given."[37] "In the perceptual . . . world . . . the object *is* not hard and cold and rough. We hope, fear, or anticipate that it will be, or at least are ready to respond to hardness, roughness, and coldness, and those features of the distance characters of the object are said to convey these contact characters."[38] Augmenting Mead I claim that perceptions that remain unfulfilled lead to an environmental alienation, a modality of uprootedness. Alienation may be thematic or non-thematic for consciousness. The manner of unfulfillment decides the issue. Since auto-mobile perceptions are of scenery the readiness for fulfillment is already dimmed, the alienation is non-thematic lived.

The perambulatory walk provides the paramount opportunity for promises of perception to emerge followed by the opportunity for fulfillment. The completion of the ongoing perceptual acts occurs through the continual overcoming of distance even in the mere process of walking. Even if nothing is actually manipulated with the hands, the feet still "pound the pavement," which at least brings many objects within the intimate sphere, and which brings many anticipated characteristics to perceptual fulfillment. Mead's discussion must be amended because we also intimately feel "space." Ambulation is the paramount activity for converting the promise of placial feel into actualities. Ambulation is the fundamental activity of the lived-body for converting the perceptual promise of the already prepared somatic and motor imagery into the concreteness of manipulatory verification. But the partitioning off of the manipulatory zone that occurs in auto-mobility denies the possibility of intimate perceptual fulfillment. Since the lived-body does not experience a series of objects passing in and out of its zone of manipulation, its anticipation, the readiness for response in somatic and motor imagery is also dimmed. This is the experiential sense of scenery. Even if one becomes interested in the scenery, because it is constituted as scenery there is not the lively involvement of anticipating its character whose reality is to become verified when the objects enter the zone of manipulation. Thus, the overly dependent employment of the automobile for traversing distances disconnects the lived-body from the primary process in which "reality" is confirmed. This perceptual alienation is another aspect of uprootedness that is detrimental to the experiential quality of the life-world through overdependence on auto-mobility. Perceptual alienation is the complement of environmental alienation.

The Observational Context of Auto-Transport

However, not the whole of the surrounding environment, i.e., the partitioned zone of actual reach, is constituted as scenery. While driving, vision is coordinated with the limbs in the operation of the equipment, which is to direct the moving compartment along a path. Objects are observed as they relate to the path of the automobile, and they are constituted according to their significance in the context of driving conduct. Some objects are encountered that have been constructed solely for the driving context, e.g., painted stripes down the center of the road. Some objects are taken into account as unwanted obstacles in the road, e.g., a loose basketball or an animal crossing the road in front of the automobile. Other objects, which are for the most part other automobiles, are meaningful according to the observational relation to one's own automobile. The meanings of objects that are encountered within the automobilist's perceptions, then, are operationally constituted according to their relation to this particular form of observation and engagement. As long as automobile travel replaces ambulation, objects are not constituted through immediate perceptual/manipulatory modalities. Instead, objects become constituted as functions of auto-mobility. Since geographical organization is constructed around auto-mobility, values other than those related to the meaning context of the road are subordinated. The hegemonic meaning-context of auto-mobility pervades life; the street is right outside the home and its domination intrudes into many contexts.

Rule Bound Contextualization

Ambulation involves observation as well as encounter and engagement. However, since there is no technological mediation between the lived-body and the objects observed, the objects do not become constituted from the point of view of a special walking context, i.e., the restructuring of the meanings in pre-predicative experience due to a specific form of mediation. The lived-body directly relates to the objects it observes during nontechnologically mediated activities. But while driving there is the primary relation between a heavy and speedy rolling object, the automobile, and the objects whose significance emerges through the mediated relation of the lived-body-cum-automobile. Walking does not require a plethora of positive rules as does driving an automobile. These rules confine the parameters of object relations from the standpoint of the automobile's general characteristics. But due to these positive rules, to be on foot also requires special positive rules in relation to those of the automobile, e.g., staying on the sidewalk and knowing when to cross the street. The parameters of perceptual observation are rule-bound due to the consequences in the restructuring of pre-predicative experience due to the mediation. The immediacy of implacement is compromised by its subordination to the rules of auto-geography, which means that the observational aspect of implacement submits to a mediated context even in its non-mediated experience. "Cars rule!"

Sensory Stimulation and Perception

The pace of walking allows for an articulation of the surrounding entities, trees, houses, or the character of the cracks in the sidewalk and the beauty of delicate flowers (i.e., the articulation of the inner horizon of objects, their details). This pace is slow enough that walking past the houses on a city block allows for the experience of their immediate presence, to relate them to the lived-body in a form of intimacy similar to a face-to-face conversation. Driving by those same houses cannot result in the same perceptions, just by the speed alone. The speed of the automobile modifies our perceptual capabilities. There is greater sensory stimulation produced by the rapid changes, but those changes merely excite the nervous system without those contents entering conscious awareness. What is actually perceived in a given "stretch" of the environment is diminished while the sensory stimulation is augmented. Due to the need to keep one's eyes on the road, the quality of the sensory stimulation is also far more restricted than what is gained when walking. The detailed articulation of the interconnection of entities within the zone of actual reach cannot occur, for in the automobile entities in this zone are passed by (i.e., articulation of the external horizon of objects, their relations). Interconnection is not merely spatial juxtaposition, and juxtaposition is the only experienced articulation from the shallow view of scenery.

Secondary Zones of Operation and a Dangerous Tendency

Schutz elucidates a structural distinction between the primary zone of operation (Mead's manipulatory area), which is the province of unmediated action and the secondary zone of operation, which presents a mediation of action and experience. Obviously, driving an automobile relates to a secondary zone of operation, the road, and as such presents "a qualitative leap in the range of experience and an enlargement of the zone of operation."[39] The path of the automobile on the road is the mediated action of the driver. Work is transferred from the primary unmediated zone to the secondary mediated zone of operation by way of the operating machinery. The work of the hands and feet coordinated to visual perception results in the traversal of space from the immobile seated position. Space traversal in this manner truncates the time for travel. Much more distance can be covered in much less time than ambulation with much less expenditure of energy. Even when travel is slowed the physical energy expended is minimal.

Entire populations in the division of single individuals or very small groups have access to this secondary zone of operation. Any mediation that allows for the transfer of action in a primary zone to the transfer of action in a secondary zone must be carefully scrutinized, for the environmental impact can be disassociated. The tendency is to associate the ease of the work in the primary environment with the effect in the secondary zone in a way that characterizes the effect on the basis of manipulative activity. One reason for this is the mystification of how the technology "works." This is why the throwing of a switch for the release of an atomic bomb is a scary situation. Imagine the ability to liquidate thousands of people with a finger motion. Or, less dramatically, the ease in the work of spraying crops with pesticides by simple controls in the primary zone of an airplane cockpit that results in quite disproportionate effects in the secondary zone of operation. The ease of the manipulation and its specific immediate effectiveness has the potential to trivialize the mediated effect, which is a tendency that is projected unless destructive ramifications are obvious or discovered (as with the case of crop dusting). The tendency is to associate the ease of auto-transport (the ease of operation and its immediate effectiveness in space-traversal) with the mediated effect in the secondary zone, which here concerns the material conditions for such travel. So, auto-mobility projects the quality of ease onto the creation of the web of paved roads across the landscape. The supporting material structuring of space for auto-transport becomes confounded with the immediate ease of auto-mobility, which is a dangerous aspect of up-rootedness. In the language of the geographical models of E. Kutter, the quality of the activity or behavioral system is superimposed on the material system.[40] The paradigm of domination superimposes the activity system onto the material system, and the dangerous mistake is to confound the value-qualities of the activity system with the value-qualities of the material system, which must be kept distinct if concerns of the environment are to be recognized.

Pre-Positional Dwelling

Interconnection, which is more than the recognition of juxtaposition, involves forms of dwelling that mediate between residing and journeying. The prepositions—around, alongside, with, between, inside, and outside—articulate concrete lived-body pre-positional interfacings with circumscribed placial-forms in the zone of actual reach, especially built forms.[41] These interconnecting forms are relational features potentially thematic for the transition from residing to journeying and vice versa. These pre-positions are paramount for the familiarization of the interconnected meanings of placial-features. The lived-body must directly experience these pre-positions in order to experience an authentic dwelling, a lived-connection to place.[42]

Auto-mobility mediates these pre-positional forms, but only in terms of the roadway. The automobile is between two trucks, alongside a gold Mercedes, on the inner loop of the beltway. It is an empty non-lived objective category to say that the automobile is traveling alongside a farm or around the city, for this use of these prepositions does not denote experienced pre-positions of the lived-body precisely by what has been said about partitioning and scenery. The transitional interconnections on the roadway have to do with jockeying for lanes, managing traffic signals, selecting routes, etc. Interconnection is only experienced according to the context of the road. The counter-places of non-roadway are experienced as a series of juxtaposed sites. This is another aspect of the uprootedness of the auto-route. The on-going interconnection of the two forms of dwelling, residing and journeying, becomes severed, which results in the devaluation of both. Through an overdependence on auto-mobility, the transitional forms of orientation are deficient. This results in the deprecation (uprootedness) of residing and journeying, for the transition from one to the other through pre-positions is alienated by the auto-mobile de-contextualization. It is more proper to say that the suburbanite lives in a single family home, but not in a neighborhood, and she dwells in neither. She has likely never set foot in the neighboring environs.[43]

Incorporation: Lived-Auto-Body

As long as the observed road does not present difficulties, pre-predicative habitudes form the basis for driving an automobile. When a difficulty arises, then a greater concern elicits the need for conscious judgment. In an immediate emergency, the lived-body acts intentionally and it is able to do so through its direct relation to the operating controls, e.g., brakes or steering. These experiences exhibit how the lived-body incorporates the automobile as a moment of its intentionality. Thus, the lived-body extends its pre-predicative experiences to the auto-body in relation to its structured environment. The environing engagement of the lived-body becomes lived-auto-mobility, which is a fundamental modification of the meaning of pre-predicative intentional experience.

A pounding object mediates between the hand and the pounded object. The hand on its own would not be able to accomplish the work and also would do physical harm to itself in the attempt. The pounding object is not merely an object-thing rather it is an object taken up into the body schema as a moment of its engagement with the world. Obviously something is gained through this mediation, but just as important and usually forgotten is that something has been lost. The same mediating tool can be used to accomplish constructive work and can be used by the hoodlum who bashes out the windshields of parked cars. The distancing that is inherent in this mediation is that the hand can produce effects without pain and damage to it; the hand loses its immediate sensitivity to its own limitations. Readily incorporated into the "handy schema" is empowerment and potency through an appropriation that becomes taken for granted and is not circumspectly appreciated. The mediation of auto-mobility involves incorporating the automobile in the body schema. Distance-from-itself is incorporated into the lived-body through any form of mediation. What is lost in auto-mobility? Lost is the appreciation for the limited capacities of the non-mediated lived-body to traverse space. The lived-body is distanced from its ambulatory capacities, which also results in a lack of appreciation for the mobility needs of other creatures. Just as hoodlums can smash things through the mediation of pounding objects based on the lived-body's distance from the unmediated capacities of the hand, a culture can appropriate the natural world for the mediation of space traversal based on the lived-body's distance from the values of non-mediated space traversal.

Kinesthesia and Locomotion

When walking, the nature of the environment determines the level and nature of energy that one must expend. Upgrades put an extra strain on the leg muscles and respiratory system. Downgrades put a strain on the knees. Bumpy or slippery terrain means that one must pay attention to footing. For high grass the gait must be modified. The lived-body feels and adjusts to the quality of the terrain and its demands. When walking on the edge of a field, the field is measured not arithmetically or geometrically but by the quality of the walk, which is not merely a question of distance. The uphill path is qualitatively assessed by the energy that is exerted. The path engenders its qualitative meaning in the direct relation to it, that is, what the path means for the ambulation. The dialectical relationship between kinesthesia and locomotion is how the lived-body measures its capacities against the demands of the geographic quality of its environment. Bundling-up, planning for provisions of refreshment, and wearing proper shoes are a few examples of taking heed of this relationship. The lived-body is oriented to its world according to its capacities. Ambulation necessarily pays respect to this orientation.

In driving an automobile the expenditure of energy is transferred to the automobile. Going up a hill is to feel slightly more pressure against the right foot as it presses against the spring of the accelerator pedal. The hill that would have exhausted me had I been on foot is easily surmounted. The leveling of energy in auto-traversal leads to a lack of appreciation for terrain. Automobile advertisements on the television display vehicles overcoming every environmental obstacle. The lived-body no longer needs to be circumspectful in its capacity for traversing. The qualities of terrain can be disregarded and in its place are the conditions of the road, which are constituted by speed limit, lanes, and traffic patterns. Paying heed to capacities has more to do with the automobile, e.g., gassing up and checking the washer fluid for the windshield. The capacities of the lived-body are oriented to driving, which takes into consideration the ability to stay alert and fatigue from sitting still. The lived-body's kinesthesia and its mediated locomotion no longer form an integral measure of the life-world in relation to the lived-body's immediate capacities for traversal. The relationship of geography to the immediate measure of body's capacities becomes severed. Energy expended by the lived-body is a product of resistance. But resistance is experienced as the turning of the steering wheel or the pressure of the foot on the brake. So, resistance, which is the "kernel" of reality that can only be experienced in the manipulatory area, is delimited and regulated by the operating conditions of the automobile. This form of rootedness, the direct measuring by the lived-body in the kinesthetic/ambulatory dialectic, is circumvented and disregarded through the over dependence on auto-mobility. It is not that the energy capacity of the lived-body is not measured in work-form of operating the automobile, that measurement, resistance in the manipulatory area, holds. The manipulatory resistance, which involves an immobile sitting posture, is transformed into mobility. What is lost, however, is an aspect of rootedness based on ambulation, which weds us to a given journey through the efforts that we must put into it. In my personal experiences of this, I can compare my different recollections of walking to the primary school that I attended and riding the bus to the secondary school I attended. The walk to the primary school is a part of me— being in the environs still resonates vividly as ghost gestures in my motor imagery. The "resistance" in the mediated traversal through which the bus made its way is only vague visual images, the lifeless quality of scenery, although I still ghost gesture the bumpiness of the ride.

Leveling the Value of the Between

When walking to a destination, the character of the between is quite important. The between must also be reckoned as a major component of the project. One learns the between walking along toward the destination. The sensory contents that fill the eyes and other sense organs are forever changing and provide a natural motivation and interest that is wedded to kinesthetic process. Today, people do not walk. For one thing the television substitutes by providing visually and auditory contents that simulates kinesthetic imagery without having to expend bodily energy. In automobile travel, point A is linked to point B. The automobile environment reduces the between to a calculation of time. The between is time in the automobile; it is not an experience of the traversed environments that link the two dwelling places.

This leads to the association of places as atomized destinations. One no longer cares about the quality of the between as a moment of lived-space. The between is something to transcend, for the partitioning of placial zones and the non-expenditure of energy in relation to the terrain makes traversal a simple transformational task. One sits in a special environment and after some time a destination is reached. Suburbanites get their automobile out of the garage that occupies the ground floor of their homes under the bedrooms and drive to the underground parking lot below their place of employment. They no longer need to experience the between as anything other than the interior of their automobile and the paved road. Thus, the actual environments that are passed by are of no concern, for the world is leveled to those atomized places that pose an interest to the motorist. One no longer needs care about those between environments, for one has a way to transcend the experience of them.

The connection of atomized sites by the auto-route modifies drastically the relation to zones of attainable reach. Because the lived-body's energy capacity in terms of the geographical terrain does not have to be taken into account, the connection of the between to the destination is trivialized. The road to . . . is now the roadway for the automobile, which levels the meaning of the between. Measured in terms of distance and time on the road, the significance of attainment is quantitatively assessed. Quality is reduced to the type of road, e.g., superhighway, single lane road.

Ranging and the Establishment of Region

By depending on the route-scape there is an uprooted sense of geographic transitions and boundaries. To be rooted to place requires a sense of region. By experiencing region, one gathers-in places and interconnects them. One must range to constitute region and this concerns the establishment of the experience of the far sphere. Even though region is usually treated as an objective category, e.g., bio-region, eco-region, and geo-region, region must be treated as a structure of implacement, otherwise it remains a reified abstraction.[44] Unless region is to be reduced to a road mapping, which is just what happens in the dependence upon auto-mobility, the far range must be explored on foot. One ranges in a region by a form of visual perception called scoping. Scoping requires a gaze that continues outward to the horizon. One is less concerned with the zone of manipulation and concentrates on connecting the zone of actual reach within the horizon and also with its relation to zones of potential reach. In this way one gets to know neighborhoods and how they are interdependent in their placial relations. Ranging is bringing to intuitive evidence the interconnection of places; separate environs become united in an act that achieves a higher level synthesis. Those who depend on automobiles to get from point A to point B may not have ever scoped their own neighborhood. Placiality is dimmed to specific meaningful spots connected by the roads that provide a way to disregard the interconnection of places. It might be thought that the speed of the automobile would allow for a better accomplishment of ranging, but the places that are connected in this fashion are to great degree emptily united. So, the world consists of a web of common route-scapes, that is, a public access for one's private interests. The "communities-in-between" are passed by and thus community is only a name. Placial transcendence complements the privatization of place traversal, which results in a communal vacuum, being-without-relational-meaning. The geographical constitution of communalization requires the perceptual act of scoping, which is concretized through ranging, a project of ambulation.

The Social Relationship of Auto-Transport

What are the social relationships, if any, that are formed between automobile drivers? Each automobile driver has her own agenda. The fact that other particular automobiles are being driven in one's same environs is fortuitous. They simply happen to be there in that vicinity at the same time that you are. Even as the drivers follow the restrictions of traffic laws, there is great variability in the drivers' intentions. There is very little possibility for collaborative effort; there is great room for individual opportunity. The road is conceived in terms of one's own projects, and the intentions of others' as indicated by the "actions" of their surrogate lived-bodies, their automobiles, are measured against one's own project. This one is driving too fast; this one is driving too slowly; this one just cut me off; etc. There is very little social interaction while driving. The relation consists of social observations and individual adjustments of each of the drivers from the partitioned-environments-on-wheels. The social observation consists in merely determining the relation of other automobilists' intentions to one's own. Most of the other automobiles remain pre-predicatively perceived unless an automobile poses an obstacle to one's intentions. Again, one's own intentions take precedence, because they are the only one's of which one is responsible and which have any meaning beyond a few moments. Reference to others usually takes the form of identifying the automobile, e.g., the blue Chevy is recklessly changing lanes. Thus, in terms of journeying, social relationships remain quite anonymous. Since most journeying is accomplished by automobile, camaraderie of the road has been virtually eliminated. What is shared is the anonymous, atomized partitioning of driving on the route-scape.[45]

These limited social relations occupy much of our daily lives. How often do we walk alongside our fellow citizens and share the walk. We do so rarely and when we do we hardly share it like it once was shared. The reason for this is when we do walk we usually are walking amidst strangers. In city life before automobiles, walks would be shared with people of whom you become familiar, due to the habits of daily life. But now when we drive somewhere and then walk, we are placed alongside those others merely by chance. The likelihood that we walk together again at the site most of the time is highly unlikely.

Conclusion

Auto-mobility offers the opportunity to traverse placial sectors in a manner that truncates time. It transfers most of the energy to the machine such that the human energy output is easily managed. It provides a comfortable private environment that shields one from the natural elements. It creates a form of life that "benefits" from these features. Auto-mobility enables people to go to places that they would never experience otherwise. However, from the standpoint of our thesis, these positive attributes are outweighed by the negative consequences of the overdependence on auto-mobility and the structuring of lived-space around the parameter of an automobile culture. The mediation of auto-mobility for the lived-body's fundamental relation to its environing world has been unexamined hitherto this chapter and the task has been to uncover the structures of this mediation. The structuring of placial qualities around the use of the automobile has led to the devaluing of the fundamental ways that we are oriented to the environment. The structuring of environments that result from a progressive deterioration of our rooted forms of placial-being also leads to the unrecognized disregard for a rooted orientation to place-scape. For the more uprootedness is incorporated into our everyday forms of life, the more we are unable to experience what rootedness is like and thus become incapable in such a state to value a rooted-placial-being. Uprootedness is taken for granted in our relative-natural world-view in a way that the solutions to environmental problems do not enter the materially conditioned form of our understanding, for the lived-body has lost the pre-predicative experience of rootedness, which is the pre-condition for a rooted existential understanding. The voices of dissent, including the pre-automobile voice of those like Thoreau, come from people who have lived-body experiences to which the average encultured person cannot relate. So their voices sound radical and far-fetched. But the fascination with being uprooted must now more than ever be called into question, because environmentally the earth can no longer support it.

Notes

1. The word, 'implacement,' and its definition have their source in the writings of Edward S. Casey. Casey's thesis that western culture has been dominated by temporocentrism at the expense of place is the general thesis that founds the research presented here. See Edward S. Casey, *Getting Back Into Place* (Bloomington: Indiana University Press, 1993).

2. Being-with and being-in are, according to Heidegger, *existentiale* of Dasein. It is important to realize that the relation with others and the relation to the worldly context are primordial structures of one's own Being. It is a serious error to begin with the transcendental monad as the fundamental ground for existence, even if such a structure is arguably the ground for knowing. Our existence is being-with and being-in, and so the use of such equipment as the automobile involves a modification of worldhood. Modification is to be understood not in the sense of objective quantifiable measurements (an analysis based on the objectivity of the world is inadequate, yet helpful), but because worldhood is a constituent of our own Being. See Martin Heidegger, *Being and Time,* trans. by John Macquarrie and Edward Robinson (New York: Harper and Row, 1962).

3. Relative-natural world-view "is the sedimented group experience that has passed the test and which does not need to be examined by individuals as regards its validity." See Alfred Schutz and Thomas Luckmann, *The Structures of the Life-World,* trans. Richard M. Zaner and H. Tristram Engelhardt Jr. (Evanston, Ill.: Northwestern University Press, 1973), 8.

4. Bracketing is a technique employed by phenomenologists that neutralizes belief in the reality of the given phenomenon such that only the contents of the experience are examined and described. In this study, I rely on structures concerning the lived-body that have been already described by other phenomenologists. Also, admittedly, the phenomenological description is geared to uncover aspects that support the critical thesis. Nevertheless, bracketing opens the experience of auto-mobility to phenomenological description.

5. The everyday and theoretical standpoints are aspects of the natural attitude. In the natural attitude, we remain object-focussed in a way that remains oblivious to the constituting processes that make possible the experience of the object. Whether through the lived-body or acts of consciousness, the experience of objects is an achievement of meaning bestowal.

6. The Marxist theory of material base-superstructure can be interpreted too narrowly, leading to the questionable reduction of economism. Some thinkers, e.g., Karl Mannheim's sociology of knowledge, have attempted to broaden the historical matrix. It is also arguable that the relation between thought and material may be dialectical, rather than a reduction to one or the other. Regardless of these debates, it was not until Merleau-Ponty that the importance of the lived-body became uncovered. Since the writings of Merleau-Ponty, there has been much written on sociocultural aspects of the lived-body. Casey advances to new levels through his work on implacement. This chapter presents a sociocultural critical analysis that is an application of the structures of implacement as well as other structures pertaining to the lived-body. Our modest point is that experiential modifications of the lived-body structures (e.g., structures of implacement) are an important aspect of ascertaining the *Weltanschauung* of a society or epoch.

7. See Peter L. Berger and Thomas Luckmann, *The Social Construction of Reality* (New York: Anchor, 1966).

8. The word, 'supermodernity,' means the values of modernity in excess, that is, the overabundance of objectivated meanings. Objectivated meanings are subjective activities that have become reified in objective culture. For a discussion of supermodernity in its

relation to implacement see, Marc Augé, *Non-Places: Introduction to an Anthropology of Supermodernity*, trans. John Howe (London: Verso, 1995).

9. Holmes Rolston III, "Challenges in Environmental Ethics," in *Environmental Philosophy*, ed. Michael E. Zimmerman (Upper Saddle River, N.J.: Prentice Hall, 1993), 142.

10. Rolston, "Challenges," 144.

11. I employ the word, 'teleonomic,' rather than, 'teleology,' because teleology implies a pre-encoded script. Some environmental philosophers too hastily have tried to argue for a teleological nature in order to reintroduce value as inherent to the system. One can avoid the metaphysics of the script through viewing nature as a dynamic system by which teleonomic structures are emergent. Teleonomic structures exhibit meaningful tendencies, yet the goals of these structures have not been prescribed in earlier or simpler levels of organization.

12. Laurie Spurling, *Phenomenology and the Social World* (London: Routledge & Kegan Paul, 1977), 116-17.

13. The pollution of automobile use is well documented. My chapter centers on the issue of geographical quality in relation to the quantification of expansion. See Kenneth P. Cantor, "Warning: The Automobile is Dangerous to Earth, Air, Fire, Water, Mind and Body," in *The Environmental Handbook*, ed. Garret DeBell (New York: Ballantine, 1970), 197-213. "The automobile and the American public are locked in a life and death struggle. The car is robbing the American people of their land, air, minds, and their very lives. It is becoming increasingly clear that solution of the transportation-automobile is of high priority if we are to come to terms with the environment, and with ourselves," 197-98.

14. See Julia Meaton and David Morrice, "The Ethics and Politics of Private Automobile Use," in *Environmental Ethics* 18, no. 1 (spring 1996): 39-54. After showing that automobile use involves other-regarding and self-regarding harm, the authors conclude: "Thus, a total ban on private automobile use is justifiable" 50.

15. See Anne and Paul Ehrlich, *Earth* (New York: Franklin Watts, 1987), 153.

16. Aldo Leopold, *A Sand County Almanac: And Sketches Here and There* (Oxford: Oxford University Press, 1977), 216.

17. J. Baird Callicott, "The Conceptual Foundations of the Land Ethic," in *Environmental Philosophy*, ed. Michael E. Zimmerman (Upper Saddle River, N.J.: Prentice Hall, 1993), 114.

18. See Norman Meyers, "The Extinction Spasm Impending: Synergisms at Work," *Conservation Biology* I (1987), 14-21.

19. Michael Soulé, "Benign Neglect: A Model of Faunal Collapse in the Game Reserves of East Africa," *Biological Conservation* 15 (1979), 259-70.

20. Edward Grumbine, "Ecosystem Management for Native Diversity," 46.

21. This quote is reported by George Sessions, "Ecosystems, Wilderness, and Global Ecosystem Protection," in Zimmerman's, *Environmental Philosophy*, 253.

22. Thomas Fleischner, "Keeping it Wild: Toward a Deeper Wilderness Management," in *Forever Wild: Conserving the Greater North Cascades Ecosystem* (Bellingham, Wash.: Mountain Hemlock Press, 1988), 79.

23. "In the early years of motoring, hardly anyone understood the automobile's potential for devastation—not just of the landscape, or the air, but of culture in general. It was assumed that cars would merely serve as wonderfully useful accessories in the human habitat as it then was, that they would make the city a better place, and cure all the troubles of rural life, without altering the arrangement of things in either place." James Howard Kunstler, *The Geography of Nowhere* (New York: Simon & Schuster, 1993), 86.

24. Again see Kunstler, *The Geography of Nowhere*. "America has now squandered its national wealth erecting a human habitat that, in all likelihood, will not be usable very much longer, and there are few unspoiled places left to retreat to in the nation's habitable reaches. Aside from its enormous social costs, which we have largely ignored, the whole system of suburban sprawl is too expensive to operate, too costly to maintain, and a threat to the ecology of living things," 114.

25. Augé, *Non-Places,* 77-79.

26. Gary Snyder, "The Place, the Region, and the Commons," in *Environmental Philosophy,* ed. Michael E. Zimmerman (Upper Saddle River, N.J.: Prentice-Hall, 1993), 449.

27. John Clark, "Political Ecology," in *Environmental Philosophy,* 356.

28. Subsequent discussion concerning the various environmental sectors as related to the lived-body is based on the work of Schutz and Luckmann and Mead. See, Alfred Schutz and Thomas Luckmann, *The Structures of the Life-World* (Evanston, Ill.: Northwestern University Press 1973), 41-52. See, George Herbert Mead, *The Philosophy of the Act* (Chicago: University of Chicago Press, 1938), 103-6, 196-97.

29. For the classic treatment of this structure of the lived-body, see, Erwin W. Straus, *Phenomenological Psychology* (New York: Basic, 1966), 137-65.

30. See Maurice Merleau-Ponty, *Phenomenology of Perception,* trans. Colin Smith (London: Routledge & Kegan Paul, 1962), 243-54.

31. See Casey, *Getting Back Into Place,* 55-56.

32. See Kunstler, *The Geography of Nowhere,* "The width and curb ratios were set in stone by traffic engineers who wanted to create streets *so* ultrasafe (for motorists) that any moron could drive them without wrecking his car. This is a good example of overspecialization. The traffic engineer is not concerned about the pedestrians. His mission is to make sure that wheeled vehicles are happy. What he deems to be ultrasafe for drivers can be dangerous for pedestrians who share the street with cars," 115.

33. Casey, *Getting Back Into Place,* 57-58.

34. See Martin Heidegger, "How the Wordly Character of the Environment Announces itself in Entities Within-the-world," in *Being and Time,* 102-7. In terms of Heidegger's concepts, scenery is present-at-hand because its possibility for readiness-to-hand has withdrawn. This relation is fixed in the mediation of auto-mobility, for scenery cannot be converted as long as one remains in the car.

35. Mead, *Act,* 104.

36. Mead, *Act,* 105.

37. Mead, *Act,* 190.

38. Mead, *Act,* 191.

39. Schutz and Luckmann, *The Structures of the Life-World,* 44.

40. See E. Kutter, "A Model for Individual Travel Behavior," in *Urban Studies* 10, 238-58.

41. Casey, *Getting Back Into Place,* 122.

42. See Kunstler, *The Geography of Nowhere*. "No thought has gone into the relationships between things—the buildings to each other, the buildings to the street, the pedestrians to the buildings," 138. The reason for this is that since we live in an automobile-centered culture, we have constructed a geography that has not considered the importance of pre-positionality, which can only be realized through ambulation. Kunstler states that the cost "has been the sacrifice of a sense of place: the idea that people and things exist in some sort of continuity, that we belong to the world physically and chronologically, and that we know where we are," 118.

43. Kunstler, *The Geography of Nowhere*, "A suburbanite could stand on her front lawn for three hours on a weekday and never have a chance for conversation," 119. Suburbanites do not walk in their neighborhoods.

44. See Casey, *Getting Back Into Place,* 60-61.

45. Kunstler, *The Geography of Nowhere.* "The extreme separation and dispersion of components that use to add up to a compact town, where everything was within a ten-minute walk, has left us with a public realm that is composed mainly of roads. And the only way to be in that public realm is to be in a car, often alone," 118-19.

Chapter 7

Having a Need to Act

John A. Scott

Speaking and Dwelling

Heidegger sees language as the house of being where we dwell awaiting the divinities and an absent good, while we lovingly cherish, protect, preserve, and care for the world. Drawing insight from Plato and others, Aristotle sees language as an architectural skill acquired through living well[1] and applied in building the changing places we need to wander within being: places like bodies, dwellings, landscapes, worlds, perhaps even internets. His *Politics* and *Ethics* profile those whose living well is achieved with language (*meta logou*). In this speculative study I consider whether Aristotle's recommended deployment of language offers hope for more satisfactory transformations in our urban and suburban landscapes than Heidegger's. The question is practical and urgent, even though it requires theoretical attention to make a start on its resolution. Hope for recovery of the landscape is vanishing, and with it any justified or good reason to act in its interest, or ours.

Heidegger's *Building Dwelling Thinking* opens by asking, What is it to dwell? How does building belong to dwelling? He answers that a human being is located in a specified place, earth, where death defines the action: "To be a human being means to be on earth as a mortal. It means to dwell . . . to cherish and protect, to preserve and care for."[2] He warns that the preservational character of placing-dwelling is not usually recognized, however. This aspect is concealed from us by language, which he says retracts the real meaning; so that confusion develops between building as production or construction and dwelling as an act. But language's "primal call does not . . . become incapable of speech; it merely falls silent." The problem is, "Man . . . fails to heed this silence."[3] Thus, human beings tend to see themselves as producing buildings rather than dwelling in places that they preserve through their act of living-there. Like Aristotle, Heidegger defines living things in terms of self-presence, as internally placing places.[4] Dwelling, as preserving, saves the earth not only by snatching it from danger, but also "setting it free into its own presencing." Heidegger describes presencing as an experience of the absence of a transcendent perpetually withdrawn good: "Mortals . . . wait for intimations of [the divinities'] coming, and do not mistake the signs of their absence. . . . They wait for the weal that has been withdrawn." Thus, mortals cultivate a good death as initiation into their transcendent nature. But, Heidegger assures us: "blindly staring toward the end" does not "mean to darken dwelling." Rather, staring toward the end preserves things to that end. "[M]ortals nurse and nurture the things that grow."

In language and other expressive arts, Heidegger says, mortals "construct things that do not grow." Such a built thing like a "bridge . . . *gathers* the earth as landscape . . . [is a] gathering or assembly . . . *that is itself a location*" which, with other locations, provides to spaces their being.[5] Heidegger sees us transforming landscapes and constructing things as an exercise of self-location not unlike a navigational process. By using things that do not grow, mortals place themselves in relation to the natural, growing world. "The relationship between man and space is . . . dwelling, strictly thought and spoken."[6] But this locating, navigational impulse appears not to sustain itself in Heidegger as firmly as it does for Socrates, Plato, and Aristotle. Heidegger generally favors more agricultural metaphors suited to those searching through clearings for hidden seeds and roots. The *"real plight of dwelling,"* he claims, lies in mortals' perennial failure to recover from its concealment in language the true meaning of dwelling. This he defines as active anticipation of the transcendent through the practice of good death. For Heidegger, language provides a place where mortals eternally search for meaning as dwellers. They search in language to recover a dwelling-defining presence concealed and withdrawn by language itself. For Heidegger mortals must "listen once more to what language says to us. . . . If we give thought . . . we obtain a clue."[7] Heidegger's strategy for dwelling in the house of language is to await intimations that will disclose what needs cherishing, caring, and preserving. His mortals speak so as to give thought to, and disclose or uncover, a concealed clue, which is brought to presence through language. Presence is critical. Heidegger has been our conversation partner[8] for the last half of the twentieth-century, and has established an influential discourse. Does Heidegger see our dwellings, like Black Forest farms, where mortals cultivate, preserve, and care for the world by landscaping it as a graveyard while they wait for a presence?

Aristotle attempts a phenomenology of the unities that natural things[9] appear to need if they are to be spoken about, and so inform our acts,[10] at all. Aristotle uses vivid biological language to express his sense of presencing when he says that thought grows to be one nature with the known object.[11] I shall argue that Aristotle, drawing on those closest to him philosophically, saw presence as accommodated in a mediated and reflective way through a mechanism, not of production and use, but of acts, based on debt and various related kinds of possession, which make it possible not just to die well, but to live well. For Aristotle as for Heidegger, mortals nurse and nurture the things that grow. We love. But for Aristotle the end that sustains loving dwellers is attained not through waiting for what is absent but through recollection of acts that are thereby made naturally, reflectively, present. Properly structured and tested recollection discloses acts in their shaping the architecture of the natural and human dwelling places that accommodate, express, and embody those acts.

Natural Economy—Debt and its Discharge

Plato too explored the dynamics of presence and absence, being and change; but was not content to wait for their accommodation. Debt was a much better investment strategy, especially a generative,[12] erotic kind of debt. At the beginning of the *Republic*, Cephalus claims that the ability to repay debts is what integrates him as a person. Debt has allowed him a fleeting acquisition of what he needs to have in order to be the human being he is. Cephalus' ability to repay the debt that sustains him depends upon his generating the resources needed to make that repayment. So the *Republic* goes on to show that the trick is to recollect precisely what was borrowed so as to be in a position to do what is needed for its repayment: that is, to do what is just. Plato designs the dialectic to facilitate recollection of those borrowed goods which, as borrowed, are neither entirely present nor entirely absent to the borrower/dweller. Recollection makes things present in a mediated way, through association. In the *Phaedo*[13] Socrates describes how learning works through recollection. He notes how the sight of Simmias often reminds one of his friend Cebes. Recollection makes learning possible because its associative action places separated, distinct elements within integrated fields.[14] It can shape a dwelling, or a republic, to integrate what is different in—and between—them. So Simmias and Socrates are not just physically proximate and present to one another. They may also be effectively integrated by a less obvious presence in the recollected Cebes.[15] Things Simmias and Socrates may do or make might be shaped and informed in various ways by Cebes' mediating, recollected, presence.

Architecture[16] affords a way to see recollection and its debt-based possibilities. Acts define and integrate architectural projects by differentiating the systems involved. A kitchen differs from a bedroom because of the different act each accommodates. And a kitchen is well integrated as a kitchen insofar it is open to change, adapting to needs as they arise. A place accommodates itself to its act;[17] and an act shapes, and continuously reshapes, its place. What architects struggle to discern is: which acts? How are they changing? How complete is the mutually dynamic fit of act and place? For an architect, whatever integrates a kitchen is disclosed in her recollection of the act to be done there. That act is good if it makes the kitchen good. The final act, the *telos* as Aristotle called it, is not so much what something is good for as it is what is good for the naturally existing subject.[18] But good needs measuring if it is to mean anything. And this means an architect must not only identify the act, but must also somehow calculate its relative value by determining how that recollected act integrates its place better than—or in some balance with—other acts that might seem to do so. Is the kitchen a key market feature that sells a house perceived primarily as a commodity? Or is the kitchen a food preparation area . . . or an entertaining area . . . or some as yet unnamed and poorly understood act embracing entertainment, cooking, and other elements? In this comparative evaluation, an architect selectively calculates which of the recollected acts-to-be-done are good, and so makes them present, allowing them to shape the place well.

Heidegger sees goods as withdrawn, and absent. But Aristotle crafts a modest observational and dialectical method for disclosing what he sees as telic, integrating, formative causes and so making them present in the natural and political worlds. Who is right? Have the divinities withdrawn, leaving us to await the end, the *eschatos*, with whatever skills of preservation we can muster? Or does *telos* possibly play some role? Do methodologically structured value judgments make present what seems to be absent?

Consensus or Measured Judgment?

David Glidden reviews what he calls a "rough-and-ready" kind of knowing, which he sees already hinted at in Aristotle's preference for integrated experience (*epagoge*), and in the use of tentative assumptions (*hypolepseis*). Some Stoics and Epicureans saw this as how we navigate through life as we cross common ground (*metabasis tou homooiou*). Such practice allows for "a way of looking and living that employed concepts, notions, forms of recognition which . . . remained sufficiently inchoate to license living without dogma." He contrasts this ancient tradition with what he sees as a cruelty prevalent in later philosophic traditions' "disdain for particulars" and over-fondness "of generality." He points to how "Heidegger's hands-on ontology . . . proved to be no respecter of persons . . . (especially Jews.)"[19] When "situating community" is at stake, Glidden encourages us to rely, as these ancients did, more on "field reports of places fleshed out in sufficient detail to make such localities come imaginatively, instructively alive."

But Glidden does not elaborate on how the choices are to be made by which we navigate across common ground. Glidden himself is obviously concerned with this issue, as his careful telling of specific stories reveals. He relies on story as the basis for consensus, and has deep faith in consensus to shape values and structure choices.[20] He concludes his study[21] by acknowledging the widely held suspicion that "the notion of a good community can be highly prejudicial locally. . . . So, modern cynics ask, what wisdom can be found in local commonplace consensus?" Roger Paden also finds a "structure of values internal to planning" at work in traditions of renaissance utopianism.[22] But he shares Glidden's view that: "If there are values internal to . . . planning then they should guide its practice and shape its institutions . . . [and] set the standards for evaluating work in the field. . . . Today, there is a widely shared belief that urban planning has no internal values." Gliddens' own response to value-neutral attitudes in community planning is to repeat his coura-geous, and modest expression of faith that "common sense is sufficiently aligned with shared experience to be at least locally reliable."[23]

But core figures in the traditions to which both Glidden and Paden appeal offer a stronger response to those who fear a good community. In what follows, I shall attempt a speculative reconstruction of that stronger response. It is also a response to Heidegger's quietism, which in my view threatens to numb our ability to respond to human, environmental, economic dangers threatening the world. But this recon-struction will take a bit of patient plodding through some old texts.

Constructing a Common Place

Plato and Aristotle try to accommodate the good.[24] At the opening of the *Republic* Cephalus identifies what gives him any integrity he appears to have as his ability to "pay my debts." He is what he is insofar as he lacks and therefore needs, and acts-as-though-he-has, and so puts himself in debt for whatever completeness or goodness he appears to have. Cephalus sets the stage for Plato's dialectic, a lens designed to explore how naturally existing things, including human beings, acquire and maintain the properties they need in order to be what they are. Neediness is the demand-side economic engine that builds the republic. Dialectic is designed to reveal how these naturally constituting need-based debts are negotiated and paid by carefully balancing needs against capabilities through divisions of labor. But we discover[25] that the republic that grows out of need is not complete and stable. It turns out to be a cruel illusion,[26] like those that justify Glidden's apprehensions about good communities. Socrates finds the integrity of the republic threatened from within by the destabilizing luxury produced by those technologists and artists whose limitless[27] skills generated the republic in the first place. Craftspeople, driven by their technological visions of the inexhaustible, unlimited[28] character of good, are seduced into unceasing improvement and progress while artists are besotted[29] by its unfathomable beauty. But unlimited pursuit of infinite beauty and inexhaustible technological progress impedes the state's capacity to measure and evaluate the integrating and sustaining acts needed for its survival. The state has finite, urgent, local needs justifying and sustaining its existence. It must be possible to limit these foundational artistic and technological forces, Plato argues, without destroying or impairing their original and continuing creative energy. There must be some measuring; otherwise a state, or any naturally existing thing, will not sustain its own generation.

So, in order to secure its survival and complete its own integration in the face of this destabilizing internal threat to its survival, Plato's state borrows what it does not have in its own right. The state accommodates itself in the place[30] provided in between the different, distinct, and separated labors of its own foundational ele-ments, its needy citizens. The state occupies and secures the place left by the divisions of their labors. It integrates itself by ensuring that the separations, the divisions, are maintained as generatively open. (We see such a place, the *chora,* more fully explored in Plato's study of space and time, the *Timaeus*, which he explicitly sets as the *Republic*'s dramatic sequel.)

The state secures its own accommodation—its place, its dwelling—by placing some limits on technologists and artists in their pursuit of the limitlessly beautiful and infinitely seductive good. The state measures out what technologists and artists themselves must not limit or measure since they must perform their necessary, foundationally generative, and creative work. The state has a place. It is to exercise justice both as a self-protection, and to protect the technologists and artists themselves against their devouring their own offspring, the state and its needy citizens, in wild pursuit of the beautifully, infinitely better that blinds us to our need to measure the good.

Both Plato and Aristotle take very seriously this need for justification. Both see its achievement in the measurement of magnitude, as we shall see Socrates suggest in a moment when he describes his own "makeshift" approach. Plato and Aristotle see mortals as needing to take the risk of measuring things.[31] Protagoras made the mistake of saying that "Man *is* the measure of all things." But neither Socrates not Plato nor Aristotle is so corrupted by anthropocentrism. They recognize Heidegger's central truth about humans: they are mortals. Humans are at risk. Humans live well by taking the risk of measuring. But mortals are not the standard of measure: good is the standard, wherever that may turn out to be in practice. Plato and Aristotle base their differing strategies for treating the cancer of infinite beauty and limitless technical progress by having mortals take the risk, and responsibility, for measuring against the standard of good. They each design strategies based on their analyses of causation and change as they observe it in nature's teleological architecture. At a critical moment in the *Pheado*, when initially promising attempts to establish the soul's immortality have foundered on failure to resolve the problem of causation, Socrates warns against misunderstanding what argumentation does and against the danger of giving up altogether on its utility.[32] He then offers an account of the "makeshift approach" that underlies Plato's, and Aristotle's, strategies for argument.

> I have worked out my own makeshift approach to the problem of causation. . . . When I was worn out with my physical investigations, it occurred to me that I must be on my guard against the same sort of risk which people run when they watch and study an eclipse of the sun; they really do sometimes injure their eyes, unless they study its reflection in water or some other medium. I conceived of something like this happening to myself, and I was afraid that by observing objects with my eyes and trying to comprehend them with each of my other senses I might blind my soul altogether. So I decided that I must have recourse to theories (*logous*) and use them in trying to discover the truth about things . . . in every case I first lay down the theory which I judge to be soundest, and then whatever seems to agree with it—with regard either to causes or to anything else I assume to be true, and whatever does not I assume not to be true . . . what I mean is this, and there is nothing new about it. I have always said it; in fact I have never stopped saying it, especially in the earlier part of this discussion. I am going

to try to explain to you the theory of causation which I have worked out myself. I propose to make a fresh start from among those principles of mine which you know so well—that is, I am assuming the existence of absolute (*auto kath hauto*) beauty and goodness and magnitude and all the rest of them. If you grant my assumption and admit that they exist (*einai tauta*), I hope with their help to explain causation to you, and to find a proof.[33]

Glidden's rough-and-ready kind of knowing echoes Socrates' makeshift approach. But there is a difference. Socrates relies on measuring goods in a way Glidden, and Protagoras, do not. Naturally existing things, like chickens, exhibit regularity and pattern that suggest they are subject to some kind of formative process, as kitchens are. If so, then chickens, like kitchens, may also be accessible by locating their unifying, integrating, differentiating acts. But their acts are not observable. Cephalus shows that such acts are neither fully present nor wholly absent, but inhabit some debt-secured territory between needing and having.[34] If architects find it difficult to recollect, identify, and calculate differentially integrating acts that complete and integrate their own projects, it will be all the more challenging to achieve something similar for naturally existing things that we do not build, like chickens or universes.[35]

In the *Timaeus* we learn what Plato thinks accommodates oneness, completeness, wholeness, limit of measure: it is emptiness.[36] Time and again Socrates says, "I know I know nothing." Nothing, emptiness, is the condition of the receptivity needed to accommodate the whole of anything. To be really in debt, as Cephalus styles it, is to have nothing except the need to have. The *Timaeus* describes such receptivity as possible only where there is a similarly radical, cathartic, generative capacity to pass-it-on . . . to give it up . . . give it back . . . to become empty again. In the *Timaeus* Plato introduces the polished mirroring receptacle or bowl as a model to explain beings in natural space and time, echoing the theme of the sun's reflective presence in the *Republic*. It is this cathartic reflective structure of being-and-knowing that Socrates mimics in his makeshift dialectical approach.[37]

In the *Phaedrus* we meet the charioteer[38] who acts as the articulating focus for the differentially integrated action joining[39] the horses. The charioteer takes-and-gives in the same act. The charioteer adds nothing, and achieves everything. He reflects the horses' motions to each other. If the charioteer adds anything he runs the risk of instant destruction. Using the language of the *Timaeus*, the charioteer is the *chora*,[40]—the receptacle—the time/place that lets the horses each do different things together as an integrated whole. Receiving everything and adding nothing, the charioteer's dynamically vanishing presence accommodates the integrated unity. If we study the makeshift approach Socrates proposes in *Phaedo* with texts like these in mind, we see a rough-and-ready kind of knowing which, like recollection, provides access to nature's architectural workings without being blinded by the sun that dazzles the artists and craftspeople of the *Republic*. Debt structures his approach, and good provides the leverage to secure that debt against its repayment. The *Phaedo* passage shows Socrates, bereft of what he needs, negotiating a loan from his companions. Somewhat like a mathematician asking us to "let there be a line AB" at the start of a theorem,[41] Socrates asks his companions to conclude a contract with him. He asks that they grant the assumption that "absolute beauty and goodness and magnitude . . . exist." In return he offers "to explain causation . . . and to find a proof" of the soul's immortality. But what Socrates asks of his companions turns out to be something different from a speculative mathematician's procedural license to build "a line, AB" so as to get on with a proof. Socrates is quite emphatic. He asks them really to take a risk,[42] and to give some things status in their own judgments—to admit that they exist. He then invokes their recollection. He reminds them that he wants them to take a risk and lend him nothing new. He wants them to share a common place with him in their recollection of an acknowledged shared experience of certain absolutes. By reference to these, he says, he hopes to locate the causes they are trying to find. If he succeeds, he will have paid off the debt. But there are risks, such as being blinded by the sun, or crashing the chariot, or going badly off course in our navigating across common ground.[43]

Socrates is not relying on something like Glidden's common sense consensus. He fears consensus produces dogmas that blind like the sun.[44] Socrates looks, rather, for the critical collaboration he needs in order to do the survey-type measuring and valuing that shapes the places where dwellers dwell.[45] Plato models that place in the *Republic*. He sees the state as founded in a generative exercise of need-based borrowing practiced by those able to see and desire the good and how to craft it, but secured against the excesses of these same appetites by the accommodating *logos,* reason and argument. But Plato is no enemy of genuinely open societies either: just of vulnerable ones that fail, or are afraid, to measure and value. Socrates relies on the common sense and creative capacity of citizens to take the risk to remember, and to participate courageously with others who are also trying to remember what dwelling is. His makeshift approach requires actually *assuming the existence of* certain things. Even Socrates is concerned about the risks posed to those who assume the existence of things like "absolute beauty and goodness and magnitude." To assume the existence of something entails not just ceasing to "withhold assent,"[46] but actually accommodating it in practice and taking the associated risks. If we really assume, for instance, that $2 + 2 = 5$, then we have to take the very acute risk of dwelling in dwellings designed according to that kind of mathematics. Our dwellings may fall down. That is the commitment, courageous or foolhardy, that Socrates asks of his companions, and for which he is willing to go into debt to them. So what is the goodness he asks them to assume?

Socrates introduces "good"[47] in the *Phaedo*[48] just a little before he describes his makeshift method. The context is his complaint that Anaxagoras fails to follow through and apply his theory about all things being only in so far as they are intelligible. If Anaxagoras really thought that were the case, says Socrates, he would try to explain things like Socrates' immediately impending death as something that makes sense for Socrates. He would not rely entirely on the approach a physiologist might use to explain it; that is, by explaining how hemlock affects a body's functions. Rather Anaxagoras should try also to analyze the issue in terms of how that death is, or is not, best for Socrates in-so-far-as-he-is-Socrates. If Anaxagoras were serious about his theory, Socrates suggests that he would work on the premise that Socrates' death should also be studied as an aspect of Socrates' intelligible existence. That is, it should be determined whether or not death was in Socrates' best interest when viewed by someone with access to what that best interest is. Socrates argues, therefore, that anyone who understood which acts make Socrates' architecture intelligible—as Anaxagoras claims it must be—would be in the best position to judge whether a dead Socrates is a good Socrates or a bad one. Such a person would truly be taking the risk, as Socrates claims Anaxagoras does not, of assuming the existence of the good. Socrates demands methodological practice incorporate the good. But is that possible? And is it possible without cruelty and blindness?

Plato and Aristotle do take Anaxagoras' theory much more seriously than Anaxagoras appears to do. They do what Socrates says Anaxagoras should have done, and proceed to explore the world not only as an object of careful observation but also on the assumption that anything able to be known is intelligible. Everything knowable, in their view, has needs that are somehow met. Aristotle tries to understand natural things by evaluating their complex architectural local dynamics. Like Plato, he warns against being lured by the obviousness and beauty of appearances, blinded by the sun, as much as against charlatans peddling their specious arguments.[49] But the fact remains we cannot actually observe the justifying acts that these three ancients would have us discern as the causally integrating differentiations that naturally existing things need in order to be. Hume was right. We do not see causes. But that may not be the end of the story.

Axioms, and How to Have Them

We catch another view of Socrates' makeshift approach in operation when we look at Aristotle's demonstrative syllogism. Plato saw the demonstrative syllogism as a debased and dangerous form of the dialectic he himself had modeled on Socrates' conversational approach. In fact, Plato refused to allow Aristotle to teach demonstration in the Academy. It is a teaching and learning[50] tool, but it works too much like a coercively expositional tool, cruelly forcing people to acquiesce in what the syllogism makes obvious. Plato may have feared people would see the syllogism as a tool to expound the world. Used in such a way it becomes cruel. It leaves no room for *aporia*, for judgments to make or ways to make them, nothing "sufficiently inchoate to license living without dogma,"[51] no measuring to do, no risks to take, no way to love, or to recognize needs, no way to remember or to be mortal. Aristotle did not design the demonstrative syllogism as an expository device; nor does it ever appear as such in any of his surviving works. Jonathan Barnes observes: "The method which Aristotle follows in his scientific and philosophical treatises and the method which he prescribes for scientific and philosophical activity in the *Posterior Analytics* seem not to coincide."[52] There are no philosophic or scientific expositions presented as syllogisms in Aristotle's extant works. But, as the tragically cruel history of dogmatic philosophy, science, and politics shows, people nonetheless mistook the method Aristotle sets out in the *Posterior Analytics* to be a method for coercively persuasive proof. But it was designed, rather, as a method to structure and defend the *epagoge* Glidden advocates. It was designed as a conversational tool used by those living, perhaps, within cities such as Paden describes built to facilitate citizens' measuring and evaluating in a way that would enable them to understand and sustain themselves and their world.

The demonstratively supported *epagoge* was designed as a reflective device for listeners to use in order to evaluate explanations offered against their own recollections and judgments. Like a mirror, or the *Meno's* sand,[53] or the *chora*, the syllogistic form allowed things to be fleetingly inscribed for consideration within a mediated presence of the good. Those listening to each other—like Socrates and his companions in the *Phaedo*, or the citizens of Paden's renaissance cities, or Glidden's actual common sense communities—are thereby equipped to take risks and evaluate the relative worth of arguments. Demonstration offers training in listening. It is about formal exposition only instrumentally, since the students must learn how to array for themselves the various competing arguments they hear on all kinds of subjects from all kinds of people. But demonstration is structured so as to allow these listeners to use their own recollection judiciously to make a measured rational selection. It is a tool for valuing carefully. An axiom, in Greek, is something worth saying. Value is measured by comparison with its competition. Aristotle's demonstrative syllogism is a tool to aid recollection in demonstrating which of the many competing middle terms mirrored fleetingly before us in the various syllogistic presentations we have noted down for ourselves for comparative consideration are the ones that let the subject be more complete and good. It is a tool for isolating and measuring which middle terms are more commensurate with all the observed phenomena. His *Prior & Posterior Analytics* explore that commensurate universality relationship. Aristotle tells us that science is a matter of chasing the right middle terms. According to his version of Socrates' makeshift approach, the right middle terms are those which, when compared with all other available explanatory middle terms, are found to be most universally commensurate with the scrupulously observed, carefully tested, and rigorously stated facts. They are most commensurately universal if they present the subject as wholly accommodated and formed within all of its own defining properties, and only by them.

Echoing the debt theme we saw in Plato, Aristotle portrays a natural thing's being as an exercise of having, of acquisition, of possession. In fact, Aristotle states his examples of logical predications using the verb "to have," not the verb "to be." Where we might say, "table is white," he would say, "white belongs to table."[54] Until the movement of the conductor's baton initiates a performance the bits and pieces of an orchestra are just its bits and pieces. The conductor's act integrates the whole complex of people and metal and wood and wind because—and to the extent that—each bit and each piece belongs wholly to the orchestra. That is, to the orchestra as a whole, as it actually is insofar as it is playing this particular piece of music, and not just as an organization that can play music. If any bit belongs less than wholly, or is out of its place, then the whole fails to be as good as it can be. So, the bits must belong in such a way that the whole is integrated. In the *Politics* Aristotle sketches how he sees the integrating role of such properties.

> A possession is an instrument for maintaining life. . . . Here, however, another distinction must be drawn; the instruments commonly so called are instruments of production, whilst a possession is an instrument of action. The shuttle, for example, is not only of use; but something else is made by it. . . . Further, as production and action are different in kind, and both require instruments, the instruments which they employ must likewise differ in kind. But life is action and not production. Again, a possession is spoken of as a part is spoken of; for the part is not only a part of something else, but wholly belongs to it; and this is also true of a possession. . . . And a possession may be defined as an instrument of action, separable from the possessor.[55]

Properties belong wholly or universally, as parts do to a whole, if they enable an act or set of acts that no part by itself (and no other whole of other parts), can do. Such wholly belonging properties integrate that which has them, so that it does something new and different. It contains within itself the principle of distinct, limited, motion. Without such a complex integrating act the subject would merely have its properties as a chaotic heap. Without an integrating act such as the one present in the movement of the conductor's baton, or of the charioteer's bridle, or the architect's discriminating memory, there would be no orchestra, no race, no city. The organization might have its musicians like a bronze statue of a person might have limbs, but lacking the acts it needs to integrate its self, it would not be an orchestra.[56] But orchestras make all kinds of noises. What turns some noises into music, and others not? What lets some acts integrate persons or cities, and other acts destroy them. Or what lets some acts make music or persons while other acts make better or worse music or persons?

Aristotle argues it is only in the presence of most commensurately universal integrating act that some sort of real music, however poor or great, or some kind of person, is to be found. The demonstrative syllogism shapes conditions under which we can provide that presence and fruitfully ask ourselves such questions. Does it reveal more of what makes a "good" Socrates to understand his death as a function of physiology, as Socrates accuses Anaxagoras of saying; or of his Athenian citizenship, as many historians suggest; or of his human character, as Socrates insists? What does my memory tell me when I recollect all that I actually experience of Socrates, and also recall his own comments on the subject in the *Phaedo*? This is the sort of question that demonstrative syllogisms are structured to allow me to answer by evaluating and measuring which of these—or countless other—true middle terms is best. It is because a particular middle term is more worth saying[57] in that it appears to me to define the place I reflectively share with the dead Socrates more commensurately and comprehensively than the other middle terms do. This makeshift triangulating, navigating approach also allows recalculations needed in changing places[58] as growth and novelty require.

The demonstrative syllogism looks as if it were an expository device for publishing compellingly packaged, blindingly dogmatic, conclusions. That has traditionally been viewed as its designed role. But as a properly didactic and dialectical tool it was to have been used by listeners[59] who follow Socrates' makeshift method, or Glidden's rough-and-ready one. Listening first to the expositions of others; then identifying and isolating the causes they propose; then exercising active, receptive, measuring, charioteer-like skills of emptiness by reflecting and recollecting and selecting which explanations are most commensurately universal in identifying acts that articulate[60] and accommodate the phenomena as actually observed. Heuristic[61] recollection, disciplined by the demonstrative syllogism, lets us accommodate and accommodate ourselves to natural things' needed goods. But we act as mortals with memories trained[62] to use good as a navigational reference for surveying the world and our place in it.

Eschatos or Telos: Testing, Testing, Testing . . .

But even if we do manage to do the calculated recollection that discloses an effectively present but safely remote good to guide our navigation and to shape our institutions and our cities and their surrounding landscapes, it is still true that any understanding we mortals might achieve will always be unfinished, always something for which we wait. This unfinished understanding is as true for Socrates, Plato, and Aristotle as it is for Heidegger. All mortals await such completed understanding. But it is easy to confuse the awaited *eschatos*, our completed understanding, with what Socrates, Plato, and Aristotle see as the already mediated presence of *telos*. Plato and Aristotle do not await divinities or the weal that has been withdrawn. Their reflective, recollective language strategies make that weal effectively present. The divinities and the weal are blindingly present to Socrates, Plato, and Aristotle. In their recollectively structured arguments they propose a way for the *telos*/good to be more safely present in the differential integrations their makeshift dialectic reveals. Thus they claim to make it possible to reveal the world in its causal needs[63] without running the risk of blindness.

While allowing that it is "important to keep such a vision of the good community ever present before our minds," Glidden adds a caveat. "So often those who rush to systematize and abstract away from examples do not then live the lives they originally envisioned . . . [in their] landscape [of] systematically organized propositions, rules, regulations."[64] Glidden is right. Abstraction is too comfortingly remote from lives lived. That fact might justify dismissing this windy old talk of reflectively rational discourse as so much cruel fiddling while the world burns. So, before tackling operational tests of his approach, we must ask Aristotle to answer the serious charge that his procedure is mere systematization and empty abstraction and does not touch lives or transform landscapes. To see how he might meet this charge, we should look first at his account of the psychology involved. It is a psychology that demands risk. Aristotle's challenge is more measured and less heroic, perhaps, than Socrates' but it is a real and demanding risk, nonetheless. It is not abstract and remote. At the end of the *Posterior Analytics,* Aristotle sketches how he understands sense-perception and knowledge to be related.

> So out of sense-perception comes to be what we call memory, and from experience again—i.e., from the universal now stabilized in its entirety within the soul, the one beside the many which is a single identity within them all—originate the skill of the craftsman and the knowledge of the man of science, skill in the sphere of coming to be and science in the sphere of being. We conclude that these states of knowledge are neither innate in a determinate form, nor developed from other higher states of knowledge, but from sense-perception. It is like a rout in battle stopped by first one man making a stand and then another, until the original formation has been restored. The soul is so constituted as to be capable of this process.[65]

Aristotle presents the turning-around as the basis both of technical skill and of scientific knowing. It is a process of stabilizing the "universal . . . in its entirety" in the *psyche*, the soul. Adopting more logical and mathematical language, he goes on to explain what he means by this talk of stabilizing the universal in its entirety. Stabilizing occurs, he says, when all of a one comes to rest[66] beside the many, to all of which it thereby provides a single identity. Translated into the language we used earlier, Aristotle's rout image amounts to saying that the architect has to stabilize in her memory whatever integrates the various acts a kitchen has to accommodate. In the *Posterior Analytics,* Aristotle tells us how to achieve that by interrogating our memories against the memories of those to whom we listen with ears trained in the exploratory use of the demonstrative syllogism.[67] The aim is to isolate a measured, and measuring, integrating middle term.[68] Such argument-based integration explains to anyone in the common[69] shared places where conversationalists dwell, why any natural thing we are studying needs the many properties it presents. This stabilizing, or resting, is a dynamic and effective resting-in-a-place. The stabilization[70] of one coming to rest beside a many, which it integrates, occurs, he says, in a place he calls a soul. Aristotle reminds us he has defined soul in the *De Anima*[71] as equipped to accommodate such mutual presence of differences. Soul is a reflective place, like the *chora*, where presence happens more safely, more reflectively, more generatively than elsewhere, and also more fleetingly. The demonstrative analytic procedure experimentally navigates us closer and closer to the middle terms that best express the causation[72] we need to save the phenomena. He advises us to identify those middle terms through analysis of the phenomena, the received opinions (*endoxa*). They are the result of collected "field reports of places fleshed out in sufficient detail to make such localities come . . . alive" like Glidden produces in his "purposeful wandering."

Living without Dogma

But such a reflective, analytic method works only for the most part. As Aristotle reminds us at the very beginning of the *Nicomachean Ethics*, the natural things and crafted products this method deals with are only "for the most part" what they appear to be. Sometimes the things we are exploring are only apparent, not actual, even if their appearances are blindingly persuasive. He warns that it is the mark of an educated person "to look for precision in each class of things just so far as the nature of the subject admits."[73] Unless we know how to test our memories we are prey to charlatans and to self-deception.[74] Martha Nussbaum sees Aristotle's method of relying on phenomena as a makeshift too. Like Glidden, she warns not to expect too much: "The method that announces appearance-saving as its goal was when it was introduced, and still is now, in danger of abrupt philosophical dismissal. It can strike us as hopelessly flat, tedious, underambitious."[75] She opens her account of the method with a passage from the *Nicomachean Ethics* reminiscent of Socrates' account of his makeshift approach, and of Glidden's.[76]

> As in all other cases, we must set down the appearances (*phainomena*) and, first working through the puzzles, in this way go on to show, if possible, the truth of all the beliefs we hold (*ta endoxa*) about these experiences; and, if this is not possible, the truth of the greatest number and the most authoritative. For if the difficulties are resolved and the beliefs (*endoxa*) are left in place, we will have done enough showing.[77]

Nussbaum might also have noted Aristotle's remarks at the opening of the *De Anima*, where he tells us that we must give an account that accords with the appearances (*apodidonai kata ten phantasian*).

> The knowledge of the essential nature of a substance is largely promoted by acquaintance with its properties: for, when we are able to give an account conformable to experience (apodidonai kata ten phantasian) of all or most of the properties of a substance, we shall be in the most favourable position to say something worth saying about the essential nature of a subject; in all demonstration a definition of the essence is required as a starting-point, so that definitions which do not enable us to discover the derived properties, or which fail to facilitate even a conjecture about them, must obviously . . . be futile.[78]

The measure[79] of success in achieving knowing on the basis of this makeshift approach lies in its ability to enable us to give an account. The extent to which our accounts "enable us to discover the derived properties, or . . . facilitate . . . a conjecture about them" is the index of whether they are futile or not. The knower takes the risk, and measures[80] the commensurateness of her expressions of recollected, reflected goods. She provides a measured place, reflectively sheltered from the dangers of the infinite good and the compulsively beautiful, where her expressions are justified in terms of—given back to—the phenomena (*apodidonai*).[81] Aristotle says she accommodates the process in her soul, her dwelling. Language shared in structured argument is the house of being after all. But it is a wanderer's place.

Aristotle makes it clear in the rout analogy and elsewhere that the reflective, turning-around process he describes is the ground both of the skill of the craftsperson and the knowledge of the scientist:[82] "skill in the sphere of coming to be and science in the sphere of being." So perhaps Heidegger's concern over our confusion of building and dwelling was anticipated and relieved in Aristotle's integration of science and practice. In her acts and productions based on this methodologically tested experience of the phenomena, the dweller/knower accommodates and measures—but is not the measure of—all things. Her practically wise[83] ability to integrate skill in the sphere of coming to be and science in the sphere of being determines whether and how well she lives. Her living well is expressed in landscapes transformed into the footprints of her wandering. She is not just waiting. In her living well, she is generatively measuring out accommodation of what is coming to be to what is in the sphere of being.

But it is not yet at all clear what living well means. Aristotle seems to say that persons rely on good as a standard[84] in their reflection by which things are both understood and are brought to be. It is how dwellers complete[85] themselves, not the duration[86] of the dwelling that is the measure of the process. But how do mortals, in their actions and productions, embody and express that living well? And what are goods? Why would we designate some vague, possibly unnamable hybrid act of cooking, entertaining, family meeting, resale facilitating, aroma generating, and a hundred or more other activities as a "good" integrating a place? If we were to focus on its integrating role, we might allow that whatever that collection of motions is it unifies—so we might, at a stretch, call it a "unity." But why call it a "good"? It might be a function or a purpose. Aristotle does use all these terms, of course. But he also sticks with good because he insists that we have to try to identify the function that best integrates the place, or the soul, of a naturally existing animate thing. But that is not the only reason he sticks to variations of the good, despite its scariness. The real reason the value-laden term is appropriate is that it is manifest always and unavoidably within a valuation exercise. An historian might more fully and truly[87] recollect and argue that Socrates' Athenian status is more commensurate as the middle term explaining the phenomenon of his death. A follower of Anaxagoras might insist that it really was the hemlock that did it, and that physiology provides the only and best account. On this ancient makeshift model, the common place these different people may come to share will not be produced by Glidden's common sense consensus, but by the fullest debate practiced by men and women educated to remember and to test their memories against each other. The common place that they may manage to build will be a function of an argued measurement about which of the three, or three thousand, middle terms is justified, in their experience, as the good dead Socrates that allows them to live well by comparison with the others' experience of dead Socrates.

Such debates, of course, look much like the ones Glidden records taking place in the communities where common sense consensus forms. The authority Glidden invokes for rough-and-ready consensus-building rests on its claim to sustain consistency in practice at least locally. So too the authority of the ancient makeshift value-based arguing depends on whether the teleological explanations produced do actually fit the landscapes, institutions, and cultural practices that accommodate and embody them. That fit must be measurable and testable. We saw Socrates invite his companions to take a real risk on the existence of such unifying dynamics. But that risk needs some safety devices if it is to be taken wisely. Aristotle, the trained biological observer, was very nervous about the ambivalently present absence of things like good which Socrates and Plato ask us to rely on. In fact, Aristotle makes it clear there can be no proof of the existence of this obviously complex integrating unity.[88] Any such integration we might seek may be very hard even to name.[89] So Aristotle insists there must be at least some way to argue a defense[90] of what may come to be seen as the defining, mediating middle terms we might come up with. There must be some way of judging whether such a reflective approach is better or worse than other approaches we have adopted or might adopt while we await the *eschatos.* History, and its record of our experience of time, may be one option for testing appropriate discursive strategies. Social science or some form of communicative action may be another. The nineteenth and twentieth centuries have explored both. Aristotle offers a different approach to these as operational tests of the adequacy of method,[91] a more logic-based one in some ways, but it really turns out to be more about our way of experiencing place: more about *telos* than *eschatos.*

In the *Metaphysics* book 4 Aristotle pointedly reformulates the challenge we earlier saw Socrates put to his companions in the *Phaedo*:

> The starting-point for all such arguments is not the demand <for a declaration> that . . . something either is or is not (for this one might perhaps take to be a begging of the question), but that he shall say something which is significant both for himself and for another; for this is necessary, if he really is to say anything. For, if he means nothing, such a man will not be capable of reasoning, either with himself or with another. But if any one grants this, demonstration will be possible; for we shall already have something definite. The person responsible for the proof, however, is not he who demonstrates but he who listens; for while disowning reason he listens to reason. And again he who admits this has admitted that something is true apart from demonstration (so that not everything will be 'so and not so'). [92]

We have noted Aristotle's statement in the *De Anima*[93] of the standard any method must meet if it is not to be dismissed as futile. He defends his version of the makeshift approach against that same standard. He claims only to offer "an account conformable to experience," and only to provide something "more worth" saying insofar as it lets a listener grasp what is "significant both for himself and for another." Is that a satisfactory standard or is it too underambitious? It is success or failure in finding what is "significant both for himself and for another" that Aristotle provides as the only test needed by anyone contemplating taking the risk Socrates lays out in the *Phaedo.*

The person of practical wisdom who accommodates what is coming to be to what is in the sphere of being is the test case for Aristotle. The *phronimos* is the one equipped to take Socrates' challenge, and enabled to take that risk more securely than were Socrates' own companions. The extent to which a person of practical wisdom lives well is the publicly verifiable index of whether the debt is repaid. But the *phronimos'* success or failure is not adjudicated as a locally acceptable common sense consensus such as Glidden offers. It is observable as a set of repeatable discursive practices that practically wise persons use to achieve effective insights into how to borrow the goods they need to sustain themselves. Insofar as these insights are observably integrated into identifiable practices, they are open to comparative evaluation by economic measures of educational and institutional success.

Managing Debt Wisely

The *phronimos* is not unlike other figures we have already met. Cephalus paying his debts reappears disguised as an architecturally sensitive charioteer, taking, and effectively establishing, possession of a fragile place with a deftly light controlling presence that allows the different horses to be integrated in their dynamic presence to each other. In the *Posterior Analytics* we met the repentant runner who stops running, turns around and, in taking a stand, creates a place where understanding and action and production occur. In the *Nicomachean Ethics* the practically wise person emerges as the one who knows she knows nothing because she is constantly subject to the cathartic play of desire that leaves her open and listening, like Socrates the midwife, (or the *Timaeus' chora*) to know, and do, and make, and live better. Such a habit defines the practically wise person who knows who and where she is.

Humphrey Carver, a prominent Canadian planner, reflected often on Canada's housing policy so much shaped by the prevailing wisdom "that the place where you live is . . . a mere material possession like cars and consumer goods; ephemeral, disposable, mortgagable, replaceable, exchangeable. . . . So little seems to be really loved and possessed by anyone."[94] It reminds him, he says, of Gertrude Stein's assessment of suburbia: "There's no there, there!" With her characteristic precision, Stein has captured the subtlety of what we might call the *phronimos'* soul. For Aristotle, living well entails possessing things that are needed; and precisely because they are needed, they are *not* mere ephemeral, disposable, mortgagable, replaceable, exchangeable possessions. For Aristotle "there" or place, or soul, is what drives growth and life. Need—or love, as it appears in the *Symposium*[95] and other dialogues—is the dynamic that drives the natural indebtedness of things, their mortality. For Aristotle, natural things are fragile.[96] They are explicable, and caused, by the ordering achieved in what he calls, in the *Politics*, "living well." Practically wise persons publicly reflect that ordering in the properties that define them, in how they possess things that let them live well. In the *Politics* book I, chapter 4[97] Aristotle distinguishes between kinds of possessions and different ways of possessing. A bed or clothing or a home accommodates and supports the integration of a person as a whole. Such possessions provide places that capacitate integrated action. Possessions like these belong wholly to a person by their presence, and thus make possible her integrated action as an organism. A weavers' shuttle, however, does not belong wholly to the weaver in this same integrating way. As a tool of production rather than of action and life, the shuttle belongs immediately to the weaving, not to the weaver.

John A. Scott

A dweller needs a home in an immediate and wholly integrating way that is different from the way a weaver needs a shuttle. Steins' suburbanite appears to think she needs a bit of real estate as a means of producing wealth like the weaver needs the shuttle. Aristotle's practically wise dweller is not enabled by the mere material possession of her dwelling in this instrumental way. The two kinds of needs[98] are of different orders. One need constitutes a "there" or a place, a soul erotically and generatively open to any and all possible satisfactions, any and all goods that actually support living well. The need for the shuttle, on the other hand, is less open. The need for the shuttle is instrumental and hypothetical, not generative. Dwelling shapes[99] and accommodates the dweller whose characteristic acts determine the architecture of the dwelling. The obvious circularity is vicious and disastrous unless it is somehow limited and measurable, as Plato demonstrates in the *Republic*. Limiting, measuring, calculating is what Aristotle's practically wise person does. In the *Nicomachean Ethics* book VI Aristotle introduces the *phronimos* standing as the one in the middle, like Plato's charioteer and the horses. "In all the states of character we have mentioned, as in all other matters, there is a mark to which the one with the rule (*logon echon*) looks, and heightens or relaxes his activity accordingly, and there is a standard which determines the mean states which we say are intermediate between excess and defect, being in accordance with the right rule."[100] There is a place where good effects action. It is in the middle where good is reflectively present. In the *phronimos'* case, that is at the junction of intellect and desire. "Intellect itself, however, moves nothing, but only the intellect which aims at an end and is practical."[101] And the *phronimos* is able to work effectively in that place, Aristotle tells us, because she is a *logon exchon*: that is literally a "word haver" or someone who has rational speech. She is capable of reasoned discourse that measures things and produces standards or rules.

Reasoned Discourse: Meta Logou

In his *Ethics* Aristotle seeks to isolate and identify the person-integrating-place-defining act. Commonplace or banal as it sounds, he finds that it is whatever act makes persons self-sufficiently happy. Self-sufficiency is key. As Socrates and Plato focused on the mechanics of debt, Aristotle focuses on the ways in which things have their properties sufficiently. We just noted Aristotle speak of "a mark to which the one who has the rule (*logon echon*) looks and heightens or relaxes his activity accordingly." The regulatory, targeting, navigational, architectural skill associated with having language and using it in an appropriately organic manner underlies this banal commonplace about happiness. In Aristotle's view, middle terms, rigorously tested for extent to which they belong wholly or universally, do integrate and successfully define[102] the matter at hand if they allow movement and rest,[103] a more-or-less, or better-and-worse. In so far as she is a "word haver," capable of rational discourse, a practically wise person is enabled by desire to distinguish between better and worse. In their calculative practical and productive acts, practically wise persons embody the relative standards, the surveyors' marks needed to allow the good to be reflectively and safely present. It is the phronimos' value-based discourse, embodied in her acts and products, that effectively expresses the rule, the measure that the *Republic* showed was needed for the good to be safely present. Jimi Hendrix's guitar playing sets the rule, the standard, for guitar playing. And it provides, too, the public test of its rightness.

But what is the rule—the measure—the *logon*, and how does the *phronimos*' act make it right? Aristotle's *phronimos* is not the artist, producer, technologist that Heidegger presents. In the *Politics* passage we looked at a few moments ago, Aristotle spoke of instrumental possessions: things we have for use but which are separable from us: things we can alienate, or be alienated from. An artist or crafts-person produces something outside, something that can be alienated, something in a place apart. An agent, on the other hand, transforms herself into the place where what can either be or not be comes to be because the agent's act itself, not some separate product, accommodates its good. She accommodates not in imagination as the artist does, or in a future-tending contract as an architect does,[104] or in a simulacrum[105] as a myth-maker. She does it in attending habitually to her own generatively erotic need to bring together things which, because she is a "word haver," she can expose as needing each other, as necessary to each other, like reason and desire.

It is not the practically wise person's production of reflective argument, but her possession of it (*echon*) that mediates and accommodates the safe presence of the good. It is the peculiar mode of possession of reflective discursive argument, "belongs wholly," that integrates her and secures her a living place. It is not so much the *phronimos*' technological or artistic imagination that effects the integrating *being* event. Aristotle repeatedly points to the difference between doing and making: between acting and producing. The *phronimos* is not primarily a producer but an agent, one who does things rather than only makes things. But the *phronimos* does not talk to—or for—herself alone. She practices logos to perform actions that architecturally measure out places that reflect and expose what is needed. She is habitually focused on discerning what needs to be done, and on allowing that need to be transformed, through desire, into act (*praxis*). How the practically wise person does this is familiar to anyone watching a two-year old. The *phronimos*' reflective mediation of good's presence in the use of appropriately structured *logos* might be compared to someone who speaks only English caught in an exclusively French-speaking community. The monolingual English speaker does not have, or speak, the French language; but she does nonetheless "have language" in that she can take a risk that the incomprehensible sounds she hears are expressions of needs to make sense. It is this sensitive alertness that Socrates asks his companions to recollect in the *Phaedo* and to exercise. The English speaker attends to, and relies on, her assumption that the babbling Frenchmen are actually trying to make sense in the noises they are making. And she acts in a manner appropriate to her skill as a word haver. She makes the kinds of responsive imitative sounds and sound patterns; and inquiring gestures like pointing to objects and speaking the English terms, inviting the French speakers to supply French equivalents. But, in Aristotle's view, sensitivity and alertness and imitation are not enough. Rational selection is required. The *phronimos* is the agent of rational selection of the fittest middle terms. Demonstrative dialectical reflective public argument is its precondition.

Training in reflective discursive listening and learning, and in the transitory character of all particular expositions of knowledge, is the social, cultural, political precondition to transformation of our urban and suburban places and landscapes: not waiting. The monolingual English speaking *phronimos* listens selectively, evaluating her own acts as better or worse in their guiding her to met her need to do things that improve comprehension. Valuing is not so much having, or expressing, a conscious or preconscious preference for something, or a strongly held opinion. It is taking the risk of acting on things to which we pay careful, reflective, analytic attention. There is always a possibility that the *phronimos* has fallen in with a particularly nasty French crowd who are pulling her leg, and just babbling incomprehensibly. That is always a risk to Socrates companions unless they adopt some protective analytic device such as Aristotle provides in demonstration. Aristotle's makeshift method trains the practically wise person how to be always on guard against charlatans. A *phronimos* has language not for speaking to her private self. She listens as its discourse leads her through evaluated choices of better or worse acts. She gives herself a place to be what she is in a world made increasingly comprehensible through her acts.

The Cruelty of the Good

Perhaps Socrates and Plato and Aristotle should have taken Nietzsche's advice and chosen a less cruel term than "good" to designate the structural dynamic of being which is revealed to and through those who are practically wise in their actions. Perhaps they should have stuck with Anaxagoras' mind. Anaximander's undefined, inexhaustible variable and Pythagoras' number have had long, creditable run. Parmenides' and Heraclitus' one remains, it seems, the grail even of contemporary physics and Democritus' atoms and void dominated the nineteenth and twentieth centuries. Or perhaps they should even have anticipated Christian grace.

But good seems to allow reflective discourse the range of movement needed. Therein lies its peculiar genius and pertinence for our incredibly cruel value-neutral age. Glidden is right. The good brings out the worst in people. Cruelty seems to be its inevitable companion. On the other hand, Aristotle's makeshift method may be too hopelessly flat, tedious, and underambitious for ancient or modern illuminati and their acolytes to practice. Aristotle's flat, tedious method, like Glidden's, is designed not for illumination but for plain, common sense, practically wise people to use. But plain, common sense, practically wise people cannot practice it either, unless supporting conditions are established and impediments removed. Scholars like Paden are right to look closely at the architectural principles shaping urban, suburban, and global landscapes and at the private and public institutions that shape contemporary dwelling in those landscapes. If architectural principles and institutions do not support or sustain practically wise people engaging in the reflective discourse they are capable of as citizens with a capacity for living well, then cruelty is licensed once again. If architecture is only about merely material possessions and planners are not able to consider how natural things and people possess and belong to each other, then practical wisdom is blocked from making sense of the world or its inhabitants.

Conclusion

If the speculation offered in this chapter is close to correct, then Aristotle would probably suggest to those who, like Glidden and Paden, seek those "values internal to . . . planning," not to rely on consensus alone, but to explore even more than they already do the mediating actions that actually do integrate actual communities, living and dead.[106] Open architecture is not just spacious or empty, but generatively, receptively, accommodating in giving back what it uses. It plays absences off against presences. It repays its debts. It renews by emptying to be refilled. Architecture and its educational institutions can support memory's lateral function by promoting attention to the betweens on which practically wise people focus in their effective desire to understand the world for which they are responsible.[107]

Notes

1. Aristotle, *Politics* Book 1, 3-13, in *The Basic Works of Aristotle*, ed. Richard McKeon (New York: Random House, 1941), 1130 ff.

2. Martin Heidegger, "Building Dwelling Thinking," in *Poetry, Language, Thought,* trans. Albert Hofstadter (New York: Harper and Row, 1971), 145-47.

3. Heidegger, "Building," 148.

4. In the *Physics* Aristotle defines the term nature as pertaining to things that have within themselves the capacity to move themselves and to stop themselves. In his study of Aristotle's *Physics* Heidegger calls nature the placing of places.

5. Heidegger, "Building," 150-55.

6. Heidegger, "Building,"157.

7. Heidegger, "Building,"148.

8. Harvey Cox, Foreword to *Man on His Own,* by Ernst Bloch, trans. E. B. Ashton (New York: Herder and Herder, 1970), 18.

9. See Heidegger's reflections on "thing" as location of assembly, "Building," 155 f.

10. See Parmenides' ways of truth and falsehood as explored in Plato's *Parmenides.*

11. "And thought thinks on itself because it shares the nature of the object of thought." Aristotle, *Metaphysics* Book 12, ch 7, 1072b15-27, in *The Basic Works of Aristotle*, ed. Richard McKeon (New York: Random House, 1941), 880. See also Aristotle, *De Anima* Book 3, chs. 4 and 5, in *Basic Works*, 589-91; and also Aristotle, *Nicomachean Ethics* Book 7, ch. 3, 1147a23 (in the context of his treatment of moral weakness *akrasia*), in *Basic*

Works, 1041. References to the Greek text are to the Bekker pagination numbers as used in the Oxford Classical Text editions of Aristotle's works.

12. It is interesting to note that the Greek word for child, *tokos,* is the same word used for the interest accruing on a debt. *Tokos* means both that rate which is charged by lenders to maintain the wholeness or completeness of the principle borrowed, and the offspring that enable repayment for their generation. The concept of best interest as Plato uses it in the *Republic* and elsewhere is a very rich pun on the teleology operating in his thought.

13. Plato, *Phaedo,* 73a-75d, in *The Collected Dialogues of Plato,* edited by Edith Hamilton and Huntington Cairns (Princeton, N.J.: Princeton University Press, 1969), 55-58. References to Plato's Greek texts are to the Stephanus pagination and page subdivisions.

14. "What distinguishes the kind of inclusion characteristic of the visible cosmos is that, unlike intelligible inclusion, it holds together in extended place beings that with respect to one another are in different places within this comprehensive place. It is as if in the transition from intelligible to visible something like place comes into play, letting things be set apart as they are gathered into the comprehensive visible cosmos. As the *chora,* which seems like place, will prove always to have come into play in the very opening of the difference." John Sallis, *Chorology: On Beginning in Plato's Timaeus* (Bloomington: Indiana University Press, 1999), 15-16.

15. In the *Republic*'s sun analogy (508d-509b) Socrates says: "This reality . . . that gives their truth to the objects of knowledge and the power of knowing to the knower, you must say is the idea of good, and you must conceive it as being the cause of knowledge, and of truth in so far as known. . . . The sun's presence . . . not only furnishes to visibles the power of visibility but it also provides for their generation and growth and nurture. . . . In like manner . . . things we know not only receive from the presence of the good their being known, but their very existence and essence is derived to them from it, though the good itself is not essence but still transcends essence." Plato, *Collected Dialogues,* 744. Socrates invokes just the sun's "presence," its "being-there," as causal. It is the good/sun as present (*parexein* 509b2-7) which provides not only for "the knownness of the things we know . . . but also their reality and their being." The sun/good is not an end for which we wait, but a condition of our present reflective action.

16. See for instance, Jacques Derrida and Peter Eisenman, *Chora L Works,* ed. Jeffrey Kipnis and Thomas Leeser (New York: Monacelli Press, 1997).

17. In Newfoundland we have a rather dangerous winter "sport." Interestingly, it is called "copying" and involves moving across open water by jumping from one ice floe to the next even though no single ice floe could sustain the jumper's weight. The act in motion sustains the bodies. The bodies borrow sustenance from the activity that thus maintains their integrity and "goodness" . . . until the process collapses, too often, in disaster.

18. I will explore below the ambiguities surrounding this obviously problematic use of the adjective, 'good.' See Roger Paden, "The Two Professions of Hippodamus of Miletus," in *Philosophy and Geography* 4, no. 1 (February 2001). Paden demonstrates the extent to which the ancients were aware of architecture and city planning as crucial to the integration of moral and political growth. Paden's article is timely, it seems to me, because it shines a strong light on the deep, and dangerous, gap between urban planning and political philosophy in our own day.

19. David Glidden, "Commonplaces," in *Philosophies of Place, Philosophy and Geography III,* ed. Andrew Light and Jonathan Smith (Lanham, Md.: Rowman & Littlefield, 1998), 169-70.

20. Glidden, "Commonplaces," 186.

21. Glidden, "Commonplaces," 189-90.

22. Roger Paden, "Values and Planning: the Argument from Renaissance Utopianism," *Ethics, Place and Environment*, 4, no. 1 (2001): 5-30. Paden provides a valuable sketch of the intellectual origins and cultural climate that have fostered the cynicism that denies what he calls a "substantive value structure" to urban planning.

23. Glidden, "Commonplaces," 190. See the same aspiration expressed on page 186.

24. There is a convention in some quarters of using an initial capital to differentiate when Plato appears to be referring to the form of "The Good" from more general adjectival uses. I will not observe that convention here since, in my view, it is rarely helpful to our understanding of Plato's actual intentions.

25. Plato, *Republic* II, 372e ff, in *Collected Dialogues*, 619.

26. Plato's *Phaedrus* explores the potential violence of relying upon language, especially written language. It has the power to institute false unities such as Parmenides and his skeptical followers, like Socrates, fought to curtail.

27. In the *Phaedo* Socrates explores why it is good for him to die. The Pythagorean concept of limit is crucial to Plato's natural philosophy. According to Plato, artist/technologists left on their own, recognize not the good but only the "better" with its inherently limitless force. Each thing existing "by nature . . . has *within itself* a principle of motion *and of stationariness*" (emphases added). See Aristotle, *Physics* 192b14, in *Basic Works*, 236. See Plato, *Phaedrus* 245e, in *Collected Dialogues*, 493.

28. Anaximander's *apeiron* is arguably an early version of the good in Plato. It is inexhaustible as well as indefinable.

29. The *Phaedrus* presents this as madness. Along with the madness of lovers, priests, and healers, the artists' madness does afford very great blessings.

30. Plato, *Republic* 433a, in *Collected Dialogues*, 674-75. In the *Timaeus*, which explicitly picks up where the *Republic* leaves off, the *chora*, the perfectly featureless, empty receptacle *(upodoxe)* is the reflective dynamic of natural physical being.

31. On this generally Pythagorean component in their thought see, inter alia, the *Phaedo* and the *Philebus*.

32. This danger may threaten Glidden's project unless the careful argumentation that lies at the heart of the accounts he crafts of what he calls his "purposeful wandering" is developed more explicitly as a measurable justification.

33. Plato, *Phaedo* 99c-d, in *Collected Dialogues*, 80-81.

34. Aristotle provides a more mathematical description of this place at *De Motu Animalium* ch. 9, 702b12 ff. Martha Craven Nussbaum, *Aristotle's De Motu Animalium* (Princeton, N.J.: Princeton University Press, 1978), 48-50.

35. This line of argument may approach an organicism which contemporary biologists might find acceptable. Cf. Ernst Mayr, *This is Biology* (Cambridge, Mass.: Belknap Press, 1997).

36. Socrates borrows his own emptiness, his own lack of knowledge, in order to ground the completeness which he needs as a natural being to relate philosophically to the neediness of other naturally existing things.

37. Ancient dialectical methods must be sharply distinguished from ninetennth-century and twentieth-century versions of "dialectic."

38. Plato, *Phaedrus* 253e, 500.

39. On the theme of "joint" in Plato's and Aristotle's methodological thought see, for example, Plato, *Phaedrus* 265, in *Collected Dialogues*, 511ff. See also *De Motu Animalium*, ch 9. Nussbaum, *Aristotle's De Motu*, 48-50.

40. For an account of a practical architectural attempt to use Plato's concept of the "chora" as the paradigm generative place see Derrida and Eisenman, *Chora*.

41. Plato, *Phaedo,* ed. with introduction and notes by John Burnet (Oxford: Clarendon Press, 1911), 109-10. Notes on 100a3-100b4.

42. Protagoras held that the human being is the measure of all things. Socrates, on the other hand, invites his companions to take his own position seriously and share his recollected experience of the presence of goods and of what cause, therefore, is. Aristotle thinks this is dangerous (*Metaphysics* 4, 1016a, 18-19), because it lays those who make the investment, in the form Socrates offers it, open to a charge of begging the question. Aristotle offers Socrates' companions a better contract: one with protections built in against that charge, and better tools for the due diligence required in making such investments responsibly.

43. Socrates' phrase at *Phaedo* 99d characterizing his approach is *"deuteron ploun."* It does mean "makeshift" in idiomatic Greek. It is a nautical phrase, literally meaning "second sailing." Navigators, in their triangulations, make remote reference points effectively present.

44. See, e.g., the *Protagoras.*

45. Both Roger Paden and David Glidden demonstrate that this aspiration circulated in the ancient world.

46. René Descartes, *Meditations on First Philosophy,* trans. Donald A. Cress (Indianapolis: Hackett, 1979), 13 and *passim.*

47. I shall concentrate for the moment on just one of the assumptions Socrates asks his companions to make, the one about the existence of "good"; but "beautiful" and "magnitude" are intimately involved, as we will see.

48. Plato, *Phaedo* 97c, in *Collected Dialogues,* 79.

49. Aristotle, *Eudemian Ethics* 1216b35ff. Book 1, ch. 6, trans. H. Rackham (Cambridge, Mass.: Harvard University Press, 1961), 219.

50. The opening phrase, "All instruction given or received. . . ." (*pasa didasklia kai pasa mathesis*), sets the didactic context for understanding the demonstrative syllogism. Aristotle, *Posterior Analytics* 74a1, in *Basic Works,* 110. For a helpful analysis of this perspective see William Wians, "Aristotle, Demonstration and Teaching," in *Ancient Philosophy* 9 (1989): 245-53.

51. Glidden, "Commonplaces," 170.

52. J. Barnes, "Aristotle's Theory of Demonstration," *Phronesis* 14, no. 2 (1969): 137.

53. Plato, *Meno* 82b, in *Collected Dialogues*, 365ff.

54. Bloch, the Marxist eschatologist, prefers "S is not yet P" to the prevailing formula, "S is P." Aristotle the teleologist insists that "P belongs to S." That is, "S" possesses its "properties" in a reflective and dynamic manner.

55. Aristotle, *Politics,* in *Basic Works,* 1131-32.

56. For a contemporary reflection that draws on some parallel themes see Gilles Deleuze, "The Simulacrum and Ancient Philosophy," in *The Logic of Sense,* trans. Mark Lester with Charles Stivale, ed. Constantin V. Boundas (New York: Columbia University Press, 1990), 253 ff.

57. See Aristotle, *De Anima* 402b21, in *Basic Works*, 536. Also see Aristotle, *Metaphysics* 1006a25, in *Basic Works*, 738.

58. On the need to be able to change places and to grow, please see the threat we earlier saw portrayed in the *Republic* as arising out of novelty and progress. See also Aristotle, *Eudemian Ethics* 1216b30, Book 1, ch. 6, 219; and Derrida and Eisenman, *Chora,* 166-67.

59. Aristotle addresses his lessons on demonstrative syllogistic (*Posterior Analytics* 71a1ff) to listeners as much as to their teachers, and he structures the pattern of the listeners' analytic listening as William Wians suggests "Aristotle, Demonstration and Teaching" in *Ancient Philosophy* 9 no. 2 (fall 1989): 245f. Aristotle renegotiates the contract between the

dialectical participants. Socrates requires admission that the listeners "let there be" certain absolutes. Aristotle requires only that the listener say something significant so the process of developing something even more worth saying can begin. (See John A. Scott, *The Problem of Demonstration in Aristotle*, Ph.D. thesis, Edinburgh University, 1975.)

60. The image of "articulation"—of the "joint" in a natural being—is important in both Plato and Aristotle. See also, for instance, Plato, *Phaedrus* 265e, in *Collected Dialogues*, 511ff.; and *De Motu Animalium*, ch. 9. Nussbaum, *Aristotle's De Motu*, 48-50.

61. Aristotle's dialectic is heuristic in the sense that it hunts and searches rather more than it expounds. Aristotle uses the term *heurein* in this sense in the *Analytics*. Nonetheless the specific kind of search is not so much the kind performed by hunters seeking a prey. It is more the kind conducted by travelers seeking signposts, or sailors navigating by the stars or other landmarks, or charioteers trying to get around the racetrack safely, or knowers trying to become one with (*symphysis*) the objects of their knowing. *Nicomachean Ethics*, Book 7, ch. 3, 1147a23; *De Anima* 429b22-430a9; *Metaphysics* 1072b15-27.

62. Aristotle calls training in the appropriately heuristic deployment of the demonstrative syllogism "*paideia*." See Aristotle, *Metaphysics* 1005b1 ff, in *Basic Works*, 736; Aristotle, *Nicomachean Ethics* 1094b27-1095a2, in *Basic Works*, 936; Aristotle, *De Partibus Animalium* 639a10 ff, in *Basic Works*, 643 ff.

63. I do not here address questions concerning the naturalistic fallacy, as I believe the concluding sections of this chapter may make them less urgent or relevant.

64. Glidden, "Commonplaces," 184.

65. Aristotle, *Posterior Analytics* II, 19, 100a 4-14, in *Basic Works*, 185.

66. For "stabilizing," coming to "rest," or "stationariness" see *De Anima* Book III and *De Motu Animalium* (especially chs. 8-9). Perhaps the most important text is *Physics* Book II, ch.1, *Cf.* Aristotle, *Physics* Book 7, 247b10ff, in *Basic Works*, 236-38 and 348.

67. Aristotle, *Posterior Analytics* Book 1, ch. 1, 71a1, in *Basic Works*, 110.

68. Aristotle's tendency to refer to middle term in the singular seems to me to be an expression of the measuring and selecting procedure demonstration facilitates. Throughout his biological and physical and philosophical works Aristotle seems to be willing to accept a plurality of causes operating within a system.

69. See Glidden, "Commonplaces," 1998.

70. Aristotle derives the Greek term *episteme* (*Physics* Book VII ch.3, 247b10 ff.) from *stenai,* "to have come to a stop." In *De Motu Animalium* chs. 8 and 9 Aristotle views soul as that which affords any animate being the required place or point of integration and touch that motion requires.

71. Aristotle, *De Anima* Book 3, in *Basic Works*, 581 f.

72. It was to explain causation that Socrates introduced his makeshift method (*deuteron ploun*) in the *Phaedo*.

73. Aristotle, *Nicomachean Ethics* Book I, ch. 3, in *Basic Works*, 936-37.

74. *Eudemian Ethics* 1216b35, 219. Cf. Descartes, "Letter of Dedication," in *Meditations,* 3.

75. Martha Nussbaum, "Saving Aristotle's Appearances" in *Language and Logos: Studies in Ancient Greek Philosophy*, ed. Malcolm Schofield and Martha Craven Nussbaum (Cambridge: Cambridge University Press, 1982), 267-93. Confirmation of Nussbaum's warning may be found Waterfield's note at 433a in his recent translation. See Robin Waterfield, *Republic* (Oxford: Oxford University Press, 1993), 402.

76. Nussbaum, "Saving Aristotle's Appearances," 267.

77. Aristotle, *Nicomachean Ethics* 1145b1 ff, in *Basic Works*, 1037.

78. Aristotle, *De Anima* 402b23f, in *Basic Works*, 536.

79. *Cf.* H. Bonitz, Index Aristotelicus (1955), 809a40 ff. for a selection of texts testifying to Aristotle's view that scientists/teachers refine their theories through this practice of *apodidonai kata ten phantasian*. See also G. E. L. Owen, "Tithenai Ta Phainomena," in *Articles on Aristotle: Vol. 1: Science,* ed. Jonathan Barnes, Malcolm Schofield, and Richard Sorabji (London: Duckworth, 1975), 113-26.

80. See, for instance, Aristotle, *Categories* 7b24-25, in *Basic Works,* 20; or *Metaphysics* 1057a9, 1053a31-35, in *Basic Works,* 837, 845.

81. Or "paid back," as Cephalus might phrase it.

82. Aristotle sees certain discontinuities within knowledge and between knowledge and practice as physiological in nature (*Nicomachean Ethics* Book 7, ch. 3), and amenable to the care and management appropriate to those impeded by inadequate time, or because they are asleep or drunk.

83. Aristotle, *Nicomachean Ethics* Books 5 and 6, in *Basic Works,* 1002 ff. Aristotle explores practical wisdom (*phronesis*) and the behavior of practically wise persons (*phronimoi*).

84. Einstein addresses issues of measurement from an earth-grounded, if not exactly anthropocentric, starting point. Albert Einstein, *Relativity: The Special and General Theory,* trans. R.W. Lawson (New York: Random House, 1961). Cf. Albert Einstein, "Space-Time," in *Encyclopædia Britannica* Thirteenth Edition (1926).

85. The *Phaedo* is a philosophical introduction to mortality-as-measure. But, anticipating Heidegger, we also have Descartes' exploration of mortality-as-limit disclosing divinity in the *Third Meditation,* Section 49: "I . . . ask myself whether I have some power through which I can bring it about that I myself, who now am, will also exist a little later? . . . If such a power were in me, then I certainly would be aware of it. But I observe there is no such power; from this fact I know most evidently that I depend upon a being other than myself." Descartes, *Meditations,* 32. Aristotle seems to find this reflected in the natural teleology of human life.

86. "But we must add 'in a complete life.' For one swallow does not make a summer, nor does one day; and so too one day, or a short time, does not make a man blessed and happy." Aristotle, *Nicomachean Ethics* I, ch. 7, in *Basic Works,* 941ff.

87. Truth, *aletheia,* is described by Heidegger as meaning the uncovered. The river Lethe is the river of "forgetfulness." *A-letheia* has a link, philologically, to "not" + "forgetting."

88. We saw Plato explored the complexity of unity in the *Republic, Timaeus, Parmenides,* and the *Philebus* and elsewhere. Aristotle mounts parallel studies in the *Physics,* in his biological writings, and in the *Metaphysics.*

89. See, e.g., *Posterior Analytics* I, ch. 5, 74 a21f, in *Basic Works,* 118. See Robert Bolton, "Definition and Scientific Method in Aristotle's Posterior Analytics and Generation of Animals," in *Philosophical Issues in Aristotle's Biology,* ed. Allan Gotthelf and James G. Lennox (Cambridge: Cambridge University Press, 1987), 133, 136-38.

90. Aristotle, *Posterior Analytics* 92a16-18, in *Basic Works,* 165.

91. See Aristotle, *Metaphysics* 1045a23-25 and b16-18, in *Basic Works,* 819-20.

92. Aristotle, *Metaphysics* Book 4, 1006a18-29, in *The Basic Works,* 737-38. Aristotle is clearly concerned to address the vulnerable condition Socrates' conversationalists were left in if they simply took the risk he asked them to take of lending him their faith in the shared recollections of the "good," etc. Aristotle very explicitly sees his approach as permitting a defense against the charge of begging the question.

93. Aristotle, *De Anima* 402b23f, in *Basic Works,* 536.

94. Humphrey Carver was doyen of Canada's post-war housing planners. His comments, including the quote from Stein, are from "Building the Suburbs: a Planner's Reflections,"

in *City Magazine* 3 (1978), 40-45. I am grateful to Dr. Chris Sharpe, Geography Department, Memorial University of Newfoundland, for this text.

95. Plato, *Symposium* 195c, in *Collected Dialogues*, 547-48.

Nussbaum's study of related themes in various of her works, but especially in her edition of *Aristotle's De Motu Animalium* and in her *Fragility of Goodness: Luck and Ethics in Greek Tragedy and Philosophy* (Cambridge: Cambridge University Press, 1986).

96. *Physics* Book II and *De Anima* are the key Aristotelian texts. See also Martha Nussbaum's study of related themes in various of her works, but especially in her edition of *Aristotle's De Motu Animalium* and in her *Fragility of Goodness: Luck and Ethics in Greek Tragedy and Philosophy* (Cambridge: Cambridge University Press, 1986).

97. Aristotle, *Basic Works*, 1131 ff.

98. See David Wiggins, *Needs, Values Truth* (Oxford: Basil Blackwell, 1987).

99. Plato might say "forms."

100. Aristotle, *Nicomachean Ethics* 1138b2, in *Basic Works*, 1022.

101. Aristotle, *Nicomachean Ethics* 1139a35-36, in *Basic Works*, 1024.

102. The Greek term for definitions is *horoi*. "Boundary markers" are reference points surveyors and builders and architects use to structure the building and landscaping.

103. *Physics* Book 2, ch.1, 92b 9-15. "'By nature' the animals and their parts exist, and the plants and the simple bodies (earth, fire, air, water) for we say that these and the like exist (*physei*) 'by nature.' (They all) present a feature in which they differ from things which are *not* constituted by nature. Each of them has *within itself* a principle of motion *and of stationariness* (*staseos*) (in respect of place, or of growth and decrease, or by way of alteration.) On the other hand, a bed and a coat . . ., *qua* receiving these designations—i.e., in so far as they are products of art—have no innate impulse to change." *Cf. Physics* Book 7, 247b10f, in *Basic Works*, 348; and Plato's *Phaedrus* 245e, in *Collected Dialogues*, 493.

104. The concluding reflective portions of the Derrida/Eisenman collaboration seem to miss—and need—this distinction. See Derrida and Eisenman, *Chora*.

105. See Deleuze, "The Simulacrum;" Dorothea Olkowski, *Gilles Deleuze and the Ruin of Representation* (Berkeley: University of California Press, 1999); Roberto Calasso, *The Marriage of Cadmus and Harmony* (New York: Vintage Random House, 1994).

106. Paden, "Values and Planning," 5-7.

107. Funding in partial support of this research was provided by the *Challenges and Opportunities in the Knowledge Based Economy* competition of the *Social Sciences and Humanities Research Council of Canada* Strategic Grants Program. I am grateful to Craig Cramm for his insightful help in reading Heidegger's treatment of place, as I am to Stephen Hawkins for his generous critique of this study; and, finally, to Professor J.G. (Peter) Dawson for his patient, revealing, and practically wise understanding of Aristotle.

Chapter 8

Municipal Parks in New York City: Olmsted, Riis, and the Transformation of the Urban Landscape, 1858-1897

Mary Hague and Nancy Siegel

Between 1858 and 1897, the landscape of New York City was transformed by the retention and addition of open spaces for municipal parks and playgrounds. This process was driven by the widespread belief that access to nature was necessary for the moral and physical health of the city's population. This paper argues that the alteration of visual and physical landscapes in New York City through the creation of public parks, as first guided by landscape architect Frederick Law Olmsted in the 1850s and later by photojournalist and activist Jacob Riis in the 1890s, represents not only the creation of cultural landscapes but of therapeutic landscapes as well. Therapeutic landscapes are defined by Robin Kearns and Wilbert Gesler as "places that have achieved lasting reputations for promoting physical, mental and spiritual healing."[1] Parks are therapeutic landscapes as re-creations of traditional healing landscapes, identified by Gesler as those offering "fresh air . . . of the countryside or magnificent scenery."[2] The urban parks of New York City reflect an additional element of the therapeutic landscape, that of providing an "atmosphere in which social distinction and social inequalities are kept at a minimum."[3] This chapter explores transformations of the New York City landscape through the creation of two public parks: Central Park and Mulberry Bend Park.[4] The approach taken here to therapeutic landscapes is that of the new cultural geography, that "landscapes reflect both human intentions and actions and the constraints and structures imposed by society."[5] Central Park and Mulberry Bend Park are also cultural landscapes, understood as both structural and humanistic landscapes, shaped by philanthropic and paternalistic humanism.[6] The dominant social and political institutions of the mid-to-late nineteenth century in New York City identified the city, especially impoverished areas, as unhealthy[7] and those same institutions devised transformations of the landscape as restorative to the health of urban neighborhoods and of the city at large. By the end of the century the park as a recreational space had become a symbol of the salutary benefits of nature. By examining the designed topographies of such public spaces, and the institutions and individuals shaping them, one can begin to frame a discussion of municipal parks as therapeutic landscapes.

Both Central Park and Mulberry Bend Park demonstrate this shared view of the salutary benefits of fresh air and exercise. Municipal parks, designed by landscape architects as grand testaments to the beauty of nature, and small neighborhood parks, as promoted by their advocates and the emerging middle class, were seen as having played a critical role in the health of New York City. Both Olmsted and Riis were committed to the democratic principle of designed open spaces. However, while Olmsted was motivated by aesthetic concerns, with collateral moral benefit, Riis was one of many small urban park advocates driven not primarily by aesthetics, but by political and moral imperatives. The changing political institutions and class structure of nineteenth-century urban America, the prevalent assumption of the salutary benefits of nature, and the paternalistic and altruistic concerns of reformers, all combined to transform the urban landscape of New York City in an attempt to create therapeutic landscapes out of undesirable sites. During the late nineteenth century, many urban reformers viewed New York City's urbanism as negative and the rural or natural setting as positive. There were two prevalent antidotes to the city: the park and the suburb. Olmsted regarded municipal parks necessary if urban residents were to maintain "a temperate, good-natured and healthy state of mind."[8] Jacob Riis hoped his 1890 publication, *How the Other Half Lives*, would educate and activate its readers, motivating them to take actions to improve the living conditions of the tenement poor. One effort to improve the lives of those living in tenements was through the addition of small neighborhood parks and playgrounds.

This study begins with a brief history of the urban development of New York City to demonstrate the perceived need for urban reform. From settlement house movements to sanitation codes and labor laws, the mid-to-late nineteenth century represents a period of vigorous reform in policy, planning, and philosophies regarding urban life.[9] The environmental effects of urbanization and the various reforms designed to ameliorate those effects were instrumental in the arguments of both Olmsted and Riis in their promotion of therapeutic landscapes.

Urbanization of New York City

The rapid and continuous urbanization of New York City began at the end of the eighteenth century. The economic heart of the city was located in lower Manhattan, which functioned as a commercial port and harbor. The city's continual use of the harbor facilitated rebuilding in the 1780s after the Revolutionary War, and also served as a magnet for new immigrants. Old buildings were restored, and new ones built, attracting both businesses and new citizens, and by 1810, New York City was the largest city in the nation. As commercial as the lower portion of the city was becoming, the northern reaches remained fairly rural. Horses had been breeding wild in the regions of upper Manhattan since the 1750s. Additionally, what is now Central Park was good pasture for cattle, which were gathered in the morning, driven downtown toward Wall Street, and returned in the evening. It was common to see sheep grazing in the Sheep Meadow of Central Park as late as 1880. New York City was replete with a menagerie of agrarian reminders and the existence of the country, manifested by the presence of cows, sheep, pigs, and horses was common in the city of the early and mid-nineteenth century.[10]

While the city maintained some signs of its rural heritage, increased commerce and growing populations were already at work transforming the urban landscape in the creation of apartment buildings and factories. With the growth of New York City, a gridiron system was adopted for street planning to maximize the profit margin for building space. Such planning reflected little concern for public spaces, much less open spaces. Increased growth was also accompanied by an increased congestion of people and conveyances on city streets. Refuse was left uncollected, making sidewalks impassable and the odor obnoxious. One particular concern was the increasing lack of exercise and fresh air afforded to the inhabitants of this urban center. Working in factories and office buildings for long hours each day left little time for family, recreation, or improving the general health of one's body and mind. The psychological as well as physical health of the city was compromised. Widespread fear of unmanaged urbanization and associated moral decay surfaced during New York's transition to a more urban and industrial city; concerned city residents sought explanation and reform.

In response, a number of theories regarding societal betterment and reform became salient. From the 1850s to the 1890s, these theories varied from Social Darwinism to the Social Gospel movement, from the worship of capitalism to the embrace of socialism. Social Darwinism and capitalism emphasized the role of the individual in creating his or her own fate while the Social Gospel movement and socialism emphasized, in the case of the former, Christian altruism, and, in the case of the latter, societal responsibilities in shaping the lives of individuals.[11] By the end of the century, the transformation of one's environment became a dominant theory of social reform, and, as will be demonstrated in the cases of Central Park and Mulberry Bend Park, this took the form of therapeutic landscapes.

Town commons and small recreational lots had existed previously in America since the seventeenth century. Until the 1840s, cemeteries were the "parks" of choice for taking in fresh air, grass, trees, and exercise. This did not detract from the need or desire for more open spaces and natural settings. In 1848, the American architect Andrew Jackson Downing was one of the first advocates to give expression to the concept of a public space dedicated for recreation in New York City. Downing published his ideas in an article titled, "A Talk about Public Parks and Gardens," in the magazine he edited at the time, *Horticulturist*.[12] Soon after, Downing traveled to England and visited the public parks of London. If England's monarchy had provided generously for its subjects through the creation of parks for public use, how then could a democracy such as the United States, with its free citizens, not have great parks and settings open to all? The concept of a free and democratic park, "a People's Park," became the ideological focus for Central Park.[13]

Andrew Jackson Downing and others interested in social reform believed that parks and other pastoral settings promoted social refinement regardless of class. From this proper association with nature, they concluded, urban residents would experience a corrective moral influence. This philosophy represented a new democratic concept for public space and its use by all classes. This would indeed distinguish Americans from the class-conscious British. As Downing elaborated:

> We have said nothing of the social influence of such a great park in New York. But this is really the most interesting phase of the whole matter. It is a fact, not a little remarkable, that ultra democratic as are the political tendencies of America, its most intelligent social tendencies are almost wholly in a contrary direction. And among the topics discussed by the advocates and opponents of the new park, none seem so poorly understood as the social aspect of the thing. It is indeed both curious and amusing to see the stand taken on the one hand by the million, that the park is made for the "upper ten," who ride in fine carriages; and, on the other hand, by the wealthy and refined, that a park in this country, will be "usurped by rowdies and low people." Shame upon our republican compatriots, who so little understand the elevating influences of the beautiful in nature and in art, when enjoyed in common by thousands and hundreds of thousands of all classes without distinction.[14]

Downing's summary of the proposed clash of the classes was at the forefront of debate over the creation of the park. The need for, and belief in, societal reform through urban planning prevailed, at least temporarily. Downing's main argument for the park was the lack of, "any breathing space for pure air, any recreation ground for healthful exercise, any pleasant roads for riding or driving, or any enjoyment of that lovely and refreshing natural beauty." He observed that "New York, and American cities generally, are voluntarily and ignorantly living in a state of complete forgetfulness of nature."[15]

Central Park: Theory and Aesthetic Design

Throughout the 1840s, Downing, among others such as the Romantic poet and editor of the *New York Post*, William Cullen Bryant, began to appeal to public officials to secure a vast tract of land to be used for the sole purpose of establishing a park for New York City residents. On July 11, 1851, the legislature of New York City under Mayor Ambrose C. Kingsland passed the Jones' Wood Park bill. A plot of waterfront property, known as Jones' Wood, located along the East River from 66th Street to 75th Street, was chosen to be converted into a public park.[16] By August of that year, opposition to Jones' Wood was so fierce that the Board of Aldermen appointed a special committee to investigate the merits or liabilities of the proscribed site. The committee strongly recommended a tract of land in the center of Manhattan Island, citing greater convenience, access, and reduced cost. On July 21, 1853, the city of New York spent over six million dollars, and took possession of 778 acres (ultimately 843 acres) of land now known as Central Park.[17] The original designs for the park were supplied by chief engineer, Egbert Viele. In September 1857, Frederick Law Olmsted applied for and was appointed to the position of superintendent under Viele. Olmsted hired over one thousand previously unemployed men to begin clearing the site designated for the park. Without much notice or concern, more than sixteen hundred inhabitants on this land, mainly Irish, German, and African Americans were summarily evicted only to be absorbed elsewhere in the city.[18] (The issue of displacement will be revisited below in the discussion of Mulberry Bend Park.) The tract of land to become this public park would have to be cleared, resculpted, and shaped as its bare condition was nothing more than raw potential (fig. 8.1).

On Olmsted's first day of work, Viele's plans were rejected by the park commissioners, who then opened a general competition for new plans. With Calvert Vaux (an associate of Andrew Jackson Downing), Olmsted submitted the winning designs in 1858 for the park, which they called "Greensward." Although Vaux was the instigator for submitting the designs, Olmsted was appointed architect-in-chief, with Vaux as consulting landscape architect. Olmsted and Vaux are credited for the design of the park, however, they were influenced greatly by Downing's design concepts for the park and relied upon surveys first arranged by Egbert Viele. Viele, too, submitted plans for the redesigned park. However, he merely resubmitted his original plans, feeling that no one could improve upon his initial designs.[19] In addition to designing a transverse system of roadways below grade level, the Olmsted/Vaux entry also took into account eighteenth-century picturesque design theories found in English parks and gardens. Olmsted had lived in London in 1850 (where he undoubtedly would have seen A. J. Downing), frequenting parks such as Birkenhead Park. Olmsted was struck immediately by the fact that the park was open to the general public.[20] This concept of applied humanism with respect to public parks remained influential throughout Olmsted's career while he focused his attention on nature theories and the spiritual effects of pleasing visual stimuli. While members of the New York literary and artistic elite, such as Washington Irving, William Cullen Bryant, and Andrew Jackson Downing became embroiled in the political aspects of designating city space for a public park, Olmsted did not consider himself foremost to be a social reformer. Through combined efforts, however, the shape of Central Park became an aesthetically motivated space for social change.

For Frederick Law Olmsted and Calvert Vaux the designs for Central Park were meant to serve as an antidote to urban life in New York City. The industrial revolution had come to America and, despite enormous advantages to the economy, the working and living environment of the city had become overwhelmingly stressful for a growing segment of the population. As thousands of workers and merchants flocked to New York in search of fame and fortune, the "simpler, less complicated" rural life became a memory, relegated to the confines of nostalgia. In addition, by the time Olmsted and Vaux designed Central Park in the late 1850s, America had been influenced by the Romantic movement and its relationship to the American landscape. By the 1850s, America was seen by many as a new Eden, and Olmsted's charge would be to design a new Garden. It is fitting then that Olmsted believed firmly that his park, through the aesthetic and healthful powers of nature, would enable others to achieve moral and social betterment. Referred to as the "lungs" of the city, the philosophy and design for Central Park, as conceived and executed by Olmsted and Vaux, were part of a progressive theory of the restorative powers of nature within an urban climate.[21] The concept for Central Park, however, comes out of the tradition of landscaped estates for the British nobility of the seventeenth and eighteenth centuries. This historical type of sculpted landscape had an enormous impact on American park design.[22]

The establishment of public parks was popularized in England by the Victorian era to serve as a foil for the lack of recreational areas, which was due to industrial growth in England's urban cities. However, the precursor to the public park comes from an established tradition of park design with the noble class in mind. In England, the concept of public parks has its origins in the seventeenth century when at mid-century, British Parliament passed ordinances for the establishment of parks for gentile walking and recreation.[23] This occurred not only on royal properties in London as a result of population increases, but also wealthy land owners opened their hunting grounds as well. By the eighteenth century, British landscape designer to the aristocracy, Lancelot "Capability" Brown was one of the first to reject formal, linear gardens and instituted softer, free-form landscape designs that incorporated the theme of a unified appearance. Brown's preferences for combining wooded pastures with open grasslands would become influential upon Olmsted's design style. Brown favored contrived irregularities in his planned landscapes to increase the "natural" appearance.[24] Brown was also in the habit of razing entire villages for the sake of his constructed parks.[25] Thus, the displacement of over sixteen hundred inhabitants for the Central Park designs was not without precedent and neither was it considered harsh nor unnecessary when done in the name of public health or beautification.

Critics denounced Brown's designs for their visual emphasis upon conspicuous wealth and consumption, arguing that a combination of the rough and rugged (the sublime) with the pastoral in park design best achieved a truly pleasing and natural effect.[26] The controversy over how much man should control nature and still maintain a "natural" appearance would ultimately have an impact upon Frederick Law Olmsted and Calvert Vaux as their designs for Central Park replicated the artificial countryside so popularized by English landscape design. Not only was English landscape design of importance to American landscape architects, but the very essence of what parks represented as symbols of elite leisure was called into question with the formation of an enormous public space like Central Park.

How the land was perceived in the eighteenth century has overarching implications as to how the landscape was received by the nineteenth century through the work of landscape architects such as Olmsted. The structured appearance of the eighteenth-century garden was viewed as an ideal landscape, a sanctum sanctorum from which to escape the harsh realities of life and a manifestation of the exercise of reason and control over nature. The land was to be reshaped for visual enjoyment and the contemplation of landscape became a pursuit no longer reserved for the wealthy alone. The casual stroll was the perfect vehicle in which to enjoy nature, but with a detached air. One should look upon nature, but not act within it.[27] The notion of physical distance and the visual gaze would be elemental in Olmsted's theory for how Central Park should be received by visitors although it would be perceived as an open park for recreational and healthful benefits. The tradition that informed Olmsted viewed the landscape in the form of the planned garden or the reshaped landscape, in which the direct imposition of man's handiwork is implied. In a shift from private to public parks, the Cartesian philosophy of detached contemplation would be combined with a "Romantic sympathy for mankind."[28] While Olmsted would himself remain detached from the visitors of Central Park, he worked to transform the natural environment of New York to allow for the interaction of people within nature as a shared emotional relationship. Olmsted would combine the planned park concept of eighteenth-century British landscapists with a late Romantic vision of nature as a healing force. By the late nineteenth century, that aesthetic would become a modern approach to therapeutic landscape design and Central Park would become a dominant symbol of nature in New York City.

In addition, the aesthetic theory for Central Park reflected the tradition of American Romanticism. As a result of the Romantic movement in America in the early nineteenth century, many Americans believed that nature itself contained restorative powers capable of soothing a weary soul. Olmsted was influenced by those who believed nature possessed a spiritual quality and the beauty one found in nature could lead one's thoughts heavenward. The harmonizing effects of nature were believed to instill the presence of God. The potential for spiritual and moral betterment as a direct result of communing with nature was an exciting prospect, particularly for Olmsted who wanted to reach out to the urban residents who felt far removed from nature's beauty or could little afford to travel in search of it. First and foremost, however, Olmsted was a landscape architect who saw the park as his palette. He saw himself an instrument of social change as an aesthetic reformer, but by no means a political activist. The role of Central Park was to function through aesthetics as a therapeutic landscape.

While New York's political and social institutions of the 1850s and 1860s would tell a different story, Olmsted was more of the theoretician than a policy maker, who touched upon a timely urban issue in much the same way that Thoreau spoke for a mass of nature lovers. Walden Pond and Central Park share a common transcendental quality. While Thoreau's Walden Pond served as the vehicle for private reflection on the beauties of nature in solitude, Olmsted replaced the definition of solitude as by one's self with the idea of solitude as communing with nature despite an urban presence. Clearly, for Olmsted, Romanticism functioned as a utopian escape from the harshness of the city by replacing reality with the picturesque. These dueling sentiments were not easily resolved but had to be recognized as coexisting. Even Ralph Waldo Emerson, (whom Olmsted admired greatly) although distrustful of the city, had to contend with the urban environment. In his journal, Emerson wrote, "I wish to have rural strength and religion for my children, and I wish city facility and polish, I find with chagrin that I cannot have both."[29] Central Park was an attempt to reconcile this Emersonian dilemma and Olmsted, too, had to contend with the noise, filth, and pollution of the city. While he found these conditions deplorable, he did believe in the moral uplift and necessity of public parks. In terms of urban development, Olmsted was concerned with population density. While the specific issue of tenement overcrowding would be left to Jacob Riis and the urban reformers later in the century, Olmsted called for comprehensive city planning as part of social welfare in order to maintain a relationship with nature in the urban environment. While Olmsted defended city life, he admitted that it was removed from nature.[30] In effect, with Central Park, and later with his designs for Prospect Park in Brooklyn, Olmsted reinstituted and reinvented the town common on an urban scale as a gathering place with therapeutic benefits: social, physical, and spiritual. Olmsted operated both with a latent Romantic, Transcendental philosophy of nature and with a form-follows-function approach to landscape design. To Olmsted, the use or function of the park would in itself dictate the form or design of the park. Olmsted, like Ralph Waldo Emerson, believed that man was capable of reform and spiritual improvement through proximity to nature and it was Olmsted's charge to design a space that would prove his point. Through his and Vaux's plans, they would channel visitors through a highly organized space (although perceived as rambling and casual) in ways that would provide moderate physical exercise along pathways leading to splendid vistas of natural beauty for spiritual enrichment.

Central Park was to be an organized landscape one-half mile wide and two and one-half miles long, north of 59th Street between 5th and 8th Avenues. The "Greensward" plan for Central Park (fig. 8.2) reveals not only the influences of the English park tradition, and the tenets of Romanticism, but ushers in a new philosophy for therapeutic landscapes in the United States. Olmsted and Vaux saw the Croton aqueduct on the park's northern end as a physical barrier and decided to leave the northern end semi-wild, while concentrating on the southern half of the park through the addition of groves, boating ponds, meadows, and walkways. The curving pedestrian walks, bridle paths, and carriage roads were arranged so that they never intersected at grade level with cross-town traffic. The design included areas for both casual promenades and more formal gatherings. In addition to the stipulated incorporation of three playing fields, a parade ground, winter skating pond, flower garden, tower, and music hall or exhibition building, Olmsted and Vaux added such pleasantries as bird cages, drinking fountains, and a zoological garden.[31] In the winter, the skating pond became a popular site for recreation for both genders. The northern end of the pond was reserved as the "Ladies' Pond" for "the more timid and delicate ones."[32] To accomplish their goals of a large, open, democratic park, Olmsted increased his work force to over two thousand men. While Olmsted's efforts were concentrated on the completion of the park, the societal benefits of providing jobs to unemployed workers is often noted as evidence of his social concern. While it is not the intent of this article to portray Olmsted as callous or disinterested, his primary impetus for change was his aesthetic design for the landscape of Central Park.

Olmsted was driven to alter the terrain in such a way as to give the convincing appearance that its variety of natural formations and plantings had always existed. To do so, he relied upon the preparatory work of Egbert Viele. Through Viele's survey of the elevations, botany, and geology of the Central Park location, Olmsted carefully selected the species of trees, plants, and shrubbery appropriate for the site.[33] He created "natural" landscapes: meadows, hills, woods, and even ponds and lakes. He included areas for genteel activities such as horseback riding, summer boating, winter skating, and year-round promenades. It must be remembered that every square foot of the park was re-shaped and molded (mostly by manual labor and horse-drawn carts) according to an elaborate plan. When reading the plan, the landscape becomes a text suggesting human movement and use. The serpentine paths would become vehicles for human transport, while the re-contoured land and elaborate placement of rocks, shrubbery, and trees would be enjoyed from a distance. In addition, the park would come to represent a symbolic landscape.[34] One could immediately associate inherent, natural factors such as trees, ponds, and rocky outcroppings with the rejuvenating effects of nature.[35] However, the imposed, more abstract features such as pathways, fences, and "keep off the grass" signs symbolize man's control of his environment. From the "Greensward" plan one can sense immediately the Cartesian reasoned control of nature blended with the Romantic sensibility of nature as a source of delight and enjoyment. Olmsted envisioned a park that would provide a sense of place for visitors. Central Park was to be a locale for aesthetic beauty, peace, and tranquility. Said Olmsted, "The Park throughout is a single work of art, and as such subject to the primary law of every work of art, namely, that it shall be framed upon a single, noble motive."[36] That motive, in theory, was the creation of a therapeutic landscape. However, the implementation of Olmsted's vision required careful negotiation of design details in order to satisfy the practical (and physical) demands of a park open to all.

The park was seen by Olmsted and Vaux as a whole. However, the parts of this whole need to be examined to better appreciate the magnitude of this collaborative design. Vaux's efforts as an architect gave shape to Olmsted's ideas and theories concerning the look and use of the park. Their collaboration was strengthened by Vaux's practical design experience in conjunction with Olmsted's enthusiasm to create an expansive picturesque retreat from urban noise and pollution. A primary concern was the issue of how to accommodate and direct various types of traffic through the park. The solution was contained in four separate traffic systems designated for carriages, horses, and pedestrians. Each of these systems was to be independent and not to intersect with the other, making for separate experiences based on mode of transportation. Carriages, horses, and pedestrians each received their own paths with an additional transverse system of moving carriages from east to west placed below grade level. This held aesthetic as well as urban planning advantages. In fact, the "Greensward" plan was the only one of thirty-three entries to place transverse roads for carriages below the grade level of the park.[37] Further, while wide, rambling drives accommodated carriages from east to west, bridal paths circled the reservoir and around the park, careful to pass under pedestrians and carriages through Vaux's constructed underpasses. The footpaths followed the carriage paths, although they did not intersect, allowing the pedestrian to stroll leisurely without fear of being knocked down by an overzealous driver.[38]

Olmsted intended the primary role for the urban dweller in the park to be that of a visual passenger. While carriage rides after work offered psychological benefits, one could surely enjoy the park's scenery as a pedestrian, and Olmsted desired to maintain as much open space as possible, not only for strolling about, but to accommodate well-placed vistas. In fact, several paths lead to structures designed as scenic lookouts as the culminating experience for the pedestrian. The Terrace, the Mall, the Ramble, the Pond, and Terrace Lake all served to move visitors around and within the great park. The Mall, for example, with its 1212 feet long and 35 feet wide promenade, was designed as a pedestrian boulevard, lined with American elms and benches, and fashioned after the elegant boulevards of Paris.[39] The Mall visually led to the Terrace and across the pond to Vista Rock—a rocky outcropping that combined a picturesque view of natural scenery with the pastoral setting of the Mall. By contrast, the Ramble was an area of the park designed to be heavily wooded, giving the illusion that it was left in a state of wilderness. Its architecture consisted of rustic bridges and shelters, a strong contrast to the elegant promenade leading to the Terrace. The combined effect was one of constantly changing but consistently pleasing views of nature as if to convince the wanderer that they were far from the city. In addition, Olmsted and Vaux were careful to position these locations on angles, creating diagonal lines of sight to detract from city buildings along Fifth and Eighth Avenues.[40]

The "Greensward" plan, with its wooded pastures and open grounds reflects in many ways the influence of Capability Brown and the English tradition. The gentle meandering shape of the pathways paralleled the internal structure. Similar to Thomas Jefferson's use of the curvilinear walkway around the west lawn at his home, Monticello, Olmsted, too, stayed away from straight lines and sharp angles, so obviously manmade and not reflective of nature's/God's plan. Olmsted's plan for the Zoological Gardens also recalls Jefferson's desire for a similar entity at Monticello. Jefferson wanted a zoological garden complete with animals:

Let it be an asylum for hares, squirrels, pheasants, partridges, and every other wild animal (except those of prey). Court them to it, by laying food for them in proper places. Procure a buck-elk, to be, as it were, monarch of the wood; but keep him shy, that his appearance may not lose its effect by too much familiarity. (A buffalo might be confined also).[41]

The zoological feature has overtones relating to the English park design that accommodated tamed creatures as part of its contrived natural setting, only to reinforce the domination of man over nature in a sophisticated manner.

Olmsted and Jefferson have another similarity of greater importance. Both landscape architects designed their land to instill a sense of pride in the American landscape. Jefferson included the vista of the mountains of Virginia as part of his panoramic view from Monticello, dissolving the boundaries between personal property and national property. In addition, he was an avid proponent of American species of trees and shrubbery. Olmsted, too, made use of the American elm and American ivy, for example, as his theory for creating a democratic public park open to all was "to speak to" the people of a nation not yet one hundred years in existence. The challenges of designing a large urban park also required Olmsted and Vaux to look beyond the immediate park boundaries to the outlying neighborhood.

Olmsted created a "fence" of planted trees along the perimeter of the park. This would provide a visual barrier for those living just outside the boundaries along Fifth Avenue while creating a sense of enclosure for those within. The selection and placement of trees surrounding the perimeter of the park served to beautify the immediate area, creating a wall or boundary to define the park's property, and presenting a rural vista from the windows of the wealthy apartment dwellers residing around the park. To counter the rectangular shape of the Park's outermost edges, the interior rambling paths and gentle undulating hills served as a natural foil for the strict, linear pattern of Manhattan's urban street system. Unlike a grand entrance proposed by Richard Morris Hunt, Olmsted placed virtually no visual importance on the "formal" entrance to Central Park off Fifth Avenue at 59th Street. The reasoning behind this was Olmsted's desire to allow city dwellers to "disappear" into the organized wilderness of the park. A gentle and visually unencumbered flow from city life to country life was the intended effect. Once within the park, Olmsted's and Vaux's order and design achieved a completely "natural" appearance.

The visitor was left to stroll casually, seemingly as if being led through nature by the sheer force of its beauty. Olmsted crafted the walkways to direct the leisurely stroller toward specific points of interest and scenic views. New Yorkers needn't travel to the Hudson Valley to find romantic scenery, Olmsted would contend; it could be found in their own urban environment. Olmsted returned the focus to the "land' in the urban landscape. Inherent in park design is the process of shaping and sculpting the landscape to replicate the desired look of natural growth and formations as found in the wilderness. The rocky marsh (fig. 8.1) that characterized the park before Olmsted set to work on this land originally contained few existing trees or shrubbery, but Olmsted designed a space that would compete with travel to the Catskill Mountains. Many who would use the park would also travel to see the wonders of the American landscape in the Catskills so long as proper fences and other safety barriers had been provided. And, this was in addition to the promise of an afternoon croquet match after partaking in the exhilarating wilds of God's handiwork. The American public wanted to experience nature as long as it posed no threat to their safety and pleasurable amenities were served alongside. Even Thomas Cole, painter of Hudson River scenery, was obliged to remove the fences and gates from his paintings although many were already in place by the time he painted his landscape views. The tourist industry thrived on members of the middle and upper classes, who found the concept of a park in their neighborhood a delightful prospect, as long as it was to be utilized by fellow gentlefolk.

In addition to the geography of the landscape, there exists a psychology related to the interior versus exterior spaces of Central Park. It was intended by Olmsted that the moral uplift of fresh air and light exercise be complemented by the ability of the visitor to leave the park and further one's moral and intellectual education through the environs outside the park's walls. The park was surrounded by museums of history, art, science, and natural history. The Astor Library, the New-York Historical Society, the Metropolitan Museum of Art, and the Museum of Natural History for example, formed the next ring of culture to be gained upon exiting the park.[42]

Olmsted firmly believed in the restorative powers of nature and felt confident that a space such as Central Park would confer social and moral benefits as a result of its aesthetic experience. In 1870 he wrote a paper, "Public Parks and the Enlargement of Towns," presented before the American Social Science Association in which he addressed this theme:

> As to the effect on public health, there is no question that it is already great. The testimony of the older physicians of the city will be found unanimous on this point. Says one: "Where I formerly ordered patients of a certain class to give up their business altogether and go out of town, I now often advise simply moderation, and prescribe a ride in the Park before going to their offices, and again a drive with their families before dinner."[43]

Olmsted was proud to report that, "except in one or two cases where the ruling policy of the management has been departed from—cases which prove the rule—not the slightest injury from wantonness, carelessness, or ruffianism has occurred."[44] Central Park served as a model for urban recreation and a respite from an industrialized society amidst growing fears of urban alienation as a result of industrialization. Olmsted seemingly solved the problem of "[retaining] proximity with nature in what was swiftly becoming a nation of cities."[45] While Olmsted was concerned about the therapeutic and social value of Central Park, it must also be noted that his vision for public use was relegated to docile play and perambulations primarily by those who lived closest to the Fifth Avenue entrance. The park was a gentle and genteel model for public intercourse, excluding rough activities and social crudities. "Crude" activities were banned, internal roads were laid to discourage racing, and children were not allowed to walk off the intended walkways. Olmsted instituted 125 varieties of signs placed around the park and enlisted an army of "keepers" to instruct and correct offensive behavior.[46]

For as casual an environment as was proposed by Olmsted for public enjoyment, the fear of moral corruption by the lower classes and poorly educated resulted in a strict policing of affairs. As one appreciative (and upper class) visitor to the park noted:

> No shows of any kind are allowed on the Park grounds; no jugglers, gamblers—except those disguised as gentlemen—puppet-shows, peddlers of flowers, players upon so-called musical instruments, ballad-singers, nor hand-organ men; in fact none of the great army of small persecutors who torment the outside world, can enter into this pleasant place to make us miserable in it.[47]

This description from 1869 provides insight into the societal restrictions present in Central Park from its earliest days and demonstrates the conflicting definitions of how a therapeutic landscape might function. Social inequalities would not exist in the ideal park setting. While there are certain healthful benefits of sitting quietly in nature, enjoying the landscape from a comfortable and non-confrontational distance, other perspectives and perceptions of recreation are equally valid in terms of the experiential qualities found within public parks. A recent observation suggests that landscape "involves as much what is *ex*cluded as what is *in*cluded in view or perception. This observation is crucially important in developing the connection between landscape and health, for people can believe a place to be healthy when, from their perspective there is simply an absence of unhealthy elements."[48] The "unhealthy elements" referred to by New York's elite gave rise to discussions of insiders versus outsiders with regard to who would benefit most from the park.

Olmsted was frustrated ultimately by politics, not for the altruistic reasons associated with Jacob Riis, but for the delays that prevented him from his ultimate vision for New York City. This is an important point to make because by the end of the nineteenth century, as Jacob Riis was pressuring Tammany Hall to establish more small neighborhood parks for the urban poor, aesthetic motivation was superseded by urgent social causes. Olmsted took a leave of absence from his position in 1861 to accept a post as general secretary of the United States Sanitary Commission.[49] Olmsted left this position in the summer of 1863, but was unable to return to his work on Central Park, as both he and Vaux had resigned in May 1863 due to irreconcilable differences with the park commissioners over resource allocations. However, both men returned to the park in 1865 to continue work at various times on this project, which was not truly completed until the late 1880s.[50] The completion of the park was hindered by the political turmoil of Tammany Hall. Political corruption and greed within the local government of New York City forced a bitter letter to the *New York Times* from Olmsted who, by 1874, had difficulties acquiring adequate funding for staff and services:

> The Mayor and Common Council elected as though reformers gave themselves up entirely to political huckstering and bargaining. Every department except Health has been shown to be chiefly ruled by regard for patronage. The Department of Parks is no exception although probably better. The evil results of this are that work costs much more than twice what it would under good government.[51]

In addition to limited resources, Olmsted was equally unsettled by the fact that although ten million people visited Central Park in 1871, its uptown location made it inaccessible to those who needed it most.[52] He responded accordingly in 1870:

> For practical every-day purposes to the great mass of the people, the park might as well be a hundred miles away. There are hundreds of thousands who have never seen it, more hundreds of thousands who have seen it only on a Sunday or holiday. The children of the city to whom it should be of the greatest use, can only get to it on holidays or in vacations, and then must pay car-fare both ways.[53]

What Olmsted failed to understand was that those children most in need of the park setting and fresh air would have neither holidays, nor vacations, nor car-fare. Without an inexpensive and extensive system of mass transit in New York City, classes tended to cluster together. To live within walking distance of one's workplace and home was commonplace. Herein lies the fallacy of the democratic principle for a therapeutic landscape. Although Olmsted truly believed that Central Park would enable the lower classes to acquire "manners and aesthetics" from their wealthier counterparts while taking in the healthful benefits of nature in the park, this social experiment would require reevaluation. Olmsted went on to design numerous parks within the five boroughs of Manhattan; however, regardless of his fear and criticism of urban population density, he never saw his park designs as for those outside of a specific class of people. Class, for Olmsted, might not have been defined by a monetary level, but it certainly carried with it specific moral and social conduct. While he firmly believed that Central Park could offer moral inspiration to the less fortunate (provided they minded their manners while in the park), he also supposed that social refinement and grace were not of the utmost importance to "the other half." Olmsted and Riis would agree that parks of all sizes were crucial for the healthful and moral benefit of all classes. But by the 1890s the location, size, and appearance of public parks were driven more by issues of class and economics, than by the aesthetic standards of Olmsted and Vaux.

Urban Reform

Between Olmsted's design of Central Park in the late 1850s and the arrival of Jacob Riis in the 1870s, New York City underwent profound changes. The population, especially of the poor and indigent, grew very rapidly from 1870 to 1890 as a result of immigration, industrialization, urbanization, and post-Civil War upheavals.[54] The extreme wealth of the upper class living on Fifth Avenue, known as "two miles of millionaires," was a stark contrast to the appalling conditions of the poorer classes living in lower Manhattan and on the Lower East Side. Tenement housing for the poor offered little light, space, or air. By 1900, there were more than 80,000 tenements in New York City proper, which housed 2.3 million out of 3.4 million city dwellers.[55] One description of the substandard living arrangements appeared in the press in 1888:

> They are prison-like structures of brick, with narrow doors and windows, cramped passages and steep rickety stairs. They are built through from one street to the other with a somewhat narrower building connecting them. . . . The narrow court-yard . . . in the middle is a damp foul-smelling place, supposed to do duty as an airshaft; had the foul fiend designed these great barracks they could not have been more villainously arranged to avoid any chance of ventilation.[56]

The impoverished sections of the city were besieged with illness, violence, alcoholism, and prostitution. Riots occurred frequently over poor wages or the high prices of food and fuel, including a 1874 riot over labor issues in Tompkins Square Park (leading to the park's redesign for easier police control).[57]

Urban environmental problems at the turn of the century, and the response of reformers to those problems, represented a shift in environmental concerns from the conservation and preservation of natural resources to issues of sanitation and public health.[58] Overcrowded tenements, streets and alleys full of animal and human waste, and air and water pollution were just a few of the noxious conditions related to public health concerns. These problems were exacerbated by increasing tenement population density, insufficient sewers and sewerage systems, a lack of municipal solid waste disposal and street cleaning, unenforced building codes, and the absence of requirements for safe working conditions. Urbanites were assaulted by smoke from factories and homes, while waste from slaughterhouses clogged nearby streams and rivers. Urban industries exposed the population to a myriad of health hazards, including "phossy jaw" (infection of the jawbones caused by exposure to phosphorous), poisoning, and the loss of limbs to machines.[59] Public health crises from communicable diseases like tuberculosis, typhoid, and cholera, resulted from densely concentrated populations and inadequate hygiene, especially in the poorer parts of the city of lower Manhattan.[60] The overwhelming hostilities of the urban environment drove urban reformers to seek remedies to, and prevention of, these public health threats. Among these remedies was the creation of additional parks and playgrounds. A large number of reform organizations in New York (the Tenement House Commissions, The Good Government Clubs, the Association for Improving the Condition of the Poor, the Outdoor Recreation League, the Federation of Churches and Christian Workers, and the Children's Aid Society, among others) saw parks as an answer to environmental and social problems. However, these organizations did not have a single view of what constituted a park or how it should be used.

> Park proponents came into conflict not only with each other but also with groups of gymnasts and pedagogues, and proponents of zoological gardens, patriotic displays, and merry-go-rounds, who wanted to determine the uses of the park. . . . With the growing importance of the park in city life and its increasing use by large numbers of people, there appeared a "strong tendency" to convert it "into a great, perpetual metropolitan Fair Ground" that disturbed those who saw it as a work of art. . . . In the long run, all supporters of the municipal park found their original ideas amended by the sheer number of people who responded to a public space in the modern city.[61]

By mid-century, the city witnessed a rapid increase in voluntary religious and secular societies designed to help the poor and rid the city of moral decay.[62] In addition to the groups mentioned above, private agencies such as the City Vigilance League, the YMCA, the Temperance Society, and the Charity Organizations Society became a constant and growing presence in New York City.[63] Many of these reformers and their societies combined social and environmental goals, viewing environmental filth and degradation as both a reflection of, and a source of, moral weaknesses. To many reformers, where one found putrid darkness, densely populated tenements, stale air, and accumulations of solid waste, one also found sin, moral temptation and decay, sloth, and physical and mental disintegration. The remedy, argued reformers, was to impose or restore order and light, and to decongest these pockets of poverty with the goal of correcting moral as well as physical infirmities.[64] The city had readily recognizable, geographically identifiable, diseased parts, abscesses of infection; these areas coincided with the neighborhoods of the poor, especially in lower Manhattan and on the Lower East Side, and required purging and exposure to the curing influences of fresh air and sunlight.

Urban reformers at the turn of the century were motivated by both altruistic concerns for the health and welfare of others, and a pragmatic concern for their own, as well as by aesthetic impulses, to clean up American cities. The degree to which urban reform efforts protected the middle class, or were expressions of paternalistic altruism, is much debated by historians.[65] Middle-class and upper-class reformers constituted most of the political activists and their goals ranged from greater political participation for the middle and lower classes to expanding and stabilizing their own security and social status. Many scholars, however, agree that the creation of urban open spaces, parks, and playgrounds as therapeutic landscapes was a means for the upper and middle classes to exert some control over the social unrest and passions of the lower classes—as "safety valves" for the discontent of the urban poor.[66] In general, however, the reformers' urban environmental cleanup effort coincided with other political and social reforms aimed at social justice. For instance, addressing public health and environmental concerns encouraged political reforms, such as the dismantling of the political machines controlling cities and the creation of a professional civil service.

Urban pollution problems and issues of public health were remedied through professionalization and public policy reforms. The new professions of public health workers, doctors of infectious diseases, transportation and sanitation engineers, and city planners and managers, all contributed to cleaning up the urban environment and thereby improving the quality of city life. Such professionals included George Waring who would reform "municipal housekeeping" in several cities by instituting municipal agencies responsible for street cleaning and the regular removal of solid waste. Waring had befriended Frederick Law Olmsted while working on Central Park as a drainage engineer in the 1850s. After his appointment as New York's Street Cleaning Commissioner in 1891, he became one of Jacob Riis's heroes in "the battle with the slum" for his willingness to challenge corruption of the municipal government and his emphasis on urban sanitation and street cleaning.[67] Several other reformers, especially women through various organizations, joined and supported the municipal housekeeping effort, with most reforms focused on street cleaning and solid waste removal.[68]

Ultimately, a combination of public and private efforts responded to the urban environmental crises, encouraging both voluntary actions and political support for reform regulations and policies. The creation of urban parks and playgrounds by municipal governments is among the most important of these policies. Additional policy reforms included building codes for tenements (which were adopted, although not always enforced), and the creation of municipal bureaus and agencies to address issues of urban environments and recreation. The creation of urban parks and playgrounds as therapeutic landscapes was championed by a number of reformers concerned about the health of those urbanites, mostly new immigrants to the United States. Many reformers were especially concerned about the effects on children of growing up in overcrowded, poorly-lit, inadequately-ventilated tenement homes, or, in the worse cases, on the streets. Reformers felt that such a life would certainly produce an adult who was less physically healthy and many concluded that there would be negative moral and intellectual effects as well. Rather than viewing vice and crime as inherent to certain people, some reformers were beginning to view these as the consequences of environmental forces. One preventative measure, reformers felt, would be to increase the exposure of urban children to the outdoors and to physical exercise and play.

The Fresh Air Fund and the Boy Scouts of America were both promoted by reformers concerned that the urban environment was unsafe for children and that if the urban environment could not be changed, then children should be removed, even if temporarily, from that environment.[69] Jacob Riis, among his many appointments and reform activities, was a member of the National Council for the Boy Scouts of America, which included other reformers such as Theodore Roosevelt and Gifford Pinchot.[70] Some of these same reformers, including

Riis, participated in the playground movement and in athletic associations, urging the creation of urban parks as the only acceptable antidote to the problems of the urban environment. Frederick Law Olmsted's vision of a municipal park in the 1850s as a natural, but grandiose, piece of landscape architecture was a far cry from the neighborhood parks and playgrounds which reformers sought at the turn of the century. A transformation was taking place, not only of the physical landscape of New York City, through additional parks, but in the understanding of the therapeutic benefits of urban parks. Aesthetic benefits would be complemented by the provision of physical necessities: fresh air, sunlight, and room for unstructured play—even *on* the grass. The evolution of a small neighborhood park, Mulberry Bend Park, in lower Manhattan, exemplifies the therapeutic effects of altering the geography of the city.

Mulberry Bend Park: Altruism and Reform

The transformation of Mulberry Bend into Mulberry Bend Park, through the advocacy of Jacob Riis, manifests the change in the role of urban parks as therapeutic landscapes. Honored as the "father of the small parks movement," and eulogized by Theodore Roosevelt as "the most useful citizen of New York," Jacob A. Riis was a journalist, photographer, and social activist.[71] At the age of twenty-one, he emigrated in 1870 from Denmark to America, where he lived in a state of near poverty for a number of years, moving from one job of hard manual labor to another. Riis finally settled in New York, finding work in 1877 as a police court reporter for the *New York Tribune*. A decade later he began to present his articles and lectures accompanied by a series of photographs of tenements, police station lodging houses, and hideaways for street children.[72] In 1890, Riis published his best-known work, *How the Other Half Lives*, an exposé of life in New York City tenements. The success of this book encouraged Riis to continue his writing on the subject, which he did in *The Children of the Poor* (1892), *A Ten Years' War* (1901), and *The Battle with the Slum* (1902), among other publications.

Jacob Riis had neither artistic nor educational training to prepare him for his career as a photojournalist and activist, yet he was extremely successful in calling public attention and governmental efforts to the plight of many urban dwellers at the turn of the century. Riis does not, however, fit the profile of a likely turn-of-the-century urban activist: he was a Danish immigrant who made his own way in the United States, unlike many members of the upper and middle classes who participated in settlement houses and other reform efforts. Although a social reformer, Riis's writing reflects the common social prejudices of his time. His stereotypes of the immigrants based on their country of origin strike readers today as inappropriate and condescending.[73] Nevertheless, Riis's publicity of the plight of the urban poor and his political activism did result in concrete reforms, especially the regulation of tenement housing and the creation of therapeutic parks and playgrounds.[74]

The catalyst for these reforms was the combination of Riis's images and his accompanying text. In *The Battle With the Slum*, Riis described a photograph of several tenements located close to Mulberry Bend as "dens of death" (fig. 8.3); he wrote:

> When the "Dens of Death" were in Baxter Street, big barracks crowded out the old shanties. More came every day, I remember the story of those shown in the picture. They had been built only a little while when complaints came to the Board of Health of smells in the houses. A sanitary inspector was sent to find the cause. He followed the smell down in the cellar, and digging there discovered that the water pipe was a blind. It had simply been run into the ground and was not connected with the sewer.[75]

Riis's photographs depicted in detail the despair, squalor, and discomfort of these crowded, dank tenement apartments. Riis used images such *Dens of Death* for the illustrated lectures he gave during the 1890s. The impact of these photographs upon his largely middle-class audience was, in many cases, much stronger than that of the poorer quality line drawings that appeared of these images in *How the Other Half Lives* and thereby fostered a stronger interest in tenement life.[76] Riis was not, however, a passive observer of the misery in New York's tenements. His effort to eliminate the tenement slums in New York City brought him into constant conflict with the political machine of Tammany Hall. He fought many battles against homelessness, slums, the terrible working and living conditions suffered by children, and against corruption in city government. As both journalist and member of several reform organizations, such as the Good Government Club, Riis's work also inspired other activists in New York City, including the members of charitable organizations, such as the Tenement House Commissions and the Citizens Union and Social Reform Club.[77]

Riis's philosophy of urban reform was that no policy or plan would succeed without the support of the general public. In this respect he clearly represents the emerging middle class, desirous of an increased political voice in expanding and protecting its own interests, and, for some, the interest of others, especially the urban poor. Riis, like sanitary consultant and reformer Caroline Bartlett Crane, credited public opinion with the ability to move city governments and hold them to their promises.[78] He used his photographs, articles, books, and lectures to call the public's attention to slum conditions and to the need for parks and playgrounds in the tenement neighborhoods. It is this insistence by Riis that the public at large concern itself with tenement life and its impact on children, that creates a collateral benefit to the immediate benefits of parks as therapeutic landscapes. A therapeutic landscape is also one that strengthens the health of society, by reducing class distinctions and inequalities. The political system and institutions of New York City were strengthened, one may argue, through the empowerment of citizens and reformers in promoting urban parks. Riis advocated parks because of their benefits for urban residents. But the means of his advocacy not only strengthened the political potential of the emerging middle class by serving as an example of what one individual can accomplish, but also encouraged political participation and expanded social awareness about "how the other half lived," among the upper and middle classes.

Jacob Riis took a special interest in the area of the city known as Mulberry Bend, referred to as early as 1869 by the New York City Board of Health as "death's thoroughfare."[79] By the 1890s, Mulberry Bend was home to Italian immigrants, a number of taverns, lodging houses, peddlers, and the homeless. The "bend" referred to the curve on the southern end of Mulberry Street as it ran south through lower Manhattan, west of the Bowery (fig. 8.4). Jacob Riis found his way there as a police reporter assigned to police headquarters on Mulberry Street. The police force of New York City, with the approval of a corrupt Tammany Hall, collected bribes from the tavern and brothel owners on Mulberry Bend and was not inclined to clean up (in any sense) this area. Riis covered not only living conditions in the tenements but also, due in part to the corruption of the police force, "crimes against poor instead of by them."[80] He considered photography as his ally in the war against the tenements, a way to witness the unlawful, immoral, and unhealthy aspects of life in the Bend.

The battle to clean up Mulberry Bend, and ultimately to transform it from "death's thoroughfare" into the opposite—a place of sunlight and fresh air and health—was one of Riis's many passions as a social reformer. Riis noted the difference that small parks and playgrounds could make in the lives of tenement children:

> It (private benevolence) has lately, by the establishment of children's playgrounds in certain tenement districts, west and east, provided a kind of open-air kinder-garten that has hit the street in a vital spot. These play-grounds do not take the place of the small parks which the city has neglected to provide, but they show what a boon these will be some day. . . . More than two hundred children were digging, swinging, see-sawing, and cavorting about the Poverty Gap playground when I looked in on a hot Saturday afternoon. . . . The street that used to swarm with mischievous imps was quiet as a church. . . . The retiring toughs have dubbed it "Holy Terror Park" in memory of what it was, not of what it is.[81]

As a proponent of the development of creativity through creative play, Riis was convinced that social problems in tenement neighborhoods could be reversed and removed by the addition of parks and playgrounds. This feature complemented the greater likelihood for physical and environmental health.[82] To secure these benefits, Riis fought to establish a park at Mulberry Bend.

Riis faced two main obstacles to his reform efforts: a complacent public and a corrupt city hall. As Riis put it, "[The fight against the slum] was a bitter fight, in which every position of the enemy had to be carried by assault. The enemy was the deadly and official inertia that was the outcome of political corruption born of the slums plus the indifference of the mass of our citizens, who probably had never seen the [Mulberry] Bend."[83] Against the first obstacle, Riis was able to use his photography to horrify, and some argue to entertain, the general public and thereby captivate their attention.[84] Riis's images expressed in graphic detail the need for reform and the provisions necessary for the children of New York. In *How the Other Half Lives*, Riis documented the lack of access to parks and playgrounds for the children of Mulberry Bend:

> I came upon a couple of youngsters in a Mulberry Street yard a while ago that were chalking on the fence their first lesson in "writin." And this is what they wrote: "Keeb of te Grass." They had it by heart, for there was not, I verily believe, a green sod within a quarter of a mile. Home to them is an empty name. Pleasure? A gentleman once catechized a ragged class in a down-town public school on this point, and recorded the results: Out of forty-eight boys twenty had never seen the Brooklyn Bridge that was scarcely five minutes' walk away, *three only had been in Central Park* [emphasis added] . . . the street, with its ash barrels and its dirt, the river that runs foul with mud, are their domain.[85]

The titles alone of images of children, such as "Minding the Baby," and "Didn't Live Nowhere," had a visceral impact on Riis's audience, promoting the need for clean, recreational environments and reinforcing the need to focus urban reform efforts on the lives of the young.

The government of New York City and Tammany Hall, on the other hand, were almost immovable obstacles, and only the combined efforts of political and social reformers were able to shake them. Riis served as an officer in the Good Government Clubs of New York, using that position to urge reforms of government and the creation of more playgrounds and parks.[86] However, political machines governing cities and states at the turn of the twentieth century derived much of their support from recent immigrants who were willing to trade either money or votes for some small level of job security or assurance of housing. The political bosses and their ward captains had no interest in improving the lives, and thus increasing the political independence, of the urban poor. Progressive era reformers were able to dislodge political machines over several years through a number of political and social changes, and many of those changes took place at the state rather than municipal government level. Such was the case with Mulberry Bend Park, where the legislation making the park possible was passed a decade before the city of New York created the park.[87]

The many urban reformers, including Riis, who urged the creation of more urban parks saw a glimmer of success on May 13, 1887, when the New York state legislature passed the Small Parks Act, a "pioneering law that enabled the city to acquire new small parks in crowded neighborhoods."[88] Riis was delighted: "[t]he Small Parks Law . . . gave us a million dollars a year to force light and air into the slum. . . ."[89] The Small Parks Act authorized a million dollars per year to the allocation of land and construction of urban parks, but that money did not accumulate if it was not spent. The city did not fully exploit this funding program until the mid-1890s and the years of inactivity by the New York City government meant less money, rather than more, for the creation of urban parks under the Small Parks Act.[90] Eventually in 1894, New York City took the steps necessary to purchase the tenements and surrounding property in Mulberry Bend from their owners.[91]

Sensing the insecurity of Mulberry Bend Park's future, Riis continued his vigilant surveillance of Mulberry Bend and his articles and photographs continued to document the health and moral dangers of the Bend. He wrote: "My scrap-book from 1883-1896 is one running comment on the Bend and upon the official indolence that delayed its demolition nearly a decade after it had been decreed. . . . [O]ne of the City Hall officials condescended to inform me of the real cause of the delay. It was simply that 'no one down there had been taking any interest in the thing.'"[92] Riis was able to generate "interest" in Mulberry Bend from time to time, although he did have to defend himself against charges of sensationalism.[93] He also had the comfort of his friendship with Theodore Roosevelt, president of the Board of New York Police Commissioners from 1895 to 1897, who shared Riis's sense of adventure and urgency in investigating life in Mulberry Bend.[94]

While these flares of progress against the Bend were followed by long periods of inactivity by the city, Riis continued his campaign to clear the slum. Riis recorded the fluctuating public interest in the Bend in *The Making of An American*:

> The editors found [Mulberry Bend] something to be indignant about when there was nothing else. Ponderous leaders about our "duty to the poor" appeared at intervals. The Grand Jury on its tours saw and protested. The City Hall felt the sting and squirmed. . . . [I allowed no chance] to pass of telling the people of New York what they were harboring [in the Bend]. They simply needed to know, I felt sure of that.[95]

Interest in the Bend, however sporadic, converted to action in 1895 when the residents of Mulberry Bend were evicted and the tenements were demolished. Those who lost their homes in the demolition moved, according to Riis, into the many vacant apartments in neighboring wards.[96] This displacement of tenement residents in the name of providing them a healthier life raises many questions about the nature of the therapeutic landscape and provides support to those who argue that the parks were simply safety valves for the protection of the social and political status quo. While the tenements had been destroyed, and the salable remnants of buildings auctioned off, debris remained and served for almost two years as a breeding ground for pests and an unsafe playground of broken bricks and discarded carts for the neighborhood children. Once again a dangerous, unhealthy landscape existed, this time as a stage in the pursuit of a healthier landscape. During 1895 and 1896, Mayor William L. Strong continued to delay the approval of the creation of the parks; as a concession to the disappointed activists, he considered the creation of a citizens' advisory committee on small parks, something which Theodore Roosevelt had urged Riis to instigate.[97]

Riis finally provoked the full implementation of the Small Parks Act by filing a complaint against the city for the "nuisance" it created at Mulberry Bend. Riis charged that the Bend presented a health hazard to the city. As the city now owned this property, Riis sought to find them responsible for its cleanup; he argued:

There is a familiar principle of sanitary law, expressed in more than one ordinance, that no citizen has a right to maintain a nuisance on his premises because he is lazy or its suits his convenience in other ways. The city is merely the aggregate of citizens in a corporation, and must be subject to the same rules.[98]

Public pressure increased on the city to clear the debris from Mulberry Bend and construct the park, when, a few days after Riis filed his complaint, boys playing in the trash managed to push over a cart resulting in the death of two playmates.[99] By the middle of 1897, the Bend had been cleared, sod and trees planted, and an open space was available for safe and salutary recreation. Mulberry Bend was finally Mulberry Bend Park (fig. 8.5), and was formally opened to the public on June 15, 1897.

Riis was not invited to the opening because he opposed municipal officials who wanted to place "keep off the grass" signs in the park. Riis, as is by now no surprise, thought that the park's very purpose was to invite free play *on* the grass. When Colonel Waring gave the final speech of the festive afternoon, he concluded with a call for three cheers for "the citizen effort" of Jacob Riis, which Riis, standing among the crowd, was gratified to hear.[100] Riis was also delighted that finally, "The Bend had become decent and orderly because the sunlight was let in, and shone upon children who had at last the right to play, even if the sign 'keep off the grass' was still there."[101] Riis's words best describe the satisfaction of successfully implementing lasting change in altering the urban landscape. "The Mulberry Bend we laid by the heels; that was the worst pigsty of all . . . since the Bend became a park . . . not once has a shot been fired or a knife been drawn. That is what it means to let the sunshine in!"[102] Reform efforts based on this sentiment continued to change New York City's landscape through the creation of small parks and playgrounds.

A geographical analysis of Mulberry Bend Park reveals, however, that the desire to revitalize an area of tenement slums for the healthful benefit of its inhabitants fell somewhat short of its goal. Unlike Olmsted's and Vaux's design for Central Park, the area of Mulberry Bend Park was not resculpted, rather, it conformed to its original geographical space. The park was designed with its bend intact but with a more healthful flow of activity space. What was to reformers a dirty, crowded street of commerce and crime was now a place of curvilinear paths intended for healthful strolling. However, whereas Olmsted and Vaux constructed their pathways to guide visitors to destinations of natural splendor in Central Park, a stroll around Mulberry Bend Park offered an open pasture-like space framed by distinctly urban views: office buildings, small trees protected by wire cages, and barriers of benches designed to prevent access to the grass. As mentioned above, and as with Central Park's creation, the creation of this park displaced an already disenfranchised population. Those who lived previously on Mulberry Bend had little access to Central Park in the northern reaches of the city; they also had little time for casual strolls and relaxing afternoons on park benches in Mulberry Bend Park. Its flat terrain afforded easy monitoring of activities, although, as in Central Park, most activities of an energetic recreational nature were banned. Mulberry Bend Park as a cultural landscape reflects the paternalist but impractical goals of upper- and middle-class reformers and therefore its therapeutic benefits were compromised. The park did indeed bring open spaces and fresh air to an area thought of as a physical and moral wasteland. Unfortunately, as in the case with Central Park, the prior inhabitants received negligible assistance in their efforts to relocate and the redesigned 'bend' offered them only moderate access to recreation.

These shortcomings of urban parks as therapeutic landscapes were not recognized by some reformers, although many strove to secure additional neighborhood parks and playgrounds designed for easy access to residents and for unrestricted physical activities. In particular, Riis's efforts to ensure additional small parks and playgrounds continued through his position as the secretary of the Small Parks Advisory Committee, created in June 1897 by Mayor William Strong.[103] Although Riis was told that the committee had as much authority as a group of "boot blacks,"[104] the committee was appointed "to advise on the acquisition of small parks and playgrounds in the crowded 'tenement districts' of Manhattan."[105] The committee report of October 1897 argued for the creation of small parks and playgrounds on the basis of statistical information regarding population density, death rates, disease, and crime rates for various wards of the city. The Small Parks Advisory Committee was especially interested in these statistics regarding children (e.g., population density of children under fifteen years old, location of public schools, and location of the nearest playgrounds and parks).[106] In the report, the committee asserted that in the planning of New York City "the children seem to have been forgotten."[107] The Small Parks Committee's recommendations for additional parks and playgrounds were also based on testimony from police that there were fewer crimes in areas of New York City where there were parks and playgrounds.[108] The Small Parks Committee and "other progressive reformers urged the creation of new small parks in congested neighborhoods of Hell's Kitchen and the Lower East Side."[109] Despite the evidence prepared by the committee, by the time their report reached the mayor's office there had been a change in government, and Riis discovered that his advisory committee in fact had limited powers to dictate specific actions.[110] However, the report encouraged reformers, along with the general public, to reward the municipal government for the creation of small parks, and so the addition of parks to New York City continued.[111]

Conclusion

Central Park and Mulberry Bend Park manifest two versions of transformations of the New York City landscape, initiated and desired as therapeutic landscapes, but executed and ultimately defined in very different ways. Both Olmsted and Riis agreed that exercise and relaxation outdoors were beneficial to urban residents. Olmsted considered the park to be a means of correcting the faults of cities and urban life, a view shared by Riis. Both supported parks which established an artificial nature: Olmsted cleared woods and squatters' shanties to construct his view of nature; Riis sought the destruction of buildings to afford an open lawn. Olmsted and Riis both faced what they considered political obstacles: Olmsted in battles over financial resources, the design features of his park, and in efforts to fight off "improvements" sought by various city agencies; Riis, as has been documented, fought the resistance of the government to demolish a section of the city that afforded it a source of income and political support.

Among their differences, however, were the benefits of therapeutic landscapes they sought to create. Olmsted viewed the outdoors setting as a designed landscape, with an eye toward the aesthetic rewards of a landscape transformed through architectural planning and opposed efforts by interfering parties such as local bureaucrats to alter what he considered the "heroic" dimensions of his and Vaux's creation. In 1869, one analyst claimed:

> "public parks may be regarded as an unerring index in the advance of a people in civilization and refinement." However, the landscape architects also considered the presence of the masses of people who made up the modern city a major obstacle in the pursuit of the fusion of city and nature. The parks' vistas re-introduced nature into the urban landscape by keeping the surrounding city and its residents out of sight, behind shields of foliage.[112]

Olmsted, for his part, hid the roadways of Central Park, and prevented the park's view from being that of a "great wall" of surrounding buildings. Riis, on the other hand, was focused on the clearing of tenements and dangerous conditions in the slums, more interested in population density and crime rates and the role of sanitation engineers than in the botanical and geological characteristics of the space. For Riis, the salutary benefits of the parks resulted from their users simply being outside, in the fresh air and sunshine; he had little concern with how the park might look or its vistas. While Olmsted had envisioned a park based on democratic principles, only those who lived close to it, mostly upper- and middle-class residents made use of its facilities. A new concept of the park as a therapeutic landscape was needed for the other half. As Jacob Riis wrote in 1891 in "Parks for the Poor," the city should provide public areas "'for the rest and recreation of the poor,' rather than 'for the pomp and parade of the wealthy.'"[113] This was provided through the creation of small urban parks, such as Mulberry Bend Park, dotting the urban landscape. The creation and use of both parks also served the therapeutic benefit of strengthening the political voice and participation of all classes. In the case of Central Park, there was vigorous public debate over its location and features, and in the case of Mulberry Bend Park, public discussion focused on social and political obligations and reform.

The two parks, Central Park and Mulberry Bend Park, and the efforts that led to their creation during the late 1800s, reflect concurrent changes in the prevailing philosophies regarding the city and the individual, the cultivated and the natural, and the significance of nature and nurture in directing human behavior. By the end of the nineteenth century, Manhattan had over 1,300 acres of parks, a testament to the consensus that parks are positive attributes of cities. However, even into the twentieth century, the tension continued between artistic design, as seen in the continual construction of urban retreats and planned neighborhoods, and calls for the practical addition of playgrounds and small parks in urban centers. Despite the different political, aesthetic, and social motivations behind the creation of Central Park and Mulberry Bend Park, both parks continue to function as therapeutic landscapes for those who use them, reflecting a continued public commitment to the salutary effects of nature.

Fig. 8.1: Central Park before construction, c. 1860. Photograph. Museum of the City of New York

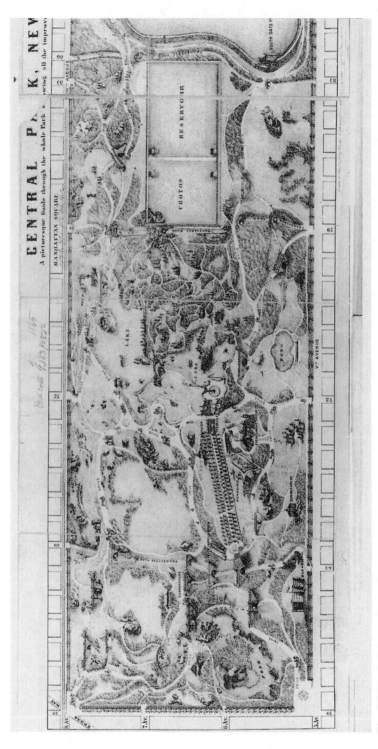

Fig. 8.2: Frederick Law Olmsted and Calvert Vaux, landscape architects, "Greensward" Plan for Central Park, New York City, 1858. Pen and ink. New York City Department of Parks, The Arsenal

Fig. 8.3: Jacob Riis, *Dens of Death*, c. 1890s. Photograph. Museum of the City of New York

Fig. 8.4: Jacob Riis, *Mulberry Bend*, c. 1880s. Photograph. Museum of the City of New York

Fig. 8.5: Jacob Riis, *The Mulberry Bend Became a Park*, c. 1897. Photograph. Museum of the City of New York

Notes

1. Robin A. Kearns and Wilbert M. Gesler, *Putting Health into Place* (Syracuse, N.Y.: Syracuse University Press, 1998), 8.

2. Wilbert M. Gesler, "Therapeutic Landscapes: Medical Issues in Light of the New Cultural Geography," *Social Science and Medicine* 34, no. 7 (1992): 736.

3. Kearns and Gesler, *Putting Health into Place,* 8. Visits to the spa at Bath, England, for example, were supposed to provide not only the restorative effects of nature, but also a mingling of classes—the aristocracy with the bourgeoisie. See Kearns and Gesler, *Putting Health into Place,* 30-32.

4. Central Park spans midtown Manhattan from 59th Street to 110th Street and Central Park West and Fifth Avenue east to west. Mulberry Bend Park, which has been renamed Columbus Park, lies between Baxter and Mulberry Streets in the current Chinatown section of lower Manhattan between Chatham and Foley Squares.

5. Gesler, "Therapeutic Landscapes," 743.

6. Edward Relph, *Rational Landscapes and Humanistic Geography* (London: Croom Helm, 1981), 44-45, and Gesler, "Therapeutic Landscapes," 737-41.

7. Except for Frederick C. Howe, who saw the city as "Hope for Democracy," in Otis Pease, ed., *The Progressive Years: The Spirit and Achievement of American Reform* (New York: George Braziller, 1962).

8. Albert Fein, ed., *Landscape into Cityscape: Frederick Law Olmsted's Plans for a Greater New York City* (Ithaca, N.Y.: Cornell University Press, 1967), 35.

9. For background information on the Social Gospel movement, and reform efforts of Progressive Era, see: David Colburn and George E. Pozzetta, eds., *Reform and Reformers in the Progressive Era* (Westport, Conn.: Greenwood, 1983); David B. Danbom, *A World of Hope: Progressives and the Struggle for an Ethical Public Life* (Philadelphia: Temple University Press, 1987); and Melvin G. Holli, "Urban Reform in the Progressive Era," in *The Progressive Era*, ed. Lewis L. Gould (Syracuse, N.Y.: Syracuse University Press, 1974), 133-51.

10. In 1819, twenty thousand pigs were estimated to be running wild through the streets of New York City. Initially employed as a mobile system of garbage removal (in addition to being a source for ham and bacon) these scavenger pigs became an unwelcome existence in the city and were partially responsible for the city streets becoming filthiest in the nation. Later, when Charles Dickens visited New York in the early 1840s, he voiced his displeasure concerning the abundance of city "swine." "Two portly sows are trotting up behind this carriage, and a select party of half-a-dozen gentlemen hogs have just now turned the corner. . . . turning up the news and small-talk of the city in the shape of cabbage stalks. . . . They are the city scavengers, these pigs." Owners were allowed to let their swine run free in the congested areas of the city until the winter of 1867. See Roger Whitehouse, *New York: Sunshine and Shadow* (New York: Harper and Row, 1974), 44; and Charles Dickens, *American Notes* (New York: Harper and Bros., 1842), 78. In 1818, a Swedish Baron visiting the city commented: "New York is not as clean as the cities of the same rank and population in Europe . . . one finds in the streets dead cats and dogs, which make the air very bad; dust and ashes are thrown out into the street, which are swept perhaps once every fortnight in the summer; only, however, in the largest and most frequent streets, otherwise, they are cleaned only once a month." In Isaac Newton Phelps Stokes, *New York Past and Present, Its History and Landmarks, 1524-1939* (New York: Plantin Press, 1939), 77.

11. See Note 9 for more information on the Social Gospel movement and the other predominant theories of social reform.

12. Cook, Clarence, *A Description of the New York Central Park* (New York: Benjamin Blom, 1869), 14.

13. Witold Rybczynski, *A Clearing in the Distance—Frederick Law Olmsted and America in the Nineteenth Century* (New York: Scribner, 1999), 93-95. See also, Edwin G. Burrows and Mike Wallace, *Gotham—A History of New York City to 1898* (New York: Oxford University Press, 1999), 790.

14. Andrew Jackson Downing, "The New York Park," in New York (City) Commissioners of Central Park, *First Annual Report on the Improvement of The Central Park* (New York: McGrath, 1857), 162-63.

15. Downing, "The New York Park," 159.

16. Burrows and Wallace, *Gotham—A History of New York City to 1898*, 791-92.

17. Cook, *A Description of the New York Central Park*, 19-20.

18. Burrows and Wallace, *Gotham—A History of New York City to 1898*, 792.

19. Rybczynski, *A Clearing in the Distance*, 158-60.

20. Relph, Edward, *Rational Landscapes and Humanistic Geography* (London: Croom Helm, 1981), 43. For a lengthier discussion of Birkenhead Park as laid out by Joseph Paxton in 1844 utilizing pastoral scenery and curving meanders see also, Rybczynski, 93-95.

21. Olmsted was outspoken about his concern that the natural environment, through the addition of open spaces such as parks, would have beneficial influences upon the health and morale of city residents. Olmsted's words will be examined later in this study regarding class issues and salutary benefits of the park.

22. The park as a designed space has a history much broader and longer than eighteenth-century England. The Italian, Dutch, and French traditions are all of great importance in American design. However, for the purposes of this article and the narrow focus of Olmsted, the designs of Lancelot "Capability" Brown are the most relevant.

23. In France this occurs after the French Revolution when the royal gardens in Paris were opened to the public.

24. John Michael Hunter, *Land into Landscape* (London: George Godwin, 1985), 114.

25. Brown destroyed parts of a village at Chatsworth and dwellings on both sides of the river for his designs at Warwick Castle. See Relph, *Rational Landscapes*, 54.

26. Sir Uvedale Price and William Gilpin wrote extensively on the picturesque. For example, see William Gilpin, *Three Essays: On Picturesque Beauty; On Picturesque Travel; and On Sketching Landscape* (London, 1792). For a discussion of landscapes in England, see Stephen Daniels, *Fields of Vision: Landscape Imagery and National Identity in England and the United States* (Princeton, N.J.: Princeton University Press, 1993).

27. Relph, *Rational Landscapes*, 15, 30.

28. Relph, *Rational Landscapes*, 45.

29. Excerpt from Perry Bliss, ed., *The Heart of Emerson's Journals* (Boston, Mass.: Houghton Mifflin, 1926), 207.

30. "It is one great purpose of the Park to supply to the hundreds of thousands of tired workers, who have no opportunity to spend their summers in the country, a specimen of God's handiwork that shall be to them, inexpensively, what a month or two in the White Mountains or the Adirondacks is, at great cost, to those in easier circumstances." See Rybczynski, 177.

31. Rybczynski, *A Clearing in the Distance*, 165.

32. Cook, *A Description of the New York Central Park*, 69.

33. Rybczynski, *A Clearing in the Distance*, 169.

34. For a discussion of new approaches to cultural geography, see Gesler, "Therapeutic Landscapes: Medical Issues in Light of the New Cultural Geography," 735-46.

35. Douglas Davies, "The evocative symbolism of trees," in *The Iconography of Landscape,* ed. Dennis Cosgrove and Stephen Daniels (Cambridge: Cambridge University Press, 1988), 33.

36. From the descriptive report by Frederick Law Olmsted and Calvert Vaux for their designs for Central Park. In, Frederick Law Olmsted Sr., *Forty Years of Landscape Architecture: Central Park* (Cambridge, Mass.: MIT Press, 1928), 45.

37. Rybczynski, *A Clearing in the Distance,* 167.

38. Cook, *A Description of the New York Central Park,* 41.

39. Cook, *A Description of the New York Central Park,* 37.

40. Rybczynski, *A Clearing in the Distance,* 166.

41. Frederick Doveton Nichols and Ralph E. Griswold, *Thomas Jefferson, Landscape Architect* (Charlottesville: University Press of Virginia, 1978), 96.

42. Cook, *A Description of the New York Central Park,* 87.

43. Frederick Law Olmsted, "Public Parks and the Establishment of Towns" (1870), in Olmsted, *Forty Years of Landscape Architecture,* 172.

44. Frederick Law Olmsted, "Public Parks and the Establishment of Towns" (1870), in S. B. Sutton, ed., *Civilizing American Cities* (Cambridge, Mass.: MIT Press, 1971), 95.

45. John F. Kasson, *Amusing the Millions* (New York: Hill & Wang, 1978), 11.

46. Burrows and Wallace, *Gotham—A History of New York City to 1898,* 795.

47. Cook, *A Description of the New York Central Park,* 87.

48. Kearns and Gesler, *Putting Health into Place,* 7.

49. A precursor to the Red Cross, sanitary commissions raised funds and assisted troops through a variety of means during the Civil War.

50. Two useful collections of Olmsted's writings are: S. B. Sutton, *Civilizing American Cities: A Selection of Frederick Law Olmsted's Writings on City Landscapes* (Cambridge, Mass.: MIT Press, 1971) and Albert Fein, ed., *Landscape into Cityscape: Frederick Law Olmsted's Plans for a Greater New York City* (Ithaca, N.Y.: Cornell University Press, 1967). Readers should consult Witold Rybczynski, *A Clearing in the Distance* (New York: Scribner, 1999) for a recent biography of Olmsted's life and work philosophy.

51. Olmsted, *Forty Years of Landscape Architecture,* 104.

52. Kasson, *Amusing the Millions,* 15.

53. Frederick Law Olmsted, "Public Parks and the Establishment of Towns" (1870), in S. B. Sutton, ed., *Civilizing American Cities,* 92.

54. "The average block density in lower Manhattan increased from 157.5 persons in 1820 to 272.50 persons in 1850. New York City's Sanitary District A averaged 986.4 people to the acre in 1894—or approximately 30,000 people in a space of 5-6 blocks [500 people per block]. In comparison, Bombay, India—the next most crowded area in the world—had 759.7 per acre and Prague, the European city with the most slum conditions, had only 485.4 people per acre." Martin V. Melosi, "Environmental Crisis in the City: The Relationship between Industrialization and Urban Pollution" in *Pollution and Reform in American Cities, 1870-1930,* ed. Martin V. Melosi (Austin: University of Texas Press, 1980), 11.

55. Sir Peter Hall, *Cities in Civilization* (New York: Pantheon Books, 1998), 752.

56. Hall, *Cities in Civilization,* 752.

57. Gunther Barth, *City People* (New York: Oxford University Press, 1980), 21. Tompkins Square Park is located between Avenues A and B in the East Village. For information on Tompkins Square Park, see "New City, New Frontier: The Lower East Side

as Wild, Wild West," by Neil Smith in *Variations On a Theme Park: The New American City and the End of Public Space,* ed. Michael Sorkin (New York: Hill & Wang, 1992).

58. The early environmental movement in the United States sought the establishment of national parks and wilderness preservation and scientific management of natural resources. In many ways, these issues primarily affected the wealthy that had investments in timber industries and those with the resources to get out of cities to travel to national parks. For further information see Robert Gottlieb, *Forcing the Spring: The Transformation of the American Environmental Movement* (Washington, D.C.: Island Press, 1993); and Melosi, *Pollution and Reform in American Cities.*

59. See Dr. Alice Hamilton's description of industrial health hazards in "The Poisonous Occupations in Illinois," <www.historymatters.gmu.edu/text/2097a-hamilton.html.> (December 13, 1999).

60. For information on the health and environmental effects of urbanization and industrialization, see: Gottlieb, *Forcing the Spring,* 47-59; Melosi, *Pollution and Reform in American Cities,* 3-31; Suellen Hoy, *Chasing Dirt: The American Pursuit of Cleanliness* (New York: Oxford University Press, 1995), 59-86; and John Opie, *Nature's Nation: An Environmental History of the United States* (New York: Harcourt Brace, 1998), 269-302.

61. Barth, *City People,* 36.

62. See Danbom, *A World of Hope.*

63. Louise Ware, *Jacob A. Riis: Police Reporter, Reformer, Useful Citizen* (New York: D. Appleton-Century, 1939), 54.

64. For reading on the American view of cities, see the following: Kenneth T. Jackson, *Crabgrass Frontier: The Suburbanization of the United States* (New York: Oxford University Press, 1985), 69-70; John F. Kasson, *Rudeness & Civility: Manners in Nineteenth-Century Urban America* (New York: Hill & Wang, 1990), 80; Richard Hofstader, *The Age of Reform* (London: Jonathon Cape, 1962), 178-79; and Robert De Forest and Lawrence Vieller, "The Tenement House Problem" in Otis Pease, ed., *The Progressive Years: The Spirit and Achievement of American Reform* (New York: George Braziller, 1962).

65. See Blaine A. Brownwell, *"Interpretations of Twentieth-Century Urban Progressive Reform"* in Colburn and Pozzetta, eds., *Reform and Reformers in the Progressive Era* and Richard Hofstader, *The Age of Reform* (London: Jonathon Cape, 1962).

66. Smith, "New City, New Frontier: The Lower East Side as Wild, Wild West," in Sorkin, ed., *Variations On a Theme Park: The New American City and the End of Public Space,* 68 and Frederick C. Howe, "The City" in Pease, ed., *The Progressive Years: The Spirit and Achievement of American Reforms.*

67. Hoy, *Chasing Dirt,*78; See also Jacob Riis, *The Battle with the Slum* (1902; reprint, Minneola, N.Y.: Dover, 1998), 267, 272; cited hereafter as *BWTS.*

68. See note 60.

69. By 1897, 17 cities offered Fresh Air relief to their children; New York City had 14 nonsectarian and 19 church-related programs, sponsoring almost 200,000 individual outings that year. These programs were extraordinarily popular and no one doubted the health effects of a day, week, or month spent outside of the city. The Boy Scouts of America (1910) emphasized the attributes of self-confidence and self-sufficiency that would derive from time spent in the great outdoors. See: Peter J Schmitt, *Back to Nature: The Arcadian Myth in Urban America* (Baltimore, Md.: Johns Hopkins University Press, 1990), 97.

70. Schmitt, *Back to Nature,* 109.

71. Riis was identified as "Father of small parks movement," according to Louise Ware, when the Playground and Recreation Association of America appointed him an honorary vice president of the organization. Ware, *Jacob A. Riis,* 165, n22. Theodore

Roosevelt was quoting a man he said was "well qualified to pass judgment;'' perhaps a reference to Roosevelt himself. See Alexander Alland, *Jacob A. Riis: Photographer & Citizen* (New York: Aperture Foundation, 1993), 33.

72. For biographies of Riis, see: Alland, *Jacob A. Riis: Photographer & Citizen*; James B. Lane, *Jacob A. Riis and the American City* (Port Washington, N.Y.: Kennikat Press, 1974); and especially useful for details of Riis's daily life is Ware, *Jacob A. Riis*. See also Riis's autobiography, *The Making of an American* (New York: Macmillan, 1902); cited hereafter as *MOAA*.

73. "The Italian comes in at the bottom, and in the generation that came over the sea he stays there. In the slums he is welcomed as a tenant who 'makes less trouble' than the contentious Irishman or the order-loving German, that is to say: is content to live in a pig-sty." Riis, *HOHL*, 48.

74. Riis and his work have been interpreted in sharply different ways. For example, he is seen by some scholars as a condescending showman, content to cater to class stereotypes and entertain his audience; on the other hand, others assess Riis as a well-meaning but narrow-minded catalyst for reform; still others credit Riis as an effective and diligent reformer. Two articles discussing the attitudes of Jacob Riis and other expositors of life in urban tenements are Bill Hug, "Walking the Ethnic Tightrope: Ethnicity and Dialectic in Jacob Riis's *How the Other Half Lives*," *Journal of American Culture* 4 (winter 1997): 41-53; and Mark Pittenger, "A World of Difference: Constructing the 'Underclass' in Progressive America," *American Quarterly* 49.1 (1997): 26-65. Additional analysis of Riis's view of his subjects and his audiences can be found in Lewis S. Fried, *Makers of the City* (Amherst: University of Massachusetts Press, 1990); Keith Gandal, *Virtues of the Vicious: Jacob Riis, Stephen Crane, and the Spectacle of the Slum* (New York: Oxford University Press, 1997); Peter B. Hales, *Silver Cities* (Philadelphia: Temple University Press, 1984); and Maren Stange, *Symbols of Ideal Life: Social Documentary Photography in America 1890-1950* (Cambridge: Cambridge University Press, 1989).

75. Riis, *BWTS,* 20.

76. Riis's pictures document the despair and unpleasantness of urban life. A typical image is "Home of an Italian Ragpicker, Jersey Street," which depicts a family working in grim, cramped conditions. Photographs such as, "Five Cents a Spot Unauthorized Lodgings in a Bayard Street Tenement" depict the horrors of life in a dark and overcrowded tenement. Lewis Fried describes Riis's photographs as "a catalog of individuals crushed by narrow alleys, of people clustered tightly while working in dilapidated rooms, of individuals thrust into the darkness of tenements. What slowly emerges is a sense of the person, the family, the gang asserting whatever frail individuality could survive these gruesome conditions." in Fried, *Makers of the City,* 41. The impact of Riis's images in his lantern-slide lectures was all the more striking for the size and proximity of the image and Riis's telling of the subjects' stories. See Hales, *Silver Cities*, 177, 193. For more information and analysis of Riis's photography, see Hales, and Stange, *Symbols of Ideal Life*.

77. See Ware, *Jacob A. Riis,* 140-56; and, Lane, *Riis and the American City*, 39-44; 105-28.

78. For additional information on Caroline Bartlett Crane, see Suellen M. Hoy "'Municipal Housekeeping': The Role of Women in Improving Urban Sanitation Practices, 1880-1917" in Melosi, ed., *Pollution and Reform in American Cities*, 181-88. Riis decried the tendency of the public to be passive and to believe that a sensible, useful idea would be implemented by the government without their active support. "[It] seems to be human nature—American human nature, at all events—to expect [a proposed reform] to carry itself through with the general good wishes but no particular life from any one. It is

a very charming expression of our faith in the power of the right to makes its way, only it is all wrong." *MOAA,* 263.

79. Lane, *Riis and American City,* 113-44.

80. Bruce Bliven, *New York: A Bicentennial History* (New York: Norton, 1981), 145.

81. Jacob Riis, *The Children of the Poor,* quoted in Alland, *Riis: Photographer & Citizen,* 204, 206.

82. Riis's support of the establishment of parks and playgrounds is discussed in Ware, *Jacob A. Riis,* 109, 162-64; and, Lane, *Riis and American City,* 124-27.

83. Riis, *BWTS,* 274.

84. As mentioned above, some analysis of Riis and the impact of his work suggest that it was truly educational and inspiration, other analysis considers Riis's works as patronizing entertainment. See note 74.

85. Riis, *HOHL,* 183.

86. See note 63 for information on Riis's role in political reform and notes 65 and 69 for Riis's use of his position as an agent of the Good Government Clubs to sponsor the creation of parks and playgrounds.

87. One example of the common delays in the reform of tenement housing is the following: "In 1901, the city managed to pass a tenement-house law that outlawed much of what had been legal since 1879, when the 'Old Law' was enacted, and the New Law served as a model for reform legislation in other cities throughout the country. The catch was that it only applied to new buildings in slum neighborhoods. Eight years after its passage, at least 600,000 New York City families were still living in Old Law tenements." Bliven, *New York,* 145. Riis tells his version of the delay and his role in instigating the creation of Mulberry Bend Park in his autobiography, *MOAA,* and *BWTS,* chapter 11, "Letting in the Light," 264-309.

88. *Park Planning for Greater New York (1870-1898)* <www.ci.nyc.ny.us/html/history 1870-1898.html> City of New York Parks & Recreation. (April 23, 1999).

89. Riis, *BWTS,* 275.

90. *Park Planning for Greater New York (1870-1898)* <www.ci.nyc.ny.us/html/history 1870-1898.html> City of New York Parks & Recreation. (April 23, 1999).

91. New York, *Laws of New York,* 110th session, 1887, chapter 320, "An Act to provide for the location, acquisition, construction and improvement of additional public parks in the city of New York," section 1, 394 (394-99); Riis, *TYW,* 178.

92. Riis, *MOAA,* 275.

93. See note 60, and see, for information on the middle-class prurient interest in slums, Kasson, *Rudeness and Civility,* 74-80.

94. Ware, *Jacob A. Riis,* 130-31; and, Gandal, *Virtues of the Vicious,* 10, 20. See Edmund Morris, *The Rise of Theodore Roosevelt* (New York: Coward, McCann & Geoghegan, 1979); and Jacob Riis, *Theodore Roosevelt the Citizen* (1903; reprint, New York: Macmillan Co., 1918), 127-54.

95. Riis, *MOAA,* 252-53.

96. Riis answered questions regarding the dislocation of the residents of Mulberry Bend in two of his works; in the quotation below from *BWTS,* he argues that not quite 12,000 were evicted; in his earlier version of *BWTS, A Ten Years' War,* he said the displaced were less than 10,000. "What became of the people who were dispossessed? . . . [When] the multitudes of Mulberry Bend . . . were put out, there was more than room enough for them in new houses ready for their use. In the Seventh, Tenth, Eleventh, Thirteenth, and Seventeenth wards, where they would naturally go if they wanted to be near home, there were 4,268 vacant apartments with room for over 18,000 tenants at our

New York average of four and a half to the family. Including the Bend, the whole number of the dispossessed was not 12,000." *BWTS*, 286-87.

97. Riis, *TR*, 132 and Lane, *Riis and American City*, 113.

98. Riis continues: "I drew up a complaint in proper official phrase, charging that the state of Mulberry Bend was 'detrimental to health and dangerous to life,' and formally arraigned the municipality before the Health Board for maintaining a nuisance upon its premises." (*MOAA*, 279) The complaint lodged with the Sanitation Bureau, included the following language:

> The Bend is a mass of wreck, a dumping-ground for all manner of filth from the surrounding tenements. The Street-Cleaning Department has no jurisdiction over it, and the Park Department, in charge of which it is, exercises none.
>
> The numerous old cellars are a source of danger to the children that swarm over the block. Water stagnating in the holes will shortly add the peril of epidemic diseases. Such a condition as that now prevailing in this block, with it dense surrounding population, would not be tolerated by your department for a single day if on private property. It has lasted here many months.
>
> The property is owned by the city, having been taken for the purposes of a park and left in this condition after the demolition of the old buildings. The undersigned respectfully represents that the city, in the proposed Mulberry Bend Park, is at present maintaining a nuisance, and that it is the duty of your honorable Board to see to it that it is forthwith abolished, to which end he prays that you will proceed at once with the enforcement of the rules of your department prohibiting the maintaining of nuisances with the city's limits. (*MOAA*, 280-81).

99. Lane, *Riis and American City*, 115.

100. Riis commented that, "The newspapers puzzled over the fact that I was not invited to the formal opening. I was secretary of the Small Parks Committee at the time, and presumably even officially entitled to be bidden to the show; though, come to think of it, our committee was a citizens' affair and not on the pay-rolls!" *MOAA*, 284. For additional details on the opening of Mulberry Bend Park, see Riis, *BWTS*, 267-68; Lane, *Riis and American City*, 115; and, Ware, *Jacob A. Riis*, 158-60.

101. Riis, *MOAA*, 283.

102. Jacob Riis, "The Peril and the Preservation of the Home," quoted in Alland, *Riis: Photographer & Citizen*, 210.

103. Ware, *Jacob A. Riis*, 160.

104. Riis, *BWTS*, 284.

105. *Park Planning for Greater New York (1870-1898)* <www.ci.nyc.ny.us/html/history1870-1898.html> City of New York Parks & Recreation. (April 23, 1999).

106. The Small Parks Advisory Committee Report analyzed: the number of children under 15; the population density of children; the death rate of ward compared to death rate of city overall; maps of parks existing or under construction, and sites of schools and planned schools; the report also included the text of the 1887 Small Parks Act. Ware, *Jacob A. Riis*, 161.

107. *Park Planning for Greater New York (1870-1898)* <www.ci.nyc.ny.us/html/history1870-1898.html> City of New York Parks & Recreation. (April 23, 1999).

108. Riis, *BWTS*, 276.

109. *Park Planning for Greater New York (1870-1898)* <www.ci.nyc.ny.us/html/history1870-1898.html> City of New York Parks & Recreation. (April 23, 1999).

110. Lane, *Riis and American City*, 126.

111. Ware, *Jacob A. Riis*, 164; Lane, *Riis and American City*, 126.

112. Barth, *City People*, 38. See Barth, 38-40, for a fuller discussion of the disputes between proponents of parks and those of playgrounds.

113. Lane, *Riis and American City*, 113, quoting Jacob Riis in "Parks for the Poor," *Christian Union*, 8 August 1891.

Chapter 9

Walking the Urban Environment: Pedestrian Practices and Peripatetic Politics

David Macauley

Ubi pedes ibi patria
—Roman law[1]

Solvitur Ambulando
—Medieval maxim[2]

Pre-amble

Perhaps even more than walking in the wilderness,[3] sauntering and strolling in the city and its suburbs involves multiple, repeated, and deeply imbricated border crossings, including nested neighborhoods, traffic flows, ethnic enclaves, residential and commercial zones, subcultures, historical sites, sacred spaces, and outcroppings of the wild in parks, cemeteries, and abandoned lots. In this sense, urban walking is by its very nature a transforming practice because the moving body and the plurality of places it inhabits are constantly conjoined and then decoupled in new ways that come to reveal the metropolitan world in its manifold dimensions. In the following essay, pedestrian practices and problems in the urban environment are explored along with their broader relation to what may be called peripatetic politics. The withdrawal of the walker's world and the decline of the walking city are described in conjunction with an attempt to uncover the close connection between walking and place. In the process, the sites and situations of urban walking are elucidated, including sidewalks and streets, promenades and parks, and outdoor or indoor malls. By contrast, we can observe

the manner that auto culture tends to change or curtail contact with our surroundings, encouraging a kind of self-absorbed "sleep walking."

Walking, though, might be re-rooted in and re-routed through the urban and
suburban landscape so as to pose a challenge to social tendencies that accentuate
forms of domestication or domination. By understanding the dynamic and
democratic dimensions of walking, we can also begin to interrogate and critically contest the opaque and authoritarian features of urban architecture, private
property, and public space. If we follow walkers through city and suburban
placescapes, we might begin to observe the implicit cultural politics at work in
various orders of ambulation. The control and maintenance of space and place,
the organization of speed and pace, and the erection or transgression of community ideas of citizenship or race are instances of such phenomena. Further, the
similarities become noticeable between pedestrian activity and linguistic speech
acts in terms of a rhetoric of walking—a trail of "foot notes" so to speak—
within the processual setting and mobile text of the city. In short, an
examination of walking in the city and suburbs shows us the many particular
and overlapping "walks of life."

At the same time, urban strolls are generally the most basic and direct mode of
apprehending our surroundings, of attuning ourselves to the ambient environment. In this sense, they both orient the lived body while ceaselessly dislocating
and relocating us within new boundaries, regions, and territories. Indeed, walking enables us to question and transform the very rigidity of such social and political borders, while at once helping to build up a stable perceptual world. The
aesthetically-inclined *flâneur* and the politically-informed drifter on a *dérive* are
several kinds of itinerant urban wayfarers who establish a critical relation to the
urban environment. However, in order to grasp more fully the diverse aspects of
walking, one must attend eventually as well to dog walkers, exercising enthusi-
asts, shuffling shoppers, and more pedestrian—common-place and foot-bound—
practices.[4] By focusing on peripatetic activities, then, it is hoped that we can
come to better understand our cities, surroundings, and circadian activities in the
borderlands that we routinely inhabit.

Withdrawal of the Walker's World

As inhabitants of a new and ever-accelerating century, we are arguably witnesses to a recession and long decline of the walking city, one that has stopped
short of its complete disappearance. The world of the walker has been withdrawing due to developments from several directions, including the rise of
swelling suburbs and now *ruburbs* (rural suburbs), the omnipresence of autos
and the ongoing elimination of public spaces. For the past fifty years, cities have
been increasingly organized for impersonal driving, private consumption, and
commercial advertising rather than human ambling, political participation, and
public revelation. Much of this change can be attributed to the transformations

of the public and private spheres and the emergence of the social sphere, which redefines the nature and relationship of the other two realms.[5]

There are at least five spatial characteristics of early "walking cities"—cities around the world in early nineteenth century, circa 1815, where the most common, cheapest and easiest means of movement was human motility—i.e., the walking body.[6] These largely centripetal (tending toward the center) dimensions encouraged people to walk and should be seen by way of contrast with the increasingly centrifugal (tending away from the center) aspects of more recent suburbanization. First, walking cities were marked by relatively high human populations, congestion, and concurrent intensity within their interiors. For example, in London, the largest city in the world at the time—with a population of 800,000—one could walk from the outer edges to the center in only two hours. The same held true in American cities, which were smaller but had equally active inner environs. Secondly and related to this feature, there existed a relatively clear distinction between the country and the town. Little to no melding or conflation of the rural and the urban could be found at the time. Thirdly, the walking city was informed by a variety of overlapping of functions. Neighborhoods were differentiated but not defined by exclusively residential, commercial, governmental, or production centers, thus encouraging rather than discouraging accessibility via foot. One did not have to travel half way across town to shop, worship, or vote, as one might need to do today. Fourth, the residents of the city tended to live a very short distance from their places of occupation. In 1815, eighty percent of the citizens were within less than a mile of their work locations. Again, the proximity of living and working spaces facilitated walking. Finally, the perceived best locations and residences were close to the center of the city rather than on the outskirts. This fact, too, heightened the value of remaining physically close to places of urban activity that were accessible through walking.

Despite the rise of the suburb and the transformation of landscapes in the process, the city still retained a sense of form and limit for as long as suburban growth was regulated by walking distances and railroads. What was undermined largely through the automobile was the habitable and livable *pedestrian scale* in the environment. "Instead of buildings set in a park, we now have buildings set in a parking lot."[7] As private cars replaced public rails, we have become dependent upon a single form of transportation that has recreated the landscape in its image. Differentiated place was increasingly subordinated to or transformed into homogeneous space. With the loss of walkable distances has disappeared the loss of walking as a regular means of circulation. "The motor car has made it unsafe and the extension of the suburb has made it impossible."[8] What we often fail to remember in this regard is that speed and power need not become autonomous values or ends in themselves but should be constantly related to human needs, local scales, and social purposes. As Lewis Mumford observes, if one desires to meet and speak with others on an urban promenade or esplanade, then three miles per hour might be too fast; whereas if a doctor is trying to get to an injured person, then three hundred miles per hour might be too slow. Correlatively, the fastest way to move a very large number of people within a limited urban environment is actually on foot, while the slowest way would be to put them in cars. Indeed, the entire population of historic Boston would have been able to assemble on foot in the Boston Commons in less than an hour's time; but if they had been transported by auto, the process would take many, many hours and probably not even have been completed unless their unparkable vehicles were abandoned to the streets.[9]

Shopping malls—a completely privatized and also deprived notion of the ancient and very political Greek *agora* or "town square" and gathering place—have reintroduced walking in the suburbs and outskirts of many small towns but now entirely indoors. They turn the walker's world inside-out or more accurately, *outside-in*. The sidewalk is rolled up and reappears in a purely commercial zone of exchange, largely absent of residences, the organic environment, and places of public appearance and display. In some cities, there are even clubs whose members now go "mall walking" each day, circling a shopping center together, circuit upon repetitious circuit, presumably in part for exercise but also to shop on their breaks from walking. In most such malls, loitering without purchasing,[10] displays of nonconformity, and political protest are strictly controlled or prohibited, in contrast to the relatively looser and freer outdoor sidewalks. A considerable amount of urban walking nevertheless does still occur within buildings themselves—in the "second story world" (third-, fourth-, fifth-story, etc.) on both vertical and horizontal axes—across interior spaces and up and down stairs between floors—like movements inside a magnificent human ant farm. We need to remain aware, then, of the troubling disappearances and unexpected re-appearances of walking in its many forms.

Place and Pace: Tracing and Effacing Our Steps

Walking locates the body in place. In the repetitious act of turning over our legs—of falling forward, then rising and collecting ourselves into a corporeal rhythm—we are as it were like large knitting (or perhaps sewing machine) needles stitching ourselves into the local fabric of the environs, grounding and rooting ourselves even if momentarily.[11] In this sense, walking tracks, outlines, or traces a place through the continuous trail left by the moving body and the memory of its motions. In route, the city is repeatedly taken in at a robust glance. The surroundings are actively synthesized in and through our bodies. We are oriented increasingly from single points to broader positions to localized regions and places. In the urban walk, there is a continuous stream of "information" parading past and through us; most of it more culturally encoded than in the countryside or wilderness. Like the catalysts and cues provided by a smell that takes us to remembrances of places past,[12] walking loosens, unties, and releases the mnemonic knots in the body, triggering an active engagement with and archival recollection of the places through which we walk. Of walking, the poet Paul Valéry has remarked:

As I went along the street where I live, I was suddenly *gripped* by a rhythm which took possession of me and soon gave me the impression of some force outside myself. It was as though someone else were making use of my *living machine*. Then another rhythm overtook and combined with the first, and certain strange *traverse* relations were set up between these two principles. . . . They combined the movement of my walking legs and some kind of song I was murmuring, or rather which was being murmured *through* me.[13]

In this description, we can observe the convergence, collaboration, and confluence of the body, mind, and place as well as the sense of being seized in the walk by something more-than and other-than oneself. There is in brief an internal processing of that externality and perhaps, more exactly, a chiasmatic crossing of inside and outside via the "living machine" of the body.

With walking, the practice is itself the path, which always takes place in a place.[14] When this link is lost, it is often because pace overtakes and supplants place. The ground is not merely re-placed with the planting of new steps, but it is dis-placed—cancelled, removed, or forgotten. Without availing ourselves of a regular walking, places are by-passed and effaced. In the process, we are courting topoclasm, place-alienation, and the creation of non-places: sites without life. To the extent to which city *sauntering* is "without the earth" (from *sans terre*)—due to the covering over, concealment, and loss of contact with the elemental ground—it needs to be in the sense of being-at-home where one walks and thus a mindful and creative internalization of the enveloping landscape and skyscape. The environment must not only be kept in mind but in the body as well. Walking thickens the perceptual scene, welcoming us into a palpable density rather than drawing us out via an attenuated celerity. Unlike being in a vehicle, the surrounding is less frequently constituted as scenery and spectacle or postcard-like picture. Rather, the world is more readily experienced as inhabited placescape.

In addition to pace, another important element of urban walking is the horizon, which is formed by the intersection of the sky and earth in the landscape (or, alternatively, the sky and water in the seascape). The horizon, in turn, defines the bounds and limits of perceptual experience, as the Greek term *horos* itself implies.[15] Several forms of this perceptual phenomenon can be distinguished including the apparent horizon—the juncture of cityscape and sky for example—and the sensible horizon—the tangent plane relative to the surface of the earth at the position of the observer. The encircling horizon for humans provides a vanishing point, an edge-line so to speak, in observation from which sight takes it reference in going out and returning. It functions and appears like an occluding edge even if it is in fact not always one for all objects. In walking, one finds the horizon progressively swallowing up or revealing celestial objects such as the moon, sun, and stars which lie in fact beyond the horizon and which wax or wane in size depending upon the motion of the earth and the time of day. When the ground surface is flat and opens up in front of us, the horizon that is formed is part of an ambient optical array. It is also, in this instance, the same as the skyline. Even when vast reaches of the city are not visible because of the outcroppings of buildings and other barriers, there exists something akin to an implicit horizon. By attending to the horizon, a feature of terrestrial perception which is stationary, we can become better oriented both in place and time during a walk by taking our bearings from the relative changes in our horizontal perceptions. The horizon and the earth-sky line from which it is often formed thus establishes us with a frame of reference, enabling us to govern our upright bodies—which ambulate perpendicularly to the horizon—through the environment. The horizon is strictly speaking neither a completely subjective nor an objective phenomenon. Rather, it represents an ongoing reciprocity of the walker with his or her surroundings and an invariant dimension of environmental perception.[16]

While the walker might move rapidly at times during rush hour or with haste in order to make an appointment, the key to being emplaced is a relative slowness that elicits attention to detail in the surroundings and a sense of relatedness of events, objects, and moments.[17] In downtown areas of large cities, men average about five feet per second, 290 to 300 feet per minute or about three and one-half miles per hour in their walking speed. Some studies have shown a general correlation between the pace of walking and city size. The relatively high premium placed upon time in large cities may help to explain some of this connection (as does the fact that ambitious and aggressive people are drawn to an environment with a fast pace), but many people also walk quickly to heighten stimulation from the environment. Time of day, too, affects tempo and pace. Pedestrians, for example, tend to walk more buoyantly and more commonly as groups before lunch than at other times, and a bit more slowly after lunch, as one might expect.[18]

One of the values of ambling in the urban environment is the face-to-face contact that it encourages as the walker moves from place to place. This interaction has been vital historically to a well-functioning democratic society, where a public sharing of ideas, beliefs, and concerns among citizens, needs to occur on a regular basis. An activity as mundane as dog walking, for example, is arguably one means of soliciting such contact and conviviality in that it facilitates social exchange and can encourage civic virtues such as friendship, neighborhood concern, and community responsibility.[19] The curious apolitical walking men and women of today, however, are often equipped with a battery-driven "companion" in the Walkman that takes them out of place and relocates them elsewhere, inside a hermetic world, in the collectively-negated nowhere of mental space. The Walkman is an escape from a shared setting, a retreat to the private realm *within* the public sphere itself. It is a withdrawal to a space that is programmed by oneself for oneself, absent of the chance sounds and surprising noises we normally find on the street, devoid of the possibility of true communication with others, who tend to avoid contact with these wired sleepwalkers. This phenomenon is evident, too, in the widespread use of mobile phones on city sidewalks, a practice which tends to inhibit association with others at street corners and intersections, where pedestrians coalesce into collective pools while waiting for a light to change or traffic to pass.

The particular places where people walk in the city are of course legion. Despite the multiple threats to them, wild and semi-wild regions are still profoundly present in our urban and suburban environs and often only accessible via walking.[20] Parks, dog-walks, cemeteries, abandoned lots, and walkable areas around rivers, reservoirs, and fountains frequently abound with animal and plant life that peep or creep out at various times of the day. For example, in Manhattan, one can still find red-tailed hawks on a stroll through Central Park; in cities in the Southwest, coyotes regularly prowl the sidewalks and streets at nights with other pedestrians; while Canada geese nest in the heart of many major urban centers. In thousands of suburbs, deer, raccoon, and even bear are commonly observed by local walkers. Apart from learning of the presence of urban animals and plants by guided walking tours through menageries, arboretums, and theme parks, it might be possible to encourage the development of city life toward reintegrating the green with the gray, and the animal with the human, in a vision of what one writer terms a *zoöpolis*—a hybrid of the wild and civilized, the biological and political.[21] Our cities are for the most part heterotopias (rather than static utopias or nightmarish dystopias), places with multiple and often contradictory functions, along with existing animal and plant communities, and walking is generally the best means of experiencing these locations and nonhuman populations with the least degree of mediation.

At the same time, we should be aware that thinking about walking potentially suffers from an over-attachment to romantic and narrowly naturalistic concerns.[22] Similarly, much writing about the environment tends to seek out and then valorize the perception of a natural world that is presumed to be autonomous from the social and human sphere. In the process, there is often a disregard of the built and especially urban realms, and a penchant to uphold natural place to the exclusion of a necessary movement through and transformation of it. On this count, many seemingly "natural" paths and places of walking in the city such as those in parks and public gardens are actually closely-constructed, highly-orchestrated, and heavily-maintained settings. In Boston, for example, the well-walked esplanade along the Charles River (and in fact the entire encompassing Back Bay area) is what might be termed an *earth work*—as opposed to *art work*—an organic and very social place that is the result of concerted human action on transported soil and dirt, which itself undergoes erosion, accretion, and ecological change.

The *Agon* with Autos: Sleepwalkers and Technomads

While walking in the contemporary world, we need to remain actively aware of the problem of "technological somnambulism"[23] and the possibility that we are *sleepwalking* through heavily occluded environments, a phenomenon and problem that is magnified in urban and suburban areas, where mediation is heightened. We are, in other words, in danger of being only half-awake in our ambling. This metaphor suggests a lack of direction, a kind of cultural blindness, errancy, and drifting brought on in part by an overreliance upon relatively opaque technologies. Technologies such as the car which—via the automotive and oil industries—has increasingly recreated cities in terms of *its* needs rather than *our* own and sewn the landscape with a network of streets and superhighways. Increasingly, we are transforming ourselves into *technomads* (technological nomads)—wanderers via the prosthetic eyes, ears, and limbs of technology as opposed to those of the walking body. Further, we are courting the risk of becoming *technobodies* (technological nobodies) where the body-environment relation is entirely reconstructed via the medium of technology, or where the body itself is greatly eclipsed. Even if the wheels of the car are considered an extension of our feet or as feet-in-rotation (as some theories of technology suggest), there is a still a numbing effect on or *narcosis* of the senses. An "autoamputation" of the body hindering self-recognition—that accompanies this (and every) attempt to extend ourselves, as Marshall McLuhan has pointed out.[24] Such technological developments and redefinitions of the body pose potential challenges to practices bound with corporeal orientation to the extent to which they raise fundamental questions about human purposiveness, teleology, functionality, posture, and locomotion. Hans Jonas, for example, has spoken of legs as "walking tools" and "external motor organs" because of the work they perform: "legs fulfill their purpose in walking as hammers do in hammering." "We can say with some confidence" he argues, "that the realm of voluntary bodily movement in man and animal (exemplified by 'walking') is a locus of real determination by purposes and goals, which are objectively executed by the same subjects that subjectively entertain them."[25]

The use of escalators, elevators, and conveyer-belt like walking machines is emblematic of a wider transformation and loss with respect to walking. In such situations, we walk (or simply stand) *in* place but do not move *through* it in the manner of actively and corporeally inhabiting it, and we walk on machines that carry and conduct us, appearing in the process to be less alive at times than our creations. The automobile driver is arguably already a kind of cybernetic organism or cyborg who (that) is encased in a heavy metal jacket and tethered to many micro-machines within the more encompassing car. As Jean Baudrillard observes in his remarks on J. G. Ballard's novel, *Crash*, "Technology is never grasped except in the (automobile) accident, that is to say in the violence done to technology itself and in the violence done to the body. It is the same: any shock, any blow, any impact, all the metallurgy of the accident can be read in the semiurgy of the body."[26]

In many regards, the *high-way* of the speeding auto is contrary to the *low-way* (and slow way) of the sauntering walker. Whereas the highway attenuates the perceptual scene, walking puts us back into the thick of things and carries us through a world of living beings. By contrast, driving ties the anchored actor and relatively passive observer to a mobile shell that narrowly limits environmental awareness while altering and often endangering the movements and lives pedestrians.[27] Driving privileges the visual mode of perception in part by dimming down and displacing the roles of other senses. It tends to numb the legs and freeze into position the lower body and torso, making it difficult to turn around or to disengage from a forward-looking posture. When we must walk the route we have driven because of an automotive breakdown or accident, this difference becomes apparent. An entirely new perspective can open around us, exfoliating many of the layers of mediation and mystification that we have learned to quietly accept, dutifully adapt to, and finally forget. Walking is thus practically (and not just theoretically) a means of overcoming the "geography of nowhere"[28] that the auto and its advocates have helped to inaugurate and implement.

Walking and driving illustrate a clash of ways of life and their attendant values. The collision or contest (*agon*) of old—perdurable and often conserving—and new—emergent and usually usurping—forms of living as defined by different technologies relative to speed, time, pace, and place is manifest throughout the day and night in the intersection and border crossings associated with walkers and cars in the city: the contested places of the sidewalks, streets, and parking lots. The political and more specifically class—and even class warfare—aspects of this *agon* were evident very early in the first auto accidents at the turn of the twentieth century. Wealthy car owners struck and killed immigrants, frequently causing community residents to retaliate against upper class "invasions" of their neighborhoods by assaulting motorists with rocks and firecrackers—sometimes to the point of riots. From 1901-1906, thirty-four anti-auto incidents were reported by the *New York Times*, including one that resulted in the death of a driver who was killed by a father of a pedestrian victim. Three-quarters of the earliest victims of auto accidents, in fact, were pedestrians and especially children playing in the streets. Many rural residents were also annoyed by the arrival of wealthy urban drivers, who injured walkers, ran over chickens and dogs, whipped up large amounts of dust, and deepened ruts in the roads. Because of such developments, New Jersey even tried to ban cars registered in New York, and the *New York Times* went as far to term autos "devil wagons" and call for an eight mile per hour speed limit in 1905.[29]

From the pedestrian's perspective, the car is less a carapace—a protective shield and shell—as it is for the driver than a potential weapon, less of means of transportation than a form of rapid transformation of the walker's world, exposing his or her vulnerability. While elevating the driver to a kind of super-human with heightened speed and power, the car degrades the pedestrian to a threatened second-class citizen. "At street level—outside a vehicle—all modern cities are violent," announces John Berger.[30] And Theodor Adorno draws this point out to its disturbing psychological implications. "Which driver is not tempted," he asks, "merely by the power of his engine, to wipe out the vermin of the street, pedestrians, children and cyclists?"[31] In his "Walk through Rotterdam," Mumford too reflects on the diminished status of peripatetic life in the United States. "We have pushed the elimination of the pedestrian to its ultimate conclusion—the drive-in market, the drive-in movie, and the drive-in bank," appending the black-humor afterthought that we are missing only the drive-in cemetery.[32] In this sense, the car has provided a machine and means to literally "drive ourselves crazy" as a culture—witness widespread road rage, frustration in traffic, and drive-by shootings—as we lose contact with one another, create environmental uniformity, and transfigure the landscape.[33]

One difficulty, of course, with overdrawing this dichotomy is that at another time and place the walker is often also a driver and vice-versa (although it is frequently only the enthusiastic peripatetic who respectfully remembers this fact). Another dilemma worth acknowledging is that with greater physical and geographic mobility (horizontal movement) provided by the car, many Americans have found a way to achieve more social mobility (vertical movement) that might otherwise have been denied to them. Nevertheless, the car poses a very real threat not only to the walking way of life but to the life of the walker him- or herself. In New York City, for example, one is more likely to be killed by a stranger in a car than by one toting a gun,[34] and nationally more children are regularly slaughtered by autos in suburbia than by firearms in the city.[35] In New York, there were 12,730 vehicle-pedestrian collisions, approximately one every forty-one minutes in 1994.[36] Ten years earlier, 293 pedestrians were killed by automobiles while 300 died in London in the same year. However, while London has taken aim at significantly reducing these fatalities by introducing cameras in high-accident zones, enforcing speed limits, aggressively broadcasting public messages about the dangers of speeding, and embracing traffic-calming projects such as widening sidewalks, installing speed bumps, and eliminating or controlling traffic on some congested streets, the efforts in New York have been much more minimal and thus less successful.[37] Indeed, the twin pursuits of pedestrian safety and reduction of traffic congestion are complementary rather than competing goals.

It may even be the case that "the swiftest traveler is he that goes a-foot"[38] when we realize the real but hidden social costs of transportation that must be factored in when calculating time in transit. In this regard, Thoreau argued that if the railroad circumnavigated the earth, he would still stay ahead of the "iron horse" by walking the same distance. In the present urban and suburban environments, we need to keep in mind the time, energy, and money we expend in working to pay for or finance the auto, car insurance, license and parking fees, traffic tickets, gas and oil, repairs and registration, costs to use turnpikes, tunnels and bridges, and road maintenance through taxes. The average American, in fact, spends up to one-fourth of his or her annual wages to enjoy the privilege (or necessity) of a keeping of a car. And while the average motorized speed in the city is roughly twice that of the pedestrian, when the social time necessary to produce the means of transport is added to time spent in transit, the average global traveling speed of modern man is less than that of Paleolithic people.[39]

In the last several decades, there have been a number of proposals to ban cars from downtown regions so as to make cities friendlier for pedestrians.[40] While this goal might be admirable even if unattainable, Jane Jacobs argues that cars are not the essential and inherent cause of urban decay. "If we would stop telling ourselves fairy tales about the suitability and charm of nineteenth-century streets for horse-and buggy traffic, we would see that the internal combustion engine, as it came on the scene was potentially an excellent instrument for abetting city intensity, and at the same time for liberating cities from one of their noxious liabilities." She continues: "We went awry by replacing, in effect, each horse on the crowded city streets with half a dozen or so mechanized vehicles, instead of using each mechanized vehicle to replace half a dozen or so horses."[41]

Still, the role of the auto in transforming urban and suburban landscapes should not be underestimated. In Boston, walkers have on average less than ten seconds (and sometimes as few as seven) to cross a street while cars receive upwards to a minute and a half to continue on their ways. Pedestrians are routinely unable to actually cross the street before the lights—which are calibrated for traffic flow rather than walking distances—switch again to "DONT WALK," and they frequently find the crosswalk blocked by the unyielding steel frame of an idling auto. In many suburban situations, the walker—unlike the auto owner—is viewed with suspicion, as a vagrant, outcast, or unwelcome outsider, and sometimes taken into custody for walking on the side of the road where no pedestrian path exists. Such social biases should at least give us pause to ask for whom (or what) our communities are organized. In cities such as Los Angeles, we may even have unwittingly constructed the environment as a kind of *autopia* (auto utopia), where the "freeway system in its totality is now a single comprehensive place, a coherent state of mind, a complete way of life."[42] Despite these developments, it is helpful to remember that every trip we take by car begins and ends on foot (even if the walk is just from the house or apartment to the garage or parking lot) and that walking is often still the most convenient mode of movement within high density areas.

Peripatetic Politics: Power, Property, and Propriety

Walking, then, should be considered a political and environmental practice. That urban walking is connected with power and politics is clear from a historical vantage point. In ancient Greece, many citizens ambled up to fifteen miles—a four hour journey by foot over rough roads in the country—to the *ekklesia* (an assembly on the Pnyx held forty times each year) in order to participate in public life, "ever delicately walking through the most pellucid air" as Euripides put it.[43] In the fourth century B.C.E., students walked out from Athens along a wide pedestrian avenue to reach the gymnasium at the Academy in the northwest suburbs. Prior to becoming Plato's celebrated school, they engaged there in physical training without clothes as part of a broad program for citizenship—a bodily belong to the *polis* (city)—that also involved an early emphasis on voice projection and oral articulation in preparation for later public debate. For the Greeks, the way one walked was considered part of personal character and thus bodily comportment was connected with political power. Long strides were viewed as an emblem of "manliness" and a sign of leadership, a point made by Homer in his admiration of Hector: "the Trojans drove forward in close throng, and Hector led them, advancing with long strides."[44] By contrast, women were supposed to walk with shorter and more abrupt steps, and men who strode in such fashion were often considered effeminate or passive homosexuals. The upright (*orthos*) and erect posture suggested purposefulness and by extension rectitude—a notion that we have inherited from the Greeks.

As Richard Sennett has shown, the Greeks tended to create links between their bodies and their buildings, between the citizens and the city, by relating physiological needs to urban political structures.[45] In addition to the gymnasium, where the bodies of boys were shaped for civic participation, the free-standing *stoa*— which helped to give ironic birth to the movement of worldly-withdrawal known as Stoicism—opened out into the *agora* and served as a place where citizens could gather to philosophize, dine, or conduct business. In this regard, it possessed both a sheltering and revelatory function for the body. Daily participation in the life of the city generally necessitated that citizens lived within walking distances of the *agora*, although by the end of the fifth century, 40 percent of the citizens were making the long trek by foot on a regular basis. Within this public sphere of action, strolling male citizens participated in the democratic workings of the *polis*, walking about in the open air so as to learn about and eventually decide pressing legal cases, ostracize or exile serious violators of law, and make speeches, among many other activities.

As in modern society, where the walker looked—that is, one's gaze—was connected normatively to social and political values of the time. Youth in Sparta, for example, were expected to cast their eyes toward the ground when walking in public—as were modest women and ashamed men in Greece generally—and to keep their hands cloaked within their garments. The politically-free and proper Greek male kept his head straight and erect, his hands held firmly, his eyes open and his gaze steadfast as he walked through the world—traits that were no doubt tied to earlier expressions or appearances of strength in battle within a warrior culture. By contrast, it was commonly believed that madmen rolled their eyes, that slaves tended to hold their heads crooked, that dangerous characters squinted, and that passive homosexuals looked around as they walked.[46] Thus, one's gait, carriage, and comportment were considered visible signs of authority or submission, of masculinity or effeminacy, and of class power or social disenfranchisement as walking came to be invested patently with notions of politics, gender, and sexuality.

Socrates is perhaps the most well-known itinerant philosopher, walking and talking so as to encourage a dialectic, but eventually sentenced to death in no small measure because of the perceived political threat he posed to democratic Athens. Indeed, Socrates only leaves the limits of the *polis* on one remarkable walking occasion, recorded by Plato in the *Phaedrus*. Aristotle, too, returned to Athens—after teaching the politically powerful Alexander of Macedon—to found his school at the Lyceum, in the precincts of a sacred grove of Apollo Lyceus and a favorite haunt of Socrates. The school was also known as the *peripatos*—a covered walking place—and its members as *peripatetikoi* due to their supposed custom of conducting conversations while walking up and down in a covered ambulatory or because much of their instruction was carried on in ambulation. Historians have traditionally held that Aristotle walked each morning with his pupils in the loggia or among the trees, discussing difficult questions of philosophy.[47] This emphasis on walking to encourage reflection—an intimacy in effect between wandering and wondering—resurfaced in his own influential writings, often with a political import. For example, in the *Nicomachean Ethics* Aristotle upholds the Athenian ideal of the leisured citizen or "gentleman" who walks slowly and with distinction through the streets. The leisured citizen is an emblem of being a "great-souled" *(megalopsychos)* individual and a paragon of one definition of man he gives in *De partibus animalium*: the animal who stands erect.[48] Finally, the role of walking as a common Greek practice with cultural significance is indicated as well by the famous riddle in Sophocles' *Oedipus Rex*: what walks with four legs in the morning, two legs in the afternoon, and three legs in the evening? The answer, of course, is the human animal: *homo erectus, homo sapiens,* or *homo faber* depending upon one's perspective.

Later, in the twelfth century, John of Salisbury spoke in his *Policraticus* of the feet of the commonwealth. "Those are called feet who discharge the humbler offices, and by whose services the members of the whole commonwealth walk upon the solid earth." Included in this category were husbandmen, farmers, cloth makers, those working in the mechanical arts and other occupations useful to the corporate commonwealth.

All these different occupations are so numerous that the commonwealth in the number of its feet exceeds not only the eight-footed crab but even the centipede, and because of their very multitude they cannot be enumerated. . . . But it applies generally to each and all of them that in their exercise they should not transgress the limits of the law, and should in all things observe constant reference to the public utility.[49]

Thus, laborers were associated with the lowest and most earthly of workers and integrated at the base of the political superstructure and body-politic, like a foot on a person. The Middle Ages were an especially peripatetic period, as many thousands of persons traveled from town to town on foot, including troubadours, monks, and wandering scholars.[50] The range of motley vagrants who roamed through Europe is evoked by Umberto Eco in his novel, *The Name of the Rose*:

false monks, charlatans, jugglers, invalid mercenaries, wandering Jews . . . lunatics, fugitives under banishment, malefactors with an ear cut off, sodomites, and along with them ambulant artisans, weavers, tinkers, chair-menders, knife-grinders, basket-weavers, masons, and also rogues of every stripe, forgers, scoundrels, cardsharps, rascals, bullies, reprobates, recreants, frauds, hooligans, simoniacal and embezzling canons and priests . . . false paralytics who lay at church doors, vagrants fleeing convents, relic-sellers, pardoners, soothsayers and fortunetellers, necromancers, healers, bogus alms-seekers, fornicators of every sort, corruptors of nuns and maidens by deception and violence, simulators of dropsy, epilepsy, hemorrhoids, gout, and sores, as well as melancholy madness.[51]

More recently, Thoreau invoked the notion that walking is related to the political sphere in his claim that he could amble for half an hour and arrive at "some portion of the earth's surface where man does not stand from one year's end to another, and there, consequently, politics are not."[52] In the city, this is clearly not the case, however, as power and politics are percolating at each corner and every stop sign.

Urban walks can lead us, too, into the border-bursting realms of crowds, solidarity, shared action, and plural subjects. Walking in the city often occurs as a form of togetherness—even when we are alone among strangers—in which we assemble, disassemble, and reassemble in shifting groups based upon happenstance or affinities of appearance and desire. Wandering out for a walk with a family member or friend, taking a turn around the block with the dog, or going on a stroll with a lover or spouse are enduring ways of establishing and maintaining intimacy and familiarity with a community. The walker in the modern or postmodern city tends to have less regular physical contact with others than amblers in earlier periods—when the streets and sidewalks were more hectic and less mediated by commercialism—though opportunities still abound in neighborhoods, parks, and public squares. Edgar Allan Poe's short story, "The Man of the Crowd" points to some of the exotic and erotic dimensions of walking among the masses as an anonymous man of the crowd disappears into the crowd itself holding within himself a secret that "does not permit itself to be read."[53] The French poet Baudelaire also suggests ways in which an urban walker might deliberately abandon his or her guard so as to be seduced, moved, excited, saddened, and eventually abandoned by a chance encounter or fantasy with a beautiful stranger or intriguing passerby on a busy sidewalk. More generally, the goal as an impassioned spectator is "to become one flesh with the crowd" and "to set up house in the heart of the multitude, amid the ebb and flow of movement, in the midst of the fugitive and the infinite." One should enter into the *hoi polloi* "as though it were an immense reservoir of electrical energy" to which one could be a mirror or kaleidoscope as expansive as the crowd itself so as to respond to and reproduce its flickering rhythms.[54]

There is even a certain public skepticism and suspicion that can arise toward the lone walker. As Ralph Waldo Emerson remarks, "Whoso goes to walk alone, accuses the whole world; he declares all to be unfit to be his companions; it is very uncivil, nay insulting; Society will retaliate."[55] In this regard, there are a variety of collective walkathons in most cities and suburbs, including those sponsored by the March of Dimes, cancer, and AIDS support groups, and organizations raising money and awareness about hunger, homelessness, and community health. Political walks in the form of demonstrations and protest marches empower people by taking to and taking back the streets.[56] City walking is tied as well to a host of social and political issues such as stalking (sexual threats), "take back the night" walks (feminism), streetwalking (prostitution), and walk-outs (labor practices and strikes).[57] In walking from neighborhood to neighborhood, one is also frequently crossing borders of ethnicity, citizenship, and race, entering worlds that are relatively unfamiliar and thus potential scenes of political and cultural education, as when one "crosses the tracks" to witness poverty and discrimination or, alternatively, affluence and privilege.[58]

Walking can be a profoundly democratic practice where all are literally placed on the same footing. This sentiment is revealed in Dostoevsky's *Notes from Underground* when the narrator, a clerk, encounters an officer on the street whose station in life clearly ranks above him:

> It tormented me that even in the street I couldn't manage to treat him as an equal. "Why must you step aside first?" I'd rant at myself . . . "Why just you, why not he?" There is, after all, no law about it. . . . Why can't it be on equal terms. . . . I was fully set to do it, but all that happened at the very last moment was that I stumbled underfoot . . . just two inches away from him . . . I made a final decision . . . I made up my mind in an instant, shut my eyes and—we collided firmly . . . I did not yield an inch and passed him by entirely on equal footing! I had achieved my goal, I had sustained my dignity, I had not yielded a step and had publicly set myself on an equal social footing with him.[59]

By contrast, some caste members in India step far in an antidemocratic direction when they treat "untouchables" as pariahs by wiping away their footprints in the dust and dirt after they have approached so as to render them *persona non grata*. In comparison with the days when many walkers were seen as vagrants, déclassé, or simply members of the underclass, because they could not afford "proper" transportation—a historical fact apparent in novels such as Jane Austen's *Pride and Prejudice* and Thomas Hardy's *Tess*—a renewed attention to walking possesses emancipatory possibilities.[60] Mao Tse Tung, Che Guevara, Moses, and other radical political figures of renown went on long walks, marches, or pilgrimages as did Buddha and Jesus. As Bruce Chatwin claims with boldness, "None of our revolutionary heroes is worth a thing until he has been on a good walk."[61]

Urban and suburban walking raise issues related to trespassing and transgression, of crossing and marking the limit of the allowable. Walking de-limits boundaries, removes and reinstates a line or time with regard to permissibility or pass-ability. Private property and public space are always at stake in the walk, and in the process and procession of human bodies, so are the borders of the appropriate and appropriated, property and propriety. On an extended walk, it is not uncommon to encounter fences, guard dogs, and alarms that hinder or prevent one's access to certain territories. The increasing surveillance of sidewalks and streets by circulating cameras and cops is in large measure maintenance for traditional lines of power, notions of propriety, and institutions of property.[62] This fact and phenomenon is evident when loiterers, vagrants, and non-consuming walkers are threatened, harassed, and arrested for not participating in the commercial spectacle, for merely being present in residential areas, or for walking across lawns, exclusive beaches, or "private communities" (an oxymoron to be sure).[63]

Walking through Walls: The City as Moving Text

Walking is a way of sidestepping domestication, of leaving the hold of the house—the household—but not necessarily the wholeness of home in the more inclusive sense of the environment. Walking methodically constitutes and yokes physical locations together in the action of the circumambulating body and surveying mind, stretching out and connecting a trail of sounds, sites, smells, and sightings—opening up and revealing a series of land-markings. Although departing from a familiar scene such as the apartment or house, the walk itself cannot be fully re-domesticated, it is always a step ahead of the interpretation. There is an excess of the signifying environment over the synthesizing activities of the walker. This is especially evident in the urban milieu where there is a superabundance of sensations that register on the walker's senses and subconscious, even if they may not be acknowledged completely upon their arrival. Thus, walking in the city can be viewed in terms of a rhetoric that recognizes the turnings and tropes, the spatial semantics and somatic styles, and the gestures and proper names inherent to the activity. As Michel de Certeau has argued, walking possesses an enunciative function. Like speech-acts, it involves an appropriation of the topography (as when speakers take on language), an acting-out of place (as when speech enacts language acoustically), and an active relating of distinct pragmatic positions (as when a verbal utterance becomes an allocution and is put into comprehensible action). We are, in other words, effectively engaged in "pedestrian speech acts," and walking can be thought of in terms of its spaces or places of enunciation.[64]

Several salient characteristics of such speech acts can be further identified in order to differentiate them from the existing system of physical spaces. According to de Certeau, three features in particular are prominent: the present, the discrete, and the phatic. Walking is first of all a present actualization of multiple spatial possibilities. These include inventive, surprising, and spontaneous acts of the walker as she or he picks and chooses a path through the city or alternatively prohibits a selection of options so as to avoid, for example, a construction zone, a dangerous neighborhood, or a heavily trafficked region. The walker simultaneously creates discreteness by making or displacing choices from among the signifiers in the linguistic landscape. Through walking, one constitutes both a "here" and a "there," a "near" and a "far," as one does in verbal communication. This dimension underscores the close parallel between pedestrian and linguistic enunciation, introduces an otherness or outside in relation to the ambling self, and articulates the conjunctive and disjunctive dimensions to the places through which we walk. Finally, urban walking possesses a phatic aspect that involves the initiation, maintenance, or disruption of contact and communication with other persons (and perhaps we can include animals and even artifacts with which one confabulates). As we walk, we regularly commune, acknowledge, and directly or indirectly converse with other walkers most obviously through utterances but also via the silent semaphores of our gestures and posture, our unfolding legs and swinging arms, our glancing eyes and flapping elbows.

These distinctions within a rhetorical ecology of ambling, too, could be expanded upon, as de Certeau suggests, so as to include an analysis of the modes of pedestrian enunciation in terms of their truth value (e.g., possible, impossible, or contingent), epistemology (e.g., plausible, questionable, excluded), and ethics or legality (e.g., the permitted, obligatory, or forbidden). "Walking affirms, suspects, tries out, transgresses, respects etc., the trajectories it 'speaks.' All the modalities [of pedestrian enunciation] sing a part in this chorus, changing from step to step, stepping in through proportions, sequences, and intensities which vary according to time, the path taken and the walker."[65] Such a theoretical framework tends to stress the opacity and blindness of the migrational and metaphoric city that is inserted between or superimposed upon the lines and grid work of a planned, coordinated, and administrated city. This phenomenon calls attention to an oddity and uncanniness that does not come to a transparent surface, except when one rises up to view the city from above.

> The ordinary practitioners of the city live 'down below,' below the thresholds at which visibility begins. They walk—an elementary form of this experience of the city; they are walkers, *Wandersmänner*, whose bodies follow the thicks and thins of an urban "text" they write without being able to read it. These practitioners make use of spaces that cannot be seen; their knowledge of them is as blind as lovers in each other's arms. The paths that correspond in this intertwining, unrecognized poems in which each body is an element signed by many others, elude legibility. It is as though the practices organizing a bustling city were characterized by their blindness. The networks of these moving, intersecting writings compose a manifold story that has neither author nor spectator, shaped out of fragments of trajectories and alterations of spaces: in relation to representations, it remains daily and indefinitely other.[66]

Indeed, it is precisely the presence of monumental "letters" in the form of concrete, steel, and glass buildings such as the 1370-foot World Trade Center situated in a massive rhetorical economy of excess and expenditure that provide for the scopic and voyeuristic possibility of a fictional reading of the complex urban text (via an aerial or bird's-eye point of view).[67]

After pressing the parallel between pedestrian processes and linguistic practices, de Certeau links walking to the realm of symbolic and mythic discourse along with aspects of "oneiric figuration," suggesting a connection between spatial practices and dreamed places—one that can be found in numerous literary writers. In describing the place of his childhood in Brooklyn, Henry Miller, for example, observes: "Suddenly, walking down a street, be it real or be it a dream, one realizes for the first time that the years have flown, that all this has passed forever and will live on only in memory; and then the memory turns inward with a strange, clutching brilliance and one goes over these scenes and incidents perpetually, in dream and reverie, while walking down a street."[68] In fact, de Certeau goes as far to suggest that to walk in the city is in some sense to admit that one is without a true place. "It is the indefinite process of being absent and in search of a proper," he writes. "The moving about that the city multiplies and concentrates makes the city itself an immense social experience of lacking a place—an experience that is, to be sure, broken up into countless tiny deportations (displacements and walks), compensated for by the relationships and intersections of these exoduses that intertwine and create an urban fabric, and placed under the sign of what ought to be, ultimately, the place but is only a name, the City."[69] The urban landscape is, in other words, as much a product of imagination as it is physical processes—it is an admixture of images (and ideas) with infrastructure, a combination of cloud and concrete.

At this juncture, the role of proper names and place-names enters into the moving *topoi* of the urban text, particularly in the toponymy of streets, boulevards, parks, apartment buildings, public squares, subway stations, churches, schools, and businesses. And while the nomenclature is not univocal or pellucid in meaning, it nevertheless assists us in making sense of our surroundings as we walk, de-marking and de-scribing zones of comfort, indicating direction, and confirming our itinerary. Such names and numbered streets can be said to form "sentences" that we compose and then enact without full awareness but which still orient our trajectories. For example, depart from 396 Beacon—cross Gloucester—turn at Massachusetts Avenue—pause and veer at Harvard Bridge —drift along Charles River footpath—and arrive at Emerson College. This phenomenon is most easily grasped perhaps in places such as "Alphabet City" in the East Village of Manhattan, in towns with streets following a lexical ordering of A, B, C, D, and so on that draw focus upon the role of lettering, and in locations such as Mexico City where street naming takes on imaginative and magical hues.[70] As de Certeau remarks, such "names create a nowhere in places; they change them into passages."[71] In the process of decorating and directing the wandering, these words and the walks to which they are wedded are transformed into "liberated spaces" so that a poetic topography is grafted onto the physical geography. "Things that amount to nothing, or almost nothing, symbolize and orient walkers' steps: names that have ceased precisely to be 'proper.'"[72]

The idea of walking as a kind of transformational encryption and inscription within the physical environment is indirectly illustrated in Paul Auster's "City of Glass," part of his *New York Trilogy*. In this short story, buildings, streets, and parks are incorporated into the emerging urban text of New York. This text is read and misread as one of the characters walks about town, seeming to trace out a daily trail of letters that suggestively spell "TOWER OF BABEL," an enigmatic reference to the problem of the diversity of tongues and the diaspora of language.[73] In this manner, the ambling serves not only as a form of physical location within the city limits and a metaphysical location within the world but also as a kind of methodological constitution of meaning. Walking, we might say, is an automatic (and often unconscious) enactment of a form of *foot-writing* as opposed to the more manual (and generally conscious) markings of handwriting, a signature of our sensuous engagement with the surroundings. In walking, we leave a series of *foot notes* in the margins (side-walks) of the urban text. In a sense, such urban walking and upright "writing" echoes, too, a much older notion of tracks as texts that can be potentially read, followed, and interpreted by the skilled traveler, hunter, or hiker given the appropriate training and patience. For the walker is not only tracking and trailing existing paths but also making and marking his or her own, in a vast over-determined but under-read palimpsest that can be followed by a wide range of pedestrians and perpipatetics as well as tourists, dogs, surveillance cameras, stalkers, detectives, and sociologists. Urban walking, then, is a turning, touring, detouring, and returning through the artifactual "canyons" and "cliffs" created by the facades of storefronts, hotels, office buildings, and arcades. It is a negotiation inside the architectural mazes and labyrinths—via short-cuts, jaywalks, backtracks, bridge-crossings, overpasses, and crowded subway undertows. And it is a movement between and through physical and perceptual walls that serve as interdictions, enticements, or endpoints for the walker and those who attempt, despite the difficulties and (de Certeau might add) impossibilities, to effectively "read" and "write" their way through the textual rhetoric of the city.

However, as we saw, the city is not only a text, but as a terrain of human traffic, a place of contested powers. While revealing, the framework offered by de Certeau is limited in terms of its ability to provide critical analysis and to suggest modes of resistance for the walker. It is on the whole more poetic than political in its approach and given toward reinstating overly sharp oppositions between a metaphoric and literal up and down, between theory and praxis, and between the macroscopic realm of the social and the microscopic domain of the individual. Still, one of the values of focusing on walking as a method of understanding the city is that it provides a "bottom-up" perspective. It ventures a street-level view from below in the shoes of ordinary citizens that counterbalances cultural and philosophical tendencies to "fall up"[74] toward the universal or immaterial and to forget the particular and familiar—i.e., the pedestrian. At the same time, it is important to keep the larger context in view and not to "fall down" and become a purveyor of a reverse-privileging. In this regard, we must also try to hold before us the broader dimensions of power and politics in the urban world. It is in this direction that the Situationists attempted to take walking while still retaining the semblances of subjectivity and creativity that are possible via bodily locomotion about a large and seemingly mechanized city. In their practice of city walking, we can discern one alternative model for critical ambling and political peripatetics.[75]

De-touring: The Path Not Taken

In formulating their critique of commodity culture and the tendency of capitalism to produce spectacles for nonparticipatory consumption, the members of the Situationist International developed a notion of the *dérive*—literally meaning "drifting" but more exactly, a method of "transient passage through varied ambiances." Such walking involves "playful-constructive behavior" and an attention to the nascent field of psycho-geography.[76] The *dérive* or drift combines both planning and chance into a kind of "organized spontaneity" as one navigates through the city. It negotiates a tension between a blind and random "letting go" and its opposite, an active awareness of psychological and placial possibilities. In this sense, it differs from the leisurely stroll or the plotted journey in that the dériving person or group must guard against becoming habituated to new routes, axes, and paths. Through a radical walking that entails a cognizance of the ambient environment, the Situationists believed that one could ascertain the fissures and breaks in a city network, the prevalence of microclimates, the nature of administrative districts, and most importantly, the manner in which sites are organized to attract or distract us. The *dérive*, too, is conceived so as to contain therapeutic potential, standing in relation to the city as a whole in a manner akin to the role of psychoanalysis at its best in relation to language. That is, it is designed to encourage a free flow of steps (words) that releases one from the banalities of ordinary life as it enacts a critique of functionalist architecture and Cartesian space upon which a dominant image of the city operates.

The *dérive* is most beneficially performed in small groups of two or three individuals who have political, aesthetic, and philosophical affinities so as to better their chances of reaching more objective conclusions about the environment. In terms of time limits, the usual duration was the length between two sleeping periods (rather than a solar day), although according to their own accounts some Situationists sustained the walking for three or four days and several even pursued it for a few months. Unlike travel, then, the *dérive* is not a continual or nonstop undertaking, and persons pursuing such radical walks are admonished to be aware of the dangers of dissolution, disintegration, and dissociation accompanying a drift. The spatial field of the *dérive* can be determinate or ill-defined, but it hinges upon the psychogeographical aims of the drifters, which can range from challenges to one's cognitive picture of the city to research on a local ambiance. Most drifts tended to occur in city regions because wandering in pastoral locales was deemed to be depressing by the Situationists—revealing their anti-ruralism. At one extreme of the realm of possibilities lies the static *dérive*—much like loitering *flânerie*—in which one might remain in a train station, for example, for an entire day, taking in the world as it walks by. Another pole is illustrated by the surrealist-like amblings of a figure who wandered through the Harz area of Germany while following a map of London, an aesthetic the Situationists seemed to tolerate as long as the automatist techniques posed a challenge to so-called bourgeois values. To the Situationists, the *dérive* is a "great game" that necessitates a certain sensibility in order to appreciate its varied dimensions. "Thus a loose lifestyle and even certain amusements considered dubious that have always been enjoyed among our entourage—slipping by night into houses undergoing demolition, hitchhiking nonstop and without destination through Paris during a transportation strike in the name of adding to the confusion, wandering in subterranean catacombs forbidden to the public, etc."[77]

As Guy Debord wrote, "That which changes our way of seeing the street is more important than that which changes our way of seeing a painting,"[78] and to this end the drift was partially directed. For the person on a *dérive* through a terrain of passion, the street unites the ordinary and extraordinary, becoming a gallery of sounds and sights that is not to be consumed in the commercial sense but rather actively engaged and even politically altered so as to reveal power relationships. Through an accompanying practice that the Situationists called *detournement*—a term suggesting a turning, diversion, or deflection as, for example, when one reads "neighborhood" as "gangland"—they hoped this could be accomplished.[79] The *dérive* helps to invest the city with human meaning, a point Debord underscored in quoting Marx's remark that "Men can see nothing around them that is not their own image: everything speaks to them of themselves. Their very landscape is alive." By deploying aerial plans, *dérives* and the insights of psychogeography, the Situationists thereby hoped to explore the uses and structures of the urban environment, offer an alternative to social alienation, and develop new readings and experiences of the city. From this perspective, maps are decidedly not neutral instruments, and the walks that track them are "not down in any map; true places never are," to borrow a line from Herman Melville. According to Debord, "Revolutionary urbanists will not limit their concern to the circulation of things and of human beings trapped in a world of things. They will try to break these topological claims, paving the way with their experiments for a human journey through authentic life."[80] In this way, the Situationists felt one could help attain the revolution of everyday life.[81]

Walking is thus potentially a form of de-touring, of undoing or unpacking the psychological and political baggage associated with the soporific dimensions of tourism, travel, and transit in the city. As Gilles Deleuze and Félix Guattari put it in their multitiered network known as *Anti-Oedipus*, "the schizophrenic out for a walk is a better model than a neurotic lying on the analyst's couch. A breath of fresh air, a relationship with the outside world."[82] Henry Miller's reflection on life in the New York streets, "The Fourteenth Ward," seems to convey the unique state of mind that walking in the city can facilitate as the ambler takes on multiple and varying lines of flight, becoming-other (nomad, child, animal, plant, music, sky) and shattering the narrow confines of the calcified self:

> Henceforward everything moves on shifting levels . . . we walk split into myriad-fragments, like an insect with a hundred feet, a centipede with soft-stirring feet that drinks in the atmosphere; we walk with sensitive filaments that drink avidly of past and future, and all things melt into music and sorrow; we walk against a united world, asserting our dividedness. All things, as we walk, splitting with us into a myriad iridescent fragments. . . . We walk the streets with a thousand legs and eyes, with furry antennae picking up the slightest clue and memory of the past. In the aimless to and fro we pause now and then, like long, sticky plants. . . . One walks the street at night with the bridge against the sky like a harp . . . every door of the cage is open and whichever way you walk is a straight line toward infinity, a straight made line over which the breakers roar.[83]

In another story, Miller further develops the parallel between a kind of healthy embrace of schizophrenia and the perceptual, psychological, and political release provided by walking:

As a human being walking around at twilight, at dawn, at strange hours, unearthly hours, the sense of being alone and unique fortifies me to such a degree that when I walk with the multitude and seem no longer to be a human but a mere speck, a gob of spit, I begin to think of myself alone . . . walking, singing, commanding the earth. I do not have to look in my vest pocket to find my soul; it is there all the time, bumping against my ribs, swelling, inflated with song. . . . The dreamers dream from the neck up, their bodies securely strapped to the electric chair. To imagine a new world is to live it daily, each thought, each glance, each step, each gesture killing and recreating, death always a step in advance. . . . These are the thoughts born of the street, *genus epileptoid*. You walk out with the guitar and the strings snap.[84]

Here we should note not just the radical walker's ostensible break with power[85] but concomitantly the severance from an orchestrated spectacle—the nonevents in non-places we increasingly find outside real time.

In this regard, Deleuze and Guattari's notion and practice of "nomadology" articulates the possibility of deterritorializing space and opening it up to qualitative multiplicities, vagabondage, and challenges to authoritarian, state, and Oedipal influences that the nomad attempts to resist. Whereas the state striates the space that it governs—formalizing it with walls, roads, or enclosures and universalizing it in the process—the nomad[86] tends to move through smooth space—which is marked only by traits that can be displaced or effaced—following vectorial fields and distributing himself or herself within it, adding to a localized but un-delimited field rather than isolating and monopolizing it. "It is a vital concern of every State not only to vanquish nomadism, but to control migrations, and more generally, to establish a zone of rights over an entire 'exterior,' over all of the flows traversing ecumenon."[87] Following such an analysis and the attendant warnings, socially-informed and politically-engaged walkers should remain vigilant in observing and then resisting the manners in which their pace is controlled, their movements are restricted, their places of circulation are regulated, and their habits are surveyed and measured.

Likewise, the idea of "dromomania" is relevant to a consideration and critique of urban peripatetics.[88] Dromomaniacs were deserters in the *ancien regime*, and the term is used in psychiatry for compulsive walkers. According to Paul Virilio—who has promulgated, extended, and interrogated the concept as it relates to speed and space—all revolutions must wrestle with the paradoxical aspects of circulation, mobilization, migration, and the moving masses. "Revolution is movement, but movement is not revolution,"[89] and so politics enters into the fray of organizing or controlling territorial and traffic flows, including the walking of foot soldiers and citizens. "We could even say," Virilio surmises, "that the rise of totalitarianism goes hand-in-hand with the development of the state's hold over the circulation of the masses."[90] The police of the *polis*, in other words, patrol the public paths, guard the gates of the city, create filters and screens against the spontaneous fluidity of the crowds, and manage the immigrations, emigrations, and internal migrations of the populace. As Deleuze and Guattari contend, the political power of the state "requires that movement . . . cease to be the absolute state of a moving body occupying a smooth space, to become the relative characteristic of a 'moved body' going from one point to another in a striated space." Thus, "the State never ceases to decompose, recompose and transform movement, or to regulate speed."[91]

Side-walks: Movement and Music in the Margins

Like all forms of travel and transit, walking in the city involves a *methodos*, a way through the world and thus a choice of routes in the environment. There are classic distinctions that can be made in the basic elements of any city, and five in particular have been identified and delineated by one noteworthy urban thinker and planner: paths, edges, districts, nodes, and landmarks. Paths are channels along which people move, whether potentially, habitually, or sporadically, and where they lack identity or are easily mistaken for one another, the entire city image can be called into question.[92] Sidewalks are one of the most prevalent manifestations of the city path. As the word itself suggests, side-walks are in one sense the exteriors and margins of the roads, the "suburbs" (so to speak) above-the-curbs of the streets. In another sense, they are the thresholds of storefronts, houses, and parks that they ring, directing people to their destinations. Sidewalks hold a vital place in our towns and cities, literally providing a platform for pubic life and an artery for regular citizen interaction. Their absence in many suburbs is a sign not only of the decline of walking but of the transformations that occur in movement toward exurbia, the domain outside the city's landscape. Sidewalks, which are understood legally as public spaces, offer needed transitional realms between the intimacy of the home and the privacy afforded by the porch on the one hand and the frenzy of traffic and the anonymity of the streets on the other hand.

> As pedestrians on the sidewalk pass in front of my property, they enter my sphere of influence. They enjoy or endure my landscaping and the architecture of my house. If I happen to be outside they might catch my gaze, and I theirs. A brief and distant intimacy connects these strangers with me because the public space of the sidewalk brings them, in a socially authorized and (usually) nonthreatening manner, into my world; when I use the sidewalk to pass in front of their houses, the intimacy is reciprocated. A very different and colder kind of relationship obtains in neighborhoods where there are no sidewalks and pedestrians must walk in the streets.[93]

Good sidewalks must be judged ultimately in terms of their integration into the communities of which they are part. It is arguable in this regard that the peace of the sidewalks and streets is not kept primarily by the police or by laws that are promulgated and enforced. Rather, as Jane Jacobs has argued, it is maintained "by an intricate, almost unconscious, network of voluntary controls and standards among the people themselves [such that] a well-used city street is apt to be a safe street. A deserted street is apt to be unsafe."[94] Following the work of urban sociologists and community planners, there seem to be a number of criteria that can be adduced and defended with regard to developing and maintaining places for walking.[95] Sidewalks should first be continuous and un-interrupted as far as this is possible in order to ensure the free movement of pedestrians. From the vantage of local businesses, a regular pedestrian flow irrigates and nourishes the city centers and sites of enterprise. In Europe, a positive result of meeting this requirement is that pedestrian cities and towns frequently retain the strongest local economies. In this sense, it might said that where the sidewalk ends, so also ceases the community.[96] In addition, sidewalks need to be both clearly-defined and safe from the threat of encroachment by cars and other vehicles, which must be reminded repeatedly that they share the world with walkers. According to federal sources, vehicle accidents involving pedestrians are twice as likely to occur in locations without sidewalks or appropriate pathways.[97] Sidewalks, moreover, must provide easy access to the destinations that pedestrians seek. The organization of walkways prior to an understanding of the places where people actually do walk or need to go can lead to problems. This dilemma is evident in parks, on college campuses, and other urban locations where sidewalks are often set up in advance of walking patterns, creating a criss-crossing and forking system of used, semi-used, and unused paths that can be visually objectionable and practically unmanageable.

Sidewalks, too, should have a rhythm that enhances, facilitates, and encourages walking and that is related aesthetically to the landscape and surrounding objects and buildings. This requirement suggests that walking may possess a musical dimension[98] that is both spatial and temporal. A dimension that is orchestrated and "played" as one is drawn by the progression of organic and inorganic "notes," architectural "scores," and visual "riffs." One encounters in the language of the landscape the arrangement, repetition, or syncopation of doors and fences, rows of trees and parking meters, clusters of benches, lines of windows, columns and telephone poles, planters and flower boxes, roof tops and even the regular cracks in the pavement. As we walk, we are propelled forward—as in a song—through expectation and anticipation and toward realization of another moment (place) that is intimately bound with and conveyed by preceding instants (locales). As Mike Greenberg suggests, "If the stride, roughly twenty-five to thirty inches for most adults, is the basic pulse of the pedestrian's encounter with the city—the beat of the music of the street—then it seems reasonable to propose that the next level of grouping might comprise events that occur at some small multiple of strides, two or three, or at most four." To this advice we may add a complicating perceptual twist: "A real building is in a state of flux as the people who see and use it are themselves in motion. As one walks along the street, buildings advance and recede, blanch and blush, spin on their toes and play hide-and-seek, reveal their seductive ankles or their proud heads."[99] Finally, sidewalks should be built to accommodate effectively the many necessary public objects that are part of daily urban and suburban life such as mailboxes, newspaper boxes, benches, utility poles, and bus shelters. This demand, of course, seems to mean that sidewalks should generally be *wide-*

walks (we might say) so that the walker is not further marginalized in the urban environment.

An MIT study—the first of its kind—in which researchers recorded the impressions and later tested the memories of twenty-seven people as they walked one by one around several blocks in Boston (along Boylston Street, through an alley, onto Newbury Street and into the Public Garden) provides some empirical information on the perceptions and attitudes of pedestrians in an urban environment.[100] Spatial form—particularly spatially dominant buildings and open areas (such as a park)—is the major impression that registers on and remains with most pedestrians, followed by the quality and characteristics of the sidewalk or city "floor" and then the details or content of the fronts of stores.[101] The spaces best remembered by walkers seem to be those that are either defined clearly or that represent breaks in an overall continuity. Sixteen of the twenty-seven participants in the study remarked on the very accommodating width of the Boylston sidewalk, including its state of repair or occasional rough surfaces, which can jar one out of a regular rhythm. The experimental pedestrians were very conscious, too, of "visual clamor" and multiple street signs. There was a widespread sense of the dramatic differences between the back alley occupations of seamstresses, for example, and the well-dressed shoppers on Newbury Street, indicating perhaps a sense of class distinctions that are visible in a short and relatively average urban walk. The walkers showed as well some awareness and concern with the presence or relative absence of trees and revealed pleasurable feelings upon entering the green space of the Public Garden (in contrast with a general distaste for the alley and an annoyance with auto traffic, though only once they had to cross it). More generally, the research indicates how walkers are constantly searching for or injecting order into their surroundings so as to make sense of their disparate impressions and to join their perceptions into a coherent picture. To this end many walkers tend to divide a walk into distinct regions—in this study three in number. Whereas relative newcomers to an urban landscape are not able to discover marked differences between spaces and places, the more experienced native is able to find similarities (though often imagined) between buildings, blocks, streets, and neighborhoods.

The Art of Walking: Pedestrian Aesthetics

To better understand the role of walking in urban contexts and other domains,[102] it is helpful to turn very briefly to a few of its representations and transformations within art, literature, and philosophy. If some walks might be conceived as rhythmic songs, the poem itself can also be construed as a kind of walk and the walk itself as form of poetic activity given their interrelated dimensions—a point made by the poet A. R. Ammons in a short essay, "A Poem is a Walk."[103] A few of these similarities include the creative use of the body and perception; the singularity, uniqueness, and un-reproducibility of most poems and many walks; the turns and returns involved in both phenomena; and the emphasis on motion which inheres in each that can be measured tellingly in by units such as feet or meters. To these aspects we should add attentiveness to the ambient surroundings, especially when the walk-poem or poem-walk is seen as a thick description or phenomenological embodiment of the landscape and topography. As it is in the case of poets like Wallace Stevens, who has gone as far to equate the ambling self with his *Umwelt* in holding that "I was the *world* in which I walked."[104] As Roger Gilbert maintains, "Like walks, poems can be seen as exploratory movements that remain uncommitted to any particular goal or outcome beyond movement itself. Both walk and poem therefore offer especially pure instances of the aesthetic, conceived as the negation of practical or end-directed activity."[105]

In addition to poetry, the use of the walk in novels has been an especially effective method of describing and detailing the city landscape. James Joyce's *Ulysses* is a paradigmatic invocation of a walk through an urban environment—very early twentieth century Dublin—that comes to reveal a distinctively modern society while at the same time recalling a lost Homeric and Greek world from which its imagery and metaphors depart.[106] The highly experimental novel takes place during the course of one day in the very walkable regions along the Liffey River. In fact, the world of Dublin as it is made manifest through the extended walk of the main characters, Stephen Dedalus and Leopold Bloom, is evoked with such verisimilitude that Joyce himself once remarked that if the city should disappear it could be recreated from the novel.

The *flâneur* as explored by Charles Baudelaire, Walter Benjamin, and other culture critics, is another kind of aesthetic walker, a spectator who discovers in the city a kind of gallery or museum. The boulevards, in other words, are places of seeing and being seen. In fact, through an active loitering and aimless strolling the *flâneur* can be said to represent a potential challenge to or critique of commodity culture with its highly regulated movements, spatial orderings, divisions of labor, and structured sense of time. Some *flâneurs* even took to walking turtles (and lobsters) down the sidewalk so as to call attention to and contest the accelerated pace of the city and modern life. Elaborating on Benjamin's idea that in the city "perception is reading," Franz Hessel writes: "The real city stroller is like a reader who reads a book simply to pass the time and for pleasure," offering in the process a theory of the *flâneur* as essayist that recalls our earlier discussion of the linkages between walking, the city, and texts. "*Flânerie* is a way of reading the street, in which people's faces, displays, shop windows, café terraces, cars, tracks, trees turn into an entire series of equivalent letters, which together form words, sentences, and pages of a book that is always new."[107]

Rousseau also employed the walk in Paris as an aesthetic avenue to what he terms "reverie," a word whose etymology implies a roaming and wandering for delight as well as a departure from habitual paths and boundaries. While completing his last work, *Reveries of the Solitary Walker*, Rousseau took pause to note on a playing card—perhaps his bookmark—an epiphanal thought. "My whole life," he noticed blithely, "has been little else than a long reverie divided into chapters by my daily walks."[108] With this idea given form, he proceeded to wander and write on—a project he had commenced in *Emile* and the *Confessions* as *promeneur solitaire* in an odd search, as he says in the "Fifth Walk" for "a state where the soul can find a resting-place."[109] In the process, he discovered that "Walking has something that animates and enlivens my ideas: I almost cannot think when I stay in place; my body needs to be in motion for my mind to be there."[110]

Post-amble

As we approach such a resting-place, we can close by raising the question whether walking is increasingly an exercise in bodily, cultural, and political nostalgia, given the near pervasive presence of the automobile, the airplane, and the internet—which seem to defeat time and denature space through the ascendancy of speed. Are we, in other words, wandering away from walking and drifting toward a post-ambling society? As Adorno puts it in *Minima Moralia*:

> the body's habituation to walking stems from the good old days. It was the bourgeois form of locomotion: physical demythologization, free of the spell of hieratic pacing, roofless wandering, breathless flight. Human dignity insisted on the right to walk, a rhythm not extorted from the body by command or terror. The walk, the stroll, were private ways of passing time, the heritage of the feudal promenade in the nineteenth century. With the liberal era walking too is dying out, even where people do not go by car.[111]

Adorno's assertion, while provocative, is surely going a bit too far. Lewis Mumford, on the hand, offers a more optimistic counterpoise to Adorno's view when he proclaims that "where walking is exciting and visually stimulating, whether it is in a Detroit shopping center or along Fifth Avenue, Americans are perfectly ready to walk." "The legs," he adds, "will come into their own again, as the ideal means of neighborhood transportation, once some provision is made for their exercise."[112] What this provision must include is not only trees for shade and overhead cover, wide sidewalks for lateral movement and traffic flow, outdoor cafes for refreshment, benches for relaxation, and flower beds for aesthetic pleasure, but also a challenge to uniform zoning practices that erect monolithic commercial, industrial, and residential areas which tend to preclude the walker. There are pedestrian outdoor "malls" in some urban areas, and solutions such as the "pedestrian pocket scheme" that attempt to counterbalance these developments have been thoughtfully proposed.[113] It should strike us as telling that many Americans will travel across the Atlantic to older European cities in part so as to experience urban settings that are scaled to a walker's sense of aesthetic appreciation, bodily needs, and desire for public participation. As Mumford himself concludes, "Nothing would do more to give life back to our blighted urban cores than to re-instate the pedestrian . . . to make circulation a delight."[114] That seems like one worthy challenge for this new century.[115]

Notes

1. Translation: "Where the feet are, there is the fatherland."
2. Roughly translated as: "The solution is through walking."
3. I consider the role of walking in the wilderness in David Macauley, "Walking the Elemental Earth: Phenomenological and Literary Foot Notes" in *Analecta Husserliana*, Vol. 71: 15-31 and David Macauley, "A Few Foot Notes on Walking," *The Trumpeter: A Journal of Ecosophy* 10, no. 1 (winter 1993): 14-16. See also David Macauley, *Walking: Philosophical Foot Notes* (Bloomington: Indiana University Press, forthcoming).
4. It is important to keep in mind that there are actually many different possible forms of movement by foot, including the ramble (e.g., a wandering in a specific locale), goal-directed walks (e.g., to the corner store), the walkabout (e.g., in the outback), the stroll (e.g., along the beach), the saunter (e.g., in a park), wilding (e.g. in the woods), circuit walks (e.g., through museums or malls), the *dérive* (e.g., a politically-engaged walk), and *flânerie* (e.g., an aesthetically-informed walk through the city).
5. On the transformations in public, private, and social space, see Hannah Arendt, *The Human Condition* (Chicago: University of Chicago Press, 1958).
6. I follow here the work of Kenneth Jackson, *Crabgrass Frontier: the Suburbanization of the United States* (New York: Oxford University Press, 1985), 14-15.
7. Lewis Mumford, *The City in History* (New York: Harcourt Brace, 1961), 506.
8. Mumford, *The City in History*, 506.
9. Mumford, *The City in History*, 506.
through the United States is in effect tantamount to a ban on gathering.
10. The ban on loitering that is increasingly common both in public and private places through the United States is in effect tantamount to a ban on gathering.
11. I elaborate on the phenomenological aspects of walking in David Macauley, "Walking the Elemental Earth," 15-31.
12. Like many other writers, Marcel Proust found much of the material for his work in walks that he took around his home.
13. Paul Valéry, "Poetry and Abstract Thought," quoted in Roger Gilbert, *Walks in the World* (Princeton, N.J.: Princeton University Press, 1991), 18-19.
14. As Siddhartha Guatama, the historical Buddha, reputedly remarked, "You cannot travel on the path before you have become the Path itself." The notion of life as a path that is walked recurs in a wide range of Eastern works, including the *Tao Te Ching* and *Dhammapada*, where to cite one example we find, "Good people keep on walking whatever happens."
15. On the notion of the horizon within phenomenology, see, for example, Edmund Husserl, *Ideas: General Introduction to Pure Phenomenology*, trans. W. R. Boyce Gibson (New York: Collier, 1962) and Maurice Merleau-Ponty, *The Phenomenology of Perception*, trans. Colin Smith (London: Routledge & Kegan Paul, 1962). For Heidegger's treatment of the horizon, especially in relation to time, see *Being and Time*, trans. John Macquarrie and Edward Robinson (New York: Harper and Row, 1962), 416ff.
16. For further consideration of ecological optics, see James J. Gibson, *The Ecological Approach to Visual Perception* (Hillsdale, N.J.: Lawrence Erlbaum, 1986).

17. Paul Virilio has described some of these dilemmas of speed relative to place, leading us into a world that is both familiar and strange. See his *Open Sky*, trans. Julie Rose (London: Verso, 1997) and *Speed and Politics*, trans. Mark Polizzotti (New York: Semiotexte, 1986).

18. See William H. Whyte, *City: Rediscovering the Center* (New York: Doubleday, 1988), 56-67.

19. On Beacon Street in Boston, where I formerly lived, a man walks his Siamese cat, Otter, twice a day or more down the sidewalk, meeting or greeting dozens of friends, acquaintances, and strangers on his way.

20. See, for example, Steven Garber, *The Urban Naturalist* (Mineola, N.Y.: Dover, 1987) and Jennifer Wolch and Joy Emel, eds., *Animal Geographies* (London: Verso, 1998).

21. Jennifer Wolch, "*Zoöpolis*" in *Animal Geographies*.

22. On romanticism in relation to walking, see Anne Wallace, *Walking, Literature, and English Culture: The Origins and Uses of the Peripatetic in Nineteenth Century* (Oxford: Clarendon Press, 1993) and Robin Jarvis, *Romantic Writing and Pedestrian Travel* (New York: St. Martin's, 1997).

23. This phrase appears in Langdon Winner, *The Whale and the Reactor* (Chicago: University of Chicago Press, 1986).

24. Marshall McLuhan, *Understanding Media: The Extensions of Man* (New York: McGraw-Hill, 1964), 52.

25. Hans Jonas, *Imperative of Responsibility: In Search of an Ethics for the Technological Age* (Chicago: University of Chicago Press, 1984), 57, 64.

26. Jean Baudrillard, *Simulacra and Simulation*, trans. Sheila Faria Glaser (Ann Arbor: University of Michigan Press, 1994), 112.

27. See also Gary Backhaus, "Auto-mobility and the Route-Scape: A Critical Phenomenology," in G. Backhaus and J. Murungi, eds., *Transformation of the Urban and Suburban Landscape* (Lanham: Md.: Lexington Books, 2001) as well as Julia Meaton and David Morrice, "The Ethics and Politics of Private Automobile Use," *Environmental Ethics* 18, no. 1 (spring 1996): 39-54. Also see Anon, "Aberration: The Automobile," *The Fifth Estate* 21, no. 2 (1987).

28. James Kunstler, *The Geography of Nowhere* (New York: Simon & Schuster, 1993).

29. See Clay McShane, *Down the Asphalt Path: The Automobile and the American City* (New York: Columbia University Press, 1994).

30. John Berger, *About Looking* (New York: Pantheon, 1980).

31. Theodor Adorno, *Minima Moralia*, trans. E. F. N. Jephcott (London: Verso, 1974).

32. Lewis Mumford, "A Walk Through Rotterdam" in *The Highway and the City* (New York: Harcourt Brace Jovanovich, 1953), 36.

33. It is a rather curious phenomenon—and a sign of the times—when many people recognize their friends and neighbors only by the cars they drive.

34. Clyde Haberman's editorial column, *New York Times*, December 10, 1996 and April 25, 1997.

35. See Roberta Brandes Gratz with Norman Mintz, *Cities Back from the Edge: New Life for Downtown* (New York: John Wiley and Sons, 1998).

36. Nationally, more than 40,000 people are killed each year in auto-related accidents, with about 20 to 25 percent of the victims being pedestrians according to figures provided by the Federal Highway Traffic Safety Commission. See Roberta Brandes Gratz, *Cities Back from the Edge*.

37. See "Danger Afoot," *New York Times*, 12 January 1998. In 1994, there were 159 pedestrian deaths in London; whereas in New York there were still 223 deaths.

38. Henry D. Thoreau, *Walden and Other Writings*, ed. Brooks Atkinson (New York: Modern Library, 1937), 47.

39. See Anon, "Aberration: The Automobile."

40. See, for example, Paul Goodman, "Banning Cars from Manhattan," in *Utopian Essays and Practical Proposals* (New York: Vintage, 1962).

41. Jane Jacobs, *Death and Life of Great American Cities* (New York: Vintage, 1961), 343.

42. Rayner Banham, *Los Angeles: The Architecture of Four Ecologies* (London: Penguin, 1973), 213.

43. Euripides, *Medea*, line 824, cited in Ernest Barker, trans., *The Politics of Aristotle* (London: Oxford University Press, 1946), xiii.

44. Homer, quoted in Richard Sennett, *Flesh and Stone: The Body and the City in Western Civilization* (New York: W.W. Norton, 1994).

45. Sennett, *Flesh and Stone*.

46. Jan Bremmer, "Walking, Standing, and Sitting in Ancient Greek Culture," in *A Cultural History of Gesture*, eds. Jan Bremmer and Herman Roodenburg (Ithaca, N.Y.: Cornell University Press, 1992), 15-35.

47. Some classicists now believe that the claim that ancient philosophers taught their students through walking may have been exaggerated.

48. Aristotle, *Nicomachean Ethics* Book 4, ch. 3, 34 and *De partibus animalium* in *The Works of Aristotle*, trans. and ed. J. A. Smith and W. D. Ross (Oxford: Clarendon Press, 1958), Book 4, ch. 10, 689b, 19-21.

49. John of Salisbury, excerpt from *Policraticus*, trans. J. Dickinson in *The Portable Medieval Reader*, ed. James Bruce Ross and Mary Martin Mclaughlin (New York: Viking, 1949), 129-30.

50. See the discussion of the lives and lyric poetry of some of these figures in Helen Waddell, *The Wandering Scholars* (New York: Doubleday, 1955).

51. Umberto Eco, *The Name of the Rose*, trans. William Weaver (New York: Harcourt Brace Jovanovich, 1983), 189.

52. Quoted in Bill McKibben, *The End of Nature* (New York: Random House, 1989), 60.

53. Edgar Allan Poe, "The Man of the Crowd" in *Great Short Works of Edgar Allan Poe*, ed. G. R. Thompson (New York: Harper and Row, 1970), 262-72.

54. Charles Baudelaire, *The Painter of Modern Life* (New York: Da Capo Press, 1964).

55. Ralph Waldo Emerson, "The Transcendentalist" in *The Portable Emerson*, ed., Carl Bode (New York: Penguin, 1946), 100.

56. "Beneath the cobblestones the beach" was a Situationist reprise during the heady days of protest in Paris in the late 1960s, suggesting that there is a world beyond the immediacy of the streets.

57. On women's issues and the notion of the gendered walk, see Deborah Nord, *Walking the Victorian Streets: Women, Representation and the City* (Ithaca, N.Y.: Cornell University Press, 1995).

58. On the subjects of race and class, see Elijah Anderson, *Streetwise: Race, Class and Change in an Urban Community* (Chicago: University of Chicago Press, 1990).

59. Fyodor Dostoevsky, *Notes from Underground*, trans. Mirra Ginsburg (New York: Bantam, 1981), 61-65. Interestingly, in the same work, Dostoevsky characterizes the dark essence of humanity in terms of our upright posture and ability to walk: "I even think that the best definition of man is: a biped ungrateful," (32).

60. Charlotte Bronte's *Jane Eyre*, for example, begins with the line: "There was no possibility of taking a walk that day."

61. Bruce Chatwin, *Anatomy of Restlessness* (New York: Penguin, 1996), 103.

62. On such issues, see Mike Davis, "Fortress Los Angeles: The Militarization of Urban Space" in Dennis R. Judd and Paul P. Kantor, *The Politics of Urban America* (Needham Heights, Mass.: Allyn and Bacon, 1998).

63. Although tending to perambulate in the woods and the wilderness rather than urban centers, Thoreau helped to show how walks might be subversive and even antinomian by challenging the notion that "good fences make good neighbors," to use a later line from Robert Frost.

64. Michel de Certeau, *The Practice of Everyday Life* (Berkeley: University of California Press, 1984).

65. de Certeau, *The Practice of Everyday Life*, 99.

66. de Certeau, *The Practice of Everyday Life*, 93.

67. One might even be inclined to ask in jaded fashion, who needs to walk or hike up mountains when we can climb or ride up skyscrapers to gain a similar view? The reference to the World Trade Center was written prior to the horrific events of September 11, 2001. I have chosen to leave it standing as the book goes to print as a small testament to the very sudden and irreversible transformations that can occur in our urban lanscapes. Having known friends who worked in the Center and having walked around the base of the buildings, and gazed in awe onto the city below from atop one of the towers, I am, like many others, unable to grasp fully the enormity of the loss in human life and the political and cultural changes that will follow in the wake of this event. I am certain, however, that pedestrians and pilgrims who walk past or journey to this landmark—a former engineering masterpiece turned postmodern 'disaster-piece'—will find their perceptions (and perhaps even their politics) dramatically altered. The catastrophic loss of the double "letters" (or haunting double digit number, 11) on the skyline has clearly created a new and no doubt disturbing visual dimension of the New York City horizon and placescape. As Ric Burns, a documentary film director on the history of New York City remarked recently, "It's our phantom limb. You feel it, but it's not there; you look to where you feel it should be."

68. Henry Miller, "The Fourteenth Ward" in *Black Spring* (New York: Grove Press, 1963), 8.

69. de Certeau, *The Practice of Everyday Life*, 103.

70. In Mexico City, common street names include Forest of Light, Tree of Fire, Forest of Secrets, and Sea of Dreams. Work Street is very long while Love and Happiness Streets are short. Good Luck crosses Hope then runs into a dead end. Comprehension Street ends in Silence.

71. de Certeau, *The Practice of Everyday Life*, 104.

72. de Certeau, *The Practice of Everyday Life*, 105.

73. Paul Auster, *The New York Trilogy* (New York: Penguin, 1990).

74. On the notion of "falling up," see Anne Wallace, *Walking, Literature, and English Culture*, 3.

75. Another way of incorporating critique into pedestrian movement about the city is radical walking tours such as those that have been conducted in the downtown areas of New York City, where participants gather to visit by foot and learn about the sites of historical labor protests, strikes, clashes with the police and government, or to commemorate events such as Stonewall.

76. Guy Debord, "Theory of the *Dérive*" in Ken Knabb, trans. and ed., *Situationist International Anthology* (Berkeley, Calif.: Bureau of Public Secrets, 1981), 50. See also Simon Sadler, *The Situationist City* (Cambridge, Mass.: MIT Press, 1998) and Guy Debord, "Two Accounts of Desire" in Elisabeth Sussman, ed. *On the Passage of a Few*

People through a Rather Brief Moment in Time:The Situationist International 1957-1972 (Cambridge, Mass.: MIT Press, 1989), 135-39.

77. Debord, "Theory of the *Dérive*," 53.

78. Guy Debord in Knabb, *Situationist International Anthology*, 25.

79. *Detournement* implies notions of detouring and subversion and is the process by which pre–existing elements (writing, cartoons, photographs, objects) are lifted out of their original contexts (which are usually heavily-coded or over-determined) and then resituated or re-territorialized via montage, erasure, insertion, or modification in unfamiliar contexts so as to reveal their hidden, latent, or "real" content. It is generally a conscious political (rather than aesthetic) re-contextualization and reassembling of ideological "texts" so as to criticize the process or culture that produces and consumes them. *Detournement*, unlike Derridean deconstruction, relies frequently, though not necessarily, on illegalist and illicit strategies that take as their starting point a kind of cultural piracy, creative plagiarism, and systematic misinterpretation in order to ferret out relations of power. In contrast to deconstructive techniques, *detournement* has few, if any, ties to the academic world; it can be practiced anonymously; and it can be exercised on a large scale by many people easily and cheaply. In Germany, for example, I have altered (rather than simply crossed out) graffiti that read "Ausländer Raus" (Foreigners Out) to say "Ausländer Rausch" (Foreigners Intoxicate/Celebrate), to cite one small example. See Kenn Knabb, ed., *Situationist International Anthology*, especially, 8-14.

80. Guy Debord, "Situationist Theses on Traffic," in Knabb, *Situationist International Anthology*, 58. Today, we might be inclined to be more skeptical toward a notion of "authentic" and "genuine" life than those writing in earlier eras.

81. Raoul Vaneigem, *The Revolution of Everyday Life* (London: Left Bank Books and Rebel Press, 1983).

82. Gilles Deleuze and Félix Guattari, *Anti-Oedipus: Capitalism and Schizophrenia*, trans. Robert Hurley et al. (Minneapolis: University of Minnesota Press, 1983), 2.

83. Henry Miller, *Black Spring*, 9-13.

84. Miller, *Black Spring*, 22-25.

85. Deleuze and Guattari, along with Michel Foucault, R. D. Laing, and other radical critics of psychiatry, seem to have over-romanticized some instances and notions of breaking with power among schizophrenics and the "mentally-ill."

86. Deleuze and Guattari make significant distinctions between nomads, itinerants, migrants, and transhumants. While these differences cannot be explored here, it is necessary to point out that the nomad is not simply a continuous walker or wanderer. In fact, the nomad is not defined by movement like the migrant who moves from point to point but rather is one "who does not move" except while seated.

87. Gilles Deleuze and Félix Guattari, *Nomadology: The War Machine*, trans. Brian Massumi (New York: Semiotexte, 1986), 59.

88. Jean-François Lyotard's idea of drifting thought which accepts no truth value and undermines legitimations of those discourses which do is also germane to a theoretical consideration of walking. See his *Driftworks* (New York: Semiotexte, 1984).

89. Virilio, *Speed and Politics*, 20.

90. Virilio, *Speed and Politics*, 16.

91. Gilles Deleuze and Félix Guattari, *Nomadology*, 60.

92. Kevin Lynch, *The Image of the City* (Cambridge, Mass.: MIT Press, 1960), 47.

93. Mike Greenberg, *The Poetics of Cities: Designing Neighborhoods that Work* (Columbus: Ohio State University Press, 1995), 14-15.

94. Jane Jacobs, *The Death and Life of Great American Cities*. See also Mitchell Duneier, *Sidewalk* (New York: Farrar, Straus and Giroux, 1999).

95. Mike Greenberg, *The Poetics of Cities.*

96. Greenberg, *The Poetics of Cities*, 81.

97. Robert Brandes Gratz, *Cities Back from the Edge.*

98. I consider the musical aspects of walking more fully in Macauley, "Walking the Elemental Earth," commenting upon the walkabout and the songlines of the Australian Aborigines and the reflections of neurologist Oliver Sacks in his *Leg to Stand On* (New York: Harper and Row, 1984) 22-23.

99. Greenberg, *The Poetics of Cities*, 92.

100. Kevin Lynch with Malcolm Rivkin, "A Walk Around the Block," *Landscape* 8, no. 3, 1959: 24-34; reprinted in Kevin Lynch, *City Sense and City Design*, ed. Tridib Banerjee and Michael Southworth (Cambridge, Mass.: MIT Press, 1995), 185-204. On each trip around the block, the interviewer informed the walkers that they were about to take a short walk and that were not to look for anything in particular but simply to talk about what they saw, heard, smelled, or more generally noticed.

101. Few walkers commented on the sky, colors, wall materials and textures, upper floor façades, overhead wires, or doorways.

102. In his considerations of ambling in the wilderness, Thoreau also treated walking as an art, rather than as mere exercise or goal-oriented traveling. See his essay, "Walking" in Thoreau, *Walden.*

103. A. R. Ammons, "A Poem is a Walk, " *Epoch* 18, no. 1 (fall 1968).

104. Wallace Stevens, quoted in Edward S. Casey, *Getting Back into Place* (Bloomington: Indiana University Press, 1993), 250.

105. Roger Gilbert, *Walks in the World*, 3.

106. James Joyce, *Ulysses*, ed. Hans Walter Gabler (New York: Vintage, 1986).

107. Franz Hessel, quoted in Anke Gleber, *The Art of Taking a Walk: Flanerie, Literature, and Film in Weimar Culture* (Princeton, N.J.: Princeton Paperbacks, 1999), 66. See also Keith Tester, *The Flaneur* (New York: Routledge, 1994).

108. Jean Jacques Rousseau, *Reveries of the Solitary Walker*, trans. Peter France (New York: Penguin, 1979), 12. See also Georges Van Den Abbeele, *Travel as Metaphor* (Minneapolis: University of Minnesota Press, 1992). Like Rousseau, Nietzsche developed a rather footloose style, finding in the process that pedestrian activity helped to generate very uncommon ideas and philosophical speculation. To Flaubert's remark, "One can think and write only when sitting down," he retorts, "Now I have you, nihilist! Assiduity is the *sin* against the holy spirit. Only ideas *won by walking* have any value," playing upon *das Sitzfleisch*, the posterior (or literally, "sitting-flesh"), with which "assiduity" (from *sedere*, to sit) is cognate. (*Twilight of the Idols*, trans. R. J. Hollingdale [New York: Penguin, 1968], 26.) Indeed, Nietzsche's self-proclaimed greatest idea, that of the "eternal recurrence of the same" and the whole of Zarathustra as man and work were acquired through walking in the area surrounding Sils-Maria, "6000 feet beyond man and time" as he says in *Ecce Homo*.

109. Rousseau, *Reveries*, 88.

110. Jean Jacques Rousseau, *Confessions*, quoted in Van Den Abbeele, *Travel as Metaphor*, 114.

111. Theodor Adorno, *Minima Moralia*, 102.

112. Lewis Mumford, *The Highway and the City*, 244.

113. See James Howard Kunstler, *The Geography of Nowhere* as well as Peter Calthorpe, "The Pedestrian Pocket" in *The City Reader*, ed. Richard T. LeGales and Frederic Stout (New York: Routledge, 1996), 351-56.

114. Mumford, *The Highway and the City*, 244.

115. I would like to thank Gary Backhaus for his sustained encouragement, Hugh Silverman for permitting me to present part of this paper at the International Association for Philosophy and Literature, and the faculty in the Department of Humanities and Social Sciences at Rose-Hulman Institute of Technology for listening to an early draft of the project. I would also like to thank Guilford Press and James O'Connor for allowing me to reprint a version of this article, which appeared originally in *Capitalism, Nature, Socialism* 11, no. 4 (December 2000): 3-43.

Chapter 10

Valid Research in Human Geography and the Image of the Ideal Science

Derek Shanahan

Introduction

Morrill has provided a brief history of the reaction to the scientific method in geography as part of a retrospective.[1] His paper describes a beleaguered group of geographers who remain staunchly "scientific" while most of the rest of the discipline of geography apparently resist a scientific approach. Morrill presents this "anti-science" viewpoint, evidenced by the continuous introduction of a variety of supposedly anti-scientific approaches, as a pervasive and widespread feature of geography. This alleged "anti-science"developed relatively quickly after the quantitative revolution.[2] For emphasis scientific geography is compared to the rise of Protestantism in Europe while alternative approaches are compared to the Catholic rejection of that Protestantism. More specifically, the humanist critique of scientific geography is seen as "very like the early, but ever recurring, movement against science, industry, cities, interdependence, technology, secularization and change."[3] Ultimately, Morrill accuses geography of returning to an exceptionalist position reminiscent of the early 1950s when, like history, geography was thought to have placed itself methodologically beyond the mainstream social sciences by apparently giving up any attempt at properly scientific research. Morrill sees contemporary geography as embracing relativistic meaning and as evidence he cites the emphasis that some geographers place on "local narratives."[4]

It is my argument that the proliferation of philosophical and methodological approaches in geography over the past three decades was not in many cases "anti-scientific," and certainly did not engage in "destructive denigration of others' motives."[5] Further, I argue, new approaches were, in an attempt to achieve some semblance of acceptance by the traditional scientists of the discipline, greatly concerned with questions of relativism and sought to avoid accusations of subjectivity at every opportunity. In fact, key researchers introducing alternative approaches to geographic research after the quantitative revolution were not only supportive of the scientific method in geography, but they also hoped to emulate that view of science in certain fundamental ways, not to reject it.

Recent debates concerning alternative methods in geography provide a clear introductory illustration of my argument. The first of these debates focused on the question of whether or not there is a unique method that could be called feminist.[6] In this debate Damaris Rose made a critically important contribution in recounting the experience of an actual faculty position interview. The applicant's avowed allegiance to feminism drew a concerned response from a member of the interviewing committee. This response placed feminism as one of many "isms" in the social sciences, and all such "isms" were explicitly (and unfavorably) compared to "scientific objectivity."[7] Feminism was seen as one of a series of approaches in geography that posed a threat to "scientific objectivity." Rose ultimately suggested that despite "epistemological sea changes" regarding subject-object distinctions and the emergence of many valid and useful approaches to social scientific research, "most practitioners and 'gatekeepers' in the social sciences . . . still regard work which blatantly blurs the distinctions between the objective and the subjective as being 'unscientific.'"[8]

Another pertinent debate in human geography concerned the research technique of the corporate interview.[9] Schoenberger's argument for its use inspired a critique of her presentation of the method.[10] In part McDowell's critique focused on Schoenberger's language. McDowell challenged particularly the way in which this language positioned the technique with regard to positivistic science. She interpreted Schoenberger's original presentation of the corporate interview as eliciting a subservient position toward conventional or "proper science." For McDowell, Schoenberger appeared to present the corporate interview almost as an apologetic; as a less rigorous attempt at science that ran the risk, perhaps, of being at best tolerated by "conventional" wisdom or, at worst, of not being accepted as a viable research technique at all. In fact McDowell, implying a sense of methodological angst in Schoenberger's words, stated at one point that it appeared that Schoenberger was "trying to convince herself of the 'scientific' nature of what she was doing."[11] Initially, a reading of Schoenberger's essay gave this author a similar reaction to that of McDowell. However, Schoenberger's subsequent reply to McDowell's critique served to recontextualise her original essay as an attempt "to speak to the positivists,"[12] and thus to gain a greater acceptance with that audience of alternative methods to research. This recontextualisation allayed fears that Schoenberger did think of her own research as having less scientific value than positivistic procedures. I understand Schoenberger did not intend to communicate a feeling of self-doubt about her research technique in the face of positivistic research. Yet, McDowell is to be commended in voicing her concern that Schoenberger *could* be read as betraying an anxiety about this alternative research method compared to positivistic science.

That traditional scientific geography has maintained a strong conceptual hold over much geographic research is attested to elsewhere. For example, as recently as the late 1980s, Mayer noted that although geographers attempt to use a variety of valid approaches to research "widespread loyalty to a positivist tradition may help explain the continuing gender blindness of our textbooks."[13] Similarly, Guelke attempted to win greater acceptance for his idealist historical geography as a rigorous approach, and to bolster the image of historical geography in the discipline as a whole. He suggested that "historians have shown that a discipline can flourish as an academic endeavor without necessarily embracing positivistic modes of reasoning."[14] Just a few years ago I was somewhat dismissively told by the editor of a geographic journal that reactions to the quantitative revolution were a result of "math anxiety." I preferred to cast these alternative research frameworks as exhibiting a real and necessary concern with blind adherence to a narrow view of what constitutes scientific research. However, at this point in the argument, my colleagues often assert that geographers have been through all of this *ad nauseam*, and to great effect. If this were the case then how do we account for measured arguments like those of Lake and Towers, which claim that a strong positivistic bias is found in much contemporary GIS research?[15] If we claim that this issue is dated, and that positivism in geography is unimportant, then do we just accept that geographers like Morrill are also merely dated? Is it enough to label Morrill an anachronism, or do we take his words more seriously? The many cogent arguments outlined above appear to defy any easy assessment of the "progress" of geographic thought as a general, inexorable, drift away from positivistic influence. To be sure there has been much change in geographic thought and methodology but it is, in my estimation, a dangerous oversimplification to subscribe to views of the so called "backlash" to the scientism of the 1950s and 1960s as a clear cut break with positivist doctrine.

Indeed, the debates introduced above appear in sharp contrast to Morrill's depiction of a pervasive anti-science viewpoint in the discipline. Not only do these examples illustrate a seemingly routine comparison with "scientific geography," but they also indicate the desire to be seen as scientific themselves. The researchers involved did not set out to present an anti-scientific viewpoint. Rather, they were attempting to find space for their preferred approaches in the face of a seemingly monolithic ideal of science. The implication here is that use of a variety of approaches to research in human geography still comes up against a widely held view that rigorous, "objective," research is the outcome of an adherence to some very narrow standards and procedures. Very often it is either "scientific objectivity," or "positivism," that is held up as the ideal for research in geography.

From an even more recent perspective Demeritt has reintroduced the science-anti-science debate in geography. He has argued that physical geographers in particular find it easy to dismiss discussions about scientific knowledge in human geography, particularly those concerning the crisis of representation. Such discussions have emphasized theory over the social practices of scientists.[16] In an article largely sympathetic to the possibility of alternative views of science in geography, Demeritt suggests that a focus on the crisis of representation is largely to blame for post modern approaches being labeled anti-scientific. Simply put these discussions are arcane to many geographers. I would agree with this assessment in many respects but theoretical issues do need to be debated and, more importantly for this chapter, not all theoretical discussions in human geography associated with representation would easily accept the label "postmodern," and some of these discussions are not really all that arcane. An exhaustive account of the range of views of how to do geography (physical or human) is becoming less and less of an option as the geographic literature burgeons with what Trevor Barnes called external critiques (the attempt to replace one "foolproof" method with another). So, this chapter will be more circumspect.[17] Demeritt and Morrill, both in different ways, point to the need for clarification concerning the practice of geography over the past few decades. While Demeritt suggests a constructive way forward, Morrill chooses to castigate the entire spirit of what has been developing. Thus the argument that is to be presented here will concern itself with two separate but related periods in the development of geography. Morrill's homily really forces us to reassess at least some of the debates in the mid-1970s. Phenomenological influences in geography will thus be addressed in order to recast Morrill's assertions of a supposed rapidly developing "attack" on scientific geography in the 1970s. And while this might seem to locate this discussion awkwardly in relation to the geographic literature of the 1990s, I do not believe that a balanced view of the importance of the crisis of representation can be had without such a partial reassessment. Demeritt focuses our attention on that crisis and thus points us, arguably, to developments in anthropological thought in the mid-1980s. Finally some examples of current phenomenological research will be presented to highlight the rigorous nature of this method, and to counter Morrill's assertion that such research is subjective and anti-scientific. The goal of this chapter is not to arbitrate between different versions of phenomenology. Rather it is to respond to Morrill's accusations concerning the scientific nature of phenomenology, the spirit of the phenomenological project (was it really anti-scientific?), and to extend Demeritt's articulation of the science-anti-science debate in geography.

Phenomenology and the Reaction "Against" Science

One of the most important reactions to the quantification and positivism of the 1950s and 1960s was the incorporation of phenomenology into geography in the 1970s. Edmund Husserl's phenomenological project is the original source of phenomenological thought in geography. But, Schutz' constitutive phenomenology and Heidegger's reformulation of Husserl's original project have taken center stage.[18] Confusion over what the phenomenological project was and its relationship to "science" occurred quickly in the geographical literature, and this retarded the acceptance and development of phenomenological insights in geography.[19]

Husserl's call for a return to the "things themselves" correctly places his philosophy as an attempt to discover the ultimate foundation for all knowledge.[20] This aim was the original goal of phenomenology, but it was a goal that was sought to benefit all intellectual inquiry, including the physical sciences. Husserl included all physical sciences in his notion of "objective-science," and was not opposed to objectivist science. Much of his work can be seen to be greatly supportive of such science. Indeed, empirical science "springs . . . from the most praiseworthy motives," with its aim to "establish the right of the self governing Reason to be the only authority in matters that concern truth."[21] Phenomenology did encompass a critique of the physical sciences. It rejected the dogmatic nature of scientific thought and its methodological exclusivity.[22] In order to make this critical point of his project clear. Husserl distinguished between the natural attitude of the sciences and the philosophical attitude, which informs all intellectual inquiry.[23] The natural attitude reduced human lives to "mere" facts and to an observable empirical "reality." The natural attitude was the proper domain of the "sciences of facts."[24] Mere facts, though, could not provide the ultimate foundation for knowledge or human experience according to Husserl. And yet the sciences essentially claimed that empirical reality, described, ordered, and "explained" by the method of science, was the highest authority for true knowledge. Husserl's call to uncover the foundation to all knowledge was also, then, a statement about the scientific method. This method derived its authority and justification from the natural attitude, and began with unstated and implicitly accepted presuppositions; a priori grounds from which to advance to new knowledge. "Empiricists appear to have overlooked the fact that the scientific demands which in their own theses they exact from all knowledge are equally addressed to these theses themselves."[25]

Husserl attempted to understand how the sciences progressed to new knowledge, and how to finally ground the claims made by those sciences, and it is here that the majority of geographers attempting to incorporate Husserlian phenomenology into the discipline misconstrued his project. In short the critique of the sciences initiated by Husserl was perceived by many geographers to be a call for an *alternative* to those sciences.[26] For example: "To counter this dominance of science Husserl wrote of phenomenology as an alternative, as a new basis for knowledge."[27]

Certainly Husserl's phenomenology imposed a radical rethinking of the foundational claims of science but it did not call for an alternative to science in the sense of its *rejection*. The philosophical attitude, the proper domain of phenomenology, took as its goal an "understanding [of] its position in regard to all empirical sciences."[28] All sciences thus had their respective intellectual domains and their respective justifications. Science was not rejected but the unexamined, a priori grounds upon which science was based were to be subject to interrogation so that we could properly understand how science helps us to understand the world. Husserl accorded the sciences their due merit, and thus his project was to subject "the scientific character of all sciences to a serious and quite necessary critique without sacrificing their primary sense of scientific discipline, so unimpeachable within the legitimacy of their methodic accomplishments."[29] Pickles clarifies this phenomenological aim. He showed that Husserl perceived the sciences as frameworks of assumptions and of propositions through which the world was abstracted so as to become intelligible.[30] All sciences, for Husserl, were positing sciences.[31] For example Pickles shows how a phenomenologist would understand the idea of a circle. "What do we mean when we say that we see a circle? . . . On the blackboard we see a diagram of a circle, but we know this to be a mere device for aiding our discussion. . . . The sketch of the circle is not what we mean when we refer to a circle."[32]

A circle has a meaning that is objective within a particular framework of propositions, that of Euclidean geometry. Similar frameworks are posited for all phenomena. Indeed Husserl made much of clarifying the scientists' aim of "grounding" their findings *within* the everyday world of scientific practice and taken for granted experience.[33] For the phenomenologist, however, inquiry must take the "path [that] leads back, here, to the primal self-evidence in which the life-world is ever pregiven."[34]

Attempting to grasp the true nature of science then, the phenomenologist must become reflective of the ways in which science creates fields of meaning. To reflect on this, for Husserl, was no easy matter and would be "comparable in the beginning to a religious conversion."[35] The phenomenological method, broader in definition than the narrowly defined notion of scientific method as a series of techniques[36] involved a series of "reductions" or philosophically rigorous reflections that would progressively bring phenomena into view unshackled from any positing framework ("the things themselves"). The objects of our inquiry are seen as constituted within the presuppositions of our taken for granted experience, and these philosophical reflections would allow us to become aware of our presuppositions and would thus provide the possibility for us to then "bracket," or "suspend belief in," those presuppositions. Thus Husserl states that while "[t]he empiricist talk" of scientists "gives the impression that the natural sciences are based on the experience of objective nature," the models of natural science are only "conceptual intermediaries" (Husserl 1970, 129) that aid our understanding of the pre-given lifeworld.[37] In other words two different, but interrelated, worlds exist for the phenomenologist; life-world and objective-scientific world.[38]

From the phenomenological viewpoint then, all science is seen as objectifying that which it studies *out of necessity*. Objectification comes about only when the researcher takes a "distance" from the world of taken for granted lived experience. This "distanciation" allows "things" to be abstracted into objects of study[39] meaning that phenomena are *created* by the sciences. For Husserl science was thus rigorous and exact, as far as it went. Of course, Husserl's phenomenology must also be subject to a phenomenological analysis of its own, and so Husserl drew a distinction between descriptive phenomenology, in which we rigorously describe the presuppositions and the objects of analysis of the sciences for example, and transcendental phenomenology. The latter's aim was to allow us to recognize universal presuppositions of the taken for granted world. It was to provide access to the ultimate foundation of knowledge and experience. Transcendental phenomenology was, however, widely criticized for embodying a complete and untenable foundationalism. Husserl aspired to "discover the real, permanent foundation of philosophy and knowledge—a foundation that will withstand historical vicissitudes, escape from 'anthropological relativism,' and satisfy the craving for ultimate constraints."[40] Further:

It is not enough to open one's eyes and live in order to find this world of original experience since what is given in the "natural attitude" is always impregnated by logical and other cognitive operations. Nor can it be revealed through a genetic psychological inquiry for that would lead only to mental processes or lived experiences as "experiences of the world, of a world in which, for this subject is already given as complete, and this means that the world is there as that on which contemporary science has already done its work of exact determination."[41]

Hindess is, of course, being critical of Husserl's belief in the possibility of achieving presuppositionless thought. Hindess' view is that this "reduction" is not possible for a human. One cannot reach an ultimate thought and analyze it, for to analyze such a thought one must introduce another thought. This critical problem is acknowledged even in considering the possibility of describing the transcendental reduction. Thus the "description of the transcendental reduction brings its performance to a halt, holds it fast, and causes it to congeal into an object."[42] Because this paradox threatens to end the possibility of phenomenology, one useful insight becomes apparent. Transcendental reduction compels us to attempt to become aware of our presuppositions (literally, our belief in the taken for granted world) and suspend our belief in them.

He who is aware of the belief in the world has already broken away from this belief, and the universal reduction serves the purpose of making him aware of this break in the first place. It is thus not a mere abstention from this belief; it is first and foremost a *discovery of this belief as a belief.* [I]t leads to a peculiar mode of consciousness, which explicitly inquires into the belief in being that functions implicitly in all natural engagement with the world, and thus allows this belief to be "*put into question*" in the positive sense. In this way, the universal reduction makes the belief in the world phenomenologically accessible in the first place; it brings this belief reflectively into view.[43]

Husserl was himself aware of the many difficulties of his transcendental turn and this is why he was clear about the distinction between descriptive phenomenology and transcendental phenomenology. Subsequent interpretations of Husserl's ideas also produced a constitutive phenomenology that revolved around an analysis of human intentionality.[44] However rigorous reflection and description are fundamental elements of all three phenomenological projects. Above all else then, phenomenology was a rigorous method that allowed the researcher to begin analysis of the taken for granted world, of the assumptions and horizons of meaning within which the world is made intelligible to us. Thus, "the world and the natural experience of it are experienced as 'phenomenon,'" and are not experienced naively.[45] In the context of geography the problem with transcendental phenomenology was recognized. Johnson for example, suggests that even though Husserl's phenomenology "goes further to the levels of 'transcendental reflection,' the geographer need not. Many of the problems of the method can thereby be avoided."[46] Overall though, Husserl's distinction was all but lost in the majority of geographic treatments of phenomenology and only the transcendental turn of Husserl, with all its attendant problems, was assessed. Pickles, through a detailed analysis of Husserl's project, and its modification by Heidegger, convincingly shows the importance of Husserl's distinction between descriptive and transcendental phenomenology, and the need to reject the latter in favor of the former. "We, like Heidegger, may choose to reject this move to transcendental phenomenology as leading to emphasis on a transcendental subject who, in the final analysis, is wordless. But also like Heidegger we cannot reject Husserl's descriptive phenomenology underpinning every empirical science of relations."[47]

Within descriptive phenomenology Husserl's notion of "phenomena" indicates that all objects have a meaning for individual human subjects. The positing sciences, and our taken for granted world, implicate human intentionality in the understanding of phenomena. All phenomena are the product of intersubjective meaning for Husserl, and while Husserl thus attempted a transcendental phenomenology to see through this intentionality in order to get to the things themselves, Pickles argues instead that the constitution of this meaning should become the focus of our studies. All descriptive phenomenology, for Pickles, is hermeneutic at base.

Within geography phenomenology took on a particular character that misrepresented Husserl's project and did so because phenomenology was cast in the mirror of positivist science; geography's ideal science. This ideal of science in geography maintains its importance, in part at least, because of what Bernstein characterized as the Cartesian anxiety. The social sciences are fundamentally oriented around a view of science that places prime importance on a Cartesian objectivity.[48] Alternative research strategies are, consequently, routinely compared to this definition of objectivity. The explicit connotation is that if the parameters of Cartesian objectivity are not met, then the research strategy must necessarily be "subjective" and will lead only to relativism. Bernstein notes that acceptance of this basic Cartesian premise is so pervasive in the social sciences that even attempts to employ different research methods, informed by different standards of validation, often actually accept basic Cartesian dictates. Subsequently these alternative research methodologies appear inferior, or inherently "subjective," because acceptance of the Cartesian basis to objectivity fundamentally *marginalizes* alternative yardsticks with which to assess their validity, and compromises the knowledge claims they make. Morrill himself asserts that traditional science is the mark of "superior" research.[49] All else is, apparently, subjective and indicative of anti-science. For Bernstein, an either/or dilemma has been created. "With a chilling clarity Descartes leads us with an apparent and ineluctable necessity to a grand and seductive Either/Or. *Either* there is some support for our being, a fixed foundation for our knowledge, or we cannot escape the forces of darkness that envelop us with madness, with intellectual and moral chaos."[50]

Widespread acceptance of Schaefer's missive, ensured that science in geography was quickly equated solely with positivist *philosophy.* The all encompassing necessity of quantitative methods so that "objectivity" could supposedly be achieved.[51] A new standard (positivist objectivity through quantitative procedures) had been imposed forcefully upon geographic research in the 1950s and 1960s. It was symbolized by the polar opposition (and polar definitions) of subjective versus objective.[52] Consequently many geographers succumbed to this prejudice. At its heart this standard of objectivity embodied the Cartesian anxiety that without an ahistorical, and acultural, neutral framework (geography borrowed a positivistic framework in which to attempt to quell the Cartesian anxiety) in which to assess competing knowledge claims only relativism presented itself.

Since the elaboration of this view of the possibilities open to geographic research, science-non-science debates have become entrenched. The either/or dilemma has produced a widespread acceptance of the subjective-objective polarization in geography and, of critical importance to phenomenology, this has often been distilled into an ever-recurring argument over description and explanation.[53] Description is seen as lacking, while explanation is the product of "true" science. Any attempts to suggest alternative approaches to study, as we saw at the beginning of this chapter, have often been met with immediate accusations from traditional scientific advocates of thrusting geography away from "real" science. For example, Moriarty accused Pickles of pursuing a "touchy feely" phenomenological approach to geography.[54] Golledge asserted that a variety of approaches to geography indicated a return to the "nonscientific dark ages of thirty years ago."[55] The description/explanation debate has also recurred, most recently between Meinig and Jordan.[56] Here Meinig sees description as part of geography's tradition while Jordan sees explanation as the inevitable outcome of a properly scientific discipline. Description is "mere description." All of these debates are strikingly similar in the propagation of one narrow view of true science on the one hand, and, on the other hand, the concerted attempt to invent new approaches while rejecting accusations of subjectivity, relativism, and anti-science.

Phenomenology in geography, especially because of its emphasis on description, was compared to positivist conceptions of science, and was quickly seen as "subjective." For example, Entrikin's assessment of phenomenology as the method of humanistic geography compared that humanism with "traditional scientific geography" defined as "an approach based upon empirical observation, public verifiability of conclusions, and the importance of isolating fact from value."[57] Further, Entrikin viewed Husserl's phenomenology as calling for the phenomenologist's "isolation from the worlds of science and naturalistic common sense."[58] Phenomenology is seen here as a pure alternative to scientific geography that seeks to isolate itself from scientific goals of objectivity and verifiability. And yet as we have seen, Husserl was at pains to be seen as objective and his phenomenology was intended to provide a method by which presuppositions contained within the strictures of traditional science, whether positivist or not, could be recognized and understood by all. Only with transcendental phenomenology might Entrikin's characterization of phenomenology hold water, and Husserl was aware of the problems of objectivity and verifiability with the transcendental reduction.

Perhaps in deference to these flaws in Husserl's transcendental methodology, Tuan and Buttimer both reduced its role in geographical research, seeing it only as a critique and not as a practical method. Entrikin agreed.[59] "Failure" of phenomenology in geography, however, was due not solely to inherent difficulties that are contained within its transcendental strictures but also to the arguments used to present descriptive phenomenology as a viable approach. Critical here was the fact that arguments presenting phenomenology were *subservient* to the existing order of positivistic research. These arguments while purportedly anti-positivistic, implicitly accepted the very assumptions they sought to distance themselves from and they even elevated traditional scientific geography.

Unable to break from the positivistic definitions of "objective" and "subjective," and to reject the objective/subjective dilemma, Buttimer did see the need to transcend the dualism between subjective and objective modes of understanding experience. But not because such a mode of thinking is false, as Husserl showed.[60] Rather, Buttimer argues that subjective and objective experience cannot be separated. In an argument supposedly anti-positivistic and highly critical of reliance on a science based on a "Cartesian grid," Buttimer ultimately denigrates phenomenology to the role of a "pre-amble to scientific procedure."[61] Tuan goes further in assessing the role of humanistic geography more generally (based on his earlier foray into phenomenology) within the discipline as a whole, apparently giving up all hope of ever escaping the shackles of positivistic research. "One of the humanist geographer's roles is that of intellectual middleman: he takes these nuggets of experience as captured in art and decomposes them into simpler themes that can be systematically ordered. Once experience is simplified and given an explicit structure, its components may yield to scientific explanation."[62]

In calling humanist geographers "middlemen," Tuan echoes and magnifies Buttimer's sentiments on phenomenology as a "pre-amble to science" in geography. Positivistic objectivism and its associated "explanations" are the mark, and standard, of superior geography. Alternative methodologies must be compared to such positivistic standards and, more to the point, must abide by positivistic, objectivist, definitions of subjectivity and relativism. For Tuan explicitly, and Buttimer implicitly, the apparent failure of phenomenology to meet Cartesian standards of objectivity renders it relativistic.

Subsequent reformulations of phenomenology also attempted to live up to scientistic standards. Billinge discussed the use of phenomenology in geography and paid particular attention to the reformulations of Husserl's work. Billinge noted that phenomenology in geography retained very little of Husserl's original work, concluding that in geography phenomenology offered us nothing. However, the argument that Billinge moved beyond phenomenology to assess the broader issue of subjectivity was that historical geographers were "no longer apologetic in pursuing a blatantly subjective approach."[63] He attempted to show that subjectivity was not wrong but he did not transcend the either/or dilemma. Rather he took sides. In calling phenomenology "negativism," Billinge attempted to ridicule phenomenology and so distance historical geography from such a methodologically unsure approach. Historical geography was seen as subjective in a positivistic sense but not in need of any particular method or philosophy to justify its research or its product. Such a view of historical geography as non-positivistic and proud is commendable in many ways, but in accepting positivistic notions of objectivity, historical geography is put in an inferior position to "serious" research. Quite simply it is "subjective." In such a scenario how could Billinge's historical geography ever gain the credibility and acceptance he craved for it? And, of course, Husserl's phenomenology rejected all forms of naively given knowledge. Uncritical "subjectivity" of the type that Billinge celebrated would find no support in either descriptive or transcendental phenomenology.

In cultural geography phenomenology was interpreted by Peter Jackson.[64] The phenomenological method apparently allowed Jackson to achieve a complete empathy with his subjects in his research on Puerto Rican identity. In explicating how "ordered segmentation" might work, Jackson tells us that the views of East Harlem in the local media upset Puerto Rican residents. "This disparaging view of a dirty East Harlem upset more established residents—myself included—not, I conjecture, because of any particular desire to romanticize the undeniably 'slum' character of much of the area's physical dilapidation, but because it was *our* neighborhood, and the negative image reflected adversely on us."[65]

This sort of ethnographic authority, which is part of Jackson's broader ploy of asserting authority in his text, implies more than Jackson thinking with the thoughts of the "natives." He talks as if he is a Puerto Rican. Such authorial moves are necessary when dealing with positivistically defined "subjective" values in a discipline with positivistically motivated objectivist tendencies. How else is Jackson to assure us that his knowledge claims are valid? While Jackson has obviously, and completely, moved away from positivist notions of foundational research, and now embraces a social constructionist view of research, in this phenomenological study he accepts positivistic definitions of "subjective" and "objective." His authority in the text must therefore speak to an objectivist myth—the completely "nativized" ethnographer—to gain a true, foundational and "objective" view of Puerto Rican identity. Without this claim to omniscience in the field his knowledge claims will appear "subjective." Phenomenology is cast as a positivistic method designed to study the subjective world of the Puerto Rican community.

Jackson also reacted to Billinge's "disparaging" attack on phenomenology.

But did not fare much better in attempting to escape positivistic notions of valid research while constructing a viable phenomenological approach.[66] The Cartesian anxiety inherent in Jackson's phenomenological approach, and shown in his textual appeals to ethnographic omniscience, also manifested itself in the question of validity of results. Ultimately Jackson stated that: "Phenomenology does, however, have useful lessons for the social geographer and the impossibility of its wholesale adoption does not mean that one need fall back by default on an unacceptable positivism. Phenomenology and positivism are, after all, not mutually exclusive alternatives; the former can indeed build critically on the latter."[67]

Jackson reiterates Tuan's position of middleman status for non-positivistic approaches and the inability to escape positivistic doctrines of objectivity, even while proposing a "non-positivistic" phenomenology is clear.[68] Phenomenology and positivism must be synthesized if knowledge claims are to be valid.

Both Billinge and Jackson had miscast phenomenology as pointing toward a more subjectivist approach to research. Both therefore became critical of its potential. The potential of phenomenology in providing validation of alternative research strategies through Husserl's intended characterization of all sciences as positing sciences, and therefore partial in their knowledge claims, was unrecognized. Jackson and Billinge, in different ways, thus fell back on positivism; Billinge in an outright acceptance of positivistically defined subjectivism, and Jackson using positivist conceptions of knowledge validation to buttress phenomenology.

Insofar as Husserl's phenomenology had any effect on the subject matter of geographic research, it was used as a justification for an emphasis on the "life-world" of individual human subjects. This was an important reorientation for geography as it stressed a greater concern for human values. Ultimately, it helped to develop one of the first steps in geography toward a view of human life as a social construction.[69] Importantly though, it is not certain that Husserl would have emphasized the social construction of the life world over the constitution of that life world. In short social constructivist studies of the life world must also be subject to a rigorous phenomenological investigation to identify the conditions under which such construction becomes intelligible to us. While the motivation for social constructivist research that Husserl has inspired in geography is laudable, Husserl's phenomenology demands a foundational basis too. This critical distinction appears to have been unseen as Husserl's phenomenology was misrepresented in geography. It was cast as a subjectivist project that provided little in the way of *method* for research, and would reduce geography to a radical relativism. Certainly human meaning and the human subject were key elements of the lifeworld that constituted the object of study for Husserl's phenomenology. But relativism was never an option. Thus Husserl rejected the characterization of the lifeworld as subjective *in a positivistic sense* by the objective-logical sciences. "The disdain with which everything "merely subjective and relative" is treated by those scientists who pursue the modern ideal of objectivity changes nothing of its own manner of being, just as it does not change the fact that the scientist himself must be satisfied with this realm whenever he has recourse, as he unavoidably must have recourse to it."[70] That Husserl recognized both the value of traditional science and the existence of many ways of understanding the world was, by and large, lost in geographical research.

To summarize, by the late 1970s phenomenology had been castigated as a subjective approach that yielded only relativist statements about the world. It was accused of having no real method. Notwithstanding researchers like Relph, Seamon, and Pickles, phenomenology all but died out in geographical research. However, a plethora of other approaches to geographical inquiry continued to challenge positivist hegemony. By the mid-1980s a "crisis of representation" was said to exist throughout the social sciences. This crisis developed out of a criticism of the textual and methodological exclusivity of traditional scientific practice that often failed to address questions of power and imperialism in social science. The scientific claim to complete authority concerning foundational truth also motivated researchers to create new approaches to the study of the human condition. (In this way philosophies like phenomenology can be seen to be closely associated with the concerns of the crisis of representation.) Thus the drive to develop alternatives to strictly traditional scientific procedures and modes of representation gathered pace. Anthropologists in particular concerned themselves with this crisis of representation because it was central to their goal of representing other people's life-worlds. The debate in anthropology would have important consequences for geography and so it is to this debate we now turn.

The Crisis of Representation

Just as geography had its positivist tradition so too did anthropology. "Scientific" cultural anthropology spawned ethnographers who believed that the goal of their discipline was to replicate the thoughts of people of other cultures. These ethnographers, in order to achieve an "objective" frame of mind, invoked a complete empathy that supposedly enabled them to think as if they actually were those "natives" under study. Difficulty emerged because fieldwork was presented as an "objective" recording and decoding of "native" life. The ethnographer emulated the scientist in the laboratory and faithfully recorded life as it unfolded before him.

The posthumous publication of Malinowski's personal diary cast serious doubt on the possibility of such ethnographic omniscience.[71] Malinowski epitomized the view of the anthropologist as an objective "walking miracle of empathy" but his diary rendered "established accounts of how anthropologists work fairly well implausible."[72] The traditional view of the anthropologist as omniscient fieldworker was replaced by an image of a fieldworker beset by informants who demanded payment for information and, amongst other things, may or may not have been lying (it was, apparently, difficult for Malinowski to be sure of this). Fieldwork and ethnography had much intellectual value of course, but the ethnographer did not, in the field, become a "scientifically objective" receptor of cultural information in the way that positivist science claimed. The ethnographer was far more involved with the creation of the ethnography than this model of fieldwork suggested. For Geertz then, the diary presented a question: if it is not possible to think like a "native," how is knowledge of the way "natives" think possible?[73]

Geertz suggests that we recognize an overt role for the ethnographer in creating the ethnography, instead of falling back on a false notion of "objectivity" which sees a detached researcher simply discovering and recording cultural facts. The ethnographer attempts to generate a plausible ethnography from the use of "experience-near" and "experience-distant" concepts.

> An experience-near concept is, roughly, one that someone—a patient, a subject, in our case an informant—might himself [sic] naturally and effortlessly use to define what he or his fellows see, feel, think, imagine and so on, and which he would readily understand when similarly applied by others. An experience-distant concept is one that specialists of one sort or another—an analyst, experimenter, an ethnographer, even a priest or an ideologist—employ to forward their scientific, philosophical, or practical aims.[74]

In other words the researcher accepts an active role in generating "local knowledge."[75] This knowledge is created using concepts and ideas. "An interpretation of the way a people lives is neither imprisoned within their mental horizons, an ethnography of witchcraft as written by a witch, nor systematically deaf to the distinctive tonalities of their existence, an ethnography of witchcraft as written by a geometer."[76] Interestingly here, Pickles sees Geertz' use of these concepts in a phenomenological way. The concepts, experience near and experience far, are thus Geertz' procedures by which he "posits" a framework within which other ways of life become intelligible to "us."[77] Essentially, for Geertz, ethnography is based more on an analogical way of thinking than on a perceived notion of a foundation of knowledge that is progressively uncovered. Theory, any kind of theory, says Geertz, is a "'seeing-as' comprehension of the less intelligible by the more (the heart is a pump, earth is a magnet)."[78]

Geertz is an interpretivist anthropologist and sees ethnographies as *products* of ethnographers, as creative acts of knowledge production. Knowledge claims are contextual and their plausibility must be ascertained through discussion and argument, and not necessarily by an appeal to some universal procedure whose superiority is sanctioned through a posited state of "scientific objectivity." With the demise of the omniscient fieldworker the alternative is not, then, necessarily merely subjective, and ultimately, relativistic, *unless* we accept the either/or dilemma presented to us by the Cartesian framework to research. Rather, Geertz would argue that Malinowski's diary shows us that far from the omniscient beings fieldworkers once thought themselves to be, "we are all natives now."[79] This interpretivist position, through its critique of traditional "objectivity," denies the validity of the foundational claim and yet attempts to take us away from notions of unavoidable relativism. That is, interpretivism rejects the either/or dilemma in favor of a hermeneutical conception of knowledge creation.

However, advocates of positivistic science see Geertz and interpretivism more generally, as validating moral and epistemological relativism. Spiro argues that anthropological relativism invokes "culture" as producing all human social and psychological characteristics. Because cultures vary then so must human social and psychological characteristics.[80] Thus, for Spiro, the interpretivist school of cultural anthropology, and Geertz in particular, seem to deny the psychic unity of humankind, and a foundational moral code by which we can judge our own, and others', cultural behavior. Spiro also believes that cultural relativism has been confused with cultural variability and diversity and in this confusion leads only to a "particularistic cultural determinism." And further:

> Because all standards are culturally constituted, there are no available *trans*cultural standards by which different cultures might be judged on a scale of merit or worth. Moreover, given the fact of cultural variability, there are no universally acceptable *pan*cultural standards by which they might be judged on such a scale. In short, since all judgments regarding the relative merit or worth of different cultures are ethnocentric, the only valid normative judgment that can be made about them is that all are of equal worth.[81]

In short superficial cultural forms are simply the external manifestation of deeper, universal, human psychological causes for Spiro, and the anthropologist must attempt to elucidate these universal features of humanity. Interpretivist anthropology appears to deny this possibility for Spiro, making meaningful cultural judgments unattainable. "Thus, for example, although the Kwakiutl exhibit a constellation of characteristics which, according to Western standards, are paranoid, the latter judgment is invalidly applied to the Kwakiutl constellation because, according to Kwakiutl standards, it is judged to be normal."[82]

Geertz calls his detractors, 'anti-relativists,' and contends that they pursue an objectivist stance that forwards a particular research method as specially placed to yield data that may be classified as foundational. This method is offered forcefully with the implicit notion "that reality has an idiom in which it prefers to be described."[83] This, of course, is the Cartesian anxiety writ large. In the anthropological context, of concern to Geertz is the return to pancultural foundations to knowledge that this position entails. Thus, in terms of "particularistic cultural determinism" Geertz favors a view of culture that focuses less on possible "deep causes" of behavior and yet does not fall into a controversial "ontological anti-realism."[84]

> The issue is not whether human beings are biological organisms with intrinsic characteristics. Men can't fly and pigeons can't talk. Nor is it whether they show commonalities in mental functioning wherever we find them. Papuans envy, Aborigines dream. The issue is, what are we to make of these undisputed facts as we go about explicating rituals, analyzing ecosystems, interpreting fossil sequences, or comparing languages."[85]

For Geertz, the anti-relativists, in true positivist fashion, have the "desire to

represent one's interpretations not as constructions brought to their objects—
societies, cultures, languages—in an effort, somehow, somewhat to comprehend
them, but as quiddities of such objects forced upon our thought."[86] For anti-
relativists, acts such as head hunting can only be properly rejected if seen as
counter to some ultimate, foundational notion of what is correct human behavior: head hunting is against "human nature" and is *therefore* wrong. Geertz
would replace this objectivist reliance on a [supposedly] foundational checklist
of "aberrant" human behaviors. Reliance on discussion and argument in which
the responsibility to judge such behavior, far from being rendered impossible
through a rejection of a foundational basis to knowledge, is brought squarely to
the door of individuals and groups. There is a responsibility to judge involved
here. To believe in foundational, pancultural, and supposedly neutral concepts,
that will make these decisions for us is to reject that responsibility. Moral relativism is avoided by Geertz in this way. Geertz makes it very clear that even
without an appeal to ultimate foundations to knowledge and "scientific objectivity" he is quite obviously not advocating epistemological relativism. Thus:

> Looking into dragons, not domesticating or abominating them, nor drowning them
> in vats of theory, is what anthropology has been all about. At least, that is what it has
> been all about, as I, no nihilist, no subjectivist, and possessed, as you can see, of
> some strong views as to what is real and what is not, what is commendable and what
> is not, what is reasonable and what is not, understand it.[87]

The problem with anti-relativism, for Geertz, is not the rejection of relativism
per se but how it is to be avoided. Anti-relativism, presented as achievable only
through adherence to traditional "scientific objectivity," is objectionable not
because "it rejects an it's-all-how-you-look-at-it-approach to knowledge or a
when-in-Rome approach to morality, but that it imagines that they can only be
defeated by placing morality beyond culture and knowledge beyond both."[88]

This debate in anthropology then, like the debate over different research
methods in geography, rested upon the idea that one special procedure exists by
which foundational knowledge can be uncovered. Any departure from this ideal
is anti-science and leads only to subjectivism and relativism. Interpretive anthropology, based as it is on hermeneutics, sees ethnography, both process and
product, as human activity and human creation respectively. Our understanding
of other cultures emerges from the dialogical process that necessarily occurs
between the anthropologist and the people she studies. And yet, as the crisis of
representation makes clear, ethnographic authority is created through the textual
practices (literally, the way the final ethnography is written) employed by the
ethnographer, so she often disappears in "the quasi-invisibility of participant-
observation." But we should never forget that the ethnographer's interpretation
is created in dialogue, in a "talking face-to-face . . . rather than reading culture
'over their shoulders.'"[89]

In an effort to eradicate "colonial styles of representation," experimentation
with textual practices is common throughout the social sciences now. Demeritt

suggests that some textual experiments in reflexivity "make a general mockery of any pretence to objective" knowledge and ultimately lead to political quietism. The question regarding why one representation is preferred over another may have been left unasked or unanswered[90] in some refexivity studies. But, the question of the politics of representation has been addressed in both cultural geography and cultural anthropology.[91] Textual authority expressed in traditional modes of writing commonly deployed tropes and a 'get to the point' analysis of complex social and cultural issues. These have long been seen as the preserve of traditional scientific practice, often in the service of colonial ideology (as Demeritt himself notes). But this analysis of the role of politics and ideology in scientific representation has not led cultural geographers, nor their counterparts in anthropology, down a slippery slope to relativism. It has provided an effective critique of the way science has dominated in the name of objectivity, and truth. It has underlined the exclusivity of scientific practice and representation, and has made a convincing argument for the need to be critical with our commonly accepted methods for research, a key element of the spirit and practice of phenomenology. Returning to Demeritt's concerns about philosophy in geography, his rendition of the science-anti-science argument too closely associates methods concerned with representation, with approaches to research broadly termed postmodern. Cutting edge research in cultural geography that effectively employs the lessons learned from the plethora of philosophical challenges to traditional scientific practice appears to have been ignored, for example. (What do physical geographers make of Said's *Orientalism*, I wonder?)[92] In short, the academic controversy over representation is not necessarily best represented by either postmodern geographers nor reflexivity studies, and an exclusive focus on these research experiments can unnecessarily bias geography's scientists about the value of research on representation and the need for alternative approaches like phenomenology.

Contemporary Phenomenological Research

Phenomenological studies have not been absent from research in philosophy and fields like design and landscape architecture. Contemporary phenomenological studies encompass rigorous description with a view to better understanding human-environment interaction, a key geographical theme. Mezga, in an effort to improve our ability to incorporate subjective design information into site development, studied the meanings attached to the Auschwitz concentration camp from a phenomenological perspective. Note that the object of study here is the subjective, qualitative values that inmates attached to various parts of the Auschwitz camp. The study itself was intended to be rigorous, not arbitrary and subjective. Using the phenomenological method developed by Relph, Mezga spent two years studying the constellation of meanings surrounding various sites in the camp.[93] The materials studied ranged from personal diaries, photographs, and historical documents to inmates' testimony. Through detailed description of various elements of the camp several sites were identified as key components of Auschwitz in terms of the inmates' experience of those sites. The camp entry gate was identified as one of the most salient features of the camp. Phenomenologically speaking this single physical site in the camp was part of the inmates' experiential structure, which the phenomenological description and analysis allowed to emerge and be recognized. Indeed the gate took on six distinct meanings.[94] Of particular importance was the way in which the gate induced an instinctive level of survival for many inmates. The orchestra's music, played just beyond the gate usually inspired hatred from the inmates and was seen as a "weapon of dehumanization."[95] Mezga concluded that phenomenological methodology was a useful component of site analysis, allowing as it does the inclusion of value and meaning in the creation of a sense of place.

Along similar lines Seamon has consistently attempted to investigate human-environment relationships through an emphasis on the sense of place that particular environments invoke in people. Seamon, for example, has studied the historic site of Olana in New York State. He isolates the physical elements of this building that most contribute to the sense of place it engenders.[96] Seamon's phenomenological study of this place had a practical goal, which was to provide information on the best possible design for a visitors' center. His phenomenological study involved intensive descriptions of site characteristics, and environmental themes that contributed to Olana's sense of place. A variety of texts were used to identify the essence of Olana's sense of place. These texts included paintings and writings about Olana, and scholarly treatises on the building and its environs. Seamon's main concern was for the trustworthiness of his interpretations. Olana's sense of place oriented around the idea of the building as a "home on high," from which its owner could "look out on the world." Indeed, as Seamon points out, Olana is the name of an ancient Persian fortress built on a hill. Ultimately, Seamon suggests that the visitors' center should reflect the related themes of "home" and "height."[97] Thus, for example, the center should be built at some elevation and should provide the public with a panoramic view of the grounds. Seamon's phenomenology of Olana is rigorous and provided practical information for problem solving. His analysis and results are clearly presented, thus allowing them to be critiqued and challenged, which is the hallmark of good science. As Pickles is at pains to point out, phenomenology, like other rigorous approaches to scientific study, must allow its findings to be "transparent," that is, open to challenge, and phenomenological knowledge must be supported by evidence and sound argument.[98]

More importantly for this argument though is Seamon's use of Hillier's space syntax to aid in the phenomenological analysis of particular urban problems, especially the pressing issue of how to create vibrant and harmonious street life in present day cities.[99] This study is important here for at least two reasons. First, Hillier's research involves complex mathematical models and computer aided simulations that attempt to describe the underlying structure of street layouts in settlement design. Seamon, as a phenomenologist, does not reject this positivistically based research, as Morrill might expect such a phenomenologist to do.

Instead Seamon's analysis is complementary to Hillier's work. That phenomenology was originally intended to be complementary to the empirical-objective sciences is also attested to by Backhaus.[100] Second, Seamon's study highlights the productive possibilities of a rigorous phenomenological analysis when used in conjunction with such empirically identified landscape forms.

Hillier studied the urban layout of the French town of Gassin. He argued particular street layouts, design of open space, and building type could contribute to increased human interaction or could retard such interaction. In fact he suggested that a "beady-ring" pattern to streets and open spaces produced increased levels of human interaction and a much improved street life.[101] Axial and convex spaces in the village were identified with the streets of greatest human movement forming what Hillier called a "deformed wheel." While this element of the morphology of Gassin was always present, individuals were, on an everyday basis, unaware of it because this formed part of their taken for granted life-world. In the everyday world of human life in Gassin the deformed wheel was unseen. It was essentially invisible, like the hand in a glove.[102] As Seamon notes this is a good example of positivist methodology allowing (in phenomenological dialect) the phenomenon to emerge rather than distorting the life-world.[103] In fact while positivist mathematical models identified this taken for granted structure of the life world of Gassin's residents, Seamon and Pickles would both argue that Hillier's scientific practice is essentially phenomenological in nature. Pickles has gone so far as to claim that all scientists, and all sciences, are phenomenological at heart. Indeed successful phenomenology, like successful science of a more traditional nature, must be able to distinguish between the world of appearances and the phenomena themselves. In other words it must be able to identify *masked* phenomena (in this case the deformed wheel) and should not be content to "treat the world as do those who live in it." Phenomenology is an inherently critical enterprise.[104]

Of course, to claim, as Hillier does, that the built environment causes certain behavior to occur is open to the criticism of environmental determinism. One role of phenomenology here is to negate the charge of determinism. A phenomenological analysis of Gassin, building on Hillier's space syntax, would investigate the actual relationships of axial and convex spaces of the deformed wheel structure of the settlement, to human activity and the human experience of that village. Seamon argues for the need to understand the connections between such a structure and the human experience of movement, rest, privacy, and interaction.[105] Thus phenomenology is seen as holding the potential of deflecting charges of determinism here, by deepening our understanding of the human encounter with the built environment.

Ultimately Hillier suggested urban problems and the perceived decline of community in cities is due, in part, to the deterioration of this "invisible" deformed wheel infrastructure in such settlements. The problem cannot be remedied unless settlements are treated holistically. And this cannot happen until planners and architects become aware of the existence of this and other morphological substructures. Until then they will continue to plan and build settlements around the western ideals of privacy and hierarchy.[106] While Seamon also documents several criticisms of Hillier's research, the essential advantages of phenomenology and positivist methodology complementing one another are manifest.

A final note on contemporary phenomenological practice should be made. Pickles warns against phenomenological research becoming too narrowly focused on practical applications. The impetus for such applications comes from the constant criticism of traditional science that phenomenology cannot provide good examples of sound research that yields "practical" results.[107] For Pickles, to restrict phenomenological research to practical applications might lead to the phenomenologist ignoring the broader purpose. Phenomenology is to investigate from the perspective of the philosophical attitude, the conditions and assumptions within which meaning is constituted for the various sciences. However, that phenomenological method can provide practical information that aids problem solving must be seen as critical evidence of its potential to geographical research.

Conclusion

As examples of contemporary phenomenological research indicate, neither phenomenology nor positivism need reject the others' assumptions or methods. Both philosophies, and methods, are rigorous and open to criticism, and the results from either type of research are amenable to modification or outright rejection. Phenomenologists, beginning with Husserl himself, never intended to reject positivist science, denigrate the motives of positivists or advocate an undisciplined subjectivity, as Morrill suggests.

Without drawing too close an analogy there are similar themes within recent anthropological discourse and the geographic debate that originally centered on phenomenology. At their heart these debates questioned the complete authority with which traditional science claimed to speak. And yet there was also much support for traditional science. What Geertz and Husserl essentially have in common is found in their respective views on the possibility of inventing new ways of seeing new objects of study in the everyday world. Both reposition traditional science. Thus for Geertz ethnographies, "like quantum mechanics or the Italian opera" are products "of the imagination."[108] Ethnographies are not imaginary, however, and similarly for Husserl the objective sciences were creative human acts:

> Objective science itself belongs to the life-world. Its theories, the logical constructs, are of course not things in the life-world like stones, houses, or trees. They are logical wholes and logical parts made up of logical elements. . . . But this or any other ideality does not change in the least the fact that these are human formations, essentially related to human actualities and potentialities, and thus belong to this concrete unity of the life-world."[109]

Returning to Demeritt, apparently physical geographers currently wonder at the "schoolboy" philosophical antics of postmodernists grappling with the crisis of representation.[110] Demeritt usefully points us in the direction of an analysis of the social practices of geographers as being a more effective challenge to the overexaggerated claims of the "scientists." He attempts to arbitrate between the two extreme positions of the science-anti-science debate. But, as Pickles argued, one of the major problems (a social practice) with the traditional scientists of geography is their very unwillingness to engage philosophical debates. And, they simultaneously dismiss those that see value and necessity in addressing these issues.[111] (In the respect, one is reminded of the adage that 'geography is what geographers do'.) The result is that alternative ways of researching the human condition, whether phenomenlogical or not, are seen as outright rejections of science, as anti-science. Any disagreement with geographers like Morrill on issues of objectivity, and what methods or approaches constitute valid research, is collapsed into the either/or conundrum, and all such alternatives are simply labeled subjective and relative. Demeritt himself confesses to having too quickly dismissed alternative claims to know as "soft-minded,"[112] and yet he also complains that human geographers have not done enough to convince physical geographers about the importance of the social construction of knowledge. Surely the unwillingness of many scientific geographers, human and physical, to closely follow philosophical debates in geography is also at the root of the "easy" dismissal of social constructivist geography.

Phenomenological research in geography cast Husserl as a subjectivist because of the very strength of positivist science in geography and the pervasiveness of the either/or dilemma. Human geographers were thus quick to reject phenomenology and to reassert the primary importance of positivistic approaches to research. Husserl himself saw the objective-logical sciences as exact, rigorous, and necessary, and did not envision a relativist methodology to replace them. The overemphasis on Husserl's transcendental turn in geography effectively denied the descriptive phenomenology that is useful to current debates on method. To argue that our ways of knowing can be extended beyond the narrow confines of traditional science, in short, to argue "that no innocent eye is available to us" is not to argue against science for relativism.[113] Morrill's reliance on the either/or dichotomy and his consequent belief that he speaks with complete "objectivity," is a particular form of authority. It allows him and his ilk to easily but wrongly view other research methods, like those of feminist geography that began this chapter, simply as irrational. If we can agree with Gregory (1989, 87) that "there have been too many calls for 'plain writing' by commentators who signally fail to understand the consequences of conventional genres and modes of representation,"[114] then Morrill's characterization of alternative geographical practice shows the importance of recognizing an ongoing crisis of representation when he asserts that, "it is as if geography before the 1950s, emphasizing region and place, was the Roman Catholic establishment. The Protestant Reformation could be viewed as the rise of science."[115] Despite his claim, he is not "implying nothing about the religions" (if it is an empty analogy then why use it?). Only 'objective science' could represent such an analogy as closed to the possibility of alternative readings.[116] His analogy directly introduces the old stereotypes of the superstitious Catholic and the hard working enlightened Protestant. What Morrill fails to realize is that when he despairs of the rise of the "ologies" and "isms" in geography his form of science, scient*ism*, is the most pervasive ism geography has known.[117]

Notes

1. Richard Morrill, "Geography, Spatial Analysis, and Social Science," *Urban Geography* 14, no. 2 (1993): 442-46.

2. Morrill, "Geography, Spatial Analysis," 442.

3. Morrill, "Geography, Spatial Analysis," 444.

4. Morrill, "Geography, Spatial Analysis," 446.

5. Morrill, "Geography, Spatial Analysis," 443.

6. Isabelle Dyck, "Ethnography: A Feminist Method?," *The Canadian Geographer* 37, (1993): 52-57. John Eyles, "Feminist and Interpretive Method: How Different?," *The Canadian Geographer* 37, (1993): 50-52. Pamela Moss, "Focus: Feminism as Method," *The Canadian Geographer* 37, (1993): 48-49. Damaris Rose, "On Feminism, Method And Methods In Human Geography: An Idiosyncratic Overview," *The Canadian Geographer* 37, (1993): 57-61.

7. Rose, "On Feminism," 57.

8. Rose, "On Feminism," 58.

9. Erica Schoenberger, "The Corporate Interview as an Evidentiary Strategy in Economic Geography," *The Professional Geographer* 43, (1991): 180-89.

10. Linda McDowell, "Valid Games? A Response to Erica Schoenberger," *The Professional Geographer* 44, (1992): 212-15.

11. McDowell, "Valid Games?," 214.

12. Erica Schoenberger, "Self-Criticism and Self Awareness in Research: A Reply to Linda McDowell," *The Professional Geographer* 44, (1992): 215-18.

13. Tamar Mayer, "Consensus and Invisibility: The Representation of Women in Human Geography Textbooks," *The Professional Geographer* 41, (1989): 397-409.

14. Leonard Guelke, "Intellectual Coherence and the Foundations of Geography," *The Professional Geographer* 41, (1989): 123-30.

15. Robert W. Lake, "Planning and Applied Geography: Positivism, Ethics and Geographic Information Systems," *Progress in Human Geography* 17, (1993): 404-13. George Towers, "GIS Versus the Community: Siting Power in Southern West Virginia," *Applied Geography* 17, (1997): 111-25.

16. David Demeritt, "Social Theory and the Reconstruction of Science and Geography," *Transactions of the Institute of British Geographers* NS 21, (1996): 484-503.

17. Trevor Barnes, "Rationality and Relativism in Economic Geography: An Interpretive Review of the Homo Economicus Assumption," *Progress in Human Geography* 12, (1988): 473-96.

18. Kay Christensen, "Geography as a Human Science: A Philosophic Critique of the Positivist-Humanist Split," in *A Search for Common Ground*, ed. Peter Gould and Gunnar Olsson (London: Pion, 1982), 37-57. David Seamon, "Using Pattern Language to

Identify Sense of Place: American Landscape Painter Frederic Church's Olana. A Test Case," in *Coming of Age: Proceedings of the Environmental Design Research Association*, ed. Richard Selby (Urbana-Champaign: University of Illinois Press, 1990). David Seamon, "The Life of the Place," *Nordisk Arkitekturforskning* 7, (1994): 35-48.

19. John Pickles, *Phenomenology, Science and Geography: Spatiality and the Human Sciences* (Cambridge: Cambridge University Press, 1985).

20. Barry Hindess, *Philosophy and Methodology in the Social Sciences* (Atlantic Highlands, N.J.: Humanities Press, 1977). Joseph Kockelmans, *Phenomenology and Physical Science: An Introduction to Philosophy of Physical Science* (Pittsburgh, Pa.: Duquesne University Press, 1966). Barry Smart, *Sociology, Phenomenology, and Marxian Analysis* (London: Routledge and Kegan Paul, 1976).

21. Edmund Husserl, *Ideas: General Introduction to Pure Phenomenology* (London: Collier Books, 1962), 72.

22. Elisabeth Ströker, *Husserl's Transcendental Phenomenology* (Stanford, Calif.: Stanford University Press, 1993).

23. Edmund Husserl, *The Crisis of European Sciences and Transcendental Phenomenology* (Evanston, Ill.: Northwestern University Press, 1970).

24. Husserl, *Ideas*, 72.

25. Husserl, *Ideas*, 77.

26. Edward Relph, "Phenomenology," in *Themes in Geographic Thought*, ed. Brian P. Harvey and Milton E. Holly (London: Croom Helm, 1981), 96-114.

27. Louise Johnson, "Bracketing Lifeworlds: Husserlian Phenomenology as Geographical Method," *Australian Geographical Studies* 21, (1983): 102-8.

28. Husserl, *Ideas*, 72.

29. Husserl, *Crisis*, 5.

30. Pickles, *Phenomenology, Science*.

31. Husserl, *Crisis*, 122-23.

32. John Pickles, "From Fact to Lifeworld," in *Qualitative Methods in Human Geography*, ed. John Eyles and David M. Smith (Cambridge: Polity Press, 1988), 233-54.

33. Husserl, *Ideas*, 74.

34. Husserl, *Crisis*, 128.

35. Husserl, *Crisis*, 137.

36. Pickles, *Phenomenology, Science*.

37. Husserl, *Crisis*, 129.

38. Husserl, *Crisis*, 130.

39. Pickles, *Phenomenology, Science*, 135-36.

40. Richard J. Bernstein, *Beyond Objectivism and Relativism: Science, Hermeneutics and Praxis* (Philadelphia: University of Pennsylvania Press, 1983), 11.

41. Hindess, *Philosophy*, 62.

42. Ströker, *Transcendental Phenomenology*, 60.

43. Ströker, *Transcendental Phenomenology*, 64.

44. Christensen, "Geography." Alfred Schutz, *Collected Papers, Volume 1* (The Hague: Martinus Nijhoff, 1962).

45. Husserl, *Crisis*, 153.

46. Johnson, *Bracketing Lifeworlds*, 104.

47. Pickles, *Phenomenology, Science*, 9.

48. Bernstein, *Beyond Objectivism*, 15.

49. Morrill, "Geography, Spatial Analysis," 443.

50. Bernstein, *Beyond Objectivism*, 18.

51. Frederick K. Schaefer, "Exceptionalism in Geography: A Methodological Exami-

nation," *Annals of the Association of American Geographers* 43, (1953): 226-49.

52. Norbert Elias, "Problems of Involvement and Detachment," *British Journal of Sociology* 7, (1956) 226-52. Alvin W. Gouldner, "Anti-Minotaur: The Myth of a Value Free Sociology," in *Sociology on Trial*, ed. Maurice Stein and Arthur Vidich (Englewood Cliffs, N.J.: Prentice Hall, 1963), 3-26. Ronald J. Johnston, *Philosophy and Human Geography* (London: Edward Arnold, 1983).

53. David Seamon, "The Phenomenological Contribution to Environmental Psychology," *Journal of Environmental Psychology* 2, (1982): 119-40.

54. Brian Moriarty, "Future Research Directions in American Human Geography," *The Professional Geographer* 33, (1981): 484-88. Brian Moriarty, "Science and the Funding of Geographical Research: The Pursuit of Reliable Knowledge," *The Professional Geographer* 35, (1983): 332-35.

55. Reginald Golledge, "Commentary on 'The Highest Form of the Geographer's Art,'" *Annals of the Association of American Geographers* 72, (1982): 557-58.

56. Terry G. Jordan, "Preadaption and European Colonization in Rural North America," *Annals of the Association of American Geographers* 79, (1989): 489-500. Donald W. Meinig, "The Historical Geography Imperative," *Annals of the Association of American Geographers* 79, (1989): 79-87.

57. J. Nicholas Entrikin, "Contemporary Humanism in Geography," *Annals of the Association of American Geographers* 66, (1976): 615-32.

58. Entrikin, "Humanism," 618.

59. Entrikin, "Humanism," 631-32.

60. Anne Buttimer, "Grasping the Dynamism of the Lifeworld," *Annals of the Association of American Geographers* 66, (1976): 277-92.

61. Buttimer, "Grasping," 289.

62. Yi Fu Tuan, "Humanistic Geography," *Annals of the Association of American Geographers* 66, (1976): 274.

63. Mark Billinge, "In Search of Negativism: Phenomenology and Historical Geography," *Journal of Historical Geography* 3, (1977): 55-67.

64. Peter Jackson, *Ethnic Groups and Boundaries* (London: Oxford University Press, 1980). Peter Jackson, "A Plea for Cultural Geography," *Area* 12, (1980): 110-13. Peter Jackson, "Phenomenology and Social Geography," *Area* 13, (1981): 299-305.

65. Jackson, *Ethnic Groups*, 7.

66. Jackson, "Social Geography," 300.

67. Jackson, "Social Geography," 302.

68. Jackson, "Social Geography," 300.

69. Buttimer, "Grasping." Johnson, "Bracketing Lifeworlds."

70. Husserl, *Crisis*, 125.

71. Bronislaw Malinowski, *A Diary in the Strict Sense of the Term* (New York: Harcourt, Brace & World, 1967).

72. Clifford Geertz, *Local Knowledge* (New York: Basic, 1983), 56.

73. Geertz, *Local Knowledge*.

74. Geertz, *Local Knowledge*, 57.

75. Clifford Geertz, *The Interpretation of Cultures* (New York: Basic, 1973).

76. Geertz, *Local Knowledge*, 57.

77. Pickles, "From Fact," 242-45.

78. Geertz, *Local Knowledge*, 22.

79. Geertz, *Local Knowledge*, 151.

80. Melford E. Spiro, "Cultural Relativism and the Future of Anthropology," *Cultural*

Anthropology 1, (1986): 259-86.

81. Spiro, "Cultural Relativism," 260.

82. Spiro "Cultural Relativism," 261.

83. Clifford Geertz, *Works and Lives: The Anthropologist as Author* (Stanford, Calif.: Stanford University Press, 1988), 140.

84. Demeritt, "Social Theory," 486.

85. Clifford Geertz, "Anti Anti-Relativism," *American Anthropologist* 86, (1984): 268.

86. Geertz, "Anti-Relativism," 272.

87. Geertz, "Anti-Relativism," 275.

88. Geertz, "Anti-Relativism," 276.

89. James E. Clifford, "On Ethnographic Authority," *Representations* 1, (1983): 133. See also, James E. Clifford and George E. Marcus, *Writing Cultures: The Poetics and Politics of Ethnography* (Berkeley: University of California Press, 1986).

90. Demeritt, "Social Theory," 496.

91. Peter Jackson, *Maps of Meaning* (London: Unwin and Hyman, 1989).

92. Edward Said, *Orientalism: Western Conceptions of the Orient* (London: Routledge & Kegan Paul, 1978).

93. Duane Mezga, "Phenomenology and Auschwitz: Seeking Practical Application of the Paradigm in Design Analysis," *Landscape Research* 18, 68.

94. Mezga, "Auschwitz," 73.

95. Mezga, "Auschwitz," 74.

96. Seamon, "Using Pattern Language."

97. Seamon, "Using Pattern Language," 172.

98. Pickles, "From Fact," 250.

99. Seamon, "Life of the Place," 35.

100. Gary Backhaus, "Georg Simmel as an Eidetic Social Scientist," *Sociological Theory* 16, 260-81.

101. Bill Hillier and Julienne Hanson, *The Social Logic of Space* (Cambridge: Cambridge University Press, 1984).

102. Hillier and Hanson, *Social Logic*, 117.

103. Seamon, "Life of the Place," 45.

104. Pickles, "From Fact," 240.

105. Seamon, "Life of the Place," 40.

106. Seamon, "Life of the Place," 43.

107. Pickles, "From Fact," 251-52.

108. Geertz, *Works and Lives*, 140.

109. Husserl, *Crisis*, 130.

110. Demeritt, "Social Theory," 486.

111. Pickles, "From Fact," 234-35.

112. Demeritt, "Social Theory," 488.

113. Pickles, *Phenomenology, Science*, x.

114. Derek Gregory, "Areal Differentiation and Post Modern Human Geography," in *Horizons in Human Geography*, ed. Derek Gregory and Rex Walford (Totowa, N.J.: Barnes & Noble, 1989), 87.

115. Morrill, "Geography, Spatial Analysis," 443.

116. Peter Jackson, "The Crisis of Representation and the Politics of Position," *Environment and Planning* 9, (1991): 131-34.

117. Morrill, "Geography, Spatial Analysis," 445.

Selected Bibliography

Abbeele, Georges van den. *Travel as Metaphor.* Minneapolis: University of Minnesota Press, 1992.

Alland, Alexander. *Jacob A. Riis: Photographer & Citizen.* New York: Aperture Foundation, 1993.

AlSayyad, Nezar, ed. *Forms of Dominance, On the Architecture and Urbanism of the Colonial Enterprise.* Aldershot, Eng.: Avebury, 1992.

Ammons, A. R., "A Poem is a Walk." *Epoch* (fall 1968).

Anderson, Elijah. *Streetwise: Race, Class and Change in an Urban Community.* Chicago: University of Chicago Press, 1990.

Arendt, Hannah. *The Human Condition.* Chicago: University of Chicago Press, 1958.

Aristotle. *Eudemian Ethics.* Translated by H. Rackham. Cambridge: Cambridge University Press, 1961.

Armstrong, Susan and Richard Botzler, eds. *Environmental Ethics: Divergence and Convergence.* New York: McGraw-Hill, 1993.

Augé, Marc. *Non-Places: Introduction to an Anthropology of Supermodernity.* Translated by John Howe. London: Verso, 1995.

Auster, Paul. *The New York Trilogy.* New York: Penguin, 1990.

Backhaus, Gary. "Georg Simmel as an Eidetic Social Scientist." *Sociological Theory* 16, no. 3 (November 1998): 260-81.

Banerjee, Tridib, and Michael Southworth, eds. *City Sense and City Design.* Cambridge, Mass.: MIT Press, 1995.

Banhan, Rayner. *Los Angeles: The Architecture of Four Ecologies.* London: Penguin, 1973.

Barnes, J. "Aristotle's Theory of Demonstration." *Phronesis* 14, no. 2 (1969).

Barnes, Jonathan, Malcolm Schofield, and Richard Sorabji, eds. *Articles on Aristotle: Vol. 1: Science.* London: Duckworth, 1975.

Barnes, Trevor. "Rationality and Relativism in Economic Geography: An Interpretive Review of the Homo Economicus Assumption." *Progress in Human Geography* 12 (1988): 473-96.

Barth, Gunther. *City People.* New York: Oxford University Press, 1980.

Baudrillard, Jean. *Simulations.* Translated by Paul Foss, Paul Patton, and Philip Beitchman. New York: Semiotexte, 1983.

Beatley, Timothy, and Kristy Manning. *The Ecology of Place.* Washington, D.C.: Island Press, 1966.

Bellah, Robert N., et al. *Habits of the Heart.* New York: Harper and Row, 1985.

Berger, Peter L., and Thomas Luckmann. *The Social Construction of Reality.* London: Anchor, 1966.

Bernstein, Richard J. *Beyond Objectivism and Relativism: Science, Hermeneutics and Praxis.* Philadelphia: University of Pennsylvania Press, 1983.

Berry, Wendell. *Life Is a Miracle.* Washington, D.C.: Counterpoint, 2000.

————. *Sex, Economy, Freedom and Community.* New York: Pantheon, 1993.

————. *What Are People For?* New York: North Point, 1990.

Billinge, Mark. "In Search of Negativism: Phenomenology and Historical Geography." *Journal of Historical Geography* 3 (1977): 55-67.

Bishir, Catherine, W. *North Carolina Architect.* Chapel Hill: University of North Carolina, 1990.

Blanchot, Maurice. *The Space of Literature.* Translated by Ann Smock. Lincoln: University of Nebraska Press, 1989.

Bremmer, Jan, and Herman Roodenburg, eds. *A Cultural History of Gesture.* Ithaca, N.Y.: Cornell University Press, 1992.

Breton, Denise, and Christopher Largent. *The Soul of Economies.* New York: Idea House, 1991.

Brown, Delmer M., ed. *The Cambridge History of Japan.* New York: Cambridge University Press, 1993.

Burrows, Edwin G., and Mike Wallace. *Gotham: A History of New York City to 1898.* New York: Oxford University Press, 1999.

Buttimer, Anne. "Grasping the Dynamism of the Lifeworld." *Annals of the Association of American Geographers* 66 (1976): 615-32.

Callicott, J. Baird, and Michael P. Nelson, eds. *The Great New Wilderness Debate.* Athens: University of Georgia Press, 1998.

Calasso, Roberto. *The Marriage of Cadmus and Harmony.* Translated by Tim Parks. New York: Vintage International, 1994.

Carver, Humphrey. "Building the Suburbs: a Planner's Reflections." *City Magazine* 3 (1978): 40-45.

Casey, Edward S. *The Fate of Place.* Berkeley: University of California Press, 1998.

Casey, Edward S. *Getting Back Into Place.* Bloomington: Indiana University Press, 1993.

Certeau, Michel de. *The Practice of Everyday Life.* Berkeley: University of California Press, 1984.

Chatwin, Bruce. *Anatomy of Restlessness.* New York: Penguin, 1996.

City of New York Parks & Recreation. *Park Planning for Greater New York (1870-1898)* <www.ci.nyc.ny.us/html/history1870-1898.html> (April 23, 1999).

Clifford, James E. "On Ethnographic Authority." *Representations 1* (1983).

Clifford, James E., and George E. Marcus. *Writing Cultures: The Poetics and Politics of Ethnography.* Berkeley: University of California Press, 1986.

Colburn, David, and George E. Pozzetta, eds. *Reform and Reformers in the Progressive Era.* Westport, Conn.: Greenwood Press, 1983.

Connell, Ruth. "Modern Political Space, Consumption and Authenticity in the Evolution of National Space, Washington, D.C." *Building as a Political Act: 1997 ACSA International Conference.* Edited by Randall Ott. New York: ACSA Press, 1998.

Cook, Clarence. *A Description of the New York Central Park.* New York: Benjamin Blom, 1869.

Cosgrove, Dennis, and Stephen Daniels, eds. *The Iconography of Landscape.* Cambridge: Cambridge University Press, 1988.

Crowe, Timothy D. *Crime Prevention Through Environmental Design.* Boston: Butterworth-Heinemann, 1991.

Crummet, Michael. *Sun Dance: The 50th Anniversary Crow Indian Sun Dance.* Helena, Mont.: Falcon Press, 1993.

Cuba, L., and D. Hummon, "A Place to Call Home: Identification with Dwelling, Community, and Region." *Sociological Quarterly* 34, no. 1 (1993): 111-32.

Czarnecki, John E. "La Crosse County Courthouse, La Crosse Wisconsin: A New County Courthouse Consolidates Law Enforcement, Incarceration, and Court Processes Within One Building." *Architectural Record* 187, no. 3 (March 1999): 126-28.

Danbom, David B. *A World of Hope: Progressives and the Struggle for an Ethical Public Life.* Philadelphia: Temple University Press, 1987.

Davis, Mike. *City of Quartz, Excavating the Future in Los Angelos.* New York: Verso, 1990.

DeBell, Garret, ed. *The Environmental Handbook.* New York: Ballantine, 1970.

Deleuze, Gilles. *The Logic of Sense.* Translated by Mark Lester with Charles Stivale. Edited by Constantin V. Boundas. New York: Columbia University Press, 1990.

Deleuze, Gilles, and Félix Guattari. *Anti-Oedipus: Capitalism and Schizophrenia.* Translated by Robert Hurley et al. Minneapolis: University of Minnesota Press, 1983.

———. *Nomadology: The War Machine.* Translated by Brian Massumi. New York: Semiotexte, 1986.

Demeritt, David. "Social Theory and the Reconstruction of Science and Geography." *Transactions of the Institute of British Geographers* NS 21 (1996): 484-503.

Derrida, Jacques. *Writing and Difference.* Translated by Alan Bass. Chicago: University of Chicago Press, 1976.

Derrida, Jacques, and Peter Eisenman. *Chora L Works.* Edited by Jeffrey Kipnis and Thomas Leeser. New York: Monacelli Press, 1997.

Descartes, René. *Meditations on First Philosophy.* Translated by Donald A. Cress. Indianapolis: Hackett, 1979.

Dietsch, Deborah K. "Capital Offense, An Overblown War Memorial will Destory a Sacred Site on the National Mall." *Architecture* (March 1997): 63.

Dorris, Virginia Kent. "Warren B. Rudman United States Courthouse, Concord, New Hampshire: With a Symmetrical Layout and a Limited Palette of Materials, a New Courthouse Recalls Traditional Civic Structures." *Architectural Record* 187, no. 3 (March 1999): 122-25.

Downing, Andrew J. "The New York Park." *First Annual Report on the Improvement of The Central Park,* New York (City) Commissioners of Central Park. New York: McGrath Publishing, 1857.

Duneier, Mitchell. *Sidewalk.* New York: Farrar, Straus, Giroux. 1999.

Dyck, Isabelle. "Ethnography: A Feminist Method?" *The Canadian Geographer* 37 (1993): 52-57.

Ehrlich, Anne and Paul Ehrlich. *Earth.* New York: Franklin Watts, 1987.

Einstein, Albert. *Relativity: The Special and General Theory.* Translated by R. W. Lawson. New York: Random House, 1961.

Elias, Norbert. "Problems of Involvement and Deatachment." *British Journal of Sociology* 7 (1956): 226-52.

Ellis, Ralph D. *Questioning Consciousness: The Interplay of Imagery, Cognition, and Emotion in the Human Brain.* Amsterdam: John Benjamins, 1995.

Entrikin, J. Nicholas. "Contemporary Humanism in Geography." *Annals of the Association of American Geographers* 66 (1976): 277-92.

Eyeles, John. "Feminist and Interpretive Method: How Different?" *The Canadian Geographer* 37 (1993): 50-52.

Farrell, David, ed. *Martin Heidegger: Basic Writings.* New York: Harper, 1991.

Fein, Albert, ed. *Landscape into Cityscape: Frederick Law Olmsted's Plans for a Greater New York City.* Ithaca, N.Y.: Cornell University Press, 1967.

Fjellman, Stephen M. *Vinyl Leaves, Walt Disney World and America.* Boulder, Colo.: Westview, 1992.

Fried, Lewis S. *Makers of the City.* Amherst: University of Massachusetts Press, 1990.

Friedman, Mitch, ed. *Forever Wild: Conserving the Greater North Cascades Ecosystem.* Bellingham, Wash.: Mountain Hemlock Press, 1988.

Friedman, Thomas L. "A Manifesto for the Fast World: From the Supercharged Financial Markets to Osama bin Laden, the Emrging Global Order Demands as Enforcer that's America's New Burden." *New York Times Magazine,* 28 March1999.

Gandal, Keith. *Virtues of the Vicious: Jacob Riis, Stephen Crane, and the Spectacle of the Slum.* New York: Oxford University Press, 1997.

Garber, Steven. *The Urban Naturalist.* Mineola, N.Y.: Dover, 1987.

Gardels, Nathan P. *At Century's End.* La Jolla, Calif.: ALTI, 1996.

Geertz, Clifford. "Anti Anti-Relativism." *American Anthropologist* 86 (1984).

———. *Local Knowledge.* New York: Basic, 1983.

———. *The Interpretation of Cultures.* New York: Basic, 1973.

———. *Works and Lives: The Anthropologist as Author.* Stanford, Calif.: Stanford University Press, 1988.

Gesler, Wilbert M. "Therapeutic Landscapes: Medical Issues in Light of the New Cultural Geography." *Social Science and Medicine* 34, no.7 (1992): 735-46.

Gibson, James J. *The Ecological Approach to Visual Perception.* Hillsdale, N.J.: Lawrence Erlbaum, 1986.

Gilbert, Roger. *Walks in the World.* Princeton, N.J.: Princeton University Press, 1991.

Gleber, Anke. *The Art of Taking a Walk: Flanerie, Literature, and Film in Weimar Culture.* Princeton, N.J.: Princeton Paperbacks, 1999.

Golledge, Reginald. "Commentary on 'The Highest Form of the Geographer's Art.'" *Annals of the Association of American Geographers* 72 (1982): 557-58.

Golledge, Reginald G., and Robert J. Stimson. *Spatial Behavior: A Geographic Perspective.* New York: Guilford, 1997.

Gotthelf, Allan, and James G. Lennox, eds. *Physical Issues in Aristotle's Biology.* Cambridge: Cambridge University Press.

Gottlieb, Robert. *Forcing the Spring: The Transformation of the American Environmental Movement.* Washington, D.C.: Island Press, 1993.

Gould, Peter, and Gunnar Olsson, ed. *A Search for Common Ground.* London: Pion, 1982.

Gouldner, Alvin W. "Anti-Minotaur: The Myth of a Value Free Sociology." *Sociology on Trial.* Edited by Maurice Stein and Arthur Vidich. Englewood Cliffs, N.J.: Prentice Hall, 1963.

Grange, Joseph. *The City An Urban Cosmology.* Albany: SUNY Press, 1999.

Gratz, Roberta Brandes, and Norman Mintz. *Cities Back From the Edge: New Life for Downtown.* New York: John Wiley and Sons, 1998.

Greenberg, Mike. *The Poetics of Cities: Designing Neighborhoods That Work.* Columbus: Ohio University Press, 1995.

Gregory, Derek, and Rex Walford, eds. *Horizons in Human Geography.* Totawa, N.J.: Barnes & Noble, 1989.

Guelke, Leonard. "Intellectual Coherence and the Foundations of Geography." *The Professional Geographer* 41 (1989): 123-30.

Hales, Peter B. *Silver Cities: The Photography of American Urbanization, 1839-1915.* Philadelphia: Temple University Press, 1989.

Harvey, Brian P., and Milton E. Holly, eds. *Themes in Geographic Thought.* London: Croom Helm, 1981.

Hegel, Georg Wilhelm Friedrich. *The Philosophy of History.* Translated by J. Sibree. New York: Dover, 1956.

Heidegger, Martin. *Being and Time.* Translated by John Macquarrie and Edward Robinson. New York: Harper and Row, 1962.

———. *Introduction to Metaphysics.* Translated by Ralph Manheim. New Haven: Yale University Press, 1959.

———. *Poetry, Language, Thought.* Translated by Albert Hofstadter. New York: Harper and Row, 1971.

Hiller, Bill, and Julienne Hanson. *The Social Logic of Space.* Cambridge: Cambridge University Press, 1984.

Hindess, Barry. *Philosophy and Methodology in the Social Sciences.* Atlantic Highlands, N.J.: Humanities Press, 1977.

Holli, Melvin G. "Urban Reform in the Progressive Era." *The Progressive Era.* Edited by Lewis L. Gould. Syracuse, N.Y.: Syracuse University Press, 1974.

Hough, Michael. *Cities and Natural Processes.* New York: Routledge, 1995.

Hoy, Suellen. *Chasing Dirt: The American Pursuit of Cleanliness.* New York: Oxford University Press, 1995.

Hunter, John Michael. *Land into Landscape.* London: George Godwin, 1985.

Husserl, Edmund. *Logical Investigations I.* Translated by J. N. Findlay. London: Routledge & Kegan Paul, 1970.

———. *Logical Investigations II.* Translated by J. N. Findlay. London: Routledge & Kegan Paul, 1970.

———. *The Crisis of European Sciences and Transcendental Phenomenology.* Translated by David Carr. Evanston, Ill.: Northwestern University Press, 1970.

Jackson, J. B. "The Westward-moving House." *Landscapes.* Edited by Ervin H. Zube. Amherst: University of Massachusetts Press, 1970.

Jackson, Kenneth T. *Crabgrass Frontier: The Suburbanization of the United States.* New York: Oxford University Press, 1985.

Jackson, Peter. "A Plea for Cultural Geography." *Area* 12 (1980): 110-13.

———. *Ethnic Groups and Boundaries.* London: Oxford University Press, 1980.

———. *Maps of Meaning.* London: Unwin and Hyman, 1989.

———. "Phenomenology and Social Geography." *Area* 13 (1981): 299-305.

———. "The Crisis of Representation and the Politics of Position." *Environmental Planning D* 9 (1991): 131-34.

Jacobs, Jane. *Death and Life of Great American Cities.* New York: Vintage, 1961.

James, William. *The Principles of Psychology, Volume Two.* New York: Dover, 1950.

Jarvis, Robin. *Romantic Writing and Pedestrian Travel.* New York: St Martin's, 1997.

Johnson, Louise. "Bracketing Lifeworlds: Husserlian Phenomenology as Geographical Method." *Australian Geographical Studies* 21 (1983): 102-8.

Johnston, Ronald J. *Philosophy and Human Geography.* London: Edward Arnold, 1983.

Jonas, Hans. *Imperative of Responsibility: In Search of an Ethics for the Technological Age.* Chicago: University of Chicago Press, 1984.

Jordan, Terry G. "Preadaption and European Colonization in Rural North America." *Annals of the Association of American Geographers* 79 (1989): 489-500.

Joyce, James. *Ulysses.* Edited by Hans Walter Gabler. New York: Vintage, 1986.

Judd, Dennis R., and Paul P. Kantor. *The Politics of Urban America.* Needham Heights, Mass.: Allyn and Bacon, 1998.

Kasson, John F. *Amusing the Millions.* New York: Hill & Wang, 1978.

———. *Rudeness and Civility: Manners in Nineteenth-Century Urban America.* New York: Hill and Wang, 1990.

Kearns, Robin A., and William M. Gessler, eds. *Putting Health into Place: Landscape, Identity, and Well-Being.* Syracuse, N.Y.: Syracuse University Press, 1998.

Klein, Naomi. *No Logo: Taking Aim at the Brand Bullies.* New York: St. Martin's, 2000.

Knabb, Ken, ed. *Situationist International Anthology.* Berkeley, Calif.: Bureau of Public Streets, 1981.

Knoop, Stuart L. "Securing the U.S. Abroad." *Architectural Record* (August 1992).

Köhler, Wolfgang. "Physical Gestalten." *A Source Book of Gestalt Psychology.* Edited by Willis D. Ellis. New York: Harcourt Brace, 1938.

Kockelmans, Joseph. *Phenomenology and Physical Science: An Introduction to Philosophy of Physical Science.* Pittsburgh, Pa.: Duquesne University Press, 1966.

Kristeva, Julia. *Strangers to Ourselves.* Translated by Leon Roudiez. New York: Columbia University Press, 1991.

Kuntsler, James Howard. *The Geography of Nowhere.* New York: Touchstone, 1993.

Kutter, E. "A Model for Individual Travel Behavior." *Urban Studies* 10: 238-58.

Lake, Robert W. "Planning and Applied Geography: Positiovism, Ethics and Geographic Information Systems." *Progress in Human Geography* 17 (1993): 404-13.

Lane, James B. *Jacob A. Riis and the American City.* Port Washington, N.Y.: Kennikat Press, 1974.

Lang, Jon. *Creating Architectural Theory: The Role of the Behavioral Sciences in Environmental Design.* New York: Van Nostrand Reinhold, 1987.

LeGales, Richard T., and Frederic Stout, eds. *The City Reader.* New York: Routledge, 1996.

Legge, James. *Confucian Analects: Great Learning and Doctrine of the Mean.* New York: Dover, 1971.

Leopold, Aldo. *A Sand County Almanac: And Sketches Here and There.* Oxford: Oxford University Press, 1977.

Light, Andrew, and Jonathan M. Smith, eds. *Philosophy and Geography I: Space, Place, and Environmental Ethics.* Lanham, Md.: Rowman & Littlefield, 1997.

———. *Philosophy and Geography III: Philosophies of Place.* Lanham, Md.: Rowman & Littlefield, 1998.

Littleton, Gregory. "Blast-Free Design." *Architecture* (May 1990): 84-85.

Loeffler, Jane C. *The Architecture of Diplomacy, Building America's Embassies.* New York: Princeton Architectural Press, 1998.

Lopez, Barry. *Of Wolves and Men.* New York: Simon & Schuster, 1978.

Lowenthal, D. "Past Time, Present Place." *The Geographic Review* 65 (1997): 1-36.

Lynch, Kevin. "A Walk Around the Block." *Landscape* 8, no. 3 (1959): 24-34.

———. *The Image of the City.* Cambridge, Mass.: MIT Press, 1960.

Lyotard, Jean-François. *Driftworks.* New York: Semiotexte, 1984.

Macy, Joanna. *World as Lover, World as Self.* Berkeley, Calif.: Parallax Press, 1991.

Malinowski, Bronislaw. *A Diary in the Strict Sense of the Term.* New York: Harcourt Brace & World, 1967.

Mander, Jerry, and Edward Goldsmith. *The Case Against the Global Economy.* San Francisco: Sierra Club, 1996.

Marx, Karl. *Capital, Volume One.* New York: Vintage, 1977.

Mayer, Tamar. "Consensus and Invisibility: The Representation of Women in Human Geography Textbooks." *The Professional Geographer* 41 (1989): 397-409.

Mayr, Ernst. *This is Biology.* Cambridge, Mass.: Belknap Press.

McDowell, Linda. "Valid Games? A Response to Erica Schoenberger." *The Professional Geographer* 44 (1992): 212-15.

McKeon, Richard, ed. *The Basic Works of Aristotle.* New York: Random House, 1941.

McKibben, Bill. *The End of Nature*. New York: Random House, 1989.

McLuhan, Marshall. *Understanding Media: The Extensions of Man*. New York: McGraw-Hill, 1964.

McShane, Clay. *Down the Asphalt Path: The Automobile and the American City*. New York: Columbia University Press, 1994.

Mead, George Herbert. *Mind, Self, and Society*. Edited by Charles W. Morris. Chicago: University of Chicago Press, 1934.

Meaton, Julia, and David Morrice. "The Ethics and Politics of Private Automobile Use." *Environmental Ethics* 18, no. 1 (spring 1996): 39-54.

———. *The Philosophy of the Act*. Chicago: University of Chicago Press, 1938.

Meinig, Donald W. "The Historical Geography Imperative." *Annals of the Association of American Geographers* 79 (1989): 79-87.

———, ed. *The Interpretation of Ordinary Landscapes: Geographical Essays*. New York: Oxford University Press, 1979.

Melosi, Martin V., ed. *Pollution and Reform in American Cities, 1870-1930*. Austin: University of Texas Press, 1980.

Merleau-Ponty, Maurice. *Phenomenology of Perception*. Translated by Colin Smith. London: Routledge & Kegan Paul, 1962.

———. *Signs*. Translated by Richard C. McCleary. Evanston, Ill.: Northwestern University Press, 1964.

———. *The Structures of Behavior*. Translated by Alden L. Fisher. Boston: Beacon Press, 1963.

Merton, Thomas. *Zen and the Birds of Appetite*. Boston: Shambhala, 1993.

Meyers, Norman. "The Extinction Spasm Impending: Synergisms at Work." *Conservation Biology I* (1987): 14-21.

Mezga, Duane. "Phenomenology and Auschwitz: Seeking Practical Application of the Paradigm in Design Analysis." *Landscape Research* 18.

Mitchell, Stephen. *Tao Te Ching*. New York: Harper, 1988.

Moriarty, Brian. "Future Research Directions in American Human Geography." *The Professional Geographer* 33 (1981): 484-88.

———. "Science and the Funding of Geographical Research: The Pursuit of Reliable Knowledge." *The Professional Geographer* 35 (1983), 332-35.

Morrill, Richard. "Geography, Spatial Analysis, and Social Science." *Urban Geography* 14, no. 2 (1993): 442-46.

Moss, Pamela. "Focus: Feminism as a Method." *The Canadian Geographer* 37 (1993): 48-49.

Mumford, Lewis. *The City in History*. New York: Harcourt Brace, 1961.

Nesbitt, Kate, ed. *Theorizing a New Agenda for Architecture: An Anthology of Architectural Theory, 1965-1995*. New York: Princeton Architectural Press, 1996.

Newman, Oscar. *Defensible Space, Crime Prevention Through Urban Design*. New York: MacMillan, 1972.

Newman, Peter, and Jeffrey Kenworthy. *Sustainability and Cities*. Washington, D.C.: Island Press, 1999.

Nietzsche, Friedrich. *Twilight of the Idols*. Translated by R. J. Hollingdale. New York: Penguin, 1968.

Norberg-Schulz, Christian. *Genius Loci: Towards a Phenomenology of Architecture*. New York: Rizzoli International, 1984.

Nord, Deborah. *Walking the Victorian Streets: Women, Representation and the City*. Ithica, N.Y.: Cornell University Press, 1995.

Nussbaum, Martha Craven. *Aristotle's De Motu Animalium.* Princeton, N.J.: Princeton University Press, 1978.

Nussbaum, Martha Craven, and Malcolm Schofield, eds. *Studies in Ancient Greek Philosophy.* Cambridge: Cambridge University Press, 1982.

O'Brien, Dennis. "The Disappearing Moral Curriculum." *The Key Reporter* 62, no. 4 (summer 1997): 1-2.

Oliver, Kelly. *Reading Kristeva.* Bloomington: Indiana University Press, 1993.

Olmsted, Frederick Law, Sr. *Forty Years of Landscape Architecture: Central Park.* Cambridge, Mass.: MIT Press, 1928.

Pease, Otis, ed. *The Progressive Years: The Spirit and Achievement of American Reform.* New York: George Braziller, 1962.

Pickles, John. "From Fact to Lifeworld." *Qualitative Methods in Human Geography.* Edited by John Eyles and David M. Smith. Cambridge: Polity Press, 1988.

———. *Phenomenology, Science and Geography: Spatiality and the Human Sciences.* Cambridge: Cambridge University Press, 1985.

Plato. *The Collected Dialogues of Plato.* Edited by Edith Hamilton and Dorion Cairns. New York: Pantheon Books, 1961.

Relph, Edward. *Rational Landscapes and Humanistic Geography.* London: Croom Helm, 1981.

Riis, Jacob. *How the Other Half Lives.* 1890. Reprint, New York: Charles Scribner's Sons, 1902.

———. *The Battle with the Slum.* 1902. Reprint, Mineola, N.Y.: Dover Publications, 1998.

———. *The Making of an American.* New York: Macmillan, 1902.

Ritzer, George. *The McDonaldization of Society.* Thousand Oaks, Calif.: Pine Forge, 1996.

Rolston, Holmes III. *Conserving Natural Value.* New York: Columbia University Press, 1994.

Rose, Damaris. "On Feminism, Method and Methods in Human Geography: An Idiosyncratic Overview." *The Canadian Geographer* 37 (1993): 57-61.

Ross, Andrew. *The Celebration Chronicles, Life, Liberty, and the Pursuit of Property Value in Disney's New Town.* New York: Ballantine, 1999.

Rotman, Brian. *Signifying Nothing: The Semiotics of Zero.* Stanford, Calif.: Stanford University Press, 1987.

Rousseau, Jean Jacques. *Reveries of the Solitary Walker.* Translated by Peter France. New York: Penguin, 1979.

Russell, James S. "Chancery and Embassy Residence, Amman, Jordan, Perry Dean Rogers, Architects." *Architectural Record* (May 1993).

Rybczynski, Witold. *A Clearing in the Distance: Frederick Law Olmsted and America in the Nineteenth Century.* New York: Scribner's, 1999.

Sadler, Simon. *The Situationist City.* Cambridge, Mass.: MIT Press, 1998.

Said, Edward. *Orientalism: Western Conceptualizations of the Orient.* London: Routledge & Kegan Paul, 1978.

Sallis, John. *Chorology: On Beginning in Plato's Timaeus.* Bloomington: Indiana University Press, 1999.

Sartre, Jean-Paul. *Being and Nothingness.* Translated by Hazel E. Barnes. New York: Washington Press, 1956.

———. *Existentialism and Human Emotions.* Translated by Hazel E. Barnes. New York: Philosophical Library, 1985.

Schaefer, Frederick K. "Exceptionalism in Geography: A Methodological Examination." *Annals of the Association of American Geographers* 43 (1953): 226-49.

Schmitt, Peter J. *Back to Nature: The Arcadian Myth in Urban America.* Baltimore: Johns Hopkins University Press, 1990.

Schoenberger, Erica. "Self-Criticism and Self Awareness in Research: A Reply to Linda McDowell." *The Professional Geographer* 44 (1992): 215-18.

———. "The Corporate Interview as an Evidentiary Strategy in Economic Geography." *The Professional Geographer* 43 (1991): 180-89.

Schumaker, E. F. *Small is Beautiful.* New York: Harper and Row, 1973.

Schutz, Alfred. *The Problem of Social Reality: Collected Papers 1.* The Hague: Martinus Nijhoff, 1962.

Schutz, Alfred, and Thomas Luckmann. *The Structures of the Life-World.* Translated by Richard M. Zaner and H. Tristram Engelhardt Jr. Evanston, Ill.: Northwestern University, 1973.

Seamon, David. "The Phenomenological Contribution to Environmental Psychology." *Journal of Environmental Psychology* 2 (1982): 119-40.

Selby, Richard, ed. *Coming of Age: Proceedings of the Environmental Design Research Association.* Urbana-Champaign: University of Illinois Press, 1990.

Sennett, Richard. *Flesh and Stone: The Body and the City in Western Civilization.* New York: Norton, 1994.

Simmel, Georg. *On Individuality and Social Forms.* Edited by Donald N. Levine. Chicago: University of Chicago Press, 1971.

Smith, Neil. "New City, New Frontier: The Lower East Side as Wild, Wild West." *Variations On a Theme Park: The New American City and the End of Public Space.* Edited by Michael Sorkin. New York: Hill & Wang, 1992.

Snyder, Gary. *The Practice of the Wild.* New York: Farrar, Straus and Giroux, 1990.

Soulé, Michael, "Benign Neglect: A Model of Faunal Collapse in the Game Reserves of East Africa." *Biological Conservation* 15 (1979): 259-70.

Spiro, Melford E. "Cultural Relativism and the Future of Anthropology." *Cultural Anthropology* 1 (1986): 259-86.

Spurling, Laurie. *Phenomenology and the Social World.* London: Routledge & Kegan Paul, 1977.

Stange, Maren. *Symbols of Ideal Life: Social Documentary Photography in America 1890-1950.* Cambridge: Cambridge University Press, 1989.

Stevanovic, Ingrid Leman. *Safeguarding Our Common Future: Rethinking Sustainable Development.* Albany: State University of New York, 2000.

Stokes, Isaac Newton Phelps. *New York Past and Present, Its History and Landmarks, 1524-1939.* New York: Plantin Press, 1939.

Straus, Erwin W. *Phenomenological Psychology.* New York: Basic Books, 1966.

Ströker, Elizabeth. *Husserl's Transcendental Phenomenology.* Stanford, Calif.: Stanford University Press, 1993.

Sussman, Elisabeth, ed. *On the Passage of a Few People Through a Rather Brief Moment in Time: The Situationist International 1957-1972.* Cambridge, Mass.: MIT Press, 1989.

Sutton, S. B. *Civilizing American Cities: A Selection of Frederick Law Olmsted's Writings on City Landscapes.* Cambridge, Mass.: MIT Press, 1971.

Tester, Kieth. *The Flaneur.* New York: Routledge, 1994.

Thoreau, Henry D. *Walden and Other Writings.* Edited by Brooks Atkinson. New York: Modern Library, 1937.

Towers, George. "GIS Versus the Community: Siting Power in Southern West Virginia." *Applied Geography* 17 (1997): 111-25.

Tuan, Yi Fu. "Humanistic Geography." *Annals of the Association of American Geographers* 66 (1976): 274.

Turner, Jack. *The Abstract Wild.* Tuscon: University of Arizona Press, 1996.

Tymieniecka, Anna-Teresa. "The Ontopoiesis of Life as a New Philosophical Paradigm." *Phenomenological Inquiry* 22 (October 1998): 12-59.

Vale, Lawrence J. *Architecture, Power and National Identity.* New Haven, Conn.: Yale University Press, 1992.

Vaneigem, Raoul. *The Revolution of Everyday Life.* London: Left Bank Books and Rebel Press, 1983.

Vergara, Camilo Jose. *The New American Ghetto.* New Brunswick, N.J.: Rutgers University Press, 1995.

Virilio, Paul. *Open Sky.* Translated by Julie Rose. London: Verso, 1997.

———. *Speed and Politics.* Translated by Mark Polizzotti. New York: Semiotexte, 1986.

Vonier, Thomas. "Security: The Next Stage." *Progressive Architecture* (April 1988): 144.

Waddell, Helen. *The Wandering Scholars.* New York: Doubleday, 1955.

Wallace, Anne. *Walking, Literature, and English Culture: The Origins and Uses of the Peripatetic in Nineteenth Century.* Oxford: Clarendon Press, 1993.

Ware, Louise. *Jacob A. Riis: Police Reporter, Reformer, Useful Citizen.* New York: D. Appleton-Century, 1939.

Waterfield, Robin. *Republic.* Oxford: Oxford University Press, 1993.

Weil, Simone. *Gravity and Grace.* New York: Routledge, 1963.

Whyte, William H. *City: Rediscovering the Center.* New York: Doubleday, 1988.

Wiggins, David. *Needs, Values Truth.* Oxford: Basil Blackwell, 1987.

Wolch, Jennifer, and Jow Emel, eds. *Animal Geographies.* London: Verso, 1998.

Wolfman, Ira. "Insecurities about Security: Face to Face with the Building-Protection Crisis." *Architectural Record* (August 1987): 129.

Zimmerman, Michael E., ed. *Environmental Philosophy.* Upper Saddle River, N.J.: Prentice Hall, 1993.

Index

Adorno, Theodor, 201, 219
Ammons, A. R., 217
Anaxagoras, 144
Anaximander, 144
Aristotle, 14, 125-27, 129-30, 133-42, 144, 203
asymmetry/symmetry of predation, 9, 12; asymmetric predatory space, 35; asymmetry of predation, 36; asymmetrical predation, 39, 47
Augé, Marc, 102
Auster, Paul, 210
Austin, Jane, 207
auto-mobility, 9, 12-13, 97-99, 101, 103-4, 106, 111-12, 114-16, 118-19

Ballard, J. G., 200
Barnes, Jonathan, 133
Barnes, Trevor, 230
Baudelaire, Charles, 206, 218
Baudrillard, Jean, 5, 200
Bellah, Robert, 92
Benjamin, Walter, 218
Berger, John, 201
Bernstein, 234
Berry, Wendell, 35-38, 40, 47-48, 88, 91, 93-94
Billinge, 236-38
Blanchot, Maurice, 44
Bryant, William Cullen, 156
Buddha, 207
Buttimer, 236

Capitalism, 29
Carver, Humphrey, 141
Casey, Edward S., 120n1
Certeau, Michel de, 208-9, 211

Chatwin, Bruce, 207
Chiasmatic, 41; chiasmatic crossing, 195; chiasmatic nature, 41
Christians, 25, 27, 29, 31, 83-84; Christian altruism, 155; Christianity, 28, 31
class-scaping, 30
Cole, Thomas, 164
Confucianism, 85
Cooley, Charles Horton, 97
CPTED (crime prevention through environmental design), 56-57, 72-73, 75-76
Crane, Caroline Bartlett, 171

Debord, Guy, 213-14
Debts, 145; debt-based possibilities, 127; debts, acts based on, 126; debt, erotic, 127; debts, need-based, 129; debt-secured security, 131
Deleuze, Gilles, 213-14
Demeritt, 229-30, 242-43, 245
Democritus, 144
Derrida, 5
Descartes, 27-28, 234; Cartesian, 28, 161, 234; Cartesian space, 212
design for security (security design), 55-56, 58, 77
deterritorialization, 3; deterritorializing space, 214
Dostoevsky, 207
Downing, Andrew Jackson, 155-57
Dwell, 14, 125; dwelling, 14, 125-26, 130, 132, 139, 142, 145

Eco, Umberto, 205
Egler, Frank, 101
Ehrlich, 100

Emerson, Ralph Waldo, 206
Entrikin, 235

Freud, 39
Friedman, Thomas, 59

Gautima, Siddhartha, 85
Geertz, 240-42; 244
gender-scaping, 30
genius loci, 1, 11
geographicity, 2
geographism, 2
Gessler, Wilbert, 14, 153
Gilbert, Robert, 218
Glidden, David, 128-29, 131-32, 134, 136-40, 144-45
Grange, Joseph, 10
Greenberg, Mike, 216
Gregory, 247
gridiron geography, 14; gridiron system, 155
Grumbine, Edward, 101
Guelke, 229
Guerva, Che, 207
Guattari, Félix, 213

Hardy, Thomas, 207
Haussman, Baron G. E., 58
Hegel, 3; Hegelian, 26
Heidegger, 5, 14, 23, 42-45, 125, 126, 128-30, 136, 138, 230, 234
Heraclitus, 144
hermeneutic(s), 10-11, 22; hermeneutics, cultural, 25
Hessel, Franz, 218
hierarchical space, 61-62
Hillier, 244-46
Hindess, 233
Hobbesian, 32
home(s), 12-14, 21, 26, 33, 44, 81, 92-93, 112, 114, 142; homeland, 26
Hough, Michael, 93
Humanism, 20, 29, 235; humanism, paternalistic, 153; humanism, philanthropic, 153
Hume, David, 86, 153
Hunt, Richard Morris, 163
Husserl, 4, 230-38, 246-47

implacement, 1, 97, 103, 105, 117

Imman, Admiral Bobby R., 72
Intertwining, 20, 31; intertwining, double understanding, 19
intrinsic-worth, 82, 84-86
Irving, Washington, 157

Jackson, J. B., 9
Jackson, Peter, 237-38
Jacobs, Jane, 202, 215
Jefferson, Thomas, 164-65
Jesus, 207
John of Salisbury, 205
Jonas, Hans, 200
Jordon, 235
Joyce, 218

Kafka, 48
Kahn, Louis I., 62
Kearns, Robin, 153
Kingsland, Ambrose C., 156
Kittleman, Earl, 37
Klein, Naomi, 94
Köhler, 7
Kristeva, 39, 42
Kuntsler, James Howard, 82, 91, 93
Kutter, E., 114

Lake and Towers, 229
Lang, John, 62
Leopold, Aldo, 100
lived-body, 1, 13, 97-98, 103, 105, 107, 109-12, 115, 117, 119
Loeffler, Jane, 72
Lowenthal, 9
Lutyens, Sir Edwin, 62

makeshift approach, 130, 131, 133, 138; makeshift method, 136
Malinowski, 239-40
Marx, 86, 213
Mayer, 229
McDonaldization, 90
McLuhan, Marshall, 200
Meinig, Donald W., 9, 235
Melville, Henry, 213-14
Merleau-Ponty, 4, 10 41-42, 44-47, 99
Mezga, 243-44
Mill, John Stuart, 86
Miller, Henry, 209, 213
Meyers, Norman, 101

Moriarity, 235
Morrill, 227, 229-31, 234, 246-48
Moses, 207
Mumford, Lewis, 195, 201, 219

Napolean III, 58
Newman, Oscar, 62
Nietzsche, 85, 144
Norberg-Schulz, 1
Nussbaum, Martha, 138

Olmsted, Frederick Law, 14, 153-54,
    157-67, 169-70, 176-77
open dynamic system(s), 4, 6, 7
orders of goodness, 12, 47

Paden, Roger, 9, 128-29, 134, 145
Parmenides, 144
Pastalin, Leon, 61
patticca samuppada, 44
phallocentric, 29
phronimos, 140-44
Pickles, 232, 234-35, 239, 246-47
Pinchot, Gifford, 169
place identity, 8
placiality, 1, 3, 6, 97, 103, 106-7, 118-
    19; placialization, lived dynamic, 98;
    placial possibilities, 212
Plato, 27, 125-27, 129-34, 142, 144;
    Platonism, 27; Platonic perspective,
    83; Platonic dialogue, 87
Poe, Edgar Allen, 206
Positivism, 2, 15, 99, 228-29, 236;
    positivist science, 234
public/private spheres, 12; private
    property and public space, 194, 207

question of land, 23, 44

race-scaping, 30
reciprocal envelopment, 4
reductionism, 33
Relph, 239, 243
reversibility, 42
Riis, Jacob, 14, 153-54, 160, 165-67,
    169-74, 176-77
Ritzer, George, 90, 93-94
Rogers, Perry Dean, 73
Rolston, Holmes, 36, 99
Roosevelt, Theodore, 169-70, 174

Rose, Damaris, 228
Rousseau, 218
route-scape, 100, 118-19
Russell, James S., 73

Sartre, 3, 32
Seamon, 239, 244, 246
Schaefer, 235
Schoenberger, 228
Schumaker, E. F., 89
Schutz, Alfred, 113, 230
security design, 12
Sennet, Richard, 204
settings-in-which-we-are-
    interchangeable-parts, 13-14, 81, 88,
    92
Simmel, Georg, 11
Simulacra, 103; simulacrum, 5
Snyder, Gary, 36, 102
social Darwinism, 155
Social Gospel Movement, 155
Socrates, 126-27, 129-36, 138-42, 144
Sophocles, 32
Soulé, Michael, 101
Speer, Albert, 70
Spiro, 239
Stein, Gertrude, 141-42
Stern, Robert, 60
Stevanovic, 8
Stevens, Wallace, 218
Strong, William C., 174
Supermodern, 100, 106;
    supermodernity, 98, 102, 106
supra-theoretical modalities, 3

technological somnambulism, 199
territorialization, 6
therapeutic landscape, 14, 153-55, 159,
    166, 169-71, 177-78
Thoreau, 46, 202, 206
transformation(s), 6-7, 9-15, 19, 22, 25-
    26, 29, 31-33, 69, 74, 100, 103, 105,
    107, 125, 153, 155, 194-95, 220;
    transformation, theoretical, 4;
    transformational currents, 11;
    transformational discovery, 8;
    transformational effects, 9;
    transformational encryption and
    description, 210; transformational
    experiences, 12; transformational

phenomenon, 10; transformational processes, 11; transformational properties, 8; transformational qualities, 8; transformational trends, 8, 11-12
Tuan, 236, 238
Tung, Mao Tse, 207
Turner, Jack, 46-47

uncanny, 12, 19-21, 41, 43, 45; uncanniness, 12, 43; uncanniness of edibility, 44; uncanny ground, 22
uprootedness, 98, 105, 110-11, 114, 119; uprooted modality, 102
utilitarian, 82-83, 86, 88; utilitarian revolution, 87

Valéry, Paul, 196
Vaux, Calvert, 157-58, 160-62, 166
Vergara, Camilo Jose, 60
Viele, Egbert, 157, 161
Virilio, Paul, 214
visibility of security, 55, 57; unseen, 12, 55, 57-58, 74, 79; seen, 55, 57, 74, 76; deceptive, 55, 58, 69; disingenuous, 55, 58, 69, 74, 76

walker's world, 14
walking city, 193, 195
Waring, George, 169
Weber, Max, 90
Weese, Harry, 72
wild being, 42

About the Contributors

Gary Backhaus received his Ph.D. in Philosophy from the American University and is a faculty member at Morgan State University in Maryland. He is a phenomenologist whose publications concern a wide range of applications including the human and social sciences, literature and the fine arts, technology, and the philosophy of dynamic systems. Some recent publications of 2001 include, "An Incongruous Life-World: A Cultural Phenomenology of *The Tailor and Ansty*," in *Analecta Husserliana* vol. 71, and "The Feel of the Flesh: Towards an Ontology of Music," in *Analecta Husserliana* vol. 73. Also, "Tymieniecka's Phenomenology of Life: The 'Imaginatio Creatrix,' Subliminal Passions, and the Moral Sense," in *Consciousness & Emotion* vol. 3. He is currently writing a reference book, *Historical Dictionary of Phenomenology* (Scarecrow Press, forthcoming).

Ruth Connell received her Master of Architecture degree from the University of Pennsylvania and is an Associate Professor for the Institute of Architecture and Planning of Morgan State University in Baltimore. Her research concerns the cultural meaning of the built environment. Recent paper titles are "An Uncanny Loss: The Diminishment of the Rural Black Church" and "Modern Political Space: Consumption and Authenticity in the Evolution of National Space, Washington, D.C." Her work includes the photographic documentation of historic black churches of the Eastern Shore of Maryland.

Francis Conroy received his Ph.D. in philosophy from the Union Institute and is Professor of Philosophy, Religion, and Sociology at Burlington County College in New Jersey. His research interests include East-West philosophy, world religions, and the environmental socialist, decentralist, and peace movements. He is currently editing for *Seventies Journal,* his existentialist/activist memoir of that period.

Mary Hague received her Ph.D. in Politics from Boston College and is Associate Professor of Politics at Juniata College in Pennsylvania. Her research interests include environmental policy and political history. She has presented several papers on environmental policy, especially addressing the Clean Water Act, and on teaching environmental politics. She is currently preparing a forthcoming article on wetlands and property rights.

James Hatley received his Ph.D. in Philosophy from the State University of New York at Stonybrook and is Associate Professor of Philosophy at Salisbury University in Maryland. Hatley's research in environmental thought is centered on developing an ethico-phenomenological account of the wilds, particularly as it pertains to hiking. In another vein, Hatley has recently published *Suffering Witness: The Quandary of Responsibility after the Irreparable*, a study of testimony about the Holocaust in the context of Emmanuel Levinas's philosophy. Hatley also is writing about the issues of forgiveness and repentance.

David Macauley received his Ph.D. in Philosophy from the State University of New York at Stony Brook and is currently a faculty member in the Environmental Studies Program at Oberlin College. He is author of *Bewildering Order: Earth, Water, Air, and Fire as Elemental Philosophy and Environmental Ideas* (State University of New York Press, 2002) and *Walking: Philosophical Foot Notes* (Indiana University Press, forthcoming). He is editor of *Minding Nature: The Philosophers of Ecology* (Guilford Press, 1996).

John Murungi received his Ph.D. in Philosophy from the Pennsylvania University, his JD at the University of Maryland Law School, and is Chairperson of the Department of Philosophy and Religious Studies at Towson University in Maryland. His research interests include Philosophy of Law, African Philosophy, and African-American Philosophy. His publications are in hermeneutics and the phenomenological aspects of African lived-experience.

John A. Scott received his Ph.D. in Philosophy from Edinburgh University and is a member of the Philosophy Department of Memorial University of Newfoundland. His research interests include ancient philosophy, place, and contemporary issues in the knowledge-based economy.

Derek Shanahan received his Ph.D. in Geography from the University of Minnesota and is Associate Professor of Geography at Millersville University in Pennsylvania. His research interests include the geography of ethnic identity, urban cultural geography, and Irish identity politics in nineteenth-century London. Publications include, "The Geography of Gender" in an edited volume entitled, *Women's Work* (Hawthorn Press, 1998), and "Race, Segregation and Restructuring" (1997) in the *Scottish Geographical Magazine.*

Nancy Siegel received her Ph.D. from Rutgers University in Art History and is Assistant Professor of Art History at Juniata College and Curator of the Juniata College Museum of Art in Pennsylvania. She specializes in American Art History, with an emphasis in nineteenth-century landscape studies. Recent books include *The Morans: The Artistry of a Nineteenth-Century Family of Painter-Etchers* (Juniata College Press, 2001), and *Uncommon Visions of Juniata's Past* (Arcadia Publishing, 2000). A recent article is "Painted Image, Inspirational Text: Thomas Cole and the Influence of John Bunyan," in *Image and Text: American Creativity and the Relationship between Writing and the Visual Arts,* edited by Mark Andrew White (Edwin A. Ulrich Museum of Art, 2000). She is currently writing a book about Thomas Cole entitled *To Walk with Nature as a Poet: Thomas Cole's Painting, Prose, and the Simultaneity of Visual/Literary Languages.*